ISABEL PERRIGO - SCHAUMBURG CONG. J.W.

Richard Perrigo
Isabel Perrigo
525 Hill Drive
Hoffman Estates, IL 60194

D1170788

GORSKIJ
529.96/8

Revelation
Its Grand Climax At Hand!

© 1988
WATCH TOWER BIBLE AND TRACT SOCIETY OF PENNSYLVANIA
All rights reserved

Publishers
WATCHTOWER BIBLE AND TRACT SOCIETY OF NEW YORK, INC.
INTERNATIONAL BIBLE STUDENTS ASSOCIATION
Brooklyn, New York, U.S.A.

First Printing in English: 3,000,000 Copies

Unless otherwise indicated, Scripture quotations are from the modern-language *New World Translation of the Holy Scriptures,* 1984 Edition

Revelation—Its Grand Climax At Hand!   English (*re-E*)   Made in the United States of America

Picture Credits

Pictures are listed by page number and, when necessary, in order of appearance on page (clockwise from top left).

Cooper-Hewitt Museum; drawing based on photo of case 9, panel A: Page 59

National Aeronautics and Space Administration, Washington, D.C.: Pages 138, 293

Pictorial Archive (Near Eastern History) Est.: Page 23 (background, 1, 4, 10)

Pictorial Archive (Near Eastern History) Est., and Survey of Israel; based on a map copyrighted by: Page 236

Staatlichen Museen zu Berlin, DDR; used with the kind permission of: Page 43 (1, 2, 3)

Revelation
Its Grand Climax
At Hand!

"Happy is he who reads aloud and those
who hear the words of this prophecy,
and who observe the things written in
it; for the appointed time is near."
—Revelation 1:3

Contents

*The entire book of Revelation is explained in this publication.
Verses being commented on appear in bold type.*

Revelation—Its Happy Climax!

A REVELATION TO JOHN—this thrilling book of the Bible brings the divine record to a happy climax. Why do we say "happy"? Well, the Author of the Bible is described as "the happy God," who entrusts "glorious good news" to those who love him. He wants us to be happy too. Thus, at the outset Revelation assures us: "Happy is he who reads . . the words of this prophecy." In its final chapter we are told: "Happy is anyone observing the words of the prophecy of this scroll."—1 Timothy 1:11; Revelation 1:3; 22:7.

² How do we find happiness through the book of Revelation? We do so by searching out the meaning of its vivid signs, or symbols, and acting in harmony therewith. Mankind's turbulent history will soon reach a catastrophic climax, as God and Jesus Christ execute judgment on today's wicked system, replacing it with "a new heaven and a new earth," where even "death will be no more." (Revelation 21:1, 4) Do not all of us want to live in such a new world, in true peace and security? We can if we build up our faith through study of God's Word, including the stirring prophecy of Revelation.

Apocalypse—What Is It?

³ Is not Revelation also called Apocalypse? That is so, "revelation" being the English translation of *a·po·ka′ly·psis* in the Greek text. Many people equate Apocalypse with world destruction by nuclear warfare. In a Texas, U.S.A., city where great numbers of

nuclear warheads are made, religiously inclined people have been saying, "We'll be the first to go." Clergymen in that area are reported to have "become convinced that Armageddon is not only inevitable but also close at hand, and that the final battle between the forces of good and bad, of God and Satan, will take place as a nuclear holocaust."*

⁴ But what really is an apocalypse? Though dictionaries define it by using terms such as "an imminent cosmic cataclysm," the Greek *a·po·ka′ly·psis* basically means "unveiling" or "uncovering." Thus, the last book of the Bible is properly entitled "A Revelation." Here we find, not a mere fatalistic message of world doom, but an uncovering of divine truths that should build in our hearts a radiant hope and an immovable faith.

⁵ True, Armageddon is described in the last book of the Bible as "the war of the great day of God the Almighty." (Revelation 16:14, 16) But it will be far different from a nuclear holocaust! Such a holocaust would likely mean the annihilation of all life on earth. On the contrary, God's Word gives the happy assurance that only wicked opposers of God will be destroyed—by forces under God's control. (Psalm 37:9, 10; 145:20) A great crowd of humans, out of all nations, will survive the climax of divine judgment

---

* *Süddeutsche Zeitung*, Munich, Germany, January 24, 1987.

1. How do we know that God wants us to be happy?
2. What must we do to find happiness through the book of Revelation?
3. What do many people think that Apocalypse and Armageddon mean?

4. What does the word "apocalypse" actually mean, and why is the last book of the Bible fittingly entitled "A Revelation"?
5. (a) Who will be destroyed at Armageddon, and who will survive? (b) What grand future awaits the Armageddon survivors?

at Armageddon. Christ Jesus will then shepherd and guide these to life everlasting in a paradise earth. Do you not want to be one of them? Happily, Revelation shows that you may be!—Revelation 7:9, 14, 17.

Searching Out Divine Secrets

6 As early as 1917, the Watch Tower Society published the book *The Finished Mystery*. This was a verse-by-verse commentary on the Bible books of Ezekiel and Revelation. Then, as world events continued to unfold in fulfillment of Bible prophecy, a timely two-volume work entitled *Light* was prepared, being released in 1930. This offered an updated study of Revelation. Light continued to 'flash up for the righteous,' so that in 1963 the Society published the 704-page book *"Babylon the Great Has Fallen!" God's Kingdom Rules!* This gave in great detail the history of the rise and fall of Babylon the Great, the world empire of false religion, and it was climaxed with a discussion of the final nine chapters of Revelation. As 'the path of the righteous ones grew brighter,' particularly with regard to congregational activity, there followed in 1969 a 384-page volume, *"Then Is Finished the Mystery of God,"* which discussed the first 13 chapters of Revelation.—Psalm 97:11; Proverbs 4:18.

7 Why should another book on Revelation be published at this present time? Much of the information that has already appeared is very detailed, and it has not been possible to translate and publish it worldwide in many languages. Hence, it was seen fit to provide a book on Revelation in just one volume and in a form that can readily be produced in a number of languages. Further, the opportunity is taken in this volume to provide teaching aids, including illustrations, charts, and summaries, that should help readers to grasp clearly the thrilling import of this marvelous prophecy.

8 An even stronger reason for publishing this book is the need to keep up-to-date with present truth. Jehovah is continually shedding greater light on the meaning of his Word, and we can expect that our understanding of Revelation, along with other prophecies, will be sharpened as we draw closer to the great tribulation. (Matthew 24:21; Revelation 7:14) It is important that we be well informed. As the apostle Peter wrote concerning divine prophecy: "You are doing well in paying attention to it as to a lamp shining in a dark place, until day dawns and a daystar rises, in your hearts."—2 Peter 1:19.

9 Revelation adds its testimony to many other Bible prophecies, showing that Jehovah God purposes to create new heavens and a new earth. (Isaiah 65:17; 66:22; 2 Peter 3:13; Revelation 21:1-5) Primarily, its message is addressed to anointed Christians, whom Jesus has bought with his blood to become corulers with him in the new heavens. (Revelation 5:9, 10) Nevertheless, this good news will also fortify the faith of those millions who look forward to everlasting life under Christ's Kingdom. Are you one of these? Then Revelation will strengthen your hope of living in Paradise, as part of the new earth, with the enjoyment of an abundance of peace, vibrant health, and an overflow of God's provisions that will never end. (Psalm 37:11, 29, 34; 72:1, 7, 8, 16) If you want to survive into that new world, it is urgent, yes, mandatory, that you pay attention to Revelation's graphic description of the epoch-making climax now at hand.—Zephaniah 2:3; John 13:17.

---

6. Over the years, what books have been published by the Watch Tower Society to shed light on Revelation?

7. (a) Why has the Society provided this book on Revelation? (b) What teaching aids are provided in the book for the benefit of readers?

8. What even stronger reason is there for publishing this book?

9. (a) Along with other prophecies, what does Revelation show that God will create? (b) What is the new world, and how may you survive into it?

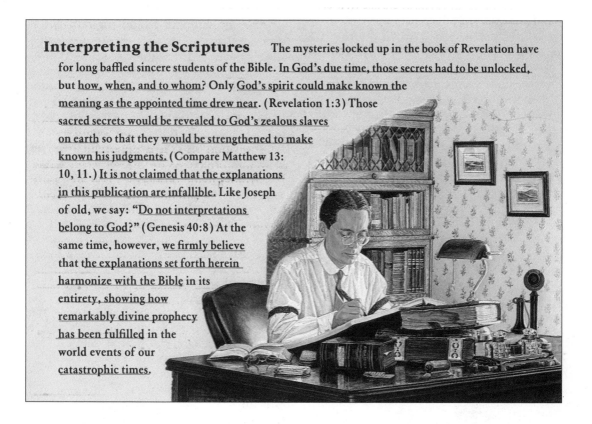

Interpreting the Scriptures   The mysteries locked up in the book of Revelation have for long baffled sincere students of the Bible. In God's due time, those secrets had to be unlocked, but how, when, and to whom? Only God's spirit could make known the meaning as the appointed time drew near. (Revelation 1:3) Those sacred secrets would be revealed to God's zealous slaves on earth so that they would be strengthened to make known his judgments. (Compare Matthew 13:10, 11.) It is not claimed that the explanations in this publication are infallible. Like Joseph of old, we say: "Do not interpretations belong to God?" (Genesis 40:8) At the same time, however, we firmly believe that the explanations set forth herein harmonize with the Bible in its entirety, showing how remarkably divine prophecy has been fulfilled in the world events of our catastrophic times.

The Grand Theme of the Bible

A BIBLE proverb says: "Better is the end afterward of a matter than its beginning." (Ecclesiastes 7:8) It is in the book of Revelation that we read of the dramatic culmination of Jehovah's grand purpose to sanctify his name before all creation. As God declared time and time again by one of his earlier prophets: "They will have to know that I am Jehovah."—Ezekiel 25:17; 38:23.

² Just as Revelation spells out the triumphant end of matters, so their beginning is described for us in earlier books of the Bible. By examining this record, we are enabled to understand the issues involved and get an overall view of God's purposes. How satisfying this is! Further, it should rouse us to action, so that we may share

---

1. What is Jehovah's grand purpose?

2. What satisfying knowledge does Revelation, along with earlier books of the Bible, help us attain?

in the marvelous future that awaits mankind. (Psalm 145:16, 20) At this point, it seems appropriate to discuss the background and theme of the entire Bible, in order that we may have in mind the paramount issue that now faces all humankind, as well as God's clearly stated purpose to resolve that issue.

³ The Bible's first book, Genesis, tells of "the beginning" and describes God's creative works, including his crowning earthly creation, man. Genesis also sets out the first divine prophecy, uttered by God himself in the garden of Eden some 6,000 years ago. A serpent had just been used to deceive the first woman, Eve; she in turn had persuaded her husband, Adam, to join her in violating Jehovah's law by eating from "the tree of the knowledge of good and bad." In passing judgment on the sinful couple, God said to the serpent: "I shall put enmity between you and the woman and between your seed and her seed. He will bruise you in the head and you will bruise him in the heel." (Genesis 1:1; 2:17; 3:1-6, 14, 15) That prophecy sets the theme for the whole Bible, including Revelation.

⁴ Immediately after uttering the prophecy, God expelled our first parents from Eden. No longer could they look forward to everlasting life in Paradise; they would have to live out their lives in the unprepared earth outside. Under sentence of death, they would produce sin-laden children. (Genesis 3:23–4:1; Romans 5:12) What, though, does the Edenic prophecy mean? Who are involved? How does it link up with Revelation? What message does it have for us today? In order to gain personal relief from the effects of the tragic event that led to

Jehovah's uttering that prophecy, it is of vital concern that we know the answers to these questions.

The Principals in the Drama

⁵ The prophecy of Genesis 3:15 was addressed to the serpent that had lied to Eve, suggesting to her that she would not die for her disobedience but that she would become independent, a goddess. The serpent thus made Jehovah out to be a liar and insinuated that humans could improve their lot by rejecting His supreme rulership. (Genesis 3:1-5) Jehovah's sovereignty was challenged and his good name besmirched. The book of Revelation describes how the righteous Judge, Jehovah, uses the Kingdom rule of his Son, Jesus Christ, to vindicate his sovereignty and clear all reproach from his name.—Revelation 12: 10; 14:7.

⁶ As for that term "serpent," does it apply only to a literal snake? Not at all! Revelation identifies for us the infamous spirit creature that spoke through that snake. It was "the great dragon . . . , the original serpent, the one called Devil and Satan, who is misleading the entire inhabited earth," that "seduced Eve by its cunning."—Revelation 12:9; 2 Corinthians 11:3.

⁷ Genesis 3:15 speaks next of "the woman." Was this Eve? Possibly she thought so. (Compare Genesis 4:1.) But a long-lasting enmity between Eve and Satan became impossible when Eve died more than 5,000 years ago. Further, since the Serpent addressed by Jehovah is an invisible spirit, we should expect that the woman also belongs to the spirit realm. Revelation 12:1, 2 confirms this, indicating that this figurative woman is Jehovah's heavenly organization of spirit creatures.—See also Isaiah 54:1, 5, 13.

---

3. What prophecy in the book of Genesis sets the theme for the whole Bible, including Revelation?

4. (a) After God uttered the first prophecy, what happened to our first parents? (b) What questions arise concerning the first prophecy, and why do we need to know the answers?

5. When the serpent deceived Eve, what developed regarding God's sovereignty and his name, and how will the controversy be resolved?

6. How does Revelation identify the one who spoke to Eve through a snake?

7. What indicates that the woman of Genesis 3:15 belongs to the spirit realm?

Two Seeds in Opposition

⁸ Two seeds appear next at Genesis 3:15. We should be deeply interested in these, for they are related to the great issue of rightful sovereignty over this earth. This involves each one of us, whether young or old. Which of these seeds do you favor?

⁹ First, there is the seed, or offspring, of the Serpent. What is this? It surely includes those other spirit creatures who joined Satan in his rebellion and who were finally "hurled down with him" to the realm of the earth. (Revelation 12:9) Since Satan, or Beelzebub, is "the ruler of the demons," it is apparent that they make up his invisible organization.—Mark 3:22; Ephesians 6:12.

¹⁰ Further, Jesus told Jewish religious leaders of his day: "You are from your father the Devil, and you wish to do the desires of your father." (John 8:44) By their opposition to God's Son Jesus, those religious leaders showed that they too were Satan's offspring. They were part of Satan's seed, serving him as their figurative father. Many other humans throughout history have similarly identified themselves by doing Satan's will, particularly in opposing and persecuting the disciples of Jesus. Collectively, these humans may be described as making up Satan's visible organization on earth.—See John 15:20; 16:33; 17:15.

☒ The Seed of the Woman Identified

¹¹ The prophecy at Genesis 3:15 refers finally to the seed of the woman. While Satan was developing his seed, Jehovah was preparing for his "woman," or wifelike celestial organization, to produce a seed. For some 4,000 years, Jehovah progressively revealed to obedient God-fearing humans details related to

the coming of the seed. (Isaiah 46:9, 10) Abraham, Isaac, Jacob, and others could thus build faith in the promise that the seed would appear in their genealogical line. (Genesis 22: 15-18; 26:4; 28:14) Satan and his henchmen often persecuted such servants of Jehovah because of their unswerving faith.—Hebrews 11:1, 2, 32-38. MEN OF OLD HAD unbelief

¹² At last, in the year 29 of our Common Era, the perfect man Jesus presented himself at the Jordan River and was baptized. Jehovah there begot Jesus with holy spirit, saying: "This is my Son, the beloved, whom I have approved." (Matthew 3:17) Jesus was there identified as having been sent forth from God's spiritual organization in heaven. He was also anointed as the King-Designate of the heavenly Kingdom that would restore rulership over the earth in Jehovah's name, thus settling once and for all the issue involving government, or sovereignty. (Revelation 11:15) Jesus, then, is the principal One of the seed of the woman, the foretold Messiah.—Compare Galatians 3:16; Daniel 9:25.

¹³ Would the woman's seed be simply one prominent person? Well, what of Satan's seed? The Bible identifies Satan's seed as ᴀ including a host of wicked angels and God-dishonoring humans. It should not surprise us, then, to learn of God's purpose to select 144,000 integrity keepers from among mankind to become priestly corulers with the Messianic Seed, Jesus Christ. Revelation refers to these when it says that the Devil, in his enmity toward God's womanly organization, "went off to wage war with the remaining ones of her seed."—Revelation 12:17; 14:1-4.

¹⁴ In the Bible, anointed Christians are

---

8. Why should we be deeply interested in what is now said about two seeds?
9. What does the seed of the Serpent surely include?
10. How does the Bible identify others as part of Satan's seed?
11. Over centuries of time, what did God reveal concerning the seed of the woman?

12. (a) When and with what event did the principal part of the seed of the woman arrive? (b) Jesus was anointed for what purpose?
13, 14. (a) Why should it not surprise us to learn that the seed of the woman would not be just one prominent person? (b) How many has God selected from among mankind to become the secondary part of the seed, and what kind of organization do they make up? (c) Who else serve in unity with the seed?

called Jesus' brothers, and as his brothers, they share the same Father and the same mother. (Hebrews 2:11) Their Father is Jehovah God. Hence, their mother must be "the woman," God's wifelike celestial organization. They become a secondary part of the seed, Christ Jesus being the primary part. The congregation of these spirit-begotten Christians on earth make up God's visible organization that serves under his womanlike organization in the heavens, where they will be united with Christ Jesus at their resurrection. (Romans 8:14-17; Galatians 3:16, 29) Though not part of the seed, millions of other sheep out of all nations are being united to serve with God's organization on earth. Are you one of these other sheep? Then your happy hope is everlasting life in a paradise earth.—John 10:16; 17:1-3.

How Enmity Developed

¹⁵ Satan's human seed began to be manifested very early in mankind's history. For example, there was Cain, the first human born, "who originated with the wicked one and slaughtered his brother" Abel. (1 John 3:12) Later, Enoch spoke of Jehovah's coming "with his holy myriads, to execute judgment against all, and to convict all the ungodly concerning all their ungodly deeds that they did in an ungodly way, and concerning all the shocking things that ungodly sinners spoke against him." (Jude 14, 15) Moreover, rebellious angels joined Satan and became part of his seed. These "forsook their own proper dwelling place" in the heavens in order to materialize fleshly bodies and marry the daughters of men. They produced a superhuman hybrid offspring of bullies. That world became filled with violence and badness, so that God destroyed it in the Deluge, faithful Noah and his family being the only human flesh to survive. The disobedient angels—now demons under Satan's control—were forced to abandon their doomed human wives and hybrid children. They dematerialized, returning to the spirit realm where they await God's fast-approaching execution of judgment on Satan and his seed.—Jude 6; Genesis 6:4-12; 7: 21-23; 2 Peter 2:4, 5.

¹⁶ Shortly after the great Deluge, a tyrant named Nimrod appeared on earth. The Bible describes him as "a mighty hunter in opposition to Jehovah"—truly part of the Serpent's seed. Like Satan, he showed a spirit of rebellion and built the city of Babel, or Babylon, in defiance of Jehovah's purpose to have mankind spread out to fill the earth. Babylon's centerpiece was to have been a great tower "with its top in the heavens." God thwarted the would-be builders of that tower. He confused their language and "scattered them from there over all the surface of the earth" but allowed Babylon itself to remain.—Genesis 9:1; 10:8-12; 11:1-9.

Political Powers Appear

¹⁷ In Babylon there appeared features of human society that developed in defiance of Jehovah's sovereignty. One of these was political. As mankind multiplied, other ambitious humans followed Nimrod's example in seizing power. Man began to dominate man to his injury. (Ecclesiastes 8:9) During the days of Abraham, for instance, Sodom, Gomorrah, and nearby cities fell under the control of kings from Shinar and other far-distant lands. (Genesis 14:1-4) Eventually, military and organizational geniuses carved out huge empires for their own enrichment and glory. The Bible refers to some of these, including Egypt, Assyria, Babylon, Medo-Persia, Greece, and Rome.

---

15. (a) Describe the development of Satan's human and angelic seed. (b) What happened to Satan's seed during the Deluge of Noah's day?

16. (a) What tyrant appeared on the scene after the Deluge, and how did he show he was part of Satan's seed? (b) How did God thwart the would-be builders of Babylon's tower?

17. As mankind multiplied, what corrupt feature of human society came to the fore, and as a result, what huge empires arose?

Darius the Mead
Cyrus the Persian

18 Jehovah tolerated the existence of those political powers, and his people rendered relative obedience to them when they lived in lands under their control. (Romans 13:1, 2) Sometimes, political authorities even served for the furtherance of God's purposes or as a protection for his people. (Ezra 1:1-4; 7:12-26; Acts 25:11, 12; Revelation 12:15, 16) Nevertheless, many political rulers have viciously opposed true worship, showing themselves to be part of the seed of the Serpent.—1 John 5:19.

19 For the most part, man-rule has failed miserably to bring happiness to us humans or to solve our problems. Jehovah has permitted mankind to experiment with every form of government, but he does not approve of corruption or the way governments have misruled the people. (Proverbs 22:22, 23) Revelation portrays oppressive world powers as making up a proud and monstrous wild beast.—Revelation 13:1, 2.

see pg 189

Selfish Commercial Traffickers

20 Closely allied to political leaders, there came into view dishonest traffickers in material goods. Records unearthed in the ruins of ancient Babylon show that business transactions exploiting the unfortunate circumstances of fellow humans were very much in vogue back there. The world's merchants have continued to work for selfish profit down to this present day, when in many lands a few have become very rich while the majority of the population languishes in poverty. In this 20th-century industrial age, the merchants and manufacturers have made great gain by supplying the political

18. (a) What attitude do God's people take toward the political rulers? (b) How have political authorities sometimes served God's interests? (c) How have many rulers shown themselves to be part of the Serpent's seed?
19. How are world powers portrayed in the book of Revelation?
20, 21. What second group must be included with the "military commanders" and "strong men" as belonging to Satan's wicked seed, and why?

powers with stockpiles of devilish military weapons of destruction, including the nuclear arsenals that now threaten mankind with annihilation. Such greedy business magnates and others of their kind must be included with the "military commanders" and "strong men" as belonging to Satan's wicked seed. They are all part of the earthly organization that God and Christ judge as deserving of execution.—Revelation 19:18.

21 To corrupt politics and greedy commercialism there must be added a third element of human society that merits God's adverse judgment. What is that? You may be surprised by what Revelation says about this well-known global structure.

Babylon the Great

22 The building of the original Babylon

22. What kind of religion developed in ancient Babylon?

Ancient cuneiform records of business transactions

The book *Ancient Near Eastern Texts*, edited by James B. Pritchard, lists almost 300 laws compiled by Hammurabi in Babylonian times. These show that it was necessary to proscribe the blatant dishonesty that apparently pervaded the commercial world in those days. To take one example: "If a seignior has purchased or he received for safe-keeping either silver or gold or a male slave or a female slave or an ox or a sheep or an ass or any sort of thing from the hand of a seignior's son or a seignior's slave without witnesses and contracts, since that seignior is a thief, he shall be put to death."

THE GRAND THEME OF THE BIBLE

was more than a political enterprise. Since that city was established in defiance of Jehovah's sovereignty, religion was involved. Indeed, ancient Babylon became a fountain of religious idolatry. Its priests taught God-dishonoring doctrines, such as the survival of a human soul after death and that the hereafter is a place of eternal horror and torment presided over by demons. They fostered the worship of creatures and of a multitude of gods and goddesses. They fabricated myths to explain the origin of the earth and man upon it and performed degrading rituals and sacrifices, supposedly to ensure fertility in childbearing and crop raising, and victory in war.

23 As the various language groups from Babylon spread out over the earth, they took Babylonish religion with them. Thus, rites and beliefs similar to those of ancient Babylon flourished among the original inhabitants of Europe, Africa, the Americas, the Far East, and the South Seas; and many of these beliefs persist to this day. Appropriately, then, Revelation refers to the world-embracing empire of false religion as a city named Babylon the Great. (Revelation, chapters 17, 18) Wherever it has been sown, false religion has sprouted oppressive priesthoods, superstition, ignorance, and immorality. It has been a powerful tool in Satan's hand. Babylon the Great has always fought fiercely against the true worship of the Sovereign Lord Jehovah.

24 As a most reprehensible part of the seed of the Serpent, the scribes and the Pharisees in first-century Judaism took the lead in persecuting and finally murdering the primary representative of the seed of the woman. Thus, the Serpent was able to "bruise him [the "seed"] in the heel." (Genesis 3:15; John 8:39-44; Acts 3:12, 15) Why is this described as only a heel wound? It is because this wounding touched him only briefly here on earth. It was not permanent because Jehovah resurrected Jesus on the third day and exalted him to spirit life. —Acts 2:32, 33; 1 Peter 3:18.

25 The glorified Jesus Christ now serves at God's right hand, judging Jehovah's enemies. He has already taken action against Satan and his angels, hurling them down and confining their activity to this earth —which accounts for the multiplying of woes in this 20th century. (Revelation 12:9, 12) But there will be the foretold removal of Satan's earthly seed when God executes judgment on Babylon the Great and all other segments of Satan's organization on earth. Finally, the Seed of God's woman, Jesus Christ, will bruise Satan, that wily old Serpent, "in the head," and that will mean his complete annihilation and his total removal from the affairs of mankind. —Romans 16:20.

26 How will all of this come about? That is what is unveiled for us in the Bible book of Revelation. It is revealed to us in a series of visions, highlighted by striking signs and symbols. Eagerly, let us examine this powerful prophecy. Happy, indeed, are we if we hear and observe the words of Revelation! By so doing, we will share in bringing honor to the name of the Sovereign Lord Jehovah and inherit his eternal blessings. Please read on and wisely apply what you learn. It can mean your salvation at this time of climax in mankind's history.

23. (a) In spreading out from Babylon, what did the people take with them, and with what result? (b) By what name does Revelation refer to a world-embracing empire of false religion? (c) Against what has false religion always fought?
24. (a) How was the Serpent able to bruise the Seed of the woman "in the heel"? (b) Why is the bruising of the woman's seed described as only a heel wound?
25. (a) How has the glorified Jesus already taken action against Satan and his angels? (b) When will there be a removal of Satan's earthly seed? (c) What will it mean when the Seed of God's woman bruises Satan, the Serpent, "in the head"?
26. Why is it most important that we examine the prophecy in Revelation?

Things That Must Shortly Take Place

YOU should be deeply concerned about world events today. Why so? Because this world cannot escape God's execution of judgment. But *you* can escape. You can do this by making yourself "no part of the world" that is doomed to destruction. This does not mean adopting an austere, monastic way of life. It means that while enjoying a wholesome, meaningful life, you separate yourself from political corruption, from greedy commercialism, and from God-dishonoring religion, as well as from violent and immoral behavior. At the same time, you must follow God's high standards of conduct and seek to do his will. (John 17: 14-16; Zephaniah 2:2, 3; Revelation 21:8) The Bible book of Revelation shows how important it is for you to apply yourself in these respects, making changes as necessary in your way of life.

² The apostle John introduces this grand prophecy with the words: *"A revelation by Jesus Christ, which God gave him, to show his slaves the things that must shortly take place."* (*Revelation 1:1a*) So it was the resurrected Jesus Christ who received this weighty message from God. Far from being part of a mystic Trinity, Jesus is here shown to be subject to his Father. In the same way, the "slaves" making up the Christian congregation are subject to Jesus Christ, so that they 'keep following him wherever he goes.' (Revelation 14:4; Ephesians 5:24) But who

today are truly "slaves" of God, and how does Revelation benefit them?

³ The apostle John, who wrote down Revelation, describes himself as such a slave. He was the last surviving apostle and one of the select spirit-anointed group of "slaves" that inherit immortal life in the heavens. Today, there are just a few thousand of these remaining on earth. God has other servants, too, a great crowd of them, men, women, and children, numbering now into the millions. Under angelic direction, these are sharing with the anointed "slaves" in declaring everlasting good news to all mankind. Oh, how all these "slaves" are expending themselves in order to help the meek ones of the earth to find salvation! (Matthew 24: 14; Revelation 7:9, 14; 14:6) Revelation indicates what you must do to benefit from the happifying good news.

⁴ How could John say, though, that these "slaves" would be shown "things that must

---

1. How can you escape God's execution of judgment upon this world?

2. How does the apostle John introduce the grand prophecy of Revelation, and to whom did God give this weighty message?

3. (a) Who are the "slaves" that are subject to Jesus Christ? (b) What work are the faithful "slaves" doing under angelic direction?

4. (a) Since it is almost 1,900 years ago that John wrote Revelation, how could he speak of "things that must shortly take place"? (b) What does the evidence now indicate about the things foretold?

To understand the book of Revelation we need

- To receive the help of Jehovah's spirit
- To discern when the Lord's day began
- To recognize the faithful and discreet slave today

shortly take place"? Were not those words spoken almost 1,900 years ago? From the viewpoint of Jehovah, in whose eyes a thousand years are but "as yesterday," 1,900 years is a short time when compared with the aeons of time that he spent in creating and preparing the earth for human habitation. (Psalm 90:4) The apostle Paul wrote of his own "eager expectation and hope," for no doubt the reality of his reward seemed close at hand to him. (Philippians 1:20) Today, however, the evidence abounds that *all* the things foretold will take place on schedule. Never before in history has the very survival of mankind been at stake. Only God has the solution!—Isaiah 45:21.

Channel of Communication

⁵ *Revelation 1:1b, 2* continues: *"And he* [Jesus] *sent forth his angel and presented it* [Revelation] *in signs through him to his slave John, who bore witness to the word God gave and to the witness Jesus Christ gave, even to all the things he saw."* Thus, John received the inspired record through an angelic messenger. He wrote it in a scroll, transmitting it to the congregations of his time. Happily for us, God has preserved it for the encouragement of the more than 50,000 congregations of his united servants on earth today.

⁶ God had a channel for communicating Revelation in John's day, and John was the earthly part of that channel. Likewise, God has a channel for giving spiritual nourishment to his 'slaves' today. In his great prophecy concerning the conclusion of the system of things, Jesus identified the earthly part of this channel as "the faithful and discreet slave whom his master appointed over his domestics, to give them their food at the proper time." (Matthew 24:3, 45-47) He uses this John class in unlocking the meaning of the prophecy.

5. How was Revelation communicated to the apostle John and then to the congregations?
6. How did Jesus identify the channel that he would use to provide spiritual food for his 'slaves' today?

⁷ The apostle John writes that Jesus presented Revelation "in signs," or symbols. These are vivid and thrilling to examine. They depict dynamic activity and should, in turn, stir us to zealous efforts in making known to others the prophecy and its meaning. Revelation presents for us a number of electrifying visions, in each of which John

7. (a) How should the signs found in Revelation affect us? (b) For how long have some of the John class shared in the fulfillment of the visions of Revelation?

INDIVIDUAL MEMBERS OF 144,000

63,000 OF 1991

16

participated either actively or as an observer. Those of the John class, some of whom have shared for upwards of 70 years in the fulfillment of these visions, are happy that God's spirit has unlocked the meaning so that they can explain it to others.

8 These visions in Revelation are not presented in chronological order. Each has its own time period of fulfillment. Many of the visions echo words of earlier prophecies that provide clues as to their interpretation. For example, Daniel's prophecy described four fearsome beasts, explaining that these portrayed ruling powers on earth. Hence, we are helped to understand that the beasts of Revelation represent political entities, including those now existing.—Daniel 7:1-8, 17; Revelation 13:2, 11-13; 17:3.

9 John was faithful in bearing witness to the message that God through Jesus Christ gave to him. He described in detail "all the things he saw." The John class has earnestly sought guidance from God and Jesus Christ in order to understand the prophecy fully and make known its fine points to God's people. For the benefit of the anointed congregation (and also of the international great crowd that God will preserve alive through the great tribulation), John writes: *"Happy is he who reads aloud and those who hear the words of this prophecy, and who observe the things written in it; for the appointed time is near."*—Revelation 1:3.

10 You will benefit greatly by reading Revelation and even more so by observing the things written in it. John explained in one of his letters: "This is what the love of God means, that we observe his commandments; and yet his commandments are not burdensome because everything that has been born from God conquers the world. And this is the conquest that has conquered the world, our faith." (1 John 5:3, 4) You can become supremely happy by building such a faith!

11 It is urgent that we observe the words of the prophecy, "for the appointed time is near." The appointed time for what? For the fulfillment of the prophecies of Revelation, including God's judgments. The time is near for God and Jesus Christ to execute final judgment on Satan's world system. When Jesus was here on earth, he stated that only his Father knew "that day or the hour." Looking ahead to the troubles that have multiplied on earth from World War I onward, Jesus also said: "This generation will by no means pass away until all these things happen." So the appointed time for executing God's decision must be drawing perilously close. (Mark 13:8, 30-32) As Habakkuk 2:3 states: "The vision is yet for the appointed time, and it keeps panting on to the end, and it will not tell a lie. Even if it should delay, keep in expectation of it; for it will without fail come true. It will not be late." Our salvation through the great tribulation depends on our observing God's prophetic Word.—Matthew 24:20-22.

---

8. (a) What is distinct about each of the visions of Revelation? (b) How does Daniel's prophecy help us to understand the identity of the beasts of Revelation?

9. (a) Like John, what attitude has the John class shown? (b) How does John show the way for us to become happy?

---

10. What must we do with regard to Revelation to attain to happiness?

11. (a) Why is it urgent that we observe the words of the prophecy? (b) What time must now be perilously close?

Jesus Comes With Encouragement

WHAT follows next should be of absorbing interest to everyone associated with the congregations of God's people today. Here is a series of messages. They have particular application as "the appointed time" draws near. (Revelation 1:3) It is to our everlasting benefit that we heed those pronouncements. The record reads: *"John to the seven congregations that are in the district of Asia: May you have undeserved kindness and peace from 'The One who is and who was and who is coming,' and from the seven spirits that are before his throne, and from Jesus Christ."—Revelation 1: 4, 5a.*

JAH

² Here John addresses "seven congregations," and these are named for us later in the prophecy. That number, "seven," is often repeated in Revelation. It signifies completeness, especially in connection with the things of God and his anointed congregation. Since the number of congregations of God's people worldwide has grown into the tens of thousands during the Lord's day, we can be sure that what is said primarily to the "seven congregations" of anointed ones also applies to all of God's people today. (Revelation 1:10) Yes, John has a vital message for all congregations of Jehovah's Witnesses and all who are associated with them, everywhere on the face of this earth.

³ "Undeserved kindness and peace"—how desirable these are and especially when we appreciate their source! The "One" from whom they flow is the Sovereign Lord Jehovah himself, "the King of eternity," who lives "from time indefinite to time indefinite." (1 Timothy 1:17; Psalm 90:2) Involved here, too, are "the seven spirits," which term indicates a fullness of operation of God's active force, or holy spirit, as it brings understanding and blessing to all who pay attention to the prophecy. Also occupying a key role is "Jesus Christ," of whom John later wrote: "He was full of undeserved kindness and truth." (John 1:14) Thus, John's greeting has the same elements that the apostle Paul mentioned in closing his second letter to the Corinthian congregation: "The undeserved kindness of the Lord Jesus Christ and the love of God and the sharing in the holy spirit be with all of you." (2 Corinthians 13:14) May those words apply also to every one of us who loves truth today!—Psalm 119:97.

"The Faithful Witness"

⁴ After Jehovah, Jesus is the most glorious person in the universe, as John recognizes, describing him as *"'the Faithful Witness,' 'The firstborn from the dead,' and 'The Ruler of the kings of the earth.'"* (*Revelation 1:5b*) Like the moon in the heavens, he has been firmly established as the greatest Witness to Jehovah's Godship. (Psalm 89:37) After he kept integrity down to a sacrificial death, he became the first from among mankind to be raised to immortal spirit life. (Colossians 1:18) Now in Jehovah's presence, he is exalted high above all earthly kings, being invest-

---

1. To whom does John now write, and who today should find his message to be of absorbing interest?
2. (a) What does the number "seven" signify? (b) During the Lord's day, to whom do the messages to the "seven congregations" apply?
3. (a) In John's greeting, where do "undeserved kindness and peace" come from? (b) What expression of the apostle Paul is similar to John's greeting?

---

4. How does John go on to describe Jesus Christ, and why are these descriptive terms so appropriate?

ed with "all authority . . . in heaven and on the earth." (Matthew 28:18; Psalm 89:27; 1 Timothy 6:15) In 1914 he was installed as King to rule among the earthly nations. —Psalm 2:6-9; Matthew 25:31-33.

[5] John continues to express appreciation for the Lord Jesus Christ in these glowing words: *"To him that loves us and that loosed us from our sins by means of his own blood —and he made us to be a kingdom, priests to his God and Father—yes, to him be the glory and the might forever. Amen."* (Revelation 1: 5c, 6) Jesus gave his perfect human life so that those of the world of mankind who exercise faith in him may be restored to perfect life. You, dear reader, can be included in this! (John 3:16) But Jesus' sacrificial death opened the way for a special blessing for those who become anointed Christians like John. These have been declared righteous on the basis of Jesus' ransom sacrifice. Renouncing all earthly life prospects, as Jesus did, those of the little flock have been begotten by God's spirit, with the expectation of being resurrected to serve as kings and priests with Jesus Christ in his Kingdom. (Luke 12:32; Romans 8:18; 1 Peter 2:5; Revelation 20:6) What a grand privilege! No wonder John exclaimed so affirmatively that the glory and the might belong to Jesus!

"Coming With the Clouds"

[6] Next, John jubilantly announces: *"Look! He is coming with the clouds, and every eye will see him, and those who pierced him; and all the tribes of the earth will beat themselves in grief because of him. Yes, Amen."* (Revelation 1:7) No doubt John was here reminded of Jesus' earlier prophecy concerning the conclusion of the system of things. Jesus there stated:

"Then the sign of the Son of man will appear in heaven, and then all the tribes of the earth will beat themselves in lamentation, and they will see the Son of man coming on the clouds of heaven with power and great glory." (Matthew 24:3, 30) Thus, Jesus 'comes' by turning his attention to the executing of Jehovah's judgments on the nations. This

---

Symbolic Numbers in Revelation

Number	Symbolic Meaning
2	Signifies solidly confirming a matter. (Revelation 11:3, 4; compare Deuteronomy 17:6.)
3	Denotes emphasis. Also indicates intensity. (Revelation 4:8; 8:13; 16:13, 19)
4	Signifies universalness or foursquareness in symmetry. (Revelation 4:6; 7:1, 2; 9:14; 20:8; 21:16)
6	Signifies imperfection, something not normal, monstrous. (Revelation 13:18; compare 2 Samuel 21:20.)
7	Signifies divinely determined completeness, as to Jehovah's purposes or to Satan's. (Revelation 1:4, 12, 16; 4:5; 5:1, 6; 10:3, 4; 12:3)
10	Signifies allness or completeness in a physical way, as to things on earth. (Revelation 2:10; 12:3; 13:1; 17:3, 12, 16)
12	Signifies a divinely constituted organization either in the heavens or on the earth. (Revelation 7:5-8; 12:1; 21:12, 16; 22:2)
24	Signifies Jehovah's abundant (doubled) organizational arrangement. (Revelation 4:4)

Some numbers mentioned in Revelation are to be understood as literal. Often, the context helps to determine this. (See Revelation 7:4, 9; 11:2, 3; 12:6, 14; 17:3, 9-11; 20:3-5.)

---

5. (a) How does John continue to express appreciation for the Lord Jesus Christ? (b) Who benefit from Jesus' gift of his perfect human life, and how have anointed Christians shared in a special blessing?
6. (a) What does John announce about Jesus' "coming with the clouds," and of what prophecy of Jesus may John have been reminded? (b) How does Jesus 'come,' and who will experience great grief on earth?

will result in momentous changes on earth, and since "all the tribes of the earth" have ignored the reality of Jesus' kingship, they will indeed experience "the anger of the wrath of God the Almighty."—Revelation 19: 11-21; Psalm 2:2, 3, 8, 9.

7 During Jesus' last evening with his disciples, he told them: "A little longer and the world will behold me no more." (John 14:19) How is it, then, that "every eye will see him"? We should not expect that Jesus' enemies would see him with physical eyes, for the apostle Paul said, after Jesus' ascension to heaven, that Jesus now "dwells in unapproachable light," and "not one of men has seen or can see" him. (1 Timothy 6:16) Evidently, John meant "see" in the sense of "discern," just as we can see, or discern, God's invisible qualities by means of his creations. (Romans 1:20) Jesus "is coming with the clouds" in that he will be just as invisible to the naked eye as the sun is when it is behind clouds. Even when the sun is hidden by clouds during daytime, we know it is there because of the daylight that surrounds us. Similarly, though the Lord Jesus is invisible, he will be revealed like 'a flaming fire, as he brings vengeance upon those who do not obey the good news about him.' These too will be compelled to "see him."—2 Thessalonians 1:6-8; 2:8.

8 Jesus will be 'seen' also by "those who pierced him." Who might these be? When Jesus was executed in 33 C.E., the Roman soldiers pierced him literally. The guilt of that murder was shared by the Jews, for Peter told some of these at Pentecost: "God made him both Lord and Christ, this Jesus whom you impaled." (Acts 2:5-11, 36; compare Zechariah 12:10; John 19:37.) Those Romans and Jews have now been dead for close to 2,000 years. So those who 'pierce him' today must represent nations and peoples that display the same hateful attitude that was shown when Jesus was impaled. Jesus is no longer here on earth. But when opposers either actively persecute Jehovah's Witnesses, who bear witness to Jesus, or passively consent to such treatment, it is just as though such opposers were 'piercing' Jesus himself.—Matthew 25:33, 41-46.

"The Alpha and the Omega"

9 Now, wonder of wonders! The Sovereign Lord Jehovah himself speaks. How appropriate this is as a preface to the visions that are about to unfold, since he is our Grand Instructor and the ultimate Source of Revelation! (Isaiah 30:20) Our God declares: *"I am the Alpha and the Omega, . . . the One who is and who was and who is coming, the Almighty."* (*Revelation 1:8*) This is the first of three times in Revelation that Jehovah himself speaks from heaven. (See also Revelation 21:5-8; 22: 12-15.) First-century Christians would quickly have recognized alpha and omega as the first and last letters of the Greek alphabet. Jehovah's calling himself by those two letters stresses that before him, there was no almighty God, and there will be none after him. He will bring to a successful conclusion, for all eternity, the issue of Godship. He will be forever vindicated as the one and only almighty God, Supreme Sovereign over all of his creation.—Compare Isaiah 46:10; 55:10, 11.

10 Confident that Jehovah will direct the outcome of matters, John tells his fellow slaves: *"I John, your brother and a sharer with you in the tribulation and kingdom and endurance in company with Jesus, came to be in the*

---

7. How will "every eye," including those of the disobedient ones, "see" Jesus?
8. (a) Who were "those who pierced him" in 33 C.E., and who are such ones today? (b) Since Jesus is no longer here on earth, how can people 'pierce him'?

9. (a) Who now speaks out, and how many times in Revelation does he do so? (b) When Jehovah calls himself "the Alpha and the Omega" and "the Almighty," what does this mean?
10. (a) How does John next describe himself, and where was he confined? (b) The scroll written by John must have been forwarded to the congregations with whose cooperation? (c) How is spiritual food often provided today?

Obtaining Spiritual Food in Difficult Times

During these last days, when Jehovah's Witnesses have suffered so much persecution and hardship, it has been vital for them to receive spiritual food in order to stay strong in faith. In most cases, adequate sustenance has been provided, often thanks to some remarkable demonstrations of Jehovah's power.

For example, in Germany under Hitler, Witnesses mimeographed and distributed copies of *The Watchtower,* which was officially banned by the cruel Nazi authorities. In Hamburg the Gestapo raided a house where such mimeographing took place. The house was small, and there was nowhere to hide anything securely. The typewriter had been left in a cupboard, and the bulky mimeograph equipment was stored in a potato bin in the basement. Moreover, behind the bin there was a suitcase full of magazines! Discovery seemed inevitable. But what happened? The officer who opened the cupboard did so in such a way that he did not see the typewriter. As for the basement, the householder reports: "The three officers stood in the middle of the room, mind you, right there where the bin stood with the suitcase full of *Watchtowers* behind it. But none of them seemed to notice it; it was as though they had been struck blind." Thanks to this remarkable providence, the household was able to continue supplying spiritual food in difficult and dangerous times.

In the 1960's, there was a civil war between Nigeria and the breakaway province of Biafra. Since Biafra was completely surrounded by Nigerian territory, the only link between it and the outside world was an airstrip. This meant that the Witnesses in Biafra were in danger of being cut off from their supply of spiritual food. Then, early in 1968, the Biafran authorities assigned one of their civil service staff to an important post in Europe and another was assigned to the Biafran airstrip. These two happened to be Jehovah's Witnesses, and now they were at both ends of the only link between Biafra and the outside world. The two recognized that the arrangement must have been from Jehovah. Hence, they volunteered for the delicate and risky task of channeling spiritual food into Biafra. And they were able to do this all through the war. One of them commented: "The arrangement was beyond something that humans could have planned."

---

isle that is called Patmos for speaking about God and bearing witness to Jesus." (Revelation 1:9) A prisoner on Patmos for the sake of the good news, enduring tribulations with his brothers, hoping firmly to have a share in the coming Kingdom, the aged John now sees the first of the visions of Revelation. No doubt he was encouraged greatly by these visions, just as the John class is stimulated today at seeing their fulfillment. We do not know how John forwarded the scroll of Revelation to the congregations, since he was in confinement at the time. (Revelation 1:11; 22:18, 19) Jehovah's angels must have cooperated in getting this done, just as they have so often protected faithful witnesses of Jehovah who serve under bans and restrictions today, so that these have been able to get timely spiritual food to their truth-hungry brothers.—Psalm 34:6, 7.

[11] How deeply John must have appreciated his privilege of being used by Jehovah as His channel of communication to the congregations! Similarly, the John class today treasures greatly its privilege of providing the household of God with spiritual "food at the proper time." (Matthew 24:45) May you be one of those strengthened by this spiritual provision so as to attain to the glorious goal of everlasting life!—Proverbs 3:13-18; John 17:3.

11. What privilege, similar to that appreciated by John, does the John class greatly treasure today?

John Beholds the Glorified Jesus

THE first vision in the book of Revelation begins with chapter 1, verse 10. This vision, like the others in Revelation, is introduced by a declaration that John hears or sees something extraordinary. (Revelation 1: 10, 12; 4:1; 6:1) This first vision is presented in a first-century framework in which messages are addressed to seven congregations contemporary with John. But John indicates the time of its real application when he says: *"By inspiration I came to be in the Lord's day."* (*Revelation 1:10a*) When is this "day"? Do the dramatic events of this tempestuous 20th century have any connection with it? If so, we should pay close attention to the prophecy, as affecting our very lives—even our survival.—1 Thessalonians 5:20, 21.

In the Lord's Day

2 In what time frame does this place the fulfillment of Revelation? Well, what is the Lord's day? The apostle Paul refers to it as a time of judgment and of fulfillment of divine promises. (1 Corinthians 1:8; 2 Corinthians 1:14; Philippians 1:6, 10; 2:16) With the arrival of that "day," Jehovah's grand purposes move progressively and triumphantly toward their climax. That "day" begins with the crowning of Jesus as heavenly King. Even after Jesus executes judgment on Satan's world, the Lord's day continues, with the restoration of Paradise and the perfecting of mankind, until Jesus finally "hands over the kingdom to his God and Father." —1 Corinthians 15:24-26; Revelation 6:1, 2.

3 The fulfillment of other Bible prophecies helps us to see when the Lord's day begins. For example, Daniel described a chopping down of rulership in the line of King David; after "seven times" it would be known "that the Most High is Ruler in the kingdom of mankind, and that to the one whom he wants to he gives it." (Daniel 4:23, 24, 31, 32) The major fulfillment of that prophecy started with the desolating of the kingdom of Judah, which is indicated by Bible evidence to have been completed by October 607 B.C.E. Revelation 12:6, 14 shows that 3 1/2 times amounts to 1,260 days; hence, seven times (twice that number) must be 2,520 days. Reckoning "a day for a year," we

---

1. How is the first vision presented, and how did John indicate the time of its real application?
2. When does the Lord's day begin, and when does it end?

3. (a) How does Daniel's prophecy of the "seven times" help us see when the Lord's day begins? (b) What events on earth confirm the year 1914 as the beginning of the Lord's day?

Vision _____ 1

Revelation 1:10–3:22

Subject: Jesus inspects spiritual Israel on earth and gives warm encouragement

Time of fulfillment: This feature of the Lord's day extends from 1914 until the last of the faithful anointed ones dies and is resurrected

Archaeological remains of the cities where the seven congregations were located confirm the Bible record. It was here that first-century Christians received Jesus' encouraging messages that today stimulate the worldwide 20th-century congregation

PERGAMUM

SMYRNA

THYATIRA

EPHESUS

SARDIS

LAODICEA

PHILADELPHIA

arrive at 2,520 years as the duration of the "seven times." (Ezekiel 4:6) Therefore, Christ Jesus began his heavenly rule in the latter part of 1914. The erupting of the first world war in that year marked "a beginning of pangs of distress" that have continued to plague mankind. Since 1914, how remarkably events in this bloodstained earth have confirmed that year to be the start of the "day" of Jesus' presence!—Matthew 24:3-14.*

⁴ Hence, this first vision and the counsel it contains are for the Lord's day, from 1914 onward. This timing is supported by the fact that, later in Revelation, the record describes the execution of God's true and righteous judgments—events in which the Lord Jesus plays an outstanding part. (Revelation 11:18; 16:15; 17:1; 19:2, 11) If the fulfillment of the first vision began in 1914, when does it end? As the messages themselves show, the organization addressed is God's congregation of anointed ones on earth. The fulfillment of this first vision ends, then, when the last faithful member of that anointed congregation dies and is raised to heavenly life. Nevertheless, the Lord's Day, with blessings to the earthly other sheep, continues till the end of Jesus Christ's Millennial Rule.—John 10:16; Revelation 20:4, 5.

⁵ In this first vision, before John sees anything, he hears something: *"And I heard behind me a strong voice like that of a trumpet, saying: 'What you see write in a scroll and send it to the seven congregations, in Ephesus and in Smyrna and in Pergamum and in Thyatira and in Sardis and in Philadelphia and in Laodicea.'"* (*Revelation 1:10b, 11*) Authoritative

and commanding as a trumpet call, a voice calls on John to write to "the seven congregations." He is to receive a series of messages and to publish the things he will see and hear. Notice that the congregations mentioned here actually existed in John's day. All of them were situated in Asia Minor, right across the sea from Patmos. They were easily accessible to one another by means of the excellent Roman roads that existed in the area. A messenger would have had no trouble carrying the scroll from one congregation to the next. These seven congregations would resemble a section of a modern-day circuit of Jehovah's Witnesses.

✗ ⁶ Most of the prophecies in Revelation were to be fulfilled after John's time. They referred to "the things that will take place after these." But the counsel to the seven congregations deals with "things that are," situations that really existed in the seven congregations at that time. The messages were valuable aids to faithful appointed elders in those seven congregations, as well as in all other congregations of anointed Christians of the time.* Since the vision has its prime application in the Lord's day, what Jesus says serves notice that similar conditions are to be expected in the congregation of anointed Christians of our own day. —Revelation 1:10, 19.

⁷ In this first vision, John sees the radiant Lord Jesus Christ in His heavenly glory. What could be more fitting for a book of prophecies relating to the great day of this Lord commissioned by heaven? And what could be more important to us, who are

---

* For a detailed explanation, see pages 128-39, 186-9 of the book *"Let Your Kingdom Come,"* distributed by the publishers of this book.

4. (a) What do the words of Revelation itself indicate as to when the first vision is fulfilled? (b) When does the fulfillment of the first vision end?
5. (a) What does a voice call on John to do? (b) Why was the location of "the seven congregations" favorable for sending a scroll to them?

* In the first century, when a congregation received a letter from an apostle, it was customary to circulate the letter to other congregations so that all could benefit from the counsel.—Compare Colossians 4:16.

6. (a) What is meant by "the things that are"? (b) Why can we be certain that conditions in the congregation of anointed Christians today must be similar to those in John's day?
7. Whom does John see in this first vision, and why is it so important and thrilling to us today?

now living in that time period and giving careful heed to his every command? Moreover, how thrilling it is for supporters of Jehovah's sovereignty to be assured that the Messianic Seed, having endured all the tests and persecutions brought by Satan and having suffered an agonizing death when His "heel" was bruised 1,900 years ago, is now alive in heaven, empowered to bring God's grand purpose to its triumphant completion! —Genesis 3:15.

8 It is evident that Jesus is now poised to go into action as enthroned King. He has been appointed as Jehovah's Chief Executioner to carry out Jehovah's final judgments against this old, wicked system of things and its diabolic god, Satan. He is also on hand to judge those of his congregation of anointed ones and the great crowd of their associates, as well as to judge the world.—Revelation 7:4, 9; Acts 17:31.

9 John turns at the sound of the loud voice, and here is what he sees: *"I turned to see the voice that was speaking with me, and, having turned, I saw seven golden lampstands."* (*Revelation 1:12*) Later, John learns what these seven lampstands symbolize. But it is the person in the midst of the lampstands that catches his eye. There was *"in the midst of the lampstands someone like a son of man, clothed with a garment that reached down to the feet, and girded at the breasts with a golden girdle."* (*Revelation 1:13*) Jesus, the "son of man," here presents himself before the awestruck witness, John, as a magnificent, glowing figure. He appears in brilliant glory among flaming golden lampstands. This templelike setting impresses on John the fact that Jesus is present in the role of Jehovah's great High Priest, with judgment powers. (Hebrews 4:14; 7:21-25) His long,

impressive garment conforms to his priestly office. Like the Jewish high priests of old, he wears a girdle—a golden girdle over his breast where it covers his heart. This signifies that he will wholeheartedly carry out his divine commission received from Jehovah God.—Exodus 28:8, 30; Hebrews 8:1, 2.

10 John's description continues: *"Moreover, his head and his hair were white as white wool, as snow, and his eyes as a fiery flame."* (*Revelation 1:14*) His snow-white hair indicates wisdom due to length of life. (Compare Proverbs 16:31.) And his fiery eyes show that he is sharp, alert, as he searches, tests, or expresses indignation. Even Jesus' feet catch John's attention: *"And his feet were like fine copper when glowing in a furnace; and his voice was as the sound of many waters."* (*Revelation 1:15*) In the vision, Jesus' feet are like copper, glowing, bright—properly so for one who walks zealously and with a fine standing in the presence of Jehovah God. Moreover, while in the Bible divine things are often pictured by gold, so things human are sometimes represented by copper.* So Jesus' glowing feet like fine copper remind us of how "comely" his feet were when he walked the earth preaching the good news. —Isaiah 52:7; Romans 10:15.

11 Indeed, as a perfect human, Jesus had a radiance that was apparent to angels and men. (John 1:14) His glorious feet also remind us that he is treading holy ground in Jehovah's organization, in which he is High Priest. (Compare Exodus 3:5.) Further, his voice resounds thunderously like a huge cascading waterfall. It is impressive, awe

---

* The interior decorations and furnishings of Solomon's temple were made of gold or overlaid with it, whereas copper was used in equipping the courtyard.—1 Kings 6: 19-23, 28-35; 7:15, 16, 27, 30, 38-50; 8:64.

8. For what action is Jesus now poised?
9. (a) How does John describe the glorified Jesus Christ amid the golden lampstands? (b) What is indicated by the templelike setting and the garment that Jesus wears? (c) What is signified by his golden girdle?

10. (a) What is indicated by Jesus' snow-white hair and fiery eyes? (b) What is the significance of Jesus' feet being like glowing copper?
11. (a) Of what do Jesus' glorious feet remind us? (b) What is indicated by the fact that Jesus' voice "was as the sound of many waters"?

ed to pronounce Jehovah's final judgments against His enemies. Decisive utterances from his mouth result in the execution of all wicked ones.—Revelation 19:13, 15.

[13] Jesus' bright, shining countenance reminds us that Moses' face emitted shining rays after Jehovah had communed with him on Mount Sinai. (Exodus 34:29, 30) Remember, too, that when Jesus was transfigured before three of his apostles 1,900 years ago, "his face shone as the sun, and his outer garments became brilliant as the light." (Matthew 17:2) Now, in a visionary representation of Jesus during the Lord's

---

13. (a) Jesus' bright, shining countenance reminds us of what? (b) What overall impression do we get from John's description of Jesus?

---

inspiring, as is fitting for the one officially called the Word of God, the one who has come "to judge the inhabited earth in righteousness."—Acts 17:31; John 1:1.

[12] **"And he had in his right hand seven stars, and out of his mouth a sharp, long two-edged sword was protruding, and his countenance was as the sun when it shines in its power. And when I saw him, I fell as dead at his feet."** (*Revelation 1:16, 17a*) Jesus himself explains the meaning of the seven stars a little later. But notice what is coming out of his mouth: "a sharp, long two-edged sword." What a fitting feature! For Jesus is the one appoint-

---

12. What is the significance of the "sharp, long two-edged sword"?

day, his face similarly reflects the radiant splendor of one who has been in Jehovah's presence. (2 Corinthians 3:18) In fact, the overall impression conveyed by John's vision is that of an effulgence of glory. From the snow-white hair, the flaming eyes, and the shining countenance down to the glowing feet, it is a superlative vision of the One who now dwells "in unapproachable light." (1 Timothy 6:16) The realism of this spectacle is so vivid! How did the overawed John react? The apostle tells us: "And when I saw him, I fell as dead at his feet."—Revelation 1:17.

14 Today, the colorful, detailed description of John's vision fills God's people with heartfelt appreciation. Already, we have passed through more than 70 years of the Lord's day, during which the vision continues to have its thrilling fulfillment. Jesus' Kingdom rule is to us a living, present reality, not a future hope. Hence, it is proper for us as loyal subjects of the Kingdom to look further with wonder at what John describes in this first vision and to listen obediently to the words of the glorified Jesus Christ.

---

14. How should we be affected when reading of John's vision of the glorified Jesus?

Unlocking a Sacred Secret

AWESOME indeed is the vision of the exalted Jesus! No doubt, if we had been spectators there with the apostle John, we too would have been overcome by that resplendent glory, prostrating ourselves as he did. (Revelation 1:10-17) This superlative inspired vision has been preserved to stimulate us to action today. Like John, we should show humble appreciation for all that the vision means. May we always have reverential respect for Jesus' position as enthroned King, High Priest, and Judge.—Philippians 2:5-11.

"The First and the Last"

2 Nevertheless, our awe need not give way to morbid fear. Jesus reassured John, as the apostle next relates. **"And he laid his right hand upon me and said: 'Do not be fearful. I am the First and the Last, and the living one.'"** (*Revelation 1:17b, 18a*) In Isaiah 44:6, Jehovah rightly describes his own position as the one and only almighty God, saying: "I am the first and I am the last, and besides me there is no God."* When Jesus presents himself by the title "the First and the Last," he is not claiming equality with Jehovah, the Grand Creator. He is using a title properly bestowed on him by God. In Isaiah, Jehovah was making a statement about His unique position as the true God. He is God eternal, and besides him there is indeed no God. (1 Timothy 1:17) In Revelation, Jesus is

---

1. How should we react to the glowing picture recorded at Revelation 1:10-17?
2. (a) By what title does Jesus present himself? (b) What is meant when Jehovah says: "I am the first and I am the last"? (c) To what does Jesus' title "the First and the Last" call attention?

---

* In the original Hebrew at Isaiah 44:6, there is no definite article with the words "first" and "last," whereas in Jesus' description of himself in the original Greek at Revelation 1:17, the definite article is found. So, grammatically, Revelation 1:17 indicates a title, whereas Isaiah 44:6 describes Jehovah's Godship.

27

talking about his bestowed title, calling attention to his unique resurrection.

[3] Jesus was indeed "the First" human to be resurrected to immortal spirit life. (Colossians 1:18) Moreover, he is "the Last" to be so resurrected by Jehovah personally. Thus, he becomes "the living one . . . living forever and ever." He enjoys immortality. In this, he is like his immortal Father, who is called "the living God." (Revelation 7:2; Psalm 42:2) For all others of humanity, Jesus himself is "the resurrection and the life." (John 11:25) In harmony with this, he says to John: *"I became dead, but, look! I am living forever and ever, and I have the keys of death and of Hades." (Revelation 1:18b)* Jehovah has given him the authority to resurrect the dead. That is why Jesus can say that he has the keys to unlock the gates for those bound by death and Hades (gravedom).—Compare Matthew 16:18.

[4] Jesus here repeats his command to record the vision, telling John: *"Write down the things you saw, and the things that are and the things that will take place after these." (Revelation 1:19)* What exciting things will John yet make known for our instruction?

The Stars and the Lampstands

[5] John has seen Jesus in the midst of seven golden lampstands with seven stars in his right hand. (Revelation 1:12, 13, 16) Now Jesus explains this: *"As for the sacred secret of the seven stars that you saw upon my right hand, and of the seven golden lampstands: The seven stars mean the angels of the seven congregations, and the seven lampstands mean seven congregations."—Revelation 1:20.*

[6] The "stars" are "the angels of the seven congregations." In Revelation, stars sometimes symbolize literal angels, but Jesus would hardly use a human penman to write to invisible spirit creatures. So the "stars" must be the human overseers, or elders, in the congregations, viewed as Jesus' messengers.* The messages are addressed to the stars, for these are responsible for the oversight of Jehovah's flock.—Acts 20:28.

[7] Since Jesus speaks to only one "angel" in each congregation, does this mean that each congregation has only one elder? No. As early as Paul's day, the Ephesian congregation had a number of elders, not just one. (Reve-

---

* The Greek word *ag'ge·los* (pronounced "an'ge·los") means "messenger" as well as "angel." At Malachi 2:7, a Levite priest is referred to as a "messenger" (Hebrew, *mal·'akh'*).—See *New World Translation Reference Bible,* footnote.

---

3. (a) In what way was Jesus "the First and the Last"? (b) What is meant by Jesus' having "the keys of death and of Hades"?
4. What command does Jesus repeat, and for whose benefit?
5. How does Jesus explain "the seven stars" and "the seven lampstands"?

6. What is represented by the seven stars, and why were the messages specifically addressed to these?
7. (a) What shows that Jesus' speaking to only one angel in each congregation does not mean that each congregation has only one elder? (b) Who, in effect, are represented by the seven stars in Jesus' right hand?

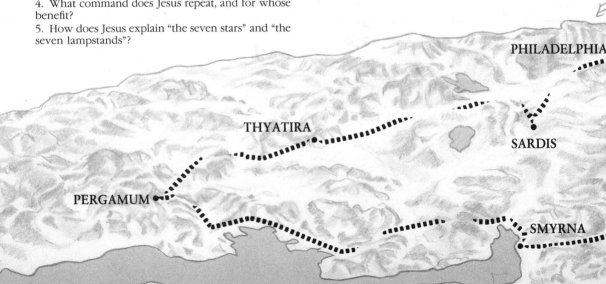

PHILADELPHIA

THYATIRA

SARDIS

PERGAMUM

SMYRNA

lation 2:1; Acts 20:17) So in John's day, when messages were sent to the seven stars to be read to the congregations (including the one in Ephesus), the stars must have stood for all those who served in the bodies of elders within Jehovah's anointed congregation. In like manner, overseers today read to their congregations letters received from the Governing Body, made up of anointed overseers who serve under Jesus' headship. The local bodies of elders have to make sure that Jesus' counsel is followed by their congregations. Of course, the counsel is for the benefit of all those associated in the congregations, not just the elders.—See Revelation 2:11a.

8 Since Jesus is the Head of the congregation, the elders are properly said to be in his right hand, that is, under his control and direction. (Colossians 1:18) He is the Chief Shepherd, and they are undershepherds. —1 Peter 5:2-4.

9 The seven lampstands are the seven congregations to whom John directs the book of Revelation: Ephesus, Smyrna, Pergamum, Thyatira, Sardis, Philadelphia, and Laodicea. Why are congregations symbolized by lampstands? Because Christians, whether individually or collectively as congregations, have to 'let their light shine before men' in this bedarkened world. (Matthew 5:14-16) Additionally, lampstands were among the furnishings of Solomon's temple. Calling the congregations lampstands would likely remind John that, in an illustrative sense, each local congregation of anointed ones is "God's temple," a dwelling place for God's spirit. (1 Corinthians 3:16) Moreover, in the antitype of the Jewish temple arrangement, members of the congregation of anointed ones serve as "a royal priesthood" in Jehovah's great spiritual temple arrangement, of which Jesus is the High Priest and where Jehovah dwells personally in the heavenly Most Holy.—1 Peter 2:4, 5, 9; Hebrews 3:1; 6:20; 9:9-14, 24.

The Great Apostasy

10 When John wrote Revelation, Christianity was upwards of 60 years old. At the outset, it had survived 40 years of constant opposition from Judaism. Then the Jewish system received a mortal blow in 70 C.E. when the unrepentant Jews lost their national identity and what was to them virtually an idol—the temple in Jerusalem.

8. What is indicated by the elders' being in the right hand of Jesus?
9. (a) What do the seven lampstands represent, and why are lampstands a fitting symbol for these? (b) Of what would the vision likely remind the apostle John?

10. What happened to the Jewish system and its unrepentant supporters in 70 C.E.?

LAODICEA

EPHESUS

¹¹ Nevertheless, the apostle Paul had foretold that there would be an apostasy among the anointed Christians, and Jesus' messages show that in John's old age this apostasy was already developing. John was the last of those who acted as a restraint on this all-out attempt by Satan to corrupt the seed of the woman. (2 Thessalonians 2:3-12; 2 Peter 3: 1-3; 2 John 7-11) So it was the appropriate time for Jehovah's Chief Shepherd to write to the elders in the congregations, warning of developing trends and encouraging right-hearted ones to stand firm for righteousness.

¹² How the congregations in 96 C.E. responded to Jesus' messages we do not know. But we do know that the apostasy developed rapidly after John's death. "Christians" ceased to use Jehovah's name and substituted "Lord" or "God" for it in Bible manuscripts. By the fourth century, the false doctrine of the Trinity had infiltrated the congregations. During this same period, the idea of an immortal soul was being adopted. Finally, Roman Emperor Constantine made "Christianity" the State religion, and this gave birth to Christendom, where Church and State joined forces in ruling for a thousand years. It was easy to become a new-style "Christian." Whole tribes adjusted their earlier pagan beliefs to versions of this religion. Many of the leaders in Christendom became oppressive political tyrants, enforcing their apostate views by the sword.

¹³ Jesus' words to the seven congregations were completely ignored by the apostatizing Christians. Jesus had warned the Ephesians to regain the love they had at first. (Revelation 2:4) Nevertheless, members of Christendom, no longer being united in love for Jehovah, fought vicious wars and persecuted one another horribly. (1 John 4:20) Jesus had warned the congregation in Pergamum against sectarianism. Yet, sects appeared even in the second century, and today Christendom has thousands of squabbling sects and religions.—Revelation 2:15.

¹⁴ Jesus had warned the Sardis congregation against being spiritually dead. (Revelation 3:1) Like those in Sardis, professed Christians quickly forgot about Christian works and soon delegated the highly important work of preaching to a small, paid clergy class. Jesus had warned the congregation in Thyatira against idolatry and fornication. (Revelation 2:20) Yet, Christendom openly sanctioned the use of images, as well as the promoting of the more subtle idolatry of nationalism and materialism. And immorality, while sometimes preached against, has always been widely tolerated.

¹⁵ Hence, Jesus' words to the seven congregations expose the total failure of all of Christendom's religions to be Jehovah's special people. Indeed, the clergy of Christendom have been the most prominent members of Satan's seed. Speaking of these as 'the lawless one,' the apostle Paul foretold that their "presence is according to the operation of Satan with every powerful work and lying signs and portents and with every unrighteous deception."—2 Thessalonians 2: 9, 10.

¹⁶ While claiming to be shepherds of the flock of God, Christendom's leaders, religious and secular, showed special hatred for anyone who tried to encourage Bible reading

---

11. Why was it so timely for the Chief Shepherd to warn the congregations of developing trends?
12. (a) How did the apostasy develop in the centuries after John's day? (b) How did Christendom come into existence?
13. Despite Jesus' warning against sectarianism, what course did the apostatizing Christians take?

---

14. (a) Though Jesus warned against being spiritually dead, what course did professed Christians take? (b) In what ways did the professed Christians fail to heed Jesus' warning against idolatry and immorality?
15. Jesus' words to the seven congregations expose what regarding Christendom's religions, and what have Christendom's clergy proved to be?
16. (a) Against whom did Christendom's leaders show special hatred? (b) What took place in Christendom during the Middle Ages? (c) Did the Protestant rebellion, or Reformation, change Christendom's apostate ways?

Christendom's religion incurred a heavy bloodguilt by persecuting and killing those who translated, read, or even owned the Bible

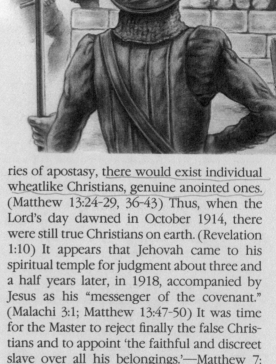

or anyone who exposed their unscriptural practices. John Hus and Bible translator William Tyndale were persecuted and martyred. During the bedarkened Middle Ages, apostate rule reached a peak in the diabolic Catholic Inquisition. Any who disputed the teachings or authority of the church were unmercifully suppressed, and countless thousands of so-called heretics were tortured to death or burned at the stake. Thus Satan endeavored to ensure that any true seed of God's womanlike organization would be quickly crushed. When the Protestant rebellion, or Reformation, occurred (from 1517 onward), many Protestant churches manifested a similar intolerant spirit. They too became bloodguilty by martyring those who endeavored to be loyal to God and Christ. Truly, "the blood of holy ones" was freely poured out!—Revelation 16:6; compare Matthew 23:33-36.

The Seed Endures

17 In his parable of the wheat and the weeds, Jesus foretold the time of darkness that would exist while Christendom reigned supreme. Nevertheless, through all the centu-

ries of apostasy, there would exist individual wheatlike Christians, genuine anointed ones. (Matthew 13:24-29, 36-43) Thus, when the Lord's day dawned in October 1914, there were still true Christians on earth. (Revelation 1:10) It appears that Jehovah came to his spiritual temple for judgment about three and a half years later, in 1918, accompanied by Jesus as his "messenger of the covenant." (Malachi 3:1; Matthew 13:47-50) It was time for the Master to reject finally the false Christians and to appoint 'the faithful and discreet slave over all his belongings.'—Matthew 7:22, 23; 24:45-47.

18 It was also time for this slave to give special attention to the things written in Jesus' messages to the seven congregations, as we see from what is stated therein. For

---

17. (a) What did Jesus' parable of the wheat and the weeds foretell? (b) What took place in 1918, resulting in what rejection and what appointment?

18. What "hour" came in 1914, and what was it time for the slave to do?

UNLOCKING A SACRED SECRET

example, Jesus refers to his coming to judge the congregations, which judgment began in 1918. (Revelation 2:5, 16, 22, 23; 3:3) He speaks of protecting the Philadelphia congregation from "the hour of test, which is to come upon the whole inhabited earth." (Revelation 3:10, 11) This "hour of test" arrives only with the dawning of the Lord's day in 1914, after which Christians were tested as to their loyalty to the established Kingdom of God.—Compare Matthew 24:3, 9-13.

¹⁹ For this reason, Jesus' words to the congregations have had their major application

---

19. (a) What do the seven congregations picture today? (b) Who have associated in large numbers with the anointed Christians, and why do Jesus' counsel and the conditions he describes apply to them also? (c) How should we view Jesus' messages to the seven first-century congregations?

since 1914. In this setting, the seven congregations picture all the congregations of anointed Christians during the Lord's day. Moreover, during the past 50 years and more, the anointed Christians pictured by John have been joined by large numbers of believers whose hope is to live forever in Paradise on earth. The counsel of the glorified Jesus Christ and the conditions he found in the seven congregations as a result of his inspection apply with equal force to these, since there is only one standard of righteousness and faithfulness for all of Jehovah's servants. (Exodus 12:49; Colossians 3:11) Thus, Jesus' messages to the seven first-century congregations in Asia Minor are not mere historical curiosities. They mean life or death to each one of us. Let us, then, listen carefully to Jesus' words.

A Time of Testing and Judging

Jesus was baptized and anointed as King-Designate at the Jordan River about October 29 C.E. Three and a half years later, in 33 C.E., he came to Jerusalem's temple and threw out those who were making it a cave of robbers. There appears to be a parallel to this in the three-and-a-half-year period from Jesus' 'sitting down on his glorious throne' in the heavens in October 1914 until his coming to inspect professed Christians as judgment began with the house of God. (Matthew 21:12, 13; 25:31-33; 1 Peter 4:17) Early in 1918 the Kingdom activity of Jehovah's people met with great opposition. It was a time of testing earth wide, and fearful ones were sifted out. In May 1918 Christendom's clergy instigated the imprisonment of officials of the Watch Tower Society, but nine months later these were released. Later, they were completely exonerated of the false charges against them. From 1919 the organization of God's people, tried and refined, moved zealously forward to proclaim Jehovah's Kingdom by Christ Jesus as the hope for mankind.—Malachi 3:1-3.

As Jesus began his inspection in 1918, the clergy of Christendom no doubt received an adverse judgment. Not only had they raised up persecution against God's people but they had also incurred heavy bloodguilt by supporting the contending nations during the first world war. (Revelation 18:21, 24) Those clergymen then placed their hope in the man-made League of Nations. Along with the entire world empire of false religion, Christendom had fallen completely from God's favor by 1919.

REVELATION CLIMAX

Rekindle That First Love!

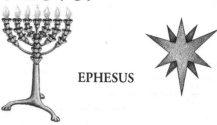

EPHESUS

JESUS' first message is to the congregation in Ephesus, at that time a thriving coastal city of Asia Minor close to the isle of Patmos. He commands John: *"To the angel of the congregation in Ephesus write: These are the things that he says who holds the seven stars in his right hand, he who walks in the midst of the seven golden lampstands."* (*Revelation 2:1*) As in the other six messages, Jesus here draws attention to a feature denoting his authoritative position. He reminds the overseers in Ephesus that all elders are under his own protective oversight and that he is inspecting all the congregations. Down into our 20th century, he has continued to exercise this loving headship, watching over the elders and kindly shepherding all associated with the congregation. From time to time, he adjusts congregational arrangements so that the light can shine more brightly. Yes, Jesus is the Chief Shepherd over the flock of God.—Matthew 11:28-30; 1 Peter 5:2-4.

[2] Jesus then sets a pattern for all but two of his seven messages by opening with warm words of commendation. For the Ephesians, he has this message: *"I know your deeds, and your labor and endurance, and that you cannot bear bad men, and that you put those to the test who say they are apostles, but they are not, and you found them liars. You are also showing endurance, and you have borne up for my name's sake and have not grown weary."* (*Revelation 2:2, 3*) Years before, the apostle Paul had warned the Ephesian elders about "oppressive wolves," apostate disturbers of the flock, and had told those elders to "keep awake," following his own tireless example. (Acts 20:29, 31) Since Jesus now commends them for their labor and endurance and for not growing weary, they must have applied that counsel.

[3] During the Lord's day, too, there have appeared "false apostles" who "speak twisted things to draw away the disciples after themselves." (2 Corinthians 11:13; Acts 20:30; Revelation 1:10) They see good in all the conflicting sectarian religions, claim that God does not have an organization, and deny that Jesus received Kingdom power in 1914. They fulfill the prophecy at 2 Peter 3: 3, 4: "In the last days there will come ridiculers with their ridicule, proceeding according to their own desires and saying: 'Where is this promised presence of his? Why, from the day our forefathers fell asleep in death, all things are continuing exactly as from creation's beginning.'"

[4] These ridiculers rebel at the thought of making public declaration of their faith.

---

1. To which congregation is Jesus' first message directed, and of what does he remind the overseers?
2. (a) For what fine things did Jesus commend the Ephesian congregation? (b) What counsel of the apostle Paul had the Ephesian elders evidently obeyed?

3. (a) How have "false apostles" sought to deceive faithful ones in our days? (b) What warning about apostates did Peter give?
4. (a) How is the pride and rebelliousness of ridiculers manifested? (b) Christians today show that they are like the Ephesians by taking what action against lying opposers?

(Romans 10:10) They have enlisted the support of Christendom's clergy and the aid of news journals and TV stations to spread lying reports about their former associates. Faithful ones soon find that the speech and conduct of these deceivers do not ring true. Like the Ephesians, Christians today "cannot bear bad men," so they disfellowship them from their congregations.*

5 Now, however, as he does with five of the seven congregations, Jesus singles out a serious problem. He says to the Ephesians: *"Nevertheless, I hold this against you, that you have left the love you had at first." (Revelation 2:4)* They should not have failed in this respect, for Paul had written them 35 years earlier referring to God's "great love with which he loved us," and he had urged them: "Become imitators of God, as beloved children, and go on walking in love, just as the Christ also loved you." (Ephesians 2:4; 5:1, 2) Further, Jesus' words should have been inscribed indelibly on their hearts: "Jehovah our God is one Jehovah, and you must love

---
* For historical details on the appearing of false apostles, see pages 37-44 of the handbook *Reasoning From the Scriptures,* available from the publishers of this book.
---

5. (a) What weakness did Jesus say the Ephesians had? (b) What words should the Ephesians have remembered?

Jehovah your God with your whole heart and with your whole soul and with your whole mind and with your whole strength." (Mark 12:29-31) The Ephesians had lost that first love.

6 Whether we are old-timers or new associates in the congregation, we must guard against losing our first love for Jehovah. How can this loss come about? We could allow attachment to our secular work, the desire to make a lot of money, or the pursuit of pleasure to become the big thing in our lives. Thus we could become fleshly minded rather than spiritually minded. (Romans 8:5-8; 1 Timothy 4:8; 6:9, 10) Our love for Jehovah should impel us to correct any such tendencies and to 'keep on seeking first God's kingdom and his righteousness,' so as to 'store up for ourselves treasures in heaven.'—Matthew 6:19-21, 31-33.

7 Let our service to Jehovah be motivated always by a deep-seated love for him. Let us have a fervent appreciation for all that Jehovah and Christ have done for us. As John

---
6. (a) Whether we are old-timers or new associates in the congregation, against what danger and tendencies must we guard? (b) What should our love for God impel us to do?
7. (a) By what should our service to Jehovah be motivated? (b) What did John say in regard to love?

Jesus' Pattern of Counsel
(citing chapters and verses of Revelation)

Message to congregation	Authority for rendering counsel	Introductory commendation	Problem clearly identified	Correction and/or encouragement	Resultant blessings
Ephesus	2:1	2:2, 3	2:4	2:5, 6	2:7
Smyrna	2:8	2:9	—	2:10	2:11
Pergamum	2:12	2:13	2:14, 15	2:16	2:17
Thyatira	2:18	2:19	2:20, 21	2:24, 25	2:26-28
Sardis	3:1	—	3:1, 2	3:3, 4	3:5
Philadelphia	3:7	3:8	—	3:8-11	3:12
Laodicea	3:14	—	3:15-17	3:18-20	3:21

himself wrote later: "The love is in this respect, not that we have loved God, but that he loved us and sent forth his Son as a propitiatory sacrifice for our sins." John goes on to tell us: "God is love, and he that remains in love remains in union with God and God remains in union with him." May we never let fade our love for Jehovah, for the Lord Jesus Christ, and for the living Word of God! This love we can express not only in zealous service to God but also by obedience to "this commandment we have from him, that the one who loves God should be loving his brother also."—1 John 4:10, 16, 21; Hebrews 4:12; see also 1 Peter 4:8; Colossians 3:10-14; Ephesians 4:15.

"Do the Former Deeds"

8 Those Ephesians must rekindle the love they once had if they do not want to lose out. *"Therefore,"* Jesus tells them, *"remember from what you have fallen, and repent and do the former deeds. If you do not, I am coming to you, and I will remove your lampstand from its place, unless you repent."* (*Revelation 2:5*) How did the Christians in the Ephesian congregation receive those words? We do not know. We hope that they repented and succeeded in reawakening their love for Jehovah. If they did not, then their lamp would be extinguished and their lampstand removed. They would lose their privilege of beaming forth the truth.

9 Nevertheless, Jesus has this encouraging word for the Ephesians: *"Still, you do have this, that you hate the deeds of the sect of Nicolaus, which I also hate."* (*Revelation 2:6*) At least they hated sectarian division, just as the Lord Jesus Christ hates it. As the years went by, however, many congregations failed to heed those words of Jesus. Lack of love for Jehovah, for the truth, and for one

another resulted in their drifting into spiritual darkness. They became fragmented into numerous quarreling sects. "Christian" copyists who had no love for Jehovah removed God's very name from Greek manuscripts of the Bible. Lack of love also allowed room for teaching Babylonish and Grecian doctrines, such as hellfire, purgatory, and the Trinity, in the name of Christianity. Having no love for God and for the truth, most of those who claimed to be Christian ceased to preach the good news of God's Kingdom. They came to be dominated by a selfish clergy class that made its own kingdom here on earth.—Compare 1 Corinthians 4:8.

10 When judgment started with the house of God in 1918, the sectarian clergy of Christendom were giving open support to World War I, urging Catholics and Protestants on both sides to slaughter one another. (1 Peter 4:17) Unlike the Ephesian congregation that hated what the sect of Nicolaus was doing, Christendom's religions had long been riddled with conflicting, anti-God doctrines, and their clergy had thrown their lot in with the world, of which Jesus said his disciples must be no part. (John 15:17-19) Their congregations, ignorant of the Bible's theme, God's Kingdom, were not lampstands beaming forth Scriptural truth, nor were their members part of the spiritual temple of Jehovah. Their leading men (and women) were not stars but were revealed to be members of "the man of lawlessness."—2 Thessalonians 2:3; Malachi 3:1-3.

11 The John class, however, emerged from the tumultuous days of the first world war with a love for Jehovah and for the truth that impelled them to serve him with flaming zeal. They resisted those who tried to introduce sectarianism through practically

---

8. How did Jesus say the Ephesians should act?
9. (a) What encouraging word did Jesus have for the Ephesians? (b) How did the congregations after John's day fail to heed Jesus' counsel to the Ephesians?

10. What was the religious situation in Christendom in 1918?
11. (a) What Christian group on the world scene in 1918 put into practice Jesus' words to the Ephesians? (b) What did the John class do from 1919 onward?

Loving Praise to Jehovah and His Son

In the songbook produced by Jehovah's people in 1905, there were twice as many songs praising Jesus as there were songs praising Jehovah God. In their 1928 songbook, the number of songs extolling Jesus was about the same as the number extolling Jehovah. But in the latest songbook of 1984, Jehovah is honored by four times as many songs as is Jesus. This is in harmony with Jesus' own words: "The Father is greater than I am." (John 14:28) Love for Jehovah must be preeminent, accompanied by deep love for Jesus and appreciation of his precious sacrifice and office as God's High Priest and King.

idolizing the first president of the Watch Tower Society, Charles T. Russell, following his death in 1916. Disciplined by persecutions and adversities, this Christian group clearly received a judgment of "well done" from their Master and an invitation to enter into his joy. (Matthew 25:21, 23) They recognized in the course of world events, and in their own experiences, the fulfillment of the sign that Jesus had given to mark his invisible presence in Kingdom power. From 1919 onward, they moved forward to share in the further fulfillment of Jesus' great prophecy: "And this good news of the kingdom will be preached in all the inhabited earth for a witness to all the nations; and then the end will come." (Matthew 6:9, 10; 24:3-14) If their love for Jehovah had been in some way lacking, it was fanned into a flame from that time onward.

[12] At a historic convention, attended by 18,000 of these Christians, at Cedar Point, Ohio, U.S.A., September 5-13, 1922, the call went out: "Back to the field, O ye sons of the most high God! . . . The world must know that Jehovah is God and that Jesus Christ is King of kings and Lord of lords. . . . Therefore advertise, advertise, advertise, the King and his kingdom." Jehovah's precious name was being made more prominent. In 1931 these Christians, assembled in convention at Columbus, Ohio, U.S.A., rejoiced to embrace and take the name indicated by God in Isaiah's prophecy—Jehovah's Witnesses. (Isaiah 43:10, 12) With its issue of March 1, 1939, the name of the organization's principal journal was changed to *The Watchtower Announcing Jehovah's Kingdom,* thus giving primary honor to our Creator and his royal government. Jehovah's Witnesses, with renewed love for Jehovah, have repented of any possible previous failure to honor and magnify his illustrious name and Kingdom. —Psalm 106:6, 47, 48.

"To Him That Conquers"

[13] Finally, as he does also in his other messages, Jesus calls attention to God's spirit as making known through Jesus the rewards for faithfulness. To the Ephesians he says: *"Let the one who has an ear hear what the spirit says to the congregations: To him that conquers I will grant to eat of the tree of life, which is in the paradise of God."* (*Revelation 2:7*) Those with hearing ears would be eager to heed that vital message, knowing that it did not come on Jesus' initiative but that it flowed from the Sovereign Lord Jehovah himself through His holy spirit, or active force. How would they 'conquer'? By following closely in the steps of Jesus, who kept integrity to the death and so could say: "Take courage! I have conquered the world." —John 8:28; 16:33; see also 1 John 5:4.

---

12. (a) At a historic convention in 1922, what call went forth? (b) What name did true Christians embrace in 1931, and of what did they repent?

13. (a) What blessing awaited the Ephesians if they 'conquered'? (b) How would Ephesian Christians 'conquer'?

¹⁴ Since they have no prospect of living in an earthly paradise, how is it that anointed Christians, such as those Ephesians, are rewarded with eating "of the tree of life, which is in the paradise of God"? This could not be the restored Paradise on earth, since the 144,000 anointed Christians, including those of the congregation at Ephesus, are bought from among mankind to rule with the Lamb, Christ Jesus, on the heavenly Mount Zion as spirit sons (Ephesians 1:5-12; Revelation 14:1, 4) Hence, the reference here must be to the heavenly gardenlike realm inherited by these conquerors. There, "in the paradise of God," yes, in the very presence of Jehovah himself, these overcomers who have been granted immortality will continue to live eternally, as symbolized here by their eating of the tree of life.

¹⁵ What, then, of the loyal earthly supporters of the 144,000 anointed ones? A great crowd of these companion Witnesses are also conquering. But their hope rests on entering an earthly paradise, where they will drink from "a river of water of life" and find healing from "the leaves of the trees" planted alongside that river. (Revelation 7:4, 9, 17; 22:1, 2) If you are one of this group, may you too express your warm love for Jehovah and win out in the conquest of faith. Thus you may attain to the happiness of everlasting life in the Paradise earth.—Compare 1 John 2:13, 14.

14. To what must "the paradise of God" mentioned by Jesus refer?

15. Why is Jesus' encouragement to conquer of vital interest to the great crowd today?

Chapter 8

Striving to Be Conquerors

TODAY, ancient Ephesus lies in ruins. But the destination of Jesus' second message is still the site of a bustling city. About 35 miles north of the ruins of Ephesus is the Turkish city of Izmir, where a zealous congregation of Jehovah's Witnesses is to be found even today. Here, in the first century, was Smyrna. Note, now, Jesus' next words: *"And to the angel of the congregation in Smyrna write: These are the things that he says, 'the First and*

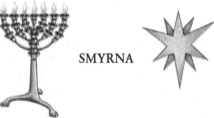

SMYRNA

the Last,' who became dead and came to life again." (Revelation 2:8) By stating this to those Christians in Smyrna, Jesus reminds them that he was the first integrity keeper that Jehovah directly resurrected to immortal spirit life and the last to be so raised. Jesus himself would resurrect all other anointed Christians. He is thus well qualified to give

1. (a) What congregation next receives a message from the glorified Jesus? (b) By calling himself "the First and the Last," of what did Jesus remind the Christians in that congregation?

counsel to his brothers, who hope to share immortal heavenly life with him.

2 Jesus led the way in enduring persecution for righteousness' sake, and he received the due reward. His faithfulness to the death and subsequent resurrection are the basis of hope for all Christians. (Acts 17:31) The fact that Jesus "became dead and came to life again" proves that whatever has to be endured in the cause of truth is not in vain. Jesus' resurrection is a source of profound encouragement for all Christians, especially when they are called on to suffer for their faith. Is this your situation? Then you can take courage also from Jesus' next words to the congregation in Smyrna:

3 *"I know your tribulation and poverty—but you are rich—and the blasphemy by those who say they themselves are Jews, and yet they are not but are a synagogue of Satan."* (Revelation 2:9) Jesus has no criticism for his brothers in Smyrna, only warm commendation. They have suffered much tribulation because of their faith. Materially they are poor, likely because of their faithfulness. (Hebrews 10: 34) Their main concern, however, is with spiritual things, and they have stored up treasures in heaven, as Jesus advised. (Matthew 6:19, 20) Hence, the Chief Shepherd views them as being "rich."—Compare James 2:5.

4 Jesus notes particularly that the Christians in Smyrna have put up with much opposition at the hands of fleshly Jews. In earlier days, many of this religion determinedly opposed the spread of Christianity. (Acts 13:44, 45; 14:19) Now, just a few decades after the fall of Jerusalem, those Jews in Smyrna are showing the same satanic spirit. No wonder Jesus views them as "a synagogue of Satan"!*

5 Faced with such hatred, the Christians in Smyrna are comforted by Jesus: *"Do not be afraid of the things you are about to suffer. Look! The Devil will keep on throwing some of YOU into prison that YOU may be fully put to the test, and that YOU may have tribulation ten days. Prove yourself faithful even to death, and I will give you the crown of life."* (Revelation 2:10) Here Jesus three times uses the Greek plural form of "you," showing that his words embrace the congregation as a whole. Jesus cannot promise that the trials of the Christians in Smyrna will soon end. Some of them will continue to be persecuted and cast into prison. They will have tribulation for "ten days." Ten is a number that symbolizes earthly completeness or entirety. Even those spiritually rich integrity keepers will receive a thorough testing while in the flesh.

6 Nevertheless, the Christians in Smyrna should not be afraid or compromise. If they remain faithful to the end, there is laid up for them as a reward "the crown of life," in their case immortal life in the heavens. (1 Corinthians 9:25; 2 Timothy 4:6-8) The apostle Paul viewed this precious prize as worth the sacrifice of everything else, even his earthly life. (Philippians 3:8) Evidently, those faithful ones in Smyrna feel the same way. Jesus concludes his message by saying: *"Let the one who has an ear hear what the spirit says to the congregations: He that conquers will*

---

* About 60 years after John died, 86-year-old Polycarp was burned to death in Smyrna because he would not recant his belief in Jesus. *The Martyrdom of Polycarp*, a work believed to be contemporaneous with this event, states that when wood was being gathered for burning, "the Jews were extremely zealous, as is their custom, in assisting at this"—even though the execution took place on "a great Sabbath day."

---

2. Why are all Christians comforted by the words of the One who "became dead and came to life again"?
3. (a) What encouragement did Jesus give the Christians in Smyrna? (b) Though the Christians in Smyrna were poor, why did Jesus say they were "rich"?
4. From whom did the Christians in Smyrna suffer much opposition, and how did Jesus view those opposers?

5. What trials lay ahead for the Christians in Smyrna?
6. (a) Why should the Christians in Smyrna not be afraid? (b) How did Jesus conclude his message to the congregation in Smyrna?

REVELATION CLIMAX

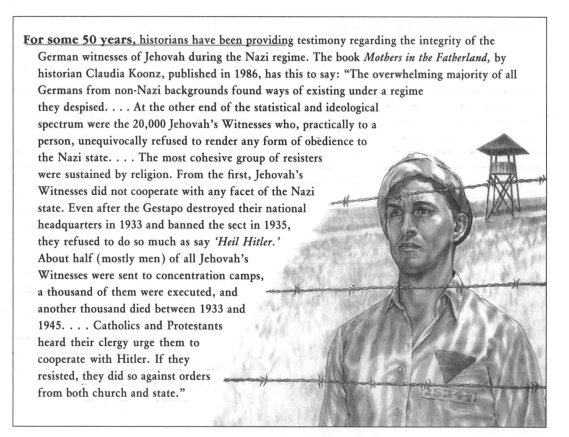

For some 50 years, historians have been providing testimony regarding the integrity of the German witnesses of Jehovah during the Nazi regime. The book *Mothers in the Fatherland*, by historian Claudia Koonz, published in 1986, has this to say: "The overwhelming majority of all Germans from non-Nazi backgrounds found ways of existing under a regime they despised. . . . At the other end of the statistical and ideological spectrum were the 20,000 Jehovah's Witnesses who, practically to a person, unequivocally refused to render any form of obedience to the Nazi state. . . . The most cohesive group of resisters were sustained by religion. From the first, Jehovah's Witnesses did not cooperate with any facet of the Nazi state. Even after the Gestapo destroyed their national headquarters in 1933 and banned the sect in 1935, they refused to do so much as say 'Heil Hitler.' About half (mostly men) of all Jehovah's Witnesses were sent to concentration camps, a thousand of them were executed, and another thousand died between 1933 and 1945. . . . Catholics and Protestants heard their clergy urge them to cooperate with Hitler. If they resisted, they did so against orders from both church and state."

by no means be harmed by the second death." (*Revelation 2:11*) The conquerors are assured of immortal heavenly life that cannot be touched by death.—1 Corinthians 15:53, 54.

"Tribulation Ten Days"

7 Much like the Christians in Smyrna, the John class and their companions today have been and continue to be "fully put to the test." Their faithfulness under trial marks them as God's own people. (Mark 13:9, 10) Shortly after the Lord's day got under way, Jesus' words to the Christians in Smyrna brought real comfort to the small interna-

tional group of Jehovah's people. (Revelation 1:10) Ever since 1879, these had been digging out from God's Word spiritual riches that they freely shared with others. But during World War I, they met up with intense hatred and opposition, partly because they did not get caught up in the war fever and partly because they were fearlessly exposing the errors of Christendom. The persecution that they received at the instigation of some of Christendom's leaders came to a head in 1918 and was comparable to what the Christians in Smyrna received from the Jewish community there.

8 A wave of persecution in the United States of America was climaxed when the new president of the Watch Tower Society, Joseph F. Rutherford, and seven associates

---

7, 8. Like the congregation in Smyrna, how was the Christian congregation "fully put to the test" in 1918?

STRIVING TO BE CONQUERORS

were sent to prison on June 22, 1918, most of them with 20-year sentences. They were released on bail nine months later. On May 14, 1919, the appeal court reversed their erroneous convictions; there were shown to be 125 errors in the trial. Roman Catholic Judge Manton, a knight of the order of St. Gregory the Great, who in 1918 had refused bail to these Christians, was sentenced later, in 1939, to two years' imprisonment and a fine of $10,000 on six charges of soliciting and accepting bribes.

9 During Nazi rule in Germany, Hitler completely banned the preaching work of Jehovah's Witnesses. For years, thousands of Witnesses were cruelly confined in concentration camps, where many died, while hundreds of young men who refused to fight in Hitler's army were executed. The clergy's support of all of this is evidenced by the words of a Catholic priest, published in the newspaper *The German* of May 29, 1938. In part, he said: "There is now one country on earth where the so-called . . . Bible Students [Jehovah's Witnesses] are forbidden. That is Germany! . . . When Adolph Hitler came to power, and the German Catholic Episcopate repeated their request, Hitler said: 'These so-called Earnest Bible Students [Jehovah's Witnesses] are troublemakers; . . . I consider them quacks; I do not tolerate that the German Catholics shall be besmirched in such a manner by this American Judge Rutherford; I dissolve [Jehovah's Witnesses] in Germany.'" To this, the priest added: "Bravo!"

10 As the Lord's day has proceeded, the Serpent and his seed have never ceased to fight against the anointed Christians and their companions. Many of these have been imprisoned and viciously persecuted. (Revelation 12:17) Those enemies have continued to 'frame mischief by law,' but Jehovah's people steadfastly insist: "We must obey God as ruler rather than men." (Psalm 94:20, *King James Version;* Acts 5:29) In 1954 the *Watchtower* magazine reported: "More than seventy countries at one time or another during the past forty years have made restrictive decrees and have persecuted Jehovah's witnesses." Where it has been possible to fight for religious freedom in the courts, these Christians have done so and have come through with resounding victories in a number of countries. In the United States Supreme Court alone, Jehovah's Witnesses have won 23 favorable decisions.

11 No other group has been so conscientious in obeying Jesus' command to pay back Caesar's things to Caesar. (Luke 20:25; Romans 13:1, 7) Yet, no other group has had members imprisoned in so many lands under so many different forms of government, and this continues to the present time in the Americas, in Europe, in Africa, and in Asia. Jesus' great prophecy concerning the sign of his presence included these words: "Then people will deliver you up to tribulation and will kill you, and you will be objects of hatred by all the nations on account of my name." (Matthew 24:3, 9) This has certainly been fulfilled upon the Christian witnesses of Jehovah during the Lord's day.

12 To fortify God's people against tribulation, the John class has continually reminded them of the substance of Jesus' words to the Christians in Smyrna. For example, as Nazi persecution started, *The Watchtower* in 1933 and 1934 carried articles such as "Fear Them Not," which discussed Matthew 10:26-33; "The Crucible," based on Daniel 3:17, 18; and

---

9. How were Jehovah's Witnesses in Nazi Germany treated by Hitler, and with what reaction by the clergy?
10. (a) As the Lord's day has proceeded, what persecution have Jehovah's Witnesses faced? (b) What often resulted when Christians fought for religious freedom in the courts?

11. What prophecy of Jesus concerning the sign of his presence has been fulfilled upon Jehovah's Witnesses during the Lord's day?
12. How has the John class fortified God's people against persecution?

"Lions' Mouths," with Daniel 6:22 as the key text. In the 1980's, during which decade Jehovah's Witnesses have suffered vicious persecution in more than 40 lands, *The Watchtower* has fortified God's people with articles such as "Happy Though Persecuted!" and "Christians Meet Persecution With Endurance."*

13 Truly, the Christian witnesses of Jeho-

---
* See *The Watchtower* of November 1, 1933; October 1 and 15, December 1 and 15, 1934; May 1, 1983.
---

13. Like the Christians in Smyrna, why have the Christian witnesses of Jehovah not been afraid of persecution?

vah are suffering physical persecution and other testings for a symbolic ten days. Like the Christians back in Smyrna, they have not been afraid; nor do any of us need to be afraid as troubles worsen here on earth. We are prepared to endure under sufferings and take even 'the plundering of our belongings' joyfully. (Hebrews 10:32-34) By studying God's Word and making it our very own, we will be equipped to stand solid in the faith. Be assured that Jehovah can and will guard you in your integrity. "Throw all your anxiety upon him, because he cares for you." —1 Peter 5:6-11.

Chapter 9

Holding Fast to Jesus' Name

TRAVELING 50 miles north up the coastal road from Smyrna and then 15 miles inland through the Caicus River valley, we come to Pergamum, now called Bergama. The city was renowned for its temple of Zeus, or Jupiter. In the 1800's, archaeologists transported the altar of that temple to Germany, where it may still be viewed, along with many statues and reliefs of pagan gods, at the Pergamon Museum in East Berlin. What message would the Lord Jesus send to the congregation living amid all that idolatry?

PERGAMUM

2 First, Jesus establishes his identity, saying: ***"And to the angel of the congregation in Pergamum write: These are the things that he says who has the sharp, long two-edged sword."*** (*Revelation 2:12*) Jesus here repeats the de-

scription given of him at Revelation 1:16. As Judge and Executioner, he will strike down those who persecute his disciples. How comforting that assurance! Regarding judgment, however, let those *within* the congregation also be warned that Jehovah, acting through this messenger of the covenant, Jesus Christ, "will become a speedy witness" against all professing Christians who practice idolatry, immorality, lying, and dishonesty and who fail to care for the needy. (Malachi 3:1, 5; Hebrews 13:1-3) The counsel and reproof that God causes Jesus to give must be heeded!

---
1. What congregation received Jesus' next message, and in what kind of city did those Christians live?
2. How does Jesus establish his identity, and what is the significance of his having 'the two-edged sword'?

41

³ Jesus now tells the congregation: *"I know where you are dwelling, that is, where the throne of Satan is."* (*Revelation 2:13a*) Truly, those Christians were surrounded by satanic worship. In addition to the temple of Zeus, there was a shrine to Aesculapius, the god of healing. Pergamum was also renowned as a center for the cult of emperor worship. The Hebrew word translated "Satan" means "Resister," and his "throne" represents his world rulership, as divinely permitted for a season. (Job 1:6, *New World Translation Reference Bible,* footnote) The profusion of idolatry in Pergamum showed that Satan's "throne" was firmly asserted in that city. How angry Satan must have felt that the Christians there did not bow to him in nationalistic worship!

⁴ Yes, "the throne of Satan" is right there in Pergamum. *"And yet,"* Jesus continues, *"you keep on holding fast my name, and you did not deny your faith in me even in the days of Antipas, my witness, the faithful one, who was killed by your side, where Satan is dwelling."* (*Revelation 2:13b*) What soul-stirring commendation! No doubt the martyrdom of Antipas resulted from his refusal to go along with demonistic practices and the worship of the Roman emperor. Not long after John received this prophecy, Pliny the Younger, personal legate to Emperor Trajan of Rome, wrote Trajan and explained his procedure for handling persons accused of being Christians—a procedure that the emperor approved. Those who denied being Christians were released when, as Pliny said, they had repeated after me an invocation to the gods, offered incense, and wine to your [Trajan's] image . . . and, in addition, cursed Christ." Any found to be Christians were executed. Even though faced by such danger, the Christians in Pergamum did not deny their faith. They 'held fast to Jesus' name' in that they continued to honor his high position as Jehovah's Vindicator and appointed Judge. Loyally, they followed in Jesus' footsteps as Kingdom witnesses.

⁵ On various occasions, Jesus had made known that Satan rules this present wicked world, but because of Jesus' integrity, Satan had no hold on him. (Matthew 4:8-11; John 14:30) In this 20th century, powerful nations, notably "the king of the north" and "the king of the south," have been struggling for world domination. (Daniel 11:40) Patriotic fervor has been whipped up, and the cult of emperor worship has a modern-day counterpart in the wave of nationalism that has swept the earth. Articles on neutrality in *The Watchtower* of November 1, 1939, and again of November 1, 1979, and September 1, 1986, have clearly stated the Bible's teaching on this issue, providing guidelines for those Christians who want to walk in the name of Jehovah and conquer the world as Jesus so courageously did.—Micah 4:1, 3, 5; John 16:33; 17:4, 6, 26; 18:36, 37; Acts 5:29.

⁶ Such counsel has been urgently needed. In the face of unreasoning patriotic fervor, Jehovah's Witnesses, both anointed ones and their companions, have had to stand firm in the faith. In the United States, hundreds of children and teachers were dismissed from schools because they did not salute the national flag, while in Germany the Witnesses were viciously persecuted for refusing to salute the swastika. As already noted, Hitler's Nazis killed thousands of Jehovah's loyal servants because they refused to share in such

---

3. What false worship took place in Pergamum, and how can it be said that "the throne of Satan" was there?

4. (a) What commendation does Jesus give to the Christians in Pergamum? (b) What did the Roman legate Pliny write to Emperor Trajan with regard to the treatment of Christians? (c) Despite danger, what course did the Christians in Pergamum take?

5. (a) What modern-day counterpart of the cult of emperor worship has caused severe tests for Christians in this 20th century? (b) What help has *The Watchtower* provided Christians?

6. Like Antipas, how have Jehovah's Witnesses taken a firm stand in modern times?

nationalistic idolatry. In the 1930's, during Japan's heyday of Shinto emperor worship, two pioneer ministers sowed much Kingdom seed in Japanese-occupied Taiwan. The military rulers threw them into prison, where one of them died because of the harsh treatment. The other was later released, only to be shot in the back—a modern-day Antipas. To this day, there are lands where worship of nationalistic symbols and exclusive devotion to the State are demanded. Many youthful Witnesses have been imprisoned, and not a few executed, because of their courageous stand as Christian neutrals. If you are a youth who faces such issues, study God's Word daily so that you may "have faith to the preserving alive of the soul," with everlasting life in view. —Hebrews 10:39–11:1; Matthew 10:28-31.

⁷ Youngsters in school have faced similar issues. In 1985, in the state of Kerala, India, three young children of Jehovah's Witnesses refused to compromise their Bible-based faith, declining to sing the national anthem. They stood respectfully while others sang, but they were nonetheless expelled from school. Their father appealed this action right up to the Supreme Court of India, where the two judges decided in favor of the children, courageously stating: "Our tradition teaches tolerance; our philosophy teaches tolerance; our constitution practices tolerance; let us not dilute it." Newspaper publicity and favorable editorials resulting from

7. How did youngsters in India face the issue of nationalistic worship, and with what result?

this case informed the entire nation of close to one fifth of the earth's population that there are Christians in that land who worship the true God Jehovah and that these stand loyally by Bible principles.

Corrupting Influences

⁸ Yes, the Christians in Pergamum are integrity keepers. *"Nevertheless,"* says Jesus, *"I have a few things against you."* What have they done to deserve censure? Jesus tells us: *"You have there those holding fast the teaching of Balaam, who went teaching Balak to put a stumbling block before the sons of Israel, to eat things sacrificed to idols and to commit fornication."*—Revelation 2:14.

⁹ In Moses' day, King Balak of Moab had hired Balaam, a non-Israelite prophet, who knew something about Jehovah's ways, to curse Israel. Jehovah resisted Balaam, compelling him to pronounce blessings for the Israelites and woes for their enemies. Balaam pacified Balak's resultant resentment by suggesting a more subtle attack: Let Moab's women seduce Israel's men into gross sexual immorality and idolatrous worship of the false god Baal of Peor! This tactic worked. Jehovah's righteous anger blazed, as he sent a scourge that killed 24,000 of those Israelite fornicators—a scourge that was stayed only when priest Phinehas took positive action to remove badness from Israel.—Numbers 24: 10, 11; 25:1-3, 6-9; 31:16.

8. What censure does Jesus find it necessary to give the Christians in Pergamum?
9. Who was Balaam, and how did his counsel put "a stumbling block before the sons of Israel"?

These evidences of rampant pagan worship are on display in the Pergamon Museum in East Berlin

¹⁰ Now, in John's day, are there similar stumbling blocks in Pergamum? There are! Immorality and idolatry have infiltrated the congregation. Those Christians have not heeded God's warnings given through the apostle Paul. (1 Corinthians 10:6-11) Since they have endured persecution, perhaps they feel that Jehovah will overlook their sexual transgressions. So Jesus makes it plain that they must shun such wickedness.

¹¹ Similarly today, Christians must guard against "turning the undeserved kindness of our God into an excuse for loose conduct." (Jude 4) We are obliged to hate what is bad and to 'pummel our bodies' in order to pursue a course of Christian virtue. (1 Corinthians 9:27; Psalm 97:10; Romans 8:6) We should never think that zeal in God's service and integrity under persecution give us a license to get involved in sexual misconduct. Over the years, offenders disfellowshipped from the worldwide Christian congregation, mostly on grounds of sexual immorality, have numbered into the tens of thousands. In some years there have been even more than fell in ancient Israel because of the Baal of Peor. May we keep up our guard so that we never fall into that company!—Romans 11:20; 1 Corinthians 10:12.

¹² Jesus also reprimands the Christians in Pergamum for 'eating things sacrificed to idols.' What would this involve? In view of Paul's words to the Corinthians, perhaps some were abusing their Christian freedom and deliberately offending the consciences of others. More likely, though, they were taking part somehow in actual idol ceremonies.

(1 Corinthians 8:4-13; 10:25-30) Faithful Christians today must show unselfish love in their exercise of Christian freedom, being careful not to stumble others. Certainly, they must avoid modern forms of idolatry, such as worshiping stars of TV, the movies, and sports, or making a god out of money, or even out of their own belly!—Matthew 6:24; Philippians 1:9, 10; 3:17-19.

Avoid Sectarianism!

¹³ Jesus further reproves the Christians in Pergamum, saying: *"So you, also, have those holding fast the teaching of the sect of Nicolaus likewise."* (*Revelation 2:15*) Previously, Jesus has commended the Ephesians for their hatred of the deeds of this sect. But the Christians in Pergamum need counsel on keeping the congregation free from sectarianism. More firmness is needed in upholding Christian standards so that the unity for which Jesus prayed at John 17:20-23 may be preserved. It is necessary "both to exhort by the teaching that is healthful and to reprove those who contradict."—Titus 1:9.

¹⁴ From early days, the Christian congregation has had to contend with proud apostates, who by smooth, deceptive speech "cause divisions and occasions for stumbling contrary to the teaching," provided through Jehovah's channel. (Romans 16:17, 18) The apostle Paul warned of this threat in almost all his letters.* In modern times, when Jesus has restored the true congregation to its Christian purity and unity, the danger of

---

* See also 1 Corinthians 3:3, 4, 18, 19; 2 Corinthians 11:13; Galatians 4:9; Ephesians 4:14, 15; Philippians 3:18, 19; Colossians 2:8; 1 Thessalonians 3:5; 2 Thessalonians 2:1-3; 1 Timothy 6:3-5; 2 Timothy 2:17; 4:3, 4; Titus 1:13, 14; 3:10; Hebrews 10:26, 27.

---

10. What stumbling blocks have infiltrated the congregation in Pergamum, and why might those Christians have felt that God would overlook their transgressions?
11. (a) Against what should Christians be on guard, and what kind of thinking must they avoid? (b) Over the years, how many have been disfellowshipped from the Christian congregation, and mostly on what grounds?
12. As with servants of God in early times, what principles apply to Christians today?

13. What words of reproof does Jesus next give the Christians in Pergamum, and why did the congregation need them?
14. (a) From early days, with whom has the Christian congregation had to contend, and how did the apostle Paul describe them? (b) What words of Jesus should be heeded by any who may have become inclined to follow a breakaway group?

REVELATION CLIMAX

A portion of manna was hidden in the ark of the covenant. Being given symbolic hidden manna means for conquering anointed ones that they receive immortality

sectarianism remains. Hence, any who may have become inclined to follow a breakaway group, thus forming a sect, should heed Jesus' next words: *"Therefore repent. If you do not, I am coming to you quickly, and I will war with them with the long sword of my mouth."—Revelation 2:16.*

15 How does sectarianism get started? Perhaps a self-styled teacher sows doubts, disputing some Bible truth (such as our being in the last days), and so a splinter group breaks off and follows him. (2 Timothy 3:1; 2 Peter 3:3, 4) Or someone criticizes the way Jehovah is having his work done and appeals to a self-sparing spirit by claiming that it is neither Scriptural nor necessary to go from house to house with the Kingdom message. Sharing in such service after the example of Jesus and his apostles would keep these ones humble; yet, they prefer to split off and take it easy, perhaps only reading the Bible occasionally as a private group. (Matthew 10:7, 11-13; Acts 5:42; 20:20, 21) Such ones concoct their own ideas about the Memorial of Jesus' death, the Scriptural command to abstain from blood, celebration of holidays, and the use of tobacco. Moreover, they downgrade Jehovah's name; very soon they fall right back into the permissive ways of Babylon the Great. Even worse, some are moved by Satan to turn upon and beat their

---

15. How does sectarianism get started?

fellow slaves, their onetime brothers.—Matthew 24:49; Acts 15:29; Revelation 17:5.

16 Any who waver because of apostate influence should be swift to heed Jesus' call to repent! Apostate propaganda must be rejected as the poison that it is! Its basis is envy and hatred, in contrast with the righteous, chaste, and lovable truths that Jesus feeds to his congregation. (Luke 12:42; Philippians 1: 15, 16; 4:8, 9) As to those who refuse to repent, the Lord Jesus does indeed "war with them with the long sword of [his] mouth." He is sifting his people in order to preserve the unity for which he prayed during his last evening with his disciples on earth. (John 17: 20-23, 26) Since apostate ones refuse the loving counsel and help offered by the stars in his right hand, Jesus judges and punishes them "with the greatest severity," consigning them to "the darkness outside." They are disfellowshipped, no more to act as leaven among God's people.—Matthew 24:48-51; 25: 30; 1 Corinthians 5:6, 9, 13; Revelation 1:16.

'Hidden Manna and a White Pebble'

17 A grand reward awaits all who heed Jesus' counsel, given by direction of Jehovah's holy spirit. Listen! *"Let the one who has*

---

16. (a) Why should those who waver because of apostate influence be swift to repent? (b) What will happen to those who refuse to repent?
17. What reward awaits anointed Christians who 'conquer,' and what did the Christians in Pergamum need to overcome?

The white pebble is for those admitted to the marriage of the Lamb

an ear hear what the spirit says to the congregations: To him that conquers I will give some of the hidden manna, and I will give him a white pebble, and upon the pebble a new name written which no one knows except the one receiving it." (*Revelation 2:17*) Thus, the Christians in Pergamum, like the Christians in Smyrna, are encouraged to 'conquer.' If they are to succeed, those in Pergamum, where the throne of Satan is, must shun idolatry. They must overcome the immorality, the sectarianism, and the apostasy linked with Balak, Balaam, and the sect of Nicolaus. So doing, those anointed Christians will be invited to eat some of "the hidden manna." What does this mean?

[18] In Moses' day, Jehovah provided manna to sustain the Israelites during their wilderness journey. That manna was not hidden, for each morning—except on the Sabbath—it appeared miraculously, like a flaky hoarfrost covering the earth. It was a divine provision to keep the Israelites alive. As a memorial, Jehovah commanded Moses to keep some of this "bread" in a golden jar inside the sacred ark of the covenant "throughout [Israel's] generations."—Exodus 16:14, 15, 23, 26, 33; Hebrews 9:3, 4.

[19] What a fitting symbol! This manna was hidden in the Most Holy compartment of the tabernacle, where the miraculous light that hovered over the Ark's cover symbolized the very presence of Jehovah. (Exodus 26:34) No one was permitted to penetrate that sacred place in order to eat the hidden manna. However, Jesus said that his anointed followers who conquer would eat "the hidden manna." Like Christ before them, they get to enter, "not into a holy place made with hands, which is a copy of the reality, but into heaven itself." (Hebrews 9:12, 24) At their resurrection, they put on incorruption and

immortality—a marvelous provision of Jehovah, symbolized by their being given the imperishable "hidden manna." How privileged that small group of overcomers is! —1 Corinthians 15:53-57.

[20] These also receive "a white pebble." In Roman courts, pebbles were used in passing judgment.* A white pebble meant acquittal, whereas a black pebble meant condemnation, often to death. Jesus' giving "a white pebble" to the Christians in Pergamum would indicate that he adjudges them innocent, pure, and clean. But Jesus' words may have a further meaning. In Roman times, pebbles were also used like tickets to gain entry to important events. So the white pebble may indicate something very special for the conquering anointed Christian—his being admitted to an honored place in heaven at the marriage of the Lamb. Only 144,000 such pebbles are provided.—Revelation 14:1; 19:7-9.

[21] Does this mean that you are left unconsidered if you are one of the great crowd of companion worshipers? Not at all! While not receiving the white pebble of admittance into heaven, you may, if you endure, come out of the great tribulation to have a part in the joyful work of restoring Paradise on earth. Sharing with you in this will be resurrected faithful ones from pre-Christian times and those of the other sheep who may have died more recently. Eventually, all the other redeemed dead will be favored with a resurrection to life on a paradise earth.—Psalm 45:16; John 10:16; Revelation 7:9, 14.

[22] What is the new name written on the pebble? A name is a means of identifying a

---

* See Acts 26:10 and footnote, *New World Translation Reference Bible*.

REVELATION CLIMAX

person and distinguishing that one from others. These anointed Christians receive the pebble after they have finished their earthly course as conquerors. Clearly, then, the name on the pebble has to do with their privilege of being united with Jesus in heaven—a most intimate position of royal service to be fully appreciated and enjoyed only by those who inherit the heavenly Kingdom. Hence, it is a name, or a designation of office, "which

STOP

no one knows except the one receiving it." —Compare Revelation 3:12.

23 What an inducement for the John class to "hear what the spirit says to the congregations" and apply it! And how this encourages their associates, the great crowd, to serve faithfully with them while they can enjoy their companionship here on earth and share with them in making known Jehovah's Kingdom!

—

6/3/91
START

Abhorring the "Deep Things of Satan"

START 12/19/94

ABOUT 40 miles southeast of Bergama (Pergamum) is the thriving Turkish town of Akhisar. Some 1,900 years ago, this town was the site of Thyatira. A traveling overseer could readily reach Thyatira by an inland road from Pergamum and then move in a circuit to the remaining congregations of Revelation chapter 3—Sardis, Philadelphia, and Laodicea. Unlike Pergamum, Thyatira does not seem to have been an important center of emperor worship, but it did have shrines and temples dedicated to pagan gods. Thyatira was noteworthy as a commercial trading center.

² When Paul was preaching in Macedonia,

THYATIRA

he met up with a Thyatiran woman named Lydia, a seller of purple. Lydia and all her household gladly accepted the message Paul was preaching and showed extraordinary hospitality. (Acts 16:14, 15) She became the first Thyatiran on record to accept Christianity. In course of time, the city itself came to have a congregation of Christians. Jesus directs his longest message there: **"And to the angel of the congregation in Thyatira write: These are the things that the Son of God says, he who has his eyes like a fiery flame, and his feet are like fine copper."—Revelation 2:18.**

³ This is the only time the expression "Son of God" appears in Revelation, although in

---

1. How was Thyatira situated in relation to other congregations, and in what kind of religious environment?
2, 3. (a) What was recorded earlier about a Thyatiran who became a Christian? (b) Of what significance is it to the Christians in Thyatira that Jesus is "the Son of God" and that he has "eyes like a fiery flame"?

47

other places Jesus does refer to Jehovah as "my Father." (Revelation 2:27; 3:5, 21) The use of the title here likely reminds the Thyatiran Christians of Jesus' intimacy with Jehovah. This Son "has his eyes like a fiery flame" —a warning to the Christians in Thyatira that his judgment will blaze against anything that he sees to be defiling in the congregation. By referring for a second time to his glowing, copperlike feet, he emphasizes his own shining example of faithfulness while walking this earth. The Christians in Thyatira no doubt heeded his counsel, and so must we today!—1 Peter 2:21.

[4] Happily, Jesus can commend those in Thyatira. He says: *"I know your deeds, and your love and faith and ministry and endurance, and that your deeds of late are more than those formerly."* (*Revelation 2:19*) Unlike the Ephesians, the anointed Christians there have not lost their first love for Jehovah. Their faith is strong. Furthermore, their deeds are more than those formerly, and like the three preceding congregations, the Christians in Thyatira are enduring. How typical of the 54,000 and more congregations of Jehovah's Witnesses throughout the earth today! Love for Jehovah shines through, as a spirit of zeal in the ministry permeates the organization, stimulating young and old. An increasing number expend themselves as pioneers, thus using wisely the yet remaining time to proclaim the glorious hope of God's incoming Kingdom!—Matthew 24:14; Mark 13:10.

[5] For decades, many faithful ones, both of the anointed remnant and of the great crowd, have been showing exemplary endurance in God's service, while the world around them has been plunging deeper and deeper into a hopeless gloom. But let us be of good courage! Revelation confirms the testimony of God's earlier prophets. "The great day of Jehovah is near. It is near, and there is a hurrying of it very much."—Zephaniah 1:14; Joel 2:1; Habakkuk 2:3; Revelation 7:9; 22:12, 13.

"That Woman Jezebel"

[6] Jesus' fiery eyes have pierced further. He notes something that needs immediate attention. *"Nevertheless,"* he tells the Christians in Thyatira, *"I do hold this against you, that you tolerate that woman Jezebel, who calls herself a prophetess, and she teaches and misleads my slaves to commit fornication and to eat things sacrificed to idols."* (*Revelation 2:20*) In the tenth century B.C.E., Queen Jezebel, the Baal-worshiping wife of King Ahab of Israel, had become notorious for her murderous, adulterous, dominating ways. Jehu, as Jehovah's anointed one, had her executed. (1 Kings 16:31; 18:4; 21:1-16; 2 Kings 9:1-7, 22, 30, 33) The idolatrous Jezebel had no claim to being a prophetess. She was not like Miriam and Deborah, who served as faithful prophetesses in Israel. (Exodus 15:20, 21; Judges 4:4; 5:1-31) And Jeho-

---

4, 5. (a) Why could Jesus commend the Christians in Thyatira? (b) How is the congregation in Thyatira typical of the more than 54,000 congregations of Jehovah's Witnesses today?

6. (a) Despite praiseworthy features, what problem does Jesus note in the congregation in Thyatira that needs immediate attention? (b) Who was Jezebel, and did she have a valid claim to being a prophetess?

REVELATION CLIMAX

vah's spirit did not move her to prophesy as it moved the aged Anna and the four daughters of Philip the evangelizer.—Luke 2:36-38; Acts 21:9.

⁷ Plainly, then, "that woman Jezebel" who claims to be a prophetess in Thyatira is a sham. She has no backing of God's spirit. Who is she? Likely, she is a woman or group of women acting as a shameless corrupting influence in the congregation. Some associated women may have been involving congregation members in immorality, while brazenly justifying their self-willed course by misapplying scriptures. False prophesying indeed! They would influence others to fall into their own ways of "fornication, uncleanness, sexual appetite, hurtful desire, and covetousness, which is idolatry." (Colossians 3:5) They would have those in the congregation indulge in an immoral, self-seeking life-style of the kind that is now countenanced, or winked at, in most of Christendom's religions.

⁸ Jesus goes on to tell the elders in Thyatira: *"And I gave her time to repent, but she is not willing to repent of her fornication. Look! I am about to throw her into a sickbed, and those committing adultery with her into great tribulation, unless they repent of her deeds."* (*Revelation 2:21, 22*) Just as the original Jezebel apparently dominated Ahab and then defied God's executioner, Jehu, so this female influence may be trying to manipulate husbands and elders. It seems that the elders in Thyatira are tolerating this immodest Jezebel influence. Jesus here sounds a strong warning for them, as well as for the global congregation of Jehovah's people today. In modern times, some such strong-willed women have induced their husbands to become apostates and have even instigated court action against Jehovah's faithful servants.—Compare Jude 5-8.

⁹ This in no way reflects unfavorably on faithful women in the Christian congregation. Nowadays, a great part of the witness work is being accomplished by faithful sisters; through the home Bible studies that they conduct, they are bringing throngs of new ones into the congregation. God himself blesses this arrangement, as is indicated by Psalm 68:11: "Jehovah himself gives the saying; the women telling the good news are a large army." Husbands may be influenced

---

7. (a) By mentioning "that woman Jezebel," Jesus is evidently referring to what influence? (b) How may some associated women have justified their self-willed course?

8. (a) What is Jesus' pronouncement about the "Jezebel" in Thyatira? (b) How has improper female influence been felt in modern times?

9. (a) Why do Jesus' words about Jezebel not reflect unfavorably on all women in the congregation? (b) When only is it that a Jezebel influence arises?

for good by the mild, respectful conduct of their wives, which "is of great value in the eyes of God." (1 Peter 3:1-4) The capable, industrious wife is praised by King Lemuel. (Proverbs 31:10-31) It is only when women step out of line by seducing men or by challenging or ignoring headship that a Jezebel influence arises.—Ephesians 5:22, 23; 1 Corinthians 11:3.

10 Referring to "that woman Jezebel," Jesus continues: *"And her children I will kill with deadly plague, so that all the congregations will know that I am he who searches the kidneys and hearts, and I will give to you individually according to your deeds."* (*Revelation 2:23*) Jesus has allowed Jezebel and her children time to repent, but they persist in their immoral ways and hence must receive judgment. There is a powerful message here for Christians today. Those who imitate Jezebel, whether men or women, and thus become her children by violating Bible principles on headship and morality or by being headstrong so as to ignore theocratic order, are spiritually in a dangerously sick condition. True, if such a one calls upon the elders in the congregation to pray over him, "the prayer of faith will make the indisposed one well, and Jehovah will raise him up"—provided he humbly acts in harmony with those prayers. But let no one think that he (or she) can fool God or Christ by attempting to conceal immoral acts or by putting on an outward show of zealous service.—James 5:14, 15.

11 Happily, most congregations of Jehovah's Witnesses today are awake to this danger. Elders are watchful of trends toward untheocratic attitudes and wrongdoing. They try to help both males and females who are in danger's way so that these may build spirituality and be readjusted before it is too late. (Galatians 5:16; 6:1) Lovingly and firmly, these Christian overseers restrain any female effort to form cliques for promoting moves similar to women's liberation. Moreover, timely counsel is periodically given in the Watch Tower Society's publications.*

12 However, where there has been gross immorality, and especially where this becomes a practice, unrepentant sinners must be disfellowshipped. We recall Jehu's zeal in getting rid of all traces of Jezebel's influence in Israel. Likewise, the John class today take firm action, setting an example for their "Jehonadab" companions and showing themselves to be far different from Christendom's permissive ministers.—2 Kings 9:22, 30-37; 10:12-17.

13 As Jehovah's Messenger and Judge, the Son of God acts rightly in identifying the modern Jezebel and throwing her into a sickbed, for her spiritual sickness is indeed a chronic one. (Malachi 3:1, 5) Those who have succumbed to this wrongful female influence will also suffer great tribulation —the sorrow of being disfellowshipped, cut off from the Christian congregation as though dead. Unless these repent, turn around, and are accepted back into the congregation, they also face physical death by "deadly plague"—at the latest, in the great tribulation. Meanwhile, restoration is possible if they fully repent of their wrong deeds. —Matthew 24:21, 22; 2 Corinthians 7:10.

14 "All the congregations" must come to

---

* See, for example, the article "Woman's Role in the First-Century Congregation" in *Awake!* of May 22, 1978.

---

10. (a) Why do Jezebel and her children receive judgment? (b) In what dangerous condition are those who become children of Jezebel, and what should such ones do?
11. How are congregations today helped to be awake to intrusion of unlawful female influence?

12. In what way does the John class today demonstrate a zeal similar to that of Jehu?
13. What will happen to those who succumb to wrongful female influence?
14. (a) How does Jesus use the elders in handling certain problems, such as any Jezebel influence? (b) How should the congregation support the elders who handle such problems?

Today, a great part of the witness work is accomplished by faithful sisters as they modestly support theocratic authority

know that Jesus searches "the kidneys," the deepest emotions, and the 'heart,' the inner-most person, including the underlying mo-tives. To this end, he uses trusted stars, or elders, in handling certain problems, such as any Jezebel influence that appears. (Revela-tion 1:20) After these elders have fully ex-amined a matter of this kind and judgment has been rendered, it is not for individu-als to probe into the whys and wherefores of the action taken. All should humbly ac-cept the elders' disposal of matters and con-tinue to be supportive of these congregation stars. Loyalty to Jehovah and his organi-zational arrangements will be rewarded. (Psalm 37:27-29; Hebrews 13:7, 17) For your own part, may your share be a blessing when Jesus gives to each one individually according to his deeds.—See also Galatians 5:19-24; 6:7-9.

START 6/3/91   START 12/26/94

"Hold Fast What You Have"

15 Jesus' next words bring comfort: *"How-ever, I say to the rest of you who are in Thyatira, all those who do not have this teach-ing, the very ones who did not get to know the 'deep things of Satan,' as they say: I am not putting upon you any other burden. Just the same, hold fast what you have until I come."* (*Revelation 2:24, 25*) There are faithful souls in Thyatira who have not been influenced by Jezebel. Similarly, for 40 years prior to 1918 and since then, not all professing Christians have tolerated the immoral, cor-rupt ways that are so rampant in Christen-dom. The small band of Bible Students, now

15. (a) What did Jesus have to say to those who had not been corrupted by Jezebel? (b) What shows that not all who claimed to be Christians back in 1918 had been corrupted by apostate Christendom?

ABHORRING THE "DEEP THINGS OF SATAN"

known as Jehovah's Witnesses, that tried to help church members see the un-Christian origin of many of Christendom's doctrines, has moved to rid itself of all Babylonish beliefs and practices received through apostate Christendom. This includes the permissive teaching of "that woman Jezebel."

16 The John class today have also encouraged their companions, the great crowd, to beware of immoral influences, such as those in the debased world of entertainment. There is no need to view or experience corruption out of curiosity or in order to learn what to avoid. It is the course of wisdom to keep far away from the "deep things of Satan." As Jesus says: "I am not putting upon you any other burden." This reminds us of the decree of the Christian governing body of the first century: "The holy spirit and we ourselves have favored adding no further burden to you, except these necessary things, to keep abstaining from things sacrificed to idols and from blood and from things strangled and from fornication. If you carefully keep yourselves from these things, you will prosper." (Acts 15:28, 29) For spiritual prosperity, avoid false religion, misuse of blood (as in blood transfusions), and immorality. And your physical health will likely be protected too.

---

16. Though Jesus and the first-century Christian governing body did not add any further burden, what things must be avoided?

17 Satan has other "deep things" today, such as complicated speculations and philosophies that flatter the intellect. In addition to permissive, immoral reasonings, these include spiritism and the theory of evolution. How does the all-wise Creator regard these "deep things"? The apostle Paul quotes him as saying: "I will destroy the wisdom of the wise ones." In contrast thereto, "the deep things of God" are simple, lucid, and heartwarming. Wise Christians shun the "deep things" of Satan's sophisticated world. Remember, "the world is passing away and so is its desire, but he that does the will of God remains forever."—1 Corinthians 1:19, *Kingdom Interlinear;* 2:10; 1 John 2:17.

18 To those Christians in Thyatira, Jesus now speaks heartwarming words. They also encourage anointed Christians today: ***"And to him that conquers and observes my deeds***

---

17. (a) How has Satan tempted people today with "deep things"? (b) What should be our attitude toward the "deep things" of Satan's sophisticated world?

18. What blessings did Jesus promise anointed Christians who remain faithful down to the end, and what privilege will these resurrected ones have at Armageddon?

REVELATION CLIMAX

down to the end I will give authority over the nations, and he shall shepherd the people with an iron rod so that they will be broken to pieces like clay vessels, the same as I have received from my Father." (*Revelation 2:26, 27*) Indeed a wonderful privilege! This authority that anointed conquerors receive at their resurrection is a sharing with Jesus in wielding the "iron rod" of destruction against the rebellious nations at Armageddon. At best, the nuclear firepower of those nations will sputter like a wet firecracker when Christ dashes his enemies to pieces as he would vessels of clay.—Psalm 2:8, 9; Revelation 16: 14, 16; 19:11-13, 15.

[19] Jesus adds: *"And I will give him the morning star."* (*Revelation 2:28*) Jesus himself later explains what this "star" is, saying: "I am the root and the offspring of David, and the bright morning star." (Revelation 22:16) Yes, it is Jesus who fulfills the prophecy that Jehovah forced from the unwilling lips of Balaam: "A star will certainly step forth out of Jacob, and a scepter will indeed rise out of Israel." (Numbers 24:17) How will Jesus give "the morning star" to those who conquer? Evidently, by giving himself to them, by taking them into the closest, most intimate relationship with him. (John 14:2, 3) Surely a powerful inducement to endure! Stimulating it is, too, for the great crowd to know that "the bright morning star" will soon exercise his Kingdom authority in restoring Paradise here on earth!

Maintain Integrity

[20] This message must have encouraged the Christians in Thyatira greatly. Just imagine —the glorified Son of God in heaven had personally spoken to the Christians in Thyatira about some of their problems! Surely, at least some in the congregation responded to such loving shepherding. This longest of the seven messages also helps us to identify the true Christian congregation today. In 1918 when Jesus came to Jehovah's temple for judgment, the vast majority of organizations claiming to be Christian were sullied by idolatry and spiritual immorality. (James 4:4) Some based their beliefs on the teachings of strong-minded women of the 19th century, such as Ellen White of the Seventh-Day Adventists and Mary Baker Eddy of the Christian Scientists, and more recently many women have been preaching from the pulpit. (Contrast 1 Timothy 2:11, 12.) Among the different forms of Catholicism, Mary is

19. (a) Who is "the morning star," and how will he be given to those who conquer? (b) What encouragement is offered to the great crowd?

20. What developments in Christendom remind us of some of the weaknesses in the congregation in Thyatira?

often honored ahead of God and Christ. Jesus did not so honor her. (John 2:4; 19:26) Could organizations that admit such unlawful female influence really be accepted as Christian?

[21] Individual Christians, whether of the John class or of the other sheep, do well to consider this message: (John 10:16) Some may find it tempting to follow an easy course, as those disciples of the Thyatiran Jezebel did. There is also the temptation to compromise. Today, issues such as eating blood products or accepting blood transfusions have to be faced. Some may feel that zeal in field service or giving talks entitles them to be less strict in other areas, such as

21. What lessons are there for individuals in Jesus' message to Thyatira?

in watching violent and immoral movies and video tapes, or overindulging in alcohol. Jesus' warning to the Christians in Thyatira tells us we must not take such liberties. Jehovah wants us to be clean, whole-souled, not divided, as many Christians were in Thyatira.

[22] Finally, Jesus declares: *"Let the one who has an ear hear what the spirit says to the congregations."* (*Revelation 2:29*) For the fourth time, Jesus here repeats this rousing refrain, and it will conclude all three messages yet to come. Do you have that responsive ear? Then keep listening intently as God, by his spirit, continues to provide counsel through his channel.

22. How does Jesus stress the importance of having a hearing ear?

Is Your Name in the Book of Life?

SOME 30 miles south of modern Akhisar (Thyatira) is the site of the next congregation to receive a message from the glorified Jesus: Sardis. In the sixth century before our Common Era, this city was the proud capital of the ancient kingdom of Lydia and seat of the enormously wealthy King Croesus. By John's day, it has fallen on hard times, and its former splendor under Croesus is mere history. Similarly, the Christian congregation there has become spiritually impoverished. For the first time, Jesus does not begin his message with a word of

1. What is the spiritual condition of the congregation in Sardis, and how does Jesus begin his message?

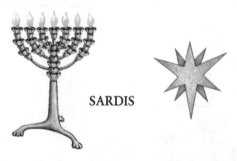

SARDIS

commendation. Instead, he says: *"And to the angel of the congregation in Sardis write: These are the things that he says who has the seven spirits of God and the seven stars, 'I know your deeds, that you have the name that you are alive, but you are dead.'"*—*Revelation 3:1*.

54

² Why does Jesus identify himself as the one "who has the seven spirits"? Because these spirits represent Jehovah's holy spirit flowing in its fullness. Later, John describes them also as "seven eyes," indicating the penetrating vision that God's holy spirit bestows on Jesus. (Revelation 5:6) Thus, he is able to uncover and handle any situation that may exist. (Matthew 10:26; 1 Corinthians 4:5) The congregation in Sardis has the reputation of being alive, active. But Jesus can see that it is spiritually dead. Evidently, most of its members have relapsed into an apathy similar to their condition before they became Christians.—Compare Ephesians 2:1-3; Hebrews 5:11-14.

³ Jesus also reminds "the angel of the congregation in Sardis" that He is the one who has "the seven stars." He holds those congregation elders in his right hand, having authority to direct them in their shepherding work. They should set their hearts to 'knowing positively the appearance of the flock.' (Proverbs 27:23) Hence, they had better listen carefully to Jesus' next words: **"Become watchful, and strengthen the things remaining that were ready to die, for I have not found your deeds fully performed before my God. Therefore, continue mindful of how you have received and how you heard, and go on keeping it, and repent. Certainly unless you wake up, I shall come as a thief, and you will not know at all at what hour I shall come upon you."** —Revelation 3:2, 3.

⁴ The elders in Sardis need to remember the joy they first had when they learned the truth and the blessings they then received.

But now they are dead as to spiritual activity. Their congregational lamp is flickering because of lack of works of faith. Years before, the apostle Peter wrote to the congregations in Asia (likely including Sardis) to build appreciation for the glorious good news that Christians had accepted and that had been declared "with holy spirit sent forth from heaven"—as represented by the seven spirits of John's vision. Peter also reminded those Asian Christians that they belonged to 'a chosen race, a royal priesthood, a holy nation, a people for special possession, that they should declare abroad the excellencies of the one that called them out of darkness into his wonderful light.' (1 Peter 1:12, 25; 2:9) Meditating on such spiritual truths will help the congregation in Sardis to repent and "strengthen the things remaining."—Compare 2 Peter 3:9.

⁵ At the moment, their appreciation and love of the truth are like a fire that has almost died out. Just a few embers continue to glow. Jesus encourages them to fan the spark, stir up the fire, repent of the sins into which their negligence has led them, and become a spiritually alive congregation once again. (Compare 2 Timothy 1:6, 7.) Otherwise, when Jesus comes unexpectedly—"as a thief"—to execute judgment, the congregation in Sardis will be unprepared.—Matthew 24:43, 44.

Coming "as a Thief"

⁶ Jesus' warning that he would come "as a thief" reaches down into modern times. It had a special application for Christians who survived into the Lord's day. Soon after 1914, there was a fulfillment of Malachi's prophecy: "'Suddenly there will come to His temple the true Lord, whom you people are seeking, and the messenger of the covenant

---

2. (a) Of what significance is it to the Christians in Sardis that Jesus has "the seven spirits"? (b) What reputation did the Sardis congregation have, but what were the facts?
3. (a) Why should "the angel of the congregation in Sardis" take special note of the fact that Jesus has "the seven stars"? (b) What strong counsel does Jesus give the congregation in Sardis?
4. How would Peter's words help the congregation in Sardis to "strengthen the things remaining"?

---

5. (a) What happened to the appreciation of the Christians in Sardis? (b) What will happen if the Sardis Christians do not respond to Jesus' counsel?
6. How did Jesus come "as a thief" in 1918, and what situation did he find among his professed followers?

in whom you are delighting. Look! He will certainly come, Jehovah of armies has said." (Malachi 3:1; Revelation 1:10) As "messenger of the covenant," Jesus came to inspect and judge those who claimed to be his followers. (1 Peter 4:17) At that time, in 1918, Christendom was embroiled in the shedding of blood in World War I and was completely dead, spiritually speaking. Even true Christians, who before the war had preached so zealously, went through a time of spiritual drowsiness. Some of their prominent elders were put into prison, and the preaching activity almost stopped. When Jehovah's spirit awakened these Christians the following year, not all were ready. Some, like the foolish virgins of Jesus' parable, were not equipped spiritually for the privilege of serving Jehovah. Happily, though, there were many who, like the discreet virgins, had heeded Jesus' warning: "Keep on the watch, therefore, because you know neither the day nor the hour."—Matthew 25:1-13.

7 The need for a Christian to be alert did not end early in the Lord's day. In his great prophecy concerning "the sign when all these things are destined to come to a conclusion," Jesus gave a strong warning: "Concerning that day or the hour nobody knows . . . Keep looking, keep awake, for you do not know when the appointed time is. But what I say to you I say to all, Keep on the watch." (Mark 13:4, 32, 33, 37) Yes, up to this very hour, each one of us, whether of the anointed or of the great crowd, needs to stay alert and fight against drifting into spiritual sleep. When Jehovah's day comes "as a thief in the night," may we be found wide awake so as to receive a favorable judgment. —1 Thessalonians 5:2, 3; Luke 21:34-36; Revelation 7:9.

8 The John class today is itself awake to the need for stimulating God's people to keep spiritually alive. To this end, special gatherings are arranged throughout the earth several times each year. In a recent year, attendance at 995 district conventions totaled 6,153,749, and 82,785 new believers were baptized. For more than a hundred years, the John class has used the *Watchtower* magazine in announcing Jehovah's name and purpose. In response to bitter persecutions during the two world wars, *The Watchtower* aroused Jehovah's Witnesses to renewed zeal by publishing articles such as "Blessed Are the Fearless" (1919), "A Call to Action" (1925), and "Defeat of Persecution" (1942).

9 As in Sardis, so in the congregations today, continued self-examination is vital for all Christians. All of us should keep asking ourselves: Are our "deeds fully performed" before our God? Without judging others, do we *personally* cultivate the spirit of self-sacrifice and strive to render whole-souled service to God? In this connection, the *Watchtower* magazine has given encouragement by discussing topics such as "Are You Self-Indulgent—Or Self-Sacrificing?" and "Exert Yourselves Vigorously."* Having such Scriptural help, let us probe our innermost selves as we try to walk humbly and prayerfully in integrity before Jehovah.—Psalm 26: 1-3; 139:23, 24.

"A Few Names"

10 Jesus' next words to the congregation in Sardis are most encouraging. He says: *"Nevertheless, you do have a few names in Sardis that did not defile their outer garments, and they shall walk with me in white ones, because they are worthy. He that conquers will*

---

* See *The Watchtower*, August 1, 1978, and January 15, 1986.

9. (a) What should all Christians be asking themselves? (b) What encouragement has *The Watchtower* given?
10. What encouraging feature did Jesus note in the congregation in Sardis, and how should this affect us?

---

7. Why do Christians today need to keep awake?
8. How has the John class today stimulated God's people to keep spiritually alive?

May your name remain
in the book of life

thus be arrayed in white outer garments; and I will by no means blot out his name from the book of life, but I will make acknowledgment of his name before my Father and before his angels." (*Revelation 3:4, 5*) Do not these words arouse us and strengthen our determination to be faithful? Because of negligence on the part of a body of elders, a congregation as a whole may fall into deep spiritual sleep. Yet, some individuals therein may strive courageously to keep their Christian identity pure and unspotted and thus continue to have a good name with Jehovah.—Proverbs 22:1.

[11] Yes, those "outer garments" refer to a person's righteous identity as a Christian. (Compare Revelation 16:15; 19:8.) It must be heartwarming for Jesus to see that, despite the apathy of the great majority, "a few names," a few anointed Christians in Sardis, still manage to keep this identity. Likewise, when professed Christians were absorbed into Babylon the Great, the world empire of false religion, during the long centuries of the great apostasy, there must always have been a few individuals who tried, against great odds, to do Jehovah's will. These were righteous like wheat hidden amid a profusion of sectarian weeds.—Revelation 17:3-6; Matthew 13:24-29.

[12] Jesus promised that he would be with these wheatlike Christians "all the days until the conclusion of the system of things." He knows who they are and what good names they made for themselves. (Matthew 28:20; Ecclesiastes 7:1) Imagine the joy of those faithful "few" who were still alive at the start of the Lord's day! They were finally separated from spiritually dead Christendom and were gathered into a righteous congregation more like the congregation in Smyrna. —Matthew 13:40-43.

[13] Those in Sardis who are faithful to the end and do not sully their Christian identity attain the realization of a wonderful hope. After the establishment of Jesus' Messianic Kingdom in 1914, they are resurrected to spirit life and as conquerors are arrayed with white outer garments in symbol of their flawless, untainted righteousness. Having

---

11, 12. (a) Even during the great apostasy, how must some have been like those faithful "few names" in Sardis? (b) What relief came to wheatlike Christians during the Lord's day?

13. What blessings are in store for anointed Christians who do not "defile their outer garments"?

IS YOUR NAME IN THE BOOK OF LIFE?

walked the cramped road that leads to life, they will enjoy an eternal reward.—Matthew 7:14; see also Revelation 6:9-11.

Forever in the Book of Life!

[14] What is "the book of life," and whose names will be retained therein? The book, or scroll, of life refers to the record of Jehovah's servants who come in line to receive the grant of everlasting life. (Malachi 3:16) Here in Revelation specific reference is made to the names of anointed Christians. But the names of those in line for everlasting life on earth are also recorded therein. Moreover, names can be 'blotted out' of that book. (Exodus 32:32, 33) Nevertheless, those of the John class whose names remain in the book of life until their death receive immortal life in heaven. (Revelation 2:10) These are the names that Jesus specially acknowledges before his Father and before His angels. How magnificent that reward!

[15] The great crowd, whose names are also written in the book of life, will come out of the great tribulation alive. By exercising faith throughout Jesus' Millennial Reign and during the decisive test that follows, these will be rewarded with life everlasting in Paradise on earth. (Daniel 12:1; Revelation 7: 9, 14; 20:15; 21:4) Their names will then remain indelibly written in the book of life. Knowing what is here presented by means of holy spirit, do you not respond with enthusiasm to Jesus' repeated exhortation: *"Let the one who has an ear hear what the spirit says to the congregations"?—Revelation 3:6.*

14. What is "the book of life," and whose names are recorded therein?

15. How will members of the great crowd get their names indelibly written in the book of life?

REVELATION CLIMAX   Chapter *12*

6/23

"Keep On Holding Fast What You Have"

PHILADELPHIA

BROTHERLY AFFECTION—what a desirable quality! No doubt Jesus has this in mind when he presents his sixth message, which is directed to the congregation in Philadelphia, for that name means "Brotherly Affection." The aged John still recalls the occasion, more than 60 years earlier, when Peter insisted three times to Jesus that he, Peter, had warm affection for his Lord. (John 21:15-17) Are the Christians in Philadelphia, on their part, showing brotherly affection? Apparently they are!

[2] Located about 30 miles southeast of Sar-

1. Jesus' sixth message was directed to the congregation in what city, and what does that city's name mean?

2. What kind of city was Philadelphia, what kind of congregation was located there, and what does Jesus say to the angel of this congregation?

dis (at the site of the modern Turkish city of Alasehir), the Philadelphia of John's day is a fairly prosperous city. More noteworthy, however, is the prosperity of the Christian congregation there. With what joy they must have received the minister that came traveling to them, likely by way of Sardis! The message he carries has stirring counsel for them. But first it refers to the authority of its illustrious Sender. He says: *"And to the angel of the congregation in Philadelphia write: These are the things he says who is holy, who is true, who has the key of David, who opens so that no one will shut, and shuts so that no one opens."—Revelation 3:7.*

3 John had heard Peter say to the man Jesus Christ: "You have sayings of everlasting life; and we have believed and come to know that you are the Holy One of God." (John 6:68, 69) Since Jehovah God is the very essence of holiness, his only-begotten Son must also be "holy." (Revelation 4:8) Jesus is also "true." The Greek word used here (*a·le·thi·nos′*) implies genuineness. In this sense, Jesus is the true light and the true bread that came down out of heaven. (John 1:9; 6:32) He is the true vine. (John 15:1) Jesus is true also in the sense that he is trustworthy. He always speaks the truth. (See John 8:14, 17, 26.) This Son of God is indeed worthy to serve as King and Judge. —Revelation 19:11, 16.

"The Key of David"

4 Jesus has "the key of David." Using it, he "opens so that no one will shut, and shuts so that no one opens." What is this "key of David"?

5 It was with King David of Israel that Jehovah made a covenant for an everlasting kingdom. (Psalm 89:1-4, 34-37) David's house ruled from Jehovah's throne in Jeru-

A Roman key of the first century

salem from 1070 to 607 B.C.E., but then God's judgment was executed upon that kingdom because it turned to wickedness. Thus Jehovah began to fulfill his prophecy at Ezekiel 21:27: "A ruin, a ruin, a ruin I shall make it [earthly Jerusalem]. As for this also, it [the scepter of kingship in David's line] will certainly become no one's until he comes who has the legal right, and I must give it to him."

6 When and how would this one with "the legal right" appear? How would the scepter of David's kingdom be given to him?

7 About 600 years later, a descendant of King David, the Jewish maiden Mary, became pregnant by holy spirit. God sent the angel Gabriel to inform Mary that she would have a son, to be named Jesus. Gabriel added: "This one will be great and will be called Son of the Most High; and Jehovah God will give him the throne of David his father, and he will rule as king over the house of Jacob forever, and there will be no end of his kingdom."—Luke 1:31-33.

8 When, in 29 C.E., Jesus was baptized in the Jordan River and anointed with holy spirit, he became King-Designate in the line of David. He showed exemplary zeal in preaching the good news of the Kingdom and commissioned his disciples likewise to preach. (Matthew 4:23; 10:7, 11) Jesus humbled himself, even to death on a torture stake, thus proving himself fully qualified to inherit the Davidic kingship. Jehovah

---

3. Why is it fitting that Jesus should be called "holy," and how can it be said that he "is true"?
4, 5. With what covenant was "the key of David" associated?

6, 7. When and how was the one with "the legal right" to appear?
8. How did Jesus prove himself qualified to inherit the Davidic kingship?

resurrected Jesus as an immortal spirit and exalted him to His own right hand in the heavens. There he inherited all the rights of the Davidic kingdom. In due time Jesus would exercise his right to "go subduing in the midst of [his] enemies."—Psalm 110:1, 2; Philippians 2:8, 9; Hebrews 10:13, 14.

9 In the meantime Jesus would have use of the key of David, opening up opportunities and privileges related to the Kingdom of God. Through Jesus, Jehovah would now deliver anointed Christians on earth "from the authority of the darkness," transferring them "into the kingdom of the Son of his love." (Colossians 1:13, 14) The key would also be used to bar such privileges to any who proved unfaithful. (2 Timothy 2:12, 13) Since this permanent heir of David's kingdom has Jehovah's backing, no creature can prevent him from fulfilling such duties. —Compare Matthew 28:18-20.

10 Coming from such an authoritative source, Jesus' words to the Christians in Philadelphia must be especially comforting! He commends them, saying: *"I know your deeds—look! I have set before you an opened door, which no one can shut—that you have a little power, and you kept my word and did not prove false to my name." (Revelation 3:8)* The congregation has been active, and a door has opened before it—doubtless a door of opportunity for ministerial service. (Compare 1 Corinthians 16:9; 2 Corinthians 2:12.) Therefore, Jesus encourages the congregation to take full advantage of the opportunity to preach. They have endured and shown that they have enough power, with help from God's spirit, to continue doing further "deeds" in Jehovah's service. (2 Corinthians 12:10; Zechariah 4:6) They have obeyed Jesus' commands and have not denied Christ, either by word or by action.

---

9. How is it that Jesus uses the key of David to open and to shut?
10. What encouragement does Jesus give the congregation in Philadelphia?

"They Will Bow Down to You"

11 Hence, Jesus promises them fruitage: *"Look! I will give those from the synagogue of Satan who say they are Jews, and yet they are not but are lying—look! I will make them come and do obeisance before your feet and make them know I have loved you." (Revelation 3:9)* Perhaps, as in Smyrna, the congregation has had problems with the local Jews. Jesus designates these as "the synagogue of Satan." Nevertheless, at least some of those Jews are about to realize that what the Christians have been preaching about Jesus is the truth. Their 'doing obeisance' will likely be in the manner described by Paul at 1 Corinthians 14:24, 25, so that they actually repent and become Christians, fully appreciating Jesus' great love in surrendering even his soul in behalf of his disciples.—John 15:12, 13.

12 Members of the Jewish synagogue in Philadelphia would likely be startled to learn that some of them were to "do obeisance" to the local Christian community. In view of the fact that there are doubtless many non-Jews in that congregation, they would expect the very opposite to take place. Why? Because Isaiah foretold: "[Non-Jewish] kings must become caretakers for you [the people of Israel], and their princesses nursing women for you. With faces to the earth they will bow down to you." (Isaiah 49:23; 45:14; 60:14) In a similar vein, Zechariah was inspired to write: "It will be in those days that ten men [non-Jews] out of all the languages of the nations will take hold, yes, they will actually take hold of the skirt of a man who is a Jew, saying: 'We will go with you people, for we have heard that God is with you people.'" (Zech-

---

11. What blessing does Jesus promise the Christians, and how was this realized?
12. Why would members of the Jewish synagogue in Philadelphia likely be startled to learn that some of them would "bow down" to the local Christian community?

ariah 8:23) Yes, non-Jews were to bow down to Jews, not the other way around!

¹³ Those prophecies were addressed to God's chosen nation. When they were uttered, fleshly Israel occupied that honored position. But when the Jewish nation rejected the Messiah, Jehovah cast them off. (Matthew 15:3-9; 21:42, 43; Luke 12:32; John 1: 10, 11) At Pentecost 33 C.E., he chose in their stead the true Israel of God, the Christian congregation. Its members are the spiritual Jews with the real circumcision of the heart. (Acts 2:1-4, 41, 42; Romans 2:28, 29; Galatians 6:16) Thereafter, the only way that individual fleshly Jews could come back to a favored relationship with Jehovah would be by putting their faith in Jesus as the Messiah. (Matthew 23:37-39) Evidently, this was about to happen with some individuals in Philadelphia.*

¹⁴ In modern times, prophecies such as Isaiah 49:23 and Zechariah 8:23 have had a very significant fulfillment. As a result of the preaching of the John class, huge numbers of people have entered through the opened door into Kingdom service.# Most of these have come out of Christendom, whose religions falsely claim to be spiritual Israel. (Compare Romans 9:6.) These, as a great crowd, wash their robes and make them white by exercising faith in Jesus' sacrificial blood. (Revelation 7:9, 10, 14) Obeying

Christ's Kingdom rule, they hope to inherit its blessings here on earth. They come to Jesus' anointed brothers and "bow down" to them, spiritually speaking, because 'they have heard that God is with them.' They minister to these anointed ones, with whom they themselves become united in a worldwide association of brothers.—Matthew 25: 34-40; 1 Peter 5:9.

"The Hour of Test" STOP →

¹⁵ Jesus goes on to say: *"Because you kept the word about my endurance, I will also keep you from the hour of test, which is to come upon the whole inhabited earth, to put a test upon those dwelling on the earth. I am coming quickly. Keep on holding fast what you have, that no one may take your crown."* (*Revelation 3:10, 11*) Although the Christians of John's day would not survive to the Lord's day (beginning in 1914), their confidence that Jesus was coming would give them power to keep on preaching. (Revelation 1:10; 2 Timothy 4:2) The "crown," or prize of everlasting life, awaited them in heaven.

---

* In Paul's time, Sosthenes, the presiding officer of the Jewish synagogue in Corinth, became a Christian brother. —Acts 18:17; 1 Corinthians 1:1.

The *Watchtower* magazine, published by the John class, has continued to highlight the urgency of seizing this opportunity and sharing as fully as possible in the preaching work; for example, see the articles "Declare Abroad the Kingdom of God" and "Urgently Needed —More Harvest Workers!" in the December 15, 1985, issue. In the February 1, 1987, issue, in the article "Doing Our Utmost to Declare the Good News," emphasis was placed on entering an "opened door" into full-time service. There was a peak of 650,095 pioneers reporting such service during one month in 1987.

---

13. Who were the Jews that would experience a fulfillment of prophecies addressed to ancient Israel?
14. How have Isaiah 49:23 and Zechariah 8:23 had a significant fulfillment in modern times?

15. (a) What did Jesus promise the Christians in Philadelphia, and what were they encouraged to do? (b) What "crown" were the Christians looking forward to receiving?

(James 1:12; Revelation 11:18) If they were faithful to death, no one could deprive them of that reward.—Revelation 2:10.

¹⁶ What, though, is "the hour of test"? No doubt, those Christians in Asia had to cope with a further wave of terrible persecution from imperial Rome.* Nevertheless, the ma-

---

* McClintock and Strong's *Cyclopedia* (Volume X, page 519) reports: "Christianity was forced upon the notice of the emperors by the tumults excited among the populace by heathen priests, who observed the remarkable progress of that faith with alarm, and Trajan [98-117 C.E.] was accordingly led to issue edicts for the gradual suppression of the new teaching which transformed men into haters of the gods. The administration of the younger Pliny as governor of Bithynia [bordering the Roman province of Asia on the north] was complicated with matters growing out of the rapid extension of Christianity and the consequent rage of the heathen population within his province."

16, 17. (a) What is "the hour of test, which is to come upon the whole inhabited earth"? (b) What was the condition of the anointed ones at the beginning of "the hour of test"?

jor fulfillment is the hour of sifting and judging that finally arrived during the Lord's day, climaxing from 1918 onward. The test has been to determine whether one is for God's established Kingdom or for Satan's world. It is for a comparatively short period, an "hour," but it is not over yet. Until it is, we must never forget that we are living in "the hour of test."—Luke 21:34-36.

¹⁷ In 1918 the John class of anointed Christians—like that staunch congregation in Philadelphia—had to face opposition from the modern-day "synagogue of Satan." Religious leaders of Christendom, who claimed to be spiritual Jews, slyly maneuvered the rulers to suppress true Christians. Nevertheless, these tried hard to 'keep the word of Jesus' endurance'; hence, with spiritual help, a significant "little power," they survived and were aroused to enter the door that now opened before them. In what way?

"An Opened Door"

START

18 In 1919 Jesus fulfilled his promise and recognized the small band of genuine anointed Christians as his "faithful and discreet slave." (Matthew 24:45-47) These entered into a privilege similar to that enjoyed by the faithful steward Eliakim in the time of King Hezekiah.* Jehovah said of Eliakim: "I will put the key of the house of David upon his shoulder, and he must open without anyone's shutting, and he must shut without anyone's opening." Eliakim shouldered heavy responsibilities for Hezekiah,

---

* The name Hezekiah means "Jehovah Strengthens." See 2 Kings 16:20, footnote, *New World Translation Reference Bible.*

---

18. What appointment did Jesus make in 1919, and how did the appointee thus become like Hezekiah's faithful steward?

the royal son of David. Similarly today, the anointed John class has had "the key of the house of David" put upon its shoulder in that it has been entrusted with the earthly interests of the Messianic Kingdom. Jehovah has strengthened his servants for this privilege, boosting their little power into dynamic energy sufficient for a gigantic global witness.—Isaiah 22:20, 22; 40:29.

19 From 1919 onward the anointed remnant, following Jesus' example, launched into a vigorous campaign of declaring abroad the good news of the Kingdom. (Matthew 4:17; Romans 10:18) As a result, some of the modern synagogue of Satan, Christendom, came to this anointed remnant, repented and 'bowed down,'

---

19. How did the John class handle the responsibilities that Jesus gave it in 1919, and with what result?

Helping Many to Bow Down

Of the 144,000 anointed ones that are to inherit the heavenly Kingdom, it appears that a remnant, the John class, of less than 9,000 have yet to complete their course on earth. At the same time, the great crowd has expanded into a multitude of 3,000,000 and more. (Revelation 7:4, 9) What has helped to bring about this vast increase? The various schools operated by Jehovah's Witnesses have made a big contribution. Far different from the seminaries of Christendom that teach worldly philosophies and downgrade the Bible, these Witness schools inculcate deep faith in God's Word. They show its practical application as to clean, moral living and dedicated service to God. Worldwide since 1943, each congregation of Jehovah's Witnesses conducts in its Kingdom Hall a local *Theocratic Ministry School.* Millions attend this school each week, following a unified program of Bible education.

Since 1959 Jehovah's Witnesses have also conducted *Kingdom Ministry Schools* for the training of congregation elders and ministerial servants. And since 1977, the *Pioneer Service Schools* have trained more than 200,000 brothers and sisters, who, with a true Philadelphian spirit, serve Jehovah full-time in the preaching work. In 1987 the *Ministerial Training School* was started for training male Witnesses for special assignments in the world field.

Outstanding among the schools operated by Jehovah's Witnesses has been the *Watchtower Bible School of Gilead.* Since 1943 this missionary school, located in New York State, has graduated two groups of students almost every year. Altogether, it has trained more than 6,000 ministers of Jehovah for foreign missionary service. The graduates of this school have served in more than a hundred lands, in many of which they were instrumental in opening up the Kingdom work. After some 40 years, many of the early missionaries are still on the job, sharing with newer missionaries in advancing the global expansion of Jehovah's organization. What a marvelous expansion this has been!

acknowledging the slave's authority. They too came to serve Jehovah in union with the older ones of the John class. This continued until the full number of Jesus' anointed brothers was gathered. Following this, "a great crowd . . . out of all nations" has come to "bow down" to the anointed slave. (Revelation 7:3, 4, 9) Together, the slave and this great crowd serve as the one flock of Jehovah's Witnesses.

20 United like the Christians in Philadelphia in a bond of genuine brotherly affection, Jehovah's Witnesses today appreciate that their work of preaching must be done urgently. Soon, the great tribulation will ring down the curtain on Satan's wicked world. At that time, may each of us be found strong in faith and active in God's service, so that our names will not be blotted out of Jehovah's book of life. (Revelation 7:14) Let us take very seriously Jesus' admonition to the congregation in Philadelphia so that we may hold fast to our service privileges and attain to the reward of everlasting life.

The Conquerors' Blessings

21 The John class today have 'kept the word about Jesus' endurance,' that is, they have followed his example and endured. (Hebrews 12:2, 3; 1 Peter 2:21) They have thus been greatly encouraged by Jesus' further words to the congregation in Philadelphia: *"The one that conquers—I will make him a pillar in the temple of my God, and he will by no means go out from it anymore."—Revelation 3:12a.*

22 What a privilege it is for one to be a pillar in the temple of Jehovah! In ancient

20. Why must Jehovah's Witnesses today be especially strong in faith and active in God's service?
21. How have anointed Christians today 'kept the word about Jesus' endurance,' and what prospect awaits them?
22. (a) What is the temple of Jesus' God? (b) How will the anointed Christians that conquer become pillars in this temple?

In 1919 the reigning King Jesus opened a door of opportunity for Christian service. An increasing number of devoted Christians have taken advantage of that opportunity.

Year	Lands Reached by Preaching	Christians Who Shared in Preaching*	Full-Time Preachers*
1918	14	3,868	591
1928	32	23,988	1,883
1938	52	47,143	4,112
1948	96	230,532	8,994
1958	175	717,088	23,772
1968	200	1,155,826	63,871
1978	205	2,086,698	115,389
1987	210	3,237,751	436,179

* The above figures are monthly averages.

Jerusalem, the literal temple was the center of Jehovah's worship. Within the temple, the high priest offered the blood of sacrificial animals, one day each year, before the miraculous light that represented Jehovah's presence in "the Most Holy." (Hebrews 9:1-7) At Jesus' baptism, there came into existence another temple, a great spiritual, templelike arrangement for worshiping Jehovah. The holy of holies of this temple is in heaven, where Jesus duly appeared "before the person of God." (Hebrews 9:24) Jesus is the High Priest, and there is only one sacrifice offered for the complete covering of sins: the shed blood of the perfect man Jesus. (Hebrews 7:26, 27; 9:25-28; 10:1-5, 12-14) As long as they remain faithful, anointed Christians on earth serve as underpriests in the earthly courtyards of this temple. (1 Peter 2:9) But once they have conquered, they too enter that heavenly holy of holies and become immovable supports, like pillars, of the templelike arrangement for worship. (Hebrews 10:19; Revelation 20:6) There is no

REVELATION CLIMAX

The activity of Jehovah's Witnesses is wholehearted. Consider, for example, the hours they have spent in preaching and teaching and the huge number of free Bible studies they have conducted in people's homes.

Year	Hours Spent Preaching (Annual Total)	Bible Studies Conducted (Monthly Average)
1918	19,116	Not Recorded
1928	2,866,164	Not Recorded
1938	10,572,086	Not Recorded
1948	49,832,205	130,281
1958	110,390,944	508,320
1968	208,666,762	977,503
1978	307,272,262	1,257,084
1987	739,019,286	3,005,048

danger that they will "go out from it anymore."

23 Jesus continues, saying: *"And I will write upon him the name of my God and the name of the city of my God, the new Jerusalem which descends out of heaven from my God, and that new name of mine."* (*Revelation 3:12b*) Yes, these conquerors have written on them the name of Jehovah—their God and Jesus' God. This shows clearly that Jehovah and Jesus are two separate persons and not two parts of a triune God, or Trinity. (John 14:28; 20:17) All creation must come to see that these anointed ones belong to Jehovah. They are *his* witnesses. They also have written on them the name of the new Jerusalem, the heavenly city that descends out of heaven in the sense that it extends its benevolent rule over all faithful mankind. (Revelation 21:9-14) All the earthly Christian sheep will

thus also know that these anointed conquerors are citizens of the Kingdom, the heavenly Jerusalem.—Psalm 87:5, 6; Matthew 25:33, 34; Philippians 3:20; Hebrews 12:22.

24 Finally, anointed overcomers have written on them Jesus' new name. This refers to Jesus' new office and the unique privileges granted to him by Jehovah. (Philippians 2:9-11; Revelation 19:12) No one else gets to know that name, in the sense that no one else has those experiences or is entrusted with those privileges. However, when Jesus writes his name on his faithful brothers, they come into an intimate relationship with him in that heavenly realm and even share in his privileges. (Luke 22:29, 30) It is no wonder that Jesus concludes his message to such anointed ones by repeating the exhortation: *"Let the one who has an ear hear what the spirit says to the congregations."*—*Revelation 3:13.*

25 What grand encouragement that message must have been to the faithful Christians in Philadelphia! And it certainly has a powerful lesson for the John class now, during the Lord's day. But its principles are important for each individual Christian, whether of the anointed or of the other sheep. (John 10:16) Each of us would do well to keep producing Kingdom fruitage as did those Christians in Philadelphia. All of us have at least a little power. All of us can do something in Jehovah's service. Let us use this power! With regard to increased Kingdom privileges, let us be alert to enter any door that opens for us. We can even pray for Jehovah to open such a door. (Colossians 4:2, 3) As we follow Jesus' pattern of endurance and prove true to his name, we will show that we, too, have an ear to hear what God's holy spirit says to the congregations.

23. (a) What promise does Jesus next make to the anointed Christians that conquer? (b) What results from the writing of Jehovah's name and the name of the new Jerusalem on Christian conquerors?

24. What is represented by Jesus' new name, and how is it written on faithful anointed Christians?
25. How can each individual Christian today apply the principle behind the counsel Jesus gave to the congregation in Philadelphia?

Buy Gold Refined by Fire

LAODICEA

start 7/8/91

LAODICEA is last of the seven congregations to receive a message from the resurrected Jesus. And what eye-opening, stimulating information it conveys!

[2] Today, you would find the ruins of Laodicea near Denizli, about 55 miles southeast of Alasehir. In the first century, Laodicea was a prosperous city. Sitting on a major road junction, it was a key center for banking and commerce. Sale of a well-known eye salve added to its wealth, and it was also famous for its high-quality garments produced locally from a fine black wool. Lack of water, a major problem for the city, had been overcome by channeling water down from hot springs some distance away. Thus, the water would be only lukewarm by the time it arrived in the city.

[3] Laodicea was near Colossae. In writing to the Colossians, the apostle Paul mentions a letter that he had sent to the Laodiceans. (Colossians 4:15, 16) We do not know what Paul wrote in that letter, but the message that Jesus now sends to the Laodiceans shows that they have fallen into a woeful spiritual condition. As usual, though, Jesus first cites his own credentials, saying: *"And to the angel of the congregation in Laodicea write: These are the things that the Amen says, the faithful and true witness, the beginning of the creation by God."—Revelation 3:14.*

[4] Why does Jesus call himself "the Amen"?

1, 2. What is the location of the last of the seven congregations to receive a message from the glorified Jesus, and what are some features of the city?

3. How does Jesus open his message to the congregation in Laodicea?

4. How is Jesus "the Amen"?

This title adds judicial weight to his message. "Amen" is a transliteration of a Hebrew word meaning "surely," "so be it," and is used at the end of prayers to affirm the sentiments expressed therein. (1 Corinthians 14:16) Jesus is "the Amen" because his flawless integrity and sacrificial death confirmed and guaranteed the fulfillment of all of Jehovah's precious promises. (2 Corinthians 1:20) Since that time, all prayers are properly addressed to Jehovah through Jesus.—John 15:16; 16:23, 24.

[5] Jesus is also "the faithful and true witness." In prophecy he is often associated with faithfulness, truth, and righteousness, for he is completely trustworthy as a servant of Jehovah God. (Psalm 45:4; Isaiah 11:4, 5; Revelation 1:5; 19:11) He is the greatest Witness for Jehovah. In fact, as "the beginning of the creation by God," Jesus has declared God's glory from the very start. (Proverbs 8:22-30) As a man on earth, he bore witness to the truth. (John 18:36, 37; 1 Timothy 6:13) After his resurrection, he promised holy spirit to his disciples and told them: "You will be witnesses of me both in Jerusalem and in all Judea and Samaria and to the most

finish

---

5. In what way is Jesus "the faithful and true witness"?

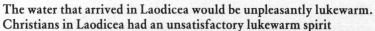
The water that arrived in Laodicea would be unpleasantly lukewarm.
Christians in Laodicea had an unsatisfactory lukewarm spirit

distant part of the earth." From Pentecost 33 C.E. onward, Jesus directed these anointed Christians in preaching the good news "in all creation that is under heaven." (Acts 1:6-8; Colossians 1:23) Truly, Jesus deserves to be called the faithful and true witness. The anointed Christians in Laodicea would benefit by listening to his words.

6 What message does Jesus have for the Laodiceans? He has no word of commendation. Frankly, he tells them: *"I know your deeds, that you are neither cold nor hot. I wish you were cold or else hot. So, because you are lukewarm and neither hot nor cold, I am going to vomit you out of my mouth."* (*Revelation 3: 15, 16*) How would you respond to such a message from the Lord Jesus Christ? Would you not awaken and examine yourself? Surely, those Laodiceans need to bestir themselves, for they have become spiritually indolent, apparently taking too much for granted. (Compare 2 Corinthians 6:1.) Jesus, whom

they as Christians should have imitated, always displays a fiery zeal for Jehovah and his service. (John 2:17) Further, meek ones have found him to be always gentle and mild, as refreshing as a cup of cold water on a swelteringly hot day. (Matthew 11:28, 29) But the Christians in Laodicea are neither hot nor cold. Like the waters that flow down into their city, they have become tepid, lukewarm. They are liable to be completely rejected by Jesus, 'vomited out of his mouth'! May we for our part always strive zealously, as did Jesus, to provide spiritual refreshment for others.—Matthew 9:35-38.

"You Say: 'I Am Rich'"

7 What really is the root of the Laodiceans' problem? We get a good idea from Jesus'

---

6. (a) How does Jesus describe the spiritual condition of the congregation in Laodicea? (b) What fine example of Jesus have the Christians in Laodicea failed to follow?

7. (a) How does Jesus identify the root of the problem of the Christians in Laodicea? (b) Why does Jesus say that Laodicean Christians are "blind and naked"?

BUY GOLD REFINED BY FIRE

next words: *"Because you say: 'I am rich and have acquired riches and do not need anything at all,' but you do not know you are miserable and pitiable and poor and blind and naked."* (*Revelation 3:17;* compare Luke 12:16-21:) Living in a wealthy city, they feel confident because of their riches. Likely, their way of life has been affected by the stadium, theaters, and gymnasiums, so that they have become "lovers of pleasures rather than lovers of God."* (2 Timothy 3:4) But the materially rich Laodiceans are impoverished spiritually. They have few, if any, 'treasures stored up in heaven.' (Matthew 6:19-21) They have not kept their eye simple, giving first place in their lives to God's Kingdom. They are really in darkness, blind, with no spiritual vision. (Matthew 6:22, 23, 33) Moreover, in spite of the fine garments that their material wealth may have purchased, in Jesus' eyes they are naked. They have no spiritual garments to identify them as Christians. —Compare Revelation 16:15.

8 What a shocking condition! But do we not often see a similar situation nowadays? What is the root cause? It is a self-confident attitude that springs from reliance upon material possessions and human resources. Like Christendom's churchgoers, some of Jehovah's people have deceived themselves, thinking that they can please God by merely attending meetings occasionally. They try to get by as merely token "doers of the word." (James 1:22) Despite repeated warnings from the John class, they set their hearts on stylish clothes, cars, and homes, and on a life centered on recreation and pleasure. (1 Timothy 6:9, 10; 1 John 2:15-17) All of this results in a dulling of spiritual perception. (Hebrews 5:11, 12) Instead of

being listlessly lukewarm, they need to rekindle "the fire of the spirit" and show refreshing eagerness to "preach the word." —1 Thessalonians 5:19; 2 Timothy 4:2, 5.

9 How does Jesus regard lukewarm Christians? His candid words should jolt them: "You do not know you are miserable and pitiable and poor and blind and naked." Their consciences are numbed to the point that they do not even realize their appalling state. (Compare Proverbs 16:2; 21:2.) This serious condition in the congregation cannot be lightly brushed aside. By setting a fine example of zeal and by shepherding in love, elders and others assigned by them may be able to awaken these straying "sheep" to their former joy of wholehearted service.—Luke 15:3-7.

Counsel on 'Becoming Rich'

10 Is there a cure for the sad situation in Laodicea? Yes, if those Christians will follow Jesus' counsel: *"I advise you to buy from me gold refined by fire that you may become rich."* (*Revelation 3:18a*) True Christian "gold," refined by fire and with all the dross removed, will make them "rich toward God." (Luke 12:21) Where can they buy such gold? Not from the local bankers but from Jesus! The apostle Paul explained what that gold is when he told Timothy to give orders to wealthy Christians "to work at good, to be rich in fine works, to be liberal, ready to share, safely treasuring up for themselves a fine foundation for the future." Only by expending themselves in this way could they "get a firm hold on the real life." (1 Timothy 6:17-19) The materially wealthy Laodiceans should have followed Paul's advice and thus become spiritually rich.—See also Proverbs 3:13-18.

---

* These places have been unearthed by archaeological diggings at the site of Laodicea.

8. (a) In what way does a situation like that in Laodicea exist also today? (b) How have some Christians deceived themselves in this greedy world?

9. (a) What words of Jesus should jolt lukewarm Christians, and why? (b) How may straying "sheep" be helped by the congregation?

10. What is the "gold" that Jesus tells the Christians in Laodicea to buy from him?

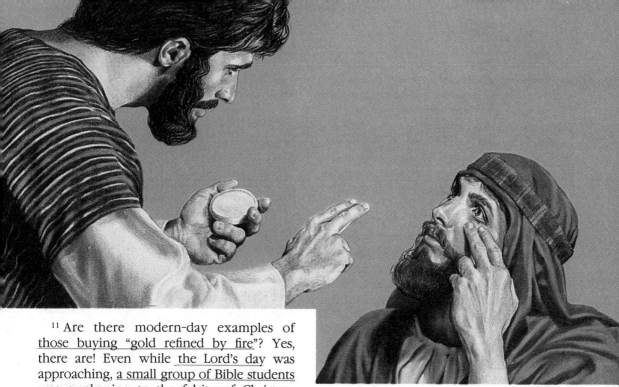

11 Are there modern-day examples of those buying "gold refined by fire"? Yes, there are! Even while the Lord's day was approaching, a small group of Bible students was awakening to the falsity of Christendom's many Babylonish teachings, such as the Trinity, immortality of the soul, hellfire torment, infant baptism, and worship of images (including the cross and those of Mary). In championing Bible truth, these Christians proclaimed Jehovah's Kingdom as mankind's only hope and Jesus' ransom sacrifice as the basis for salvation. Almost 40 years ahead of time, they pointed to 1914 as the year marked in Bible prophecy as the end of the times of the Gentiles, when civil and ecclesiastical powers would be shaken. —Revelation 1:10; Luke 21:24-26, *King James Version.*

STOP 12 Taking the lead among these awakening Christians was Charles Taze Russell, who, in the early 1870's, formed a Bible study class in Allegheny (now part of Pittsburgh), Pennsylvania, U.S.A. When he started his search for truth, Russell was in partnership with his father and on his way to becoming a millionaire. But he sold out his chain-store business interests and spent his fortune in helping to finance the publishing of God's Kingdom in all the earth. In 1884 Russell became the first president of the corporation now known as the Watch Tower Bible and Tract Society of Pennsylvania. In 1916 he died on a train near El Paso, Texas, en route to New York, exhausted by his final preaching tour of the western United States. He set an outstanding example of storing up spiritual treasures in heaven, an example that is followed by hundreds of thousands of self-sacrificing pioneer ministers in these late 1900's.—Hebrews 13:7; Luke 12:33, 34; compare 1 Corinthians 9:16; 11:1.

Applying Spiritual Eye Salve

Start 7/15/91

13 Jesus also sternly admonishes those

---

11. What modern-day examples do we have of those buying "gold refined by fire"?
12. Who was one of those taking the lead among awakening Christians, and how did he set an outstanding example in storing up treasures in heaven?

13. (a) How will spiritual eye salve improve the condition of the Laodiceans? (b) What kind of garments does Jesus recommend, and why?

Laodiceans: *"Buy . . . white outer garments that you may become dressed and that the shame of your nakedness may not become manifested, and eyesalve to rub in your eyes that you may see." (Revelation 3:18b)* They should seek a cure for their spiritual blindness by purchasing curative eye salve, not that of the local healers, but of the kind that only Jesus can provide. This would help them to get spiritual discernment, helping them to walk in "the path of the righteous ones" with their beaming eyes focused on doing God's will. (Proverbs 4:18, 25-27) Thus, they may put on, not the costly garments of black wool made locally in Laodicea, but fine "white outer garments" that proclaim their privileged identity as followers of Jesus Christ. —Compare 1 Timothy 2:9, 10; 1 Peter 3:3-5.

¹⁴ Is spiritual eye salve available in modern times? Assuredly it is! In 1879 Pastor Russell, as he was affectionately called, began to publish in defense of truth the magazine that is known worldwide today as *The Watchtower Announcing Jehovah's Kingdom.* In its second issue, he declared: "[This magazine] has, we believe, JEHOVAH for its backer, and while this is the case it will never *beg* nor *petition* men for support. When He who says: 'All the gold and silver of the mountains are mine,' fails to provide necessary funds, we will understand it to be time to suspend the publication." Some 20th-century television evangelists have amassed vast fortunes and lived in shameless (and sometimes immoral) luxury. (Compare Revelation 18:3.) In contrast, the Bible Students, known today as Jehovah's Witnesses, have used all the unsolicited contributions received to organize and advance the worldwide preaching of Jehovah's incoming Kingdom. The John class to this day directs the

14. (a) What spiritual eye salve has been available since 1879? (b) What has been the ultimate source of the financial backing of Jehovah's Witnesses? (c) In the use of contributions, how do Jehovah's Witnesses differ from others?

publishing of *The Watchtower* and *Awake!*, which magazines had a combined circulation in 1988 of more than 20 million. *The Watchtower* is available in more than a hundred languages. It is the official journal of a congregation of more than three million Christians who have used such spiritual eye salve in getting their eyes opened to false religion and to the urgency of preaching the good news in all the nations.—Mark 13:10.

Benefiting From Reproof and Discipline

¹⁵ Let us return to the Laodiceans. How will they respond to the severe counsel from Jesus? Should they be disheartened and feel that Jesus no longer wants them as his followers? No, that is not the case at all. The message goes on to say: *"All those for whom I have affection I reprove and discipline. Therefore be zealous and repent."* (*Revelation 3:19*) As with discipline from Jehovah, Jesus' discipline is a sign of his love. (Hebrews 12:4-7) The Laodicean congregation should take advantage of his affectionate concern and apply his counsel. They should repent, recognizing that their lukewarmness amounts to sinning. (Hebrews 3:12, 13; James 4:17) Let their elders put materialistic ways behind them and "stir up like a fire" the gift they have from God. With the spiritual eye salve taking effect, let all in the congregation find refreshment as from a cooling draft of cold springwater.—2 Timothy 1:6; Proverbs 3:5-8; Luke 21:34. *Pay attention to yourself*—

¹⁶ What of us today? Jesus continues to 'love his own that are in the world.' This he will do "all the days until the conclusion of the system of things." (John 13:1; Matthew 28:20) His love and affection are displayed

through the modern-day John class and the stars, or elders, in the Christian congregation. (Revelation 1:20) In these very trying times, the elders are deeply interested in helping all of us, old and young, to keep within the confines of the theocratic fold, resisting the independence, the materialistic greed, and the immoral filth of the world. If we receive strong counsel or discipline at times, remember that "the reproofs of discipline are the way of life." (Proverbs 6:23) All of us are imperfect and should be zealous to repent as necessary so that we may be readjusted and remain in God's love.—2 Corinthians 13:11.

¹⁷ We must not allow materialism, riches, or the lack of riches to make us lukewarm. Wealth can aid in opening up new possibilities of service, but it can also be dangerous. (Matthew 19:24) A well-to-do person may feel that he does not need to be as zealous in the preaching work as others, provided that he makes sizable donations from time to time. Or he may feel that being wealthy entitles him to favors. Additionally, there are many pleasures and pastimes open to a wealthy person that others cannot afford. But those diversions take up time and may draw the unwary away from the Christian ministry, thus making the indiscreet one lukewarm. May we avoid all such snares and keep "working hard and exerting ourselves" wholeheartedly, with everlasting life in view.—1 Timothy 4:8-10; 6:9-12.

'Taking the Evening Meal'

¹⁸ Jesus goes on to say: *"Look! I am standing at the door and knocking. If anyone hears my voice and opens the door, I will come into his house and take the evening meal with him and he with me."* (*Revelation 3:20*) If the Laodicean Christians will only welcome Jesus into their congregation, he will help them to

---

15. Why does Jesus give strong counsel to the Christians in Laodicea, and how should the congregation react to it?
16. (a) How are Jesus' love and affection displayed today? (b) If we receive strong counsel, how should we react?

17. How can wealth be spiritually dangerous to us?
18. What opportunity does Jesus set before the Christians in Laodicea?

overcome their lukewarmness!—Matthew 18:20.

¹⁹ Jesus' mention of the evening meal doubtless reminds the Laodiceans of the times when he ate meals with his disciples. (John 12:1-8) Such occasions always brought spiritual blessings for those present. Likewise, there were notable occasions after Jesus' resurrection when he was present at a meal with his disciples, which occasions greatly strengthened them. (Luke 24:28-32; John 21:9-19) Hence, his promise to come into the Laodicean congregation and take the evening meal with them is a promise to bring them rich spiritual benefits if only they will receive him.

²⁰ Jesus' loving exhortation to the Laodiceans has great significance for the remaining anointed Christians today. Some of these remember that, as the Lord's day began, Christendom's religionists were lukewarm to an appalling degree. Instead of welcoming our Lord's return in 1914, her clergy got embroiled in the slaughter of World War I, in which 24 of the 28 contending nations claimed to be Christian. How great their bloodguilt! During World War II, which was also fought largely in Christendom, false religion's sins again "massed together clear up to heaven." (Revelation 18:5) Further, the clergy have turned their back on Jehovah's incoming Kingdom by supporting the League of Nations, the United Nations, and nationalistic, revolutionary movements, none of which can solve mankind's problems. Jesus has long since rejected the clergy, judging them adversely and throwing them away, just as a fisherman disposes of unsuitable fish caught in his dragnet. The miserable plight of Christendom's churches today testifies to that judgment of her. May

her eventual fate serve as a warning to us! —Matthew 13:47-50.

²¹ Even within the true congregation, there have been lukewarm individuals who are like a drink that is neither stimulatingly hot nor refreshingly cold. But Jesus still warmly loves his congregation. He makes himself available to Christians who respond hospitably, and many have welcomed him, as though to an evening meal. As a result, from 1919 onward their eyes have been opened to the meaning of Bible prophecies. They have enjoyed a period of great enlightenment.—Psalm 97:11; 2 Peter 1:19.

²² In addressing the Laodiceans, Jesus may also have had another evening meal in mind. Later in Revelation we read: "Happy are those invited to the evening meal of the Lamb's marriage." This is the majestic victory banquet in praise of Jehovah after he has executed judgment on false religion—a banquet shared in by Christ and his completed bride of 144,000 in heaven. (Revelation 19:1-9) Responsive members of that ancient Laodicean congregation—yes, and faithful brothers of Christ Jesus today, who wear clean garments of identification as genuine anointed Christians—will all feast with their Bridegroom at that evening meal. (Matthew 22:2-13) What a powerful inducement to be zealous and repent!

A Throne for the Conquerors

²³ Jesus speaks of a further reward, saying: *"To the one that conquers I will grant to sit down with me on my throne, even as I conquered and sat down with my Father on his*

---

19. What does Jesus imply when he promises to take the evening meal with the congregation in Laodicea?

20. (a) At the beginning of the Lord's day, what resulted from Christendom's lukewarmness? (b) How has Jesus' judgment affected Christendom?

21. From 1919 onward, how have Christians in the true congregation responded to Jesus' words to the Christians in Laodicea?

22. What future evening meal may Jesus have had in mind, and who will share in it?

23, 24. (a) Of what further reward does Jesus speak? (b) When did Jesus sit down on his Messianic throne, and when did he begin the judgment of professed Christians? (c) What marvelous promise did Jesus make to his disciples when he instituted the Memorial of his death?

throne." (*Revelation 3:21*) In fulfillment of David's words at Psalm 110:1, 2, the integrity-keeping Jesus, having conquered the world, was resurrected in 33 C.E. and exalted to sit down with his Father on His heavenly throne. (Acts 2:32, 33) In another crucial year, 1914, Jesus arrived to sit down on his own Messianic throne as King and Judge. The judgment began in 1918 with professed Christians. Anointed conquerors who died before that time would then be resurrected and join Jesus in his Kingdom. (Matthew 25:31; 1 Peter 4:17) He had promised this to them when instituting the Memorial of his death, saying to his disciples: "I make a covenant with you, just as my Father has made a covenant with me, for a kingdom, that you may eat and drink at my table in my kingdom, and sit on thrones to judge the twelve tribes of Israel."—Luke 22:28-30.

Materialism Versus Wisdom

Back in 1956, a news columnist wrote: "It is estimated that a century ago the average man had 72 wants, of which 16 were regarded as necessities. Today, the average man is estimated to have 474 wants, 94 of which are regarded as necessities. A century ago, 200 articles were urged upon the average man by salesmanship—but today there are 32,000 articles which require sales resistance. Man's necessities are few—his wants, infinite." Today, people are bombarded with the idea that material wealth and possessions are the principal thing in life. Thus, many come to ignore the wise advice of Ecclesiastes 7:12: "Wisdom is for a protection the same as money is for a protection; but the advantage of knowledge is that wisdom itself preserves alive its owners."

---

24 What a marvelous assignment—to sit with the reigning King during "the re-creation" and share with him, on the basis of his perfect sacrifice, in raising the world of obedient mankind to Edenic perfection! (Matthew 19:28; 20:28) As John informs us, Jesus makes those who conquer to be "a kingdom, priests to his God and Father," to occupy thrones around Jehovah's own magnificent heavenly throne. (Revelation 1:6; 4:4) Let all of us—whether of the anointed or of the new earth society that hopes to share in restoring Paradise—take to heart the words of Jesus to the Laodiceans!—2 Peter 3:13; Acts 3:19-21.

25 As with previous messages, Jesus ends this one with words of exhortation: ***"Let the one who has an ear hear what the spirit says to the congregations."*** (*Revelation 3:22*) We are living deep in the time of the end. The evidence is all around us that Christendom is cold as far as love is concerned. In contrast, may we as true Christians respond fervently to Jesus' message to the congregation in Laodicea, yes, to all seven of our Lord's messages to the congregations. This we can do by having a vigorous share in the fulfillment of Jesus' great prophecy for our day: "And this good news of the kingdom will be preached in all the inhabited earth for a witness to all the nations; and then the end will come."—Matthew 24:12-14.

26 Jesus' counsel to the seven congregations is ended. He does not speak to John again in Revelation until the final chapter; but he participates in many of the visions, for example, in executing Jehovah's judgments. Let us now join the John class in examining the second remarkable vision revealed by the Lord Jesus Christ.

25. (a) As with previous messages, how does Jesus end his message to Laodicea? (b) How should individual Christians today respond to Jesus' words to the congregation in Laodicea?
26. When does Jesus again speak directly to John, but in what does he participate?

The Magnificence
of Jehovah's Celestial Throne

JOHN begins to share with us further soul-stirring visions. By inspiration he is still in the Lord's day. So, what he describes has deep meaning for us who are actually living in that day. By means of these visions, Jehovah lifts the veil of invisibility on heavenly realities and gives us his own view of his judgments to be executed on earth. Moreover, whether we have a heavenly or an earthly hope, these revelations help us to see our place in Jehovah's purpose. All of us, therefore, should continue to be keenly interested in John's expression: "Happy is he who reads aloud and those who hear the words of this prophecy, and who observe the things written in it."—Revelation 1:3.

2 What John next beholds surpasses anything presented by video to 20th-century man! He writes: *"After these things I saw, and, look! an opened door in heaven, and the first voice that I heard was as of a trumpet, speaking*

1. Why should we be keenly interested in the visions John shares with us?
2. What experience does John now have?

Vision _____ 2

Revelation 4:1–5:14

Subject: Awesome happenings before God's throne of judgment

Time of fulfillment: This vision features events taking place from 1914 until the end of the Millennium and beyond, when every creature that is in heaven and on earth will praise Jehovah.—Revelation 5:13

with me, saying: 'Come on up here, and I shall show you the things that must take place.'" (*Revelation 4:1*) John in vision penetrates the invisible heavens of Jehovah's presence, exalted far above physical outer space as explored by modern astronauts, even far above the galaxies of the material universe. As though by entering an opened door, John is invited to feast his eyes on a breathtaking panorama of the ultimate spirit heavens where Jehovah himself is enthroned. (Psalm 11:4; Isaiah 66:1) What a privilege!

3 The Bible does not identify this "first voice." Like Jesus' strong voice heard earlier, it has a commanding trumpetlike sound. (Revelation 1:10, 11) It brings to mind the penetrating horn blast that signaled Jehovah's presence at Mount Sinai. (Exodus 19:18-20) Undoubtedly, Jehovah is the majestic Source of the summons. (Revelation 1:1) He has opened the door so that John, in vision, can enter the most holy location in all the vast realm of Jehovah's sovereignty.

Jehovah's Resplendent Presence

4 What does John see? Listen, as he now shares with us his grand experience: *"After these things I immediately came to be in the power of the spirit: and, look! a throne was in its position in heaven, and there is one seated upon the throne."* (*Revelation 4:2*) In an in-

3. What does the voice "as of a trumpet" bring to mind, and who is undoubtedly the Source of it?
4. (a) What meaning does John's vision have for anointed Christians? (b) What meaning does the vision have for those whose hope it is to live forever on earth?

stant of time, John is spiritually transported by God's active force to the very throne of Jehovah. How thrilling for John! Here he is given a dazzling preview of those very heavens wherein he and other anointed Christians have reserved for them "an incorruptible and undefiled and unfading inheritance." (1 Peter 1:3-5; Philippians 3:20) For those whose hope it is to live forever on earth, John's vision also has profound meaning. It helps them to comprehend the glory of Jehovah's presence and of the heavenly ruling structure used by Jehovah in judging the nations and afterward in governing human lives on earth. Jehovah is indeed the God of superb organization!

5 Much of what John observes up there in heaven resembles features of the tabernacle in the wilderness. This was constructed about 1,600 years earlier as a sanctuary of true worship for the Israelites. In the Holy of Holies of that tabernacle was the ark of the covenant, and it was from above the solid gold cover of that Ark that Jehovah himself spoke. (Exodus 25:17-22; Hebrews 9:5) Hence, the cover of the Ark served as a symbol of Jehovah's throne. John now sees the reality of that symbolic representation: the Sovereign Lord Jehovah himself sitting in exquisite grandeur on his lofty heavenly throne.

6 Unlike earlier prophets who had visions of Jehovah's throne, John does not describe in detail the Holy One who occupies it. (Ezekiel 1:26, 27; Daniel 7:9, 10) But John gives us his impression of the enthroned One in these words: *"And the one seated is, in appearance, like a jasper stone and a precious red-colored stone, and round about the throne there is a rainbow like an emerald in appearance."* (*Revelation 4:3*) What incomparable magnif-

icence! John perceives a serene, scintillating beauty like that of lustrous, gleaming gemstones. How appropriately this agrees with the disciple James' description of Jehovah as "the Father of the celestial lights"! (James 1:17) Shortly after writing Revelation, John himself stated: "God is light and there is no darkness at all in union with him." (1 John 1:5) What a superbly glorious Personage Jehovah really is!

7 Notice that John sees around the throne a rainbow, colored emerald green. The Greek word here translated rainbow (*ir'is*) suggests a completely circular form. The rainbow is first mentioned in the Bible in connection with Noah's day. After the waters of the Deluge subsided, Jehovah caused a rainbow to appear in the cloud, and he explained what it symbolized in these words: "My rainbow I do give in the cloud, and it must serve as a sign of the covenant between me and the earth. And I shall certainly remember my covenant which is between me and you and every living soul among all flesh; and no more will the waters become a deluge to bring all flesh to ruin." (Genesis 9:13, 15) What, then, would the heavenly vision bring to John's mind? The rainbow that he saw must have reminded him of the need for a peaceful relationship with Jehovah, such as the John class enjoys today. It would also impress him with the serenity and peace of Jehovah's presence, a serenity that will extend to all obedient humans when Jehovah spreads his tent over mankind in the new earth society.—Psalm 119:165; Philippians 4:7; Revelation 21:1-4.

Identifying the 24 Elders

8 John knew that priests were appointed to serve in the ancient tabernacle. So he may have been surprised at seeing what he de-

---

5. What reality does John see that was symbolized by the cover of the ark of the covenant?
6. What impression of Jehovah does John give us, and why is this fitting?

7. What can we learn from the fact that there is a rainbow around Jehovah's throne?
8. Whom does John see round about the throne, and whom do these represent?

REVELATION CLIMAX

scribes next: *"And round about the throne there are twenty-four thrones, and upon these thrones I saw seated twenty-four elders dressed in white outer garments, and upon their heads golden crowns."* (Revelation 4:4) Yes, instead of priests, there are 24 elders, enthroned and crowned like kings. Who are these elders? They are none other than anointed ones of the Christian congregation, resurrected and occupying the heavenly position Jehovah promised them. How do we know that?

⁹ First of all, they are wearing crowns. The Bible speaks of anointed Christians as gaining 'an incorruptible crown' and attaining to an endless life—immortality. (1 Corinthians 9:25; 15:53, 54) But since these 24 elders are sitting on thrones, the golden crowns in this context represent royal authority. (Compare Revelation 6:2; 14:14.) This supports the conclusion that the 24 elders portray Jesus' anointed footstep followers in their heavenly position, for Jesus made a covenant with them to sit on thrones in his Kingdom. (Luke 22: 28-30) Only Jesus and these 24 elders—not even the angels—are described as ruling in heaven in Jehovah's presence.

¹⁰ This harmonizes with the promise that Jesus made to the Laodicean congregation: "To the one that conquers I will grant to sit down with me on my throne." (Revelation 3:21) But the heavenly assignment of the 24 elders is not limited to governmental rule. In the introduction to the book of Revelation, John said of Jesus: "He made us to be a kingdom, priests to his God and Father." (Revelation 1:5, 6) These ones are both kings and priests. "They will be priests of God and of the Christ, and will rule as kings with him for the thousand years."—Revelation 20:6.

¹¹ What is significant about the number 24, in that John sees 24 elders around the throne? In many respects, these were foreshadowed by the faithful priests of ancient Israel. The apostle Peter wrote to anointed Christians: "You are 'a chosen race, a royal priesthood, a holy nation, a people for special possession.'" (1 Peter 2:9) Interestingly, that ancient Jewish priesthood came to be divided into 24 divisions. Each division was assigned its own weeks in the year to serve before Jehovah, so that sacred service was rendered without a break. (1 Chronicles 24: 5-19) It is fitting, then, that there are 24 elders depicted in John's vision of the heavenly priesthood because this priesthood serves Jehovah continually, without ceasing. When completed, there will be 24 divisions, each with 6,000 conquerors, for Revelation 14:1-4 tells us that 144,000 (24 x 6,000) are "bought from among mankind" to stand on the heavenly Mount Zion with the Lamb, Jesus Christ. Since the number 12 signifies a divinely balanced organization, 24 doubles—or strengthens—such an arrangement.

Lightnings, Voices, and Thunders

¹² What does John next see and hear? *"And out of the throne there are proceeding lightnings and voices and thunders."* (Revelation 4:5a) How reminiscent of other awesome manifestations of Jehovah's celestial power! For example, when Jehovah "came down" on Mount Sinai, Moses reported: "On the third day when it became morning it came about that thunders and lightnings began occurring, and a heavy cloud upon the mountain and a very loud sound of a horn. . . . When the sound of the horn became continually louder and louder, Moses began to speak, and the true God began to answer him with a voice."—Exodus 19:16-19.

9, 10. How do we know that the 24 elders represent the anointed Christian congregation in its glorious heavenly position?

11. Why is it fitting that the number of elders is 24, and what does that number signify?

12. What does John next see and hear, and what do the "lightnings and voices and thunders" call to mind?

¹³ During the Lord's day, Jehovah makes his power and presence manifest in a sublime way. No, not by literal lightning, for John is seeing signs. What, then, do the lightnings represent? Well, flashes of lightning can illuminate, but they can also strike one dead. Therefore, these lightnings issuing from Jehovah's throne well picture the flashes of enlightenment that he has continually granted his people and, even more significantly, his fiery judgment messages.—Compare Psalm 18:14; 144:5, 6; Matthew 4:14-17; 24:27.

¹⁴ What of the voices? During Jehovah's descent onto Mount Sinai, a voice spoke to Moses. (Exodus 19:19) Voices from heaven issued many of the commands and proclamations in the book of Revelation. (Revelation 4:1; 10:4, 8; 11:12; 12:10; 14:13; 16:1, 17; 18:4; 19:5; 21:3) Today, Jehovah has also issued commands and proclamations to his people, illuminating their understanding of Bible prophecies and principles. Enlightening information has often been disclosed at international conventions, and such Bible truths have, in turn, been proclaimed worldwide. The apostle Paul said of faithful preachers of the good news: "Why, in fact, 'into all the earth their sound went out, and to the extremities of the inhabited earth their utterances.'"—Romans 10:18.

¹⁵ Thunder usually follows lightning. David referred to literal thunder as "the voice of Jehovah." (Psalm 29:3, 4) When Jehovah fought for David against his enemies, thunder was said to come from Him. (2 Samuel 22:14; Psalm 18:13) Elihu told Job that Jehovah's voice sounded like thunder, as He does "great things that we cannot know." (Job 37: 4, 5) During this part of the Lord's day,

Jehovah has 'thundered,' warning of the great acts he will perform against his enemies. These symbolic peals of thunder have echoed and reechoed throughout the earth. Happy you are if you have paid attention to these thunderous proclamations and are making wise use of your tongue in adding to their volume!—Isaiah 50:4, 5; 61:1, 2.

Lamps of Fire and a Glassy Sea

¹⁶ What does John further see? This: *"And there are seven lamps of fire burning before the throne, and these mean the seven spirits of God. And before the throne there is, as it were, a glassy sea like crystal."* (Revelation 4:5b, 6a) John himself tells us the significance of the seven lamps: "These mean the seven spirits of God." The number seven symbolizes divine completeness; so the seven lamps must represent the fullness of the enlightening force of the holy spirit. How grateful the John class today is that it has been entrusted with this enlightenment, together with the responsibility to pass it on to the spiritually hungry peoples of earth! How glad we are that each year over 200 million copies of the *Watchtower* magazine continue to beam forth this light in more than a hundred languages!—Psalm 43:3.

¹⁷ John sees also a "glassy sea like crystal." What would this symbolize with regard to those invited into Jehovah's heavenly court? Paul spoke of the way that Jesus sanctified the congregation, "cleansing it with the bath of water by means of the word." (Ephesians 5:26) Before his death, Jesus told his disciples: "You are already clean because of the word that I have spoken to you." (John 15:3) Hence, this glassy sea like crystal must represent the cleansing, recorded Word of God. Those of the royal priesthood who come into Jehovah's presence must have been thoroughly cleansed by his Word.

---

13. What is pictured by the lightnings issuing from Jehovah's throne?
14. How have voices sounded out today?
15. What thunders have proceeded from the throne during this part of the Lord's day?

16. What is signified by the "seven lamps of fire"?
17. What does the "glassy sea like crystal" symbolize?

Behold—"Four Living Creatures"!

START. 7/31/89

[18] John now observes another feature. He writes: *"And in the midst of the throne and around the throne there are four living creatures that are full of eyes in front and behind."* —Revelation 4:6b.

[19] What do these creatures picture? A vision reported by another prophet, Ezekiel, helps us to find the answer. Ezekiel saw Jehovah enthroned on a celestial chariot, which was accompanied by living creatures embodying characteristics similar to those described by John. (Ezekiel 1:5-11, 22-28) Later, Ezekiel again saw that chariot throne accompanied by the living creatures. This time, however, he referred to the living creatures as cherubs. (Ezekiel 10:9-15) The four living creatures that John sees must represent the many cherubs of God—creatures of high rank in His spirit organization. John would not think it unusual to see cherubs positioned so close to Jehovah's person, since in the ancient tabernacle arrangement, two cherubs of gold were displayed upon the lid of the ark of the covenant, which represented Jehovah's throne. From between these cherubs, Jehovah's voice issued commandments to the nation.—Exodus 25:22; Psalm 80:1.

[20] These four living creatures are "in the midst of the throne and around the throne." Exactly what does this mean? It could signify that they are positioned around the throne in such a way that one is standing in the middle of each side. Thus, the translators of *Today's English Version* paraphrased the original Greek expression in this way: "surrounding the throne on each of its sides." Alternatively, the expression could mean

that the four living creatures are in the central position in heaven where the throne is. Likely, that is why *The Jerusalem Bible* renders the phrase: "in the centre, grouped round the throne itself." The important thing is the closeness of the cherubs to Jehovah's throne, comparable to that of the cherubs that Ezekiel saw at each corner of Jehovah's organizational chariot. (Ezekiel 1:15-22) All of this harmonizes with the words of Psalm 99:1: "Jehovah himself has become king. . . . He is sitting upon the cherubs."

[21] John continues: *"And the first living creature is like a lion, and the second living creature is like a young bull, and the third living creature has a face like a man's, and the fourth living creature is like a flying eagle."* (Revelation 4:7) Why do these four living creatures look so different, one from another? These distinctive living creatures evidently highlight specific godly qualities. First, there is the lion. A lion is used in the Bible as a symbol of courage, especially in the pursuit of justice and righteousness. (2 Samuel 17:10; Proverbs 28:1) Thus, the lion well represents the godly quality of courageous justice. (Deuteronomy 32:4; Psalm 89:14) The second living creature resembles a young bull. What quality does a bull bring to your mind? To the Israelites the bull was a valuable possession because of its power. (Proverbs 14:4; see also Job 39:9-11.) The young bull, then, represents power, dynamic energy as supplied by Jehovah. —Psalm 62:11; Isaiah 40:26.

[22] The third living creature has a face like a man's. This must represent godlike love, since on earth man alone was created in God's image, with the superlative quality of love. (Genesis 1:26-28; Matthew 22:36-40; 1 John 4:8, 16) Undoubtedly, the cherubs display this quality as they serve around

18. What does John see in the midst of and around the throne?

19. What is pictured by the four living creatures, and how do we know this?

20. In what way can it be said that the four living creatures are "in the midst of the throne and around the throne"?

21, 22. (a) How does John describe the four living creatures? (b) What is represented by the appearance of each of the four living creatures?

Jehovah's throne. What now of the fourth living creature? This one is like a flying eagle in appearance. Jehovah himself calls attention to the eagle's great vision: "Far into the distance its eyes keep looking." (Job 39:29) Hence, the eagle well symbolizes farsighted wisdom. Jehovah is the Source of wisdom. His cherubs exercise divine wisdom as they obey his commands.—Proverbs 2:6; James 3:17.

Jehovah's Praises Ring Out

23 John continues his description: *"And as for the four living creatures, each one of them respectively has six wings; round about and underneath they are full of eyes. And they have no rest day and night as they say: 'Holy, holy, holy is Jehovah God, the Almighty, who was and who is and who is coming.'"* (*Revelation 4:8*) This fullness of eyes suggests complete and farsighted vision. The four living creatures exercise this unceasingly, as they have no need of sleep. They imitate the One of whom it is written: "As regards Jehovah, his eyes are roving about through all the earth to show his strength in behalf of those whose heart is complete toward him." (2 Chronicles 16:9) Having so great a number of eyes, the cherubs can see everywhere. Nothing escapes their attention. Thus they are well-equipped to serve God in his work of judging. Of him it is said: "The eyes of Jehovah are in every place, keeping watch upon the bad ones and the good ones." (Proverbs 15:3) And with three pairs of wings—the number three being used in the Bible for emphasis—the cherubs can move with lightning swiftness to herald Jehovah's judgments and execute them.

24 Listen! Melodious, soul stirring, is the song of praise that the cherubs render to Jehovah: "Holy, holy, holy is Jehovah God, the Almighty, who was and who is and who is coming." Again, the threeness indicates intensity. The cherubs strongly affirm the holiness of Jehovah God. He is the Source and the ultimate Standard of holiness. He is also "the King of eternity," always "the Alpha and the Omega, the first and the last, the beginning and the end." (1 Timothy 1:17; Revelation 22:13) The cherubs take no rest periods as they proclaim the matchless qualities of Jehovah before all creation.

25 The heaven of heavens resounds with praises to Jehovah! John's description continues: *"And whenever the living creatures offer glory and honor and thanksgiving to the one seated upon the throne, the one that lives forever and ever, the twenty-four elders fall down before the One seated upon the throne and worship the One that lives forever and ever, and they cast their crowns before the throne, saying: 'You are worthy, Jehovah, even our God, to receive the glory and the honor and the power, because you created all things, and because of your will they existed and were created.'"* (*Revelation 4:9-11*) In all Scripture, this is one of the grandest declarations of homage to Jehovah, our God and Sovereign Lord!

26 The 24 elders have the same mental attitude that Jesus displays, even casting their crowns down before Jehovah. It is furthest from their minds to exalt themselves in the presence of God. They humbly recognize that the only purpose of their kingship is to bring honor and glory to him, just as Jesus always does. (Philippians 2:5, 6, 9-11) Submissively, they acknowledge their own inferiority and confess that their rulership is dependent on the sovereignty of Jehovah. Thus, they are in heartfelt harmony with the cherubs and the rest of faithful creation in giving praise

---

23. What is symbolized by the fact that the four living creatures are "full of eyes," and what is emphasized by their having three pairs of wings?
24. How do the cherubs praise Jehovah, and with what significance?

25. How do the living creatures and the 24 elders unite in adoring Jehovah?
26. Why do the 24 elders cast their crowns before Jehovah?

and glory to the God who created all things.—Psalm 150:1-6.

27 Who can remain unmoved at reading John's account of this vision? It is splendorous, grand! But what must the reality be like? Jehovah's very majesty must enliven anyone with an appreciative heart to join the four living creatures and the 24 elders in praising Him, both in prayer and by publicly proclaiming His name. This is the God for whom Christians are privileged to be witnesses today. (Isaiah 43:10) Remember that John's vision applies to the Lord's day, where we now are. "The seven spirits" are ever at hand to guide and strengthen us. (Galatians 5:16-18) God's Word is available

today to help us be holy in serving a holy God. (1 Peter 1:14-16) Certainly, we are happy to read aloud the words of this prophecy. (Revelation 1:3) What an inducement they provide to be faithful to Jehovah and not allow the world to distract us from actively singing his praises!—1 John 2:15-17.

28 So far, John has described what he sees when he is invited to approach through that opened door in heaven. Most outstandingly, he reports that Jehovah, in all the magnificence of His majesty and dignity, is seated on His celestial throne. He is surrounded by the mightiest of all organizations—radiant in its splendor and loyalty. The divine Court is in session. (Daniel 7:9, 10, 18) The stage is set for something extraordinary to happen. What is it, and how does it affect us today? Let us watch as the scene unfolds!

27, 28. (a) How should John's description of this vision affect us? (b) What questions arise as to what John next sees and hears?

"Who Is Worthy to Open the Scroll?"

SUBLIME! AWE INSPIRING! Such is the stirring vision of Jehovah's throne in its setting amid the lamps of fire, the cherubs, the 24 elders, and the glassy sea. But John, what do you see next? John focuses on the very center of this heavenly scene, telling us: _"And I saw in the right hand of the One seated upon the throne a scroll written within and on the reverse side, sealed tight with seven seals. And I saw a strong angel proclaiming with a loud voice: 'Who is worthy to open the scroll and loose its seals?' But neither in heaven nor upon_

earth nor underneath the earth was there a single one able to open the scroll or to look into it. And I gave way to a great deal of weeping because no one was found worthy to open the scroll or to look into it."—Revelation 5:1-4.

2 Jehovah himself, Sovereign Lord of all creation, is holding out that scroll. It must be full of vital information, for it has writing on the front and on the back. Our curiosity is aroused. What does the scroll contain? We

1. What happens now in John's vision?

2, 3. (a) Why is John eager that someone be found to open the scroll, but what appears to be the prospect for that? (b) For what have God's anointed people eagerly waited in our time?

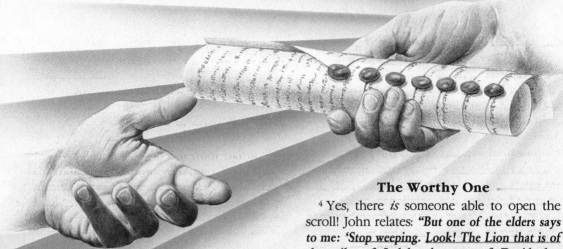

The Worthy One

[4] Yes, there *is* someone able to open the scroll! John relates: *"But one of the elders says to me: 'Stop weeping. Look! The Lion that is of the tribe of Judah, the root of David, has conquered so as to open the scroll and its seven seals.'"* (*Revelation 5:5*) So John, dry those tears! The John class and their loyal companions today have also endured decades of severe trials while waiting patiently for enlightenment. What a comforting reward we now have in understanding the vision, and what a privilege to share in its fulfillment by proclaiming its message to others!

[5] Ah, "the Lion that is of the tribe of Judah"! John is familiar with the prophecy that Jacob, ancestor of the Jewish race, pronounced concerning his fourth son, Judah: "A lion cub Judah is. From the prey, my son, you will certainly go up. He bowed down, he stretched himself out like a lion and, like a lion, who dares rouse him? The scepter will not turn aside from Judah, neither the commander's staff from between his feet, until Shiloh comes; and to him the obedience of the peoples will belong." (Genesis 49:9, 10) The royal line of God's people stemmed from Judah. Starting with David, all the kings who ruled in Jerusalem until the Babylonians destroyed that city were Judah's

recall Jehovah's invitation to John: "Come on up here, and I shall show you the things that must take place." (Revelation 4:1) With tingling expectation, we look forward to learning about those things. But alas, the scroll is tightly closed, sealed shut with seven seals!

[3] Will the strong angel find someone worthy to open the scroll? According to the *Kingdom Interlinear,* the scroll is located "upon the right hand" of Jehovah. This suggests that he holds it out on his open palm. But it appears that no one in heaven or on earth is worthy to accept and open that scroll. Not even underneath the earth, among faithful servants of God who have died, is anyone qualified for this high honor. No wonder that John is visibly upset! Perhaps he is not going to learn "the things that must take place" after all. In our day, too, God's anointed people have anxiously waited for Jehovah to send forth his light and truth on Revelation. This he would do progressively at the appointed time for the prophecy's fulfillment, in order to lead his people in the way of a "grand salvation."—Psalm 43:3, 5.

4. (a) Who is discovered that is worthy to open the scroll and its seals? (b) In what reward and privilege do the John class and their companions now share?
5. (a) What prophecy was spoken concerning Judah, and where did Judah's descendants rule? (b) Who is Shiloh?

descendants. But not one of them was the Shiloh prophesied by Jacob. Shiloh means "He Whose [Right] It Is." Prophetically, this name pointed to Jesus, the one to whom the Davidic Kingdom now permanently belongs. —Ezekiel 21:25-27; Luke 1:32, 33; Revelation 19:16.

6 John quickly recognizes the reference to "the root of David." The promised Messiah is prophetically called both "a twig out of the stump of Jesse [father of King David] . . . a sprout" and "the root of Jesse that will be standing up as a signal for the peoples." (Isaiah 11:1, 10) Jesus was a twig of Jesse, being born into the royal line of David, son of Jesse. Further, as a root of Jesse, he was the One that caused the Davidic dynasty to sprout again, giving it life and sustenance forever.—2 Samuel 7:16.

7 Jesus preeminently is the one who, as a perfect human, served Jehovah in integrity and under excruciating trials. He supplied the complete answer to Satan's challenge. (Proverbs 27:11) Thus, he could say as he did on the night before his sacrificial death, "I have conquered the world." (John 16:33) For this reason, Jehovah entrusted the resurrected Jesus with "all authority . . . in heaven and on the earth." He alone of all servants of God is qualified to receive the scroll, with a view to making known its momentous message.—Matthew 28:18.

8 It is appropriate, indeed, that Jesus should open the scroll. Since 1914 he has been enthroned as King of God's Messianic Kingdom, and that scroll reveals so much concerning the Kingdom and what it will accomplish. Jesus faithfully bore witness to

---

6. In what way was Jesus "a twig" of Jesse and also "the root of David"?
7. What makes Jesus worthy to take the scroll from the hand of the One seated upon the throne?
8. (a) With regard to the Kingdom, what shows Jesus' worthiness? (b) Why is it appropriate that one of the 24 elders reveals to John the person who is worthy to open the scroll?

Kingdom truth while he was here on earth. (John 18:36, 37) He taught his followers to pray for the coming of the Kingdom. (Matthew 6:9, 10) He initiated the preaching of the good news of the Kingdom at the beginning of the Christian era and prophesied the culmination of that preaching work during the time of the end. (Matthew 4:23; Mark 13:10) It is likewise appropriate that one of the 24 elders should reveal to John that Jesus is the one to open the seals. Why? Because these elders sit on thrones and wear crowns, being joint heirs with Christ in his Kingdom. —Romans 8:17; Revelation 4:4.

'The Lamb That Was Slaughtered'

9 John looks to see this "Lion that is of the tribe of Judah." But how astounding! A completely different symbolic figure appears: **"And I saw standing in the midst of the throne and of the four living creatures and in the midst of the elders a lamb as though it had been slaughtered, having seven horns and seven eyes, which eyes mean the seven spirits of God that have been sent forth into the whole earth."** —Revelation 5:6.

10 Right in the center, beside the throne, within the circles formed by the four living creatures and the 24 elders, there is a lamb! Doubtless John quickly identifies this lamb with "the Lion that is of the tribe of Judah" and "the root of David." He knows that, more than 60 years earlier, John the Baptizer introduced Jesus to onlooking Jews as "the Lamb of God that takes away the sin of the world!" (John 1:29) All during his life on earth, Jesus remained untainted by the world —just like an unblemished lamb—so that he could offer his blameless life as a sacrifice for mankind.—1 Corinthians 5:7; Hebrews 7:26.

---

9. Instead of a lion, what does John see standing "in the midst of the throne," and how did he describe it?
10. Who is the "lamb" that John saw, and why is the term appropriate?

REVELATION CLIMAX

11 Is it somehow belittling or undignified to represent the glorified Jesus as "a lamb as though it had been slaughtered"? Not at all! The fact that Jesus stayed faithful to the death was a major defeat for Satan and a great triumph for Jehovah God. Representing Jesus in this way vividly portrays his conquest of Satan's world and is a reminder of the deep love that Jehovah and Jesus have for mankind. (John 3:16; 15:13; compare Colossians 2:15.) Jesus is thus pointed to, as the promised Seed, outstandingly qualified to open the scroll.—Genesis 3:15. •

12 What else adds to our appreciation of this "lamb"? He has seven horns. Horns in the Bible are often a symbol of power or authority, and seven would indicate completeness. (Compare 1 Samuel 2:1, 10; Psalm 112:9; 148:14.) Hence, the Lamb's seven horns represent the fullness of power that Jehovah has entrusted to Jesus. He is "far above every government and authority and power and lordship and every name named, not only in this system of things, but also in that to come." (Ephesians 1:20-23; 1 Peter 3:22) Jesus has particularly exercised power, governmental power, since 1914 when Jehovah enthroned him as heavenly King. —Psalm 2:6.

13 Moreover, Jesus is filled to completeness with holy spirit, as pictured by the Lamb's seven eyes, which "mean the seven spirits of God." Jesus is a channel through whom the fullness of Jehovah's active force flows to His earthly servants. (Titus 3:6) Evidently, it is by this same spirit that he sees from heaven what is happening here on earth. Like his Father, Jesus has perfect discernment. Nothing escapes his notice. (Compare Psalm 11:4; Zechariah 4:10.) Clearly, this Son—the integrity keeper who conquered the world; the Lion of the tribe of Judah; the root of David; the one who offered his life for mankind; the one with complete authority, fullness of holy spirit, and perfect discernment from Jehovah God—yes, this one is outstandingly worthy to take the scroll from Jehovah's hand. Does he hesitate to accept this commission of service in Jehovah's lofty organization? No! Rather, "he went and at once took it [the scroll] out of the right hand of the One seated on the throne." (Revelation 5:7) What a fine example of willing compliance!

Songs of Praise

14 How do those others before Jehovah's throne react? "And when he took the scroll, the four living creatures and the twenty-four elders fell down before the Lamb, having each one a harp and golden bowls that were full of incense, and the incense means the prayers of the holy ones," (Revelation 5:8) Like the four cherubic living creatures before God's throne, the 24 elders bow to Jesus in acknowledgment of his authority. But these elders are alone in having harps and bowls of incense.* And they alone now sing a new song. (Revelation 5:9) Thus they resemble the 144,000 of the holy "Israel of God," who also carry harps and sing a new song. (Galatians 6:16; Colossians 1:12; Revelation 7:3-8; 14:1-4) Further, the 24 elders are shown to fulfill a heavenly, priestly function, pictured by that of the priests in ancient Israel who burned incense to Jehovah in the tabernacle—a function that ended on earth when God took the Mosaic Law out of the way, nailing it to Jesus' torture stake. (Colossians 2:14) What conclusion do we draw from all of this? That here

---

* Grammatically speaking, the expression "having each one a harp and golden bowls that were full of incense" could refer both to the elders and to the four living creatures. The context, however, makes it clear that the expression refers only to the 24 elders.

---

11. Why is it not undignified to represent the glorified Jesus as "a lamb as though it had been slaughtered"?
12. What do the seven horns of the Lamb picture?
13. (a) What do the seven eyes of the Lamb picture? (b) What does the Lamb proceed to do?

14. (a) How do the four living creatures and the 24 elders react to Jesus' taking the scroll? (b) How does the information John receives about the 24 elders confirm their identity and position?

the anointed overcomers are seen in their ultimate assignment as 'priests of God and of the Christ, ruling as kings with him for the thousand years.'—Revelation 20:6.

15 In ancient Israel, entry into the Most Holy before the symbolic presence of Jehovah was limited to the high priest. For him, carrying incense was a life-or-death matter. Jehovah's law said: "[Aaron] must take the fire holder full of burning coals of fire from off the altar before Jehovah, and the hollows of both his hands full of fine perfumed incense, and he must bring them inside the curtain. He must also put the incense upon the fire before Jehovah, and the cloud of the incense must overspread the Ark cover, which is upon the Testimony, that he may not die." (Leviticus 16:12, 13) It was impossible for the high priest to penetrate successfully into the Most Holy unless he burned incense.

16 In the Christian system of things not only the antitypical High Priest, Jesus Christ, but also each of the 144,000 underpriests eventually gets to enter the antitypical Most Holy, the place of Jehovah's presence in heaven. (Hebrews 10:19-23) Entry into this Most Holy is impossible for these priests, as represented here by the 24 elders, unless they 'burn incense,' that is, constantly offer up prayers and supplications to Jehovah. —Hebrews 5:7; Jude 20, 21; compare Psalm 141:2.

A New Song

17 A melodic song now rings forth. It is sung to the Lamb by his priestly associates, the 24 elders: "*And they sing a new song,*

saying: '*You are worthy to take the scroll and open its seals, because you were slaughtered and with your blood you bought persons for God out of every tribe and tongue and people and nation.*'" (*Revelation 5:9*) The expression "new song" occurs several times in the Bible and usually refers to praising Jehovah for some mighty act of deliverance. (Psalm 96:1; 98:1; 144:9) Thus, the song is new because the singer can now proclaim additional wonderful works of Jehovah and express renewed appreciation for His glorious name.

18 Here, though, the 24 elders sing a new song before Jesus rather than before Jehovah. But the principle is the same. They praise Jesus for the new things that he, as God's Son, has done in their behalf. By means of his blood, he mediated the new covenant and thus made possible the bringing forth of a new nation as Jehovah's special possession. (Romans 2:28, 29; 1 Corinthians 11:25; Hebrews 7:18-25) Members of this new spiritual nation came from many fleshly nations, but Jesus united them into one congregation as one nation.—Isaiah 26:2; 1 Peter 2:9, 10.

19 When Jehovah formed the Israelites into a nation back in the days of Moses, he made a covenant with them and promised that if they would remain faithful to that covenant, they would become a kingdom of priests before him. (Exodus 19:5, 6) The Israelites were not faithful and never experienced the realization of that promise. On the other hand, the new nation, formed by virtue of the new covenant mediated by Jesus, has remained faithful. Its members therefore get to rule over the earth as kings and also to serve as priests, helping righthearted ones among mankind to be reconciled to Jehovah. (Colossians 1:20) It is just as the new song

---

15. (a) In Israel, who only was privileged to go into the Most Holy of the tabernacle? (b) Why was it a matter of life or death for the high priest to burn incense before entering the Most Holy?
16. (a) In the Christian system of things, who penetrate the antitypical Most Holy? (b) Why do anointed Christians have to 'burn incense'?
17. (a) What new song do the 24 elders sing? (b) How is the expression "new song" usually used in the Bible?

18. For what do the 24 elders praise Jesus with their new song?
19. (a) What blessing did fleshly Israel fail to realize because of their unfaithfulness? (b) What blessing does Jehovah's new nation get to enjoy?

expresses it: *"And you made them to be a kingdom and priests to our God, and they are to rule as kings over the earth."* (*Revelation 5:10*) What joy those 24 elders have in singing this new song of praise to the glorified Jesus!

A Heavenly Chorus

START

20 How do others of the vast heavenly host of Jehovah's organization respond to this new song? John thrills to behold their heartfelt accord: *"And I saw, and I heard a voice of many angels around the throne and the living creatures and the elders, and the number of them was myriads of myriads and thousands of thousands, saying with a loud voice: 'The Lamb that was slaughtered is worthy to receive the power and riches and wisdom and strength and honor and glory and blessing.'"* (*Revelation 5: 11, 12*) What an impressive song of praise!

21 Does this mean that now Jesus has somehow replaced Jehovah God and that all creation has turned to praising him rather than his Father? Far from it! Rather, this song of praise is in harmony with what the apostle Paul wrote: *"God exalted [Jesus] to a superior position and kindly gave him the name that is above every other name, so that in the name of Jesus every knee should bend of those in heaven and those on earth and those under the ground, and every tongue should openly acknowledge that Jesus Christ is Lord to the glory of God the Father."* (Philippians 2:9-11) Jesus is here extolled because of his part in settling the primary issue before all creation—the vindication of Jehovah's rightful sovereignty. What glory, indeed, this has brought to his Father!

A Swelling Anthem

22 In the scene described by John, the hosts of heaven are rendering melodious acclaim to Jesus in acknowledgment of his faithfulness and his heavenly authority. In this, they are joined by voices from the earthly realm as these too share in praising both the Father and the Son. Just as the achievements of a human son can bring great credit to parents, so Jesus' loyal course redounds among all creation "to the glory of God the Father." Thus, John goes on to report: *"And every creature that is in heaven and on earth and underneath the earth and on the sea, and all the things in them, I heard saying: 'To the One sitting on the throne and to the Lamb be the blessing and the honor and the glory and the might forever and ever.'"*—*Revelation 5:13.*

23 When does this superb anthem sound forth? It began early in the Lord's day. After Satan and his demons were cast out of the heavens, "every creature that is in heaven" could unite in this song of praise. And, as the record shows, since 1919 a growing multitude on earth have united their voices in praising Jehovah, increasing from a few thousand to well over three million by the late 1980's.* After Satan's earthly system has been destroyed, "every creature . . . on earth" will be singing the praises of Jehovah and his Son. In Jehovah's own due time, the resurrection of the countless millions of dead will begin, and then "every creature . . . underneath the earth" that is in the memory of God will have the opportunity to join in singing the anthem.

24 Already, "from the extremity of the earth . . . the sea and . . . islands," millions of humans are singing a new song in association with Jehovah's global organization. (Isaiah 42:10; Psalm 150:1-6) This joyous praise will reach a crescendo at the end of the Millennium, when mankind has been raised to perfection. That old Serpent, the arch-

---

20. What song of praise to the Lamb is now sounded?
21. Does the praising of the Lamb detract from Jehovah's sovereignty or position? Explain.
22. In what anthem do voices from the earthly realm join?

---

* See the chart on page 64.

23, 24. (a) What indicates when the anthem would begin in heaven, and when on earth? (b) How does the anthem swell in volume as the years pass?

deceiver, Satan himself, will thereafter be destroyed in complete fulfillment of Genesis 3:15, and in a triumphant climax, all living creation, spirit and human, will sing in unison: "To the One sitting on the throne and to the Lamb be the blessing and the honor and the glory and the might forever and ever." There will be no dissenting voice in all the universe.

²⁵ What a joyful time that will be! Surely, what John describes here makes our hearts swell with happiness and stimulates us to join the heavenly hosts in singing heartfelt praises to Jehovah God and Jesus Christ. Are we not more determined than ever to endure in right works? If we do so, we can expect that, with Jehovah's help, we will be there individually

---

25. (a) Reading John's account of the universal anthem moves us to do what? (b) What splendid example is set for us by the four living creatures and the 24 elders as the vision ends?

at the happy climax, adding our voices to that universal chorus of praise. Certainly, the cherubic four living creatures and the resurrected anointed Christians are in full accord, for the vision ends with the words: *"And the four living creatures went saying: 'Amen!' and the elders fell down and worshiped."—Revelation 5:14.*

²⁶ May you, dear reader, exercise faith in the sacrifice of the Lamb—the 'worthy one'—and be blessed in your humble efforts to worship and serve Jehovah—"the One seated upon the throne." Let the John class help you today as it provides the needed "measure of [spiritual] food supplies at the proper time." (Luke 12:42) But look! The Lamb prepares to open the seven seals. What exciting disclosures are now in store for us?

---

26. In what should we exercise faith, and what is the Lamb preparing to do?

Chapter 16

Four Horsemen at the Gallop!

IN THIS day of crisis, are we not intensely interested in "the things that must shortly take place"? Surely we are, for we ourselves

---

1. How does Jehovah reveal to John the contents of the intriguing scroll that Jesus opens?

Vision 3
Revelation 6:1-17
Subject: The ride of the four horsemen, the martyred witnesses underneath the altar, and the great day of wrath
Time of fulfillment: From 1914 up to the destruction of this system of things

are involved! So let us now accompany John as Jesus proceeds to open that intriguing scroll. Remarkably, John does not have to read it. Why not? Because its contents are conveyed to him "in signs" by a series of dynamic, action-packed scenes.—Revelation 1:1, 10.

² Listen to John as Jesus opens the first seal of the scroll: *"And I saw when the Lamb opened one of the seven seals, and I heard one of the four living creatures say with a voice as of thunder: 'Come!'"* (*Revelation 6:1*) This is

---

2. (a) What does John see and hear, and what does the appearance of the cherub suggest? (b) To whom is the command of the first cherub addressed, and why do you so answer?

the voice of the first cherub. Its lionlike appearance would suggest to John that Jehovah's organization will act with courage in executing His righteous judgments. And to whom is that command addressed? It could not be to John, for John has already been invited to share in these prophetic scenes. (Revelation 4:1) That "voice as of thunder" is calling forth other participants in the first of a series of four rousing episodes.

The White Horse and Its Illustrious Rider

3 John, and with him the zealous John class and companions of today, is privileged to see a fast-moving drama! John says: *"And I saw, and, look! a white horse; and the one seated upon it had a bow; and a crown was given him, and he went forth conquering and to complete his conquest."* (*Revelation 6:2*) Yes, in answer to that thunderous "Come!" a white horse charges forth. In the Bible, the horse often symbolizes warfare. (Psalm 20:7; Proverbs 21:31; Isaiah 31:1) This horse, likely a beautiful stallion, gleams with a whiteness that indicates unblemished holiness. (Compare Revelation 1:14; 4:4; 7:9; 20:11.) How appropriate this is, for it portrays warfare that is clean and righteous in Jehovah's holy eyes!—See also Revelation 19:11, 14.

4 Who is the Rider of this horse? He has a bow, an offensive weapon of war, but he is also given a crown. The only righteous ones seen wearing crowns during the Lord's day are Jesus and the class represented by the 24 elders. (Daniel 7:13, 14, 27; Luke 1:31-33; Revelation 4:4, 10; 14:14)* It is unlikely that a member of the group of 24 elders would

* Note, however, that the "woman" of Revelation 12:1 has a figurative "crown of twelve stars."

3. (a) What does John now describe? (b) In harmony with Bible symbolism, what must the white horse picture?
4. Who is the Rider of the white horse? Explain.

be pictured as receiving a crown on his own merit. Hence, this lone horseman must be *Jesus Christ* and no other. John sees him in heaven at the historic moment in 1914 when Jehovah declares, "I, even I, have installed my king," and tells him that this is for the purpose "that I may give nations as your inheritance." (Psalm 2:6-8)* Thus, in opening the first seal Jesus reveals how he himself, as the newly crowned King, sallies forth to war at God's appointed time.

5 This scene harmonizes beautifully with Psalm 45:4-7, addressed to the King enthroned by Jehovah: "And in your splendor go on to success; ride in the cause of truth and humility and righteousness, and your right hand will instruct you in fear-inspiring things. Your arrows are sharp—under you peoples keep falling—in the heart of the enemies of the king. God is your throne to time indefinite, even forever; the scepter of your kingship is a scepter of uprightness. You have loved righteousness and you hate wickedness. That is why God, your God, has anointed you with the oil of exultation more than your partners." Being familiar with that prophetic description, John would appreciate that it applies to Jesus' activity as King. —Compare Hebrews 1:1, 2, 8, 9.

Going Forth Conquering

6 Why, though, must the newly crowned King ride forth to war? It is because his kingship is established in the face of bitter opposition from Jehovah's chief adversary, Satan the Devil, and those on earth who —knowingly or unknowingly—serve Satan's ends. The birth of the Kingdom itself calls for a major war in heaven. Fighting under

* For detailed proof that Jesus came into his Kingdom in 1914, see chapter 14 and the appendix of the book *"Let Your Kingdom Come,"* published by the Watchtower Bible and Tract Society of New York, Inc.

5. How does the psalmist describe the Rider in a way similar to Revelation 6:2?
6. (a) Why must the Rider go forth conquering? (b) Through which years does the ride of conquest continue?

the name Michael (meaning "Who Is Like God?"), Jesus overcomes Satan and his demons and hurls them down to the earth. (Revelation 12:7-12) Jesus' ride of conquest continues through the opening decades of the Lord's day while the nations and peoples of earth are being judged and sheeplike humans are being gathered to the King's side for salvation. Though the whole world still lies "in the power of the wicked one," Jesus lovingly continues to shepherd his anointed brothers and their companions, helping each to achieve the conquest of faith.—1 John 5:19; Matthew 25:31-33.

⁷ What other conquests has Jesus made during the past 70-and-more years of the Lord's day? Around the globe, individually and as a congregation, Jehovah's people have experienced many hardships, pressures, and persecutions, similar to those described by the apostle Paul in giving proof of his ministry. (2 Corinthians 11:23-28) Jehovah's Witnesses have needed "power beyond what is normal," especially in theaters of war and violence, in order to endure. (2 Corinthians 4:7) But even in the most trying situations, faithful Witnesses have been able to say as did Paul: "The Lord stood near me and infused power into me, that through me the preaching might be fully accomplished." (2 Timothy 4:17) Yes, Jesus conquered on their behalf. And he will continue to go forth conquering in our behalf, as long as we are resolved to complete *our* conquest of faith. —1 John 5:4.

⁸ The global congregation of Jehovah's Witnesses has shared in many conquests under the guidance of its conquering King. Outstandingly, he protected these Bible Students from annihilation in 1918, when they

themselves were 'conquered' temporarily by Satan's political organization. In 1919, however, he broke prison bars to rescue them, and he then enlivened them to proclaim the good news "to the most distant part of the earth."—Revelation 13:7; Acts 1:8.

⁹ Before and during World War II, the dictatorial Axis powers tried to wipe out Jehovah's Witnesses in many lands where religious leaders, particularly those of the Roman Catholic hierarchy, gave open or tacit support to oppressive dictators. But the 71,-509 Witnesses who were preaching when the war started in 1939 became 141,606 by its end in 1945, even though upwards of 10,000 had spent long years in prisons and concentration camps, and other thousands

---

7. What conquests has Jesus made on earth in the first decades of the Lord's day, and what should be our resolve?

8, 9. (a) In what conquests has the global congregation of Jehovah's Witnesses shared? (b) Where has growth of Jehovah's Witnesses been truly outstanding?

had been killed. The number of active Witnesses earth wide has expanded to well over three million today. Growth has been outstanding in Catholic lands and in countries where persecutions were most bitter—such as Germany, Italy, and Japan, in each of which the Witnesses are now reporting well over 100,000 active field ministers.—Isaiah 54:17; Jeremiah 1:17-19.

[10] Our conquering King has also blessed

10. With what victories has the conquering King blessed his people "in the defending and legally establishing of the good news"?

The King Rides Victorious

During the 1930's and 1940's, determined enemies tried to make it appear that the ministry of Jehovah's Witnesses was illegal, criminal, or even subversive. (Psalm 94:20) In the year 1936 alone, there were 1,149 arrests recorded in the United States. The Witnesses fought many legal cases all the way to the United States Supreme Court, and following are some of their outstanding victories.

On May 3, 1943, the Supreme Court in the case of *Murdock v. Pennsylvania* decided that the Witnesses did not need a license in order to place literature for money. On that same day, the decision in the case of *Martin v. City of Struthers* held that it was not unlawful to ring doorbells while participating in the door-to-door distribution of handbills and other advertising matter.

On June 14, 1943, the Supreme Court decided in the *Taylor v. Mississippi* case that the Witnesses did not encourage disloyalty to the government by their preaching. On that same day, in *West Virginia State Board of Education v. Barnette,* the Court held that a school board did not have the right to expel from school children of Jehovah's Witnesses who refused to salute the flag. The very next day, the full High Court of Australia removed that country's ban on Jehovah's Witnesses, this being declared "arbitrary, capricious and oppressive."

---

his zealous people by leading them to many victories "in the defending and legally establishing of the good news" in courts of law and before rulers. (Philippians 1:7; Matthew 10:18; 24:9) This has been on an international scale—in Australia, Argentina, Canada, Greece, India, Swaziland, Switzerland, Turkey, and other lands. Among 23 legal victories gained by Jehovah's Witnesses in the United States Supreme Court have been those guaranteeing the right to declare the good news "publicly and from house to house" and to desist from idolatrous patriotic ceremonies. (Acts 5:42; 20:20; 1 Corinthians 10:14) Thus, the way has been kept open for an expanding global witness.

[11] How does Jesus "complete his conquest"?* This he does, as we shall see, by disposing of false religion and then hurling every remaining segment of Satan's visible organization into a symbolic "fiery lake" of destruction, in vindication of Jehovah's sovereignty. Confidently, we now look forward to that day at Armageddon when our "King of kings" will gain the final victory over Satan's oppressive political organization! (Revelation 16:16; 17:14; 19:2, 14-21; Ezekiel 25:17) In the meantime, the invincible Conqueror on the white horse continues to ride forth as Jehovah keeps adding honesthearted ones to His righteous nation on earth. (Isaiah 26:2; 60:22) Are you sharing with the anointed John class in that joyful Kingdom expansion? In that event, what the apostle John sees when the next three seals are opened will no doubt stir you to have an even greater share in Jehovah's work for this day.

---

* While many translations render this phrase "to conquer" (*Revised Standard, The New English Bible, King James Version*) or "bent on conquest" (*Phillips, New International Version*), the use of the aorist subjunctive here in the original Greek gives a sense of completion or finality. Hence, Robertson's *Word Pictures in the New Testament* comments: "The aorist tense here points to ultimate victory."

11. (a) How does the Rider "complete his conquest"? (b) What effect should the opening of the second, third, and fourth seals have upon us?

Behold, the Fiery-Colored Horse!

[12] Toward the end of Jesus' ministry on earth, his disciples asked him privately: "What will be the sign of your presence and of the conclusion of the system of things?" In reply, he foretold calamities that would be "a beginning of pangs of distress." Said Jesus: "Nation will rise against nation, and kingdom against kingdom; and there will be great earthquakes, and in one place after another pestilences and food shortages; and there will be fearful sights and from heaven great signs." (Matthew 24:3, 7, 8; Luke 21:10, 11) The things John sees when the remaining seals of the scroll are opened provide a remarkable parallel to that prophecy. Watch now as the glorified Jesus opens the second seal!

[13] *"And when he opened the second seal, I heard the second living creature say: 'Come!'"* (*Revelation 6:3*) It is the second cherub, with the appearance of a bull, that issues the command. Power is the quality here symbolized, but power used righteously. In contrast, though, John is now to see a hideous, death-dealing display of power.

[14] How, then, is this second summons to "Come!" answered? In this way: *"And another came forth, a fiery-colored horse; and to the one seated upon it there was granted to take peace away from the earth so that they should slaughter one another; and a great sword was given him."* (*Revelation 6:4*) A grim vision indeed! And there is no doubt as to what it pictures: *war!* Not the righteous, victorious warfare of Jehovah's conquering King but cruel, man-made, international warfare with needless bloodshed and pain. How appropriate that this rider is mounted on a fire-red horse!

[15] Certainly, John would want no part with this horseman and his headlong ride, for it had been prophesied concerning God's people: "Neither will they learn war anymore." (Isaiah 2:4) Though still "in the world," John and, by extension, the John class and the great crowd today are "no part" of this bloodstained system. Our weapons are spiritual and "powerful by God" for actively proclaiming the truth, apart from carnal warfare. —John 17:11, 14; 2 Corinthians 10:3, 4.

[16] There had been many wars before 1914, the year when the Rider of the white horse

---

12. What did Jesus say would mark his invisible presence as King?

13. What contrast is about to become evident to John?

14. What horse and rider does John next see, and what does this vision picture?

15. Why should we want no part of the ride of the second horseman?

16. When and how was the rider of the red horse given "a great sword"?

received his crown. But now the rider of the red horse is given "a great sword." What does this imply? With the eruption of World War I, human warfare becomes more sanguinary, more destructive than ever before. During the 1914-18 bloodbath, tanks, poison gas, airplanes, submarines, huge cannons, and automatic weapons were used either for the first time or on an unprecedented scale. In some 28 nations, whole populations, not just professional soldiers, were pressed into the war effort. Casualties were horrendous. More than nine million soldiers were slaughtered, and civilian casualties were astronomical.

"Granted to Take Peace Away From the Earth"

Where is technology leading? *The Globe and Mail,* Toronto, Canada, January 22, 1987, reported the following from a speech by Ivan L. Head, president of the International Development Research Centre:

"It is reliably estimated that one out of every four scientists and technologists in the world engaged in research and development is working on weapons. . . . At 1986 rates, the expenditure is more than $1.5-million a minute. . . . Are we all more secure as a result of this kind of technological emphasis? The nuclear arsenals possessed by the superpowers contain the explosive force of all the munitions expended by all the combatants in all of the Second World War —times 6,000. Six thousand Second World Wars. Since 1945, there have been less than seven weeks when the world has been free of military activity. There have been more than 150 wars of an international or a civil nature, which are estimated to have claimed 19.3 million lives, most of them as the result of the efficient new technologies that have emerged in this era of the United Nations."

Even with the end of the war, there was no return to real peace on earth. More than 50 years after that war, German statesman Konrad Adenauer commented: "Security and quiet have disappeared from the lives of men since 1914." It was, indeed, granted to the rider of the fiery-colored horse to take peace away from the earth!

[17] Then, with his thirst for blood whetted, the rider of the red horse plunged into World War II. Instruments of slaughter became ever more fiendish, and casualties skyrocketed to four times those of World War I. In 1945 two atom bombs burst over Japan, each one annihilating—in a flash—tens of thousands of victims. During the second world war, the rider of the red horse reaped a huge harvest of some 55 million lives, and even then he was not satisfied. It is reliably reported that at least 19 million souls have fallen under the "great sword" since World War II.

[18] Could we call this a triumph for military technology? It is, rather, a testimony that the merciless red horse is at the gallop. And where will that gallop end? Some scientists forecast mathematically that an accidental nuclear war is virtually certain to take place within the next 25 years—let alone a planned nuclear conflagration! But happily the conquering Rider of the white horse has other thoughts about this.

[19] As long as society is based on nationalistic pride and hatred, mankind must continue to sit on a keg of nuclear peril. Even if the nations, out of desperation, should scrap all nuclear firepower, they would retain the know-how. In short order, they could reproduce their murderous nuclear devices; hence, any war with conventional weapons could

---

17. How has the use of the "great sword" continued, following World War I?
18, 19. (a) Rather than its being a triumph for military technology, to what fact is the slaughter since World War II a testimony? (b) What peril confronts mankind, but what will the Rider of the white horse do to offset it?

REVELATION CLIMAX

soon mushroom into a holocaust. The pride and hatred that envelop the nations today must lead to humanity's suicide, unless—ah, yes, unless the Rider of the white horse should head off the mad gallop of the fiery-colored mount. Let us be confident that Christ the King will ride, both to complete his conquest over the world controlled by Satan and to establish a new earthly society based on love—love of God and neighbor—a force for peace far, far superior to the shaky nuclear deterrents of our maddened times.—Psalm 37:9-11; Mark 12:29-31; Revelation 21:1-5.

A Black Horse Plunges Forth

[20] Jesus now opens the third seal! John, what do you observe? ***And when he opened the third seal, I heard the third living creature say: 'Come!' '' (Revelation 6:5a)*** Happily, this third cherub "has a face like a man's," depicting the quality of love. Principled love will abound in God's new world, even as that fine quality permeates all of Jehovah's organization today. (Revelation 4:7; 1 John 4:16) We can be sure that the Rider of the white horse, who "must rule as king until God has put all enemies under his feet," will lovingly remove the calamitous situation that is next brought to John's scrutiny.—1 Corinthians 15:25.

[21] What does John see, then, as the third summons to "Come!" is answered? ***And I saw, and, look! a black horse; and the one seated upon it had a pair of scales in his hand."*** (***Revelation 6:5b***) Stark famine! That is the dire message of this prophetic scene. It points forward to situations early in the Lord's day when food must be rationed out by scales. Since 1914 famine has been a continuing worldwide problem. Modern warfare brings famine in its wake, for re-

sources normally used in feeding the hungry are often diverted to supplying war weapons. Farm workers are conscripted, and battle-scarred fields and scorched-earth policies curtail food production. How true this was during the first world war, when millions suffered from hunger and died. Moreover, the rider of the black horse of hunger did not relent with the end of the war. During the 1930's, five million perished in just one famine in the Ukraine. The second world war brought in its wake more food shortages and famines. As the black horse continued its gallop, The World Food Council reported in mid-1987 that 512 million humans were starving and that 40,000 children die of hunger-related causes every day.

[22] John has more to tell us: ***"And I heard a***

---

20. What assurance do we have that the Rider of the white horse will cope with any calamitous situation?
21. (a) What is pictured by the black horse and its rider? (b) What proves that the black horse is still on the rampage?

22. (a) What does a voice say, expressing what need? (b) What is implied by the cost of a quart of wheat and of three quarts of barley?

voice as if in the midst of the four living creatures say: '*A quart of wheat for a denarius, and three quarts of barley for a denarius; and do not harm the olive oil and the wine.*'" (*Revelation 6:6*) All four cherubs are united in expressing a need to watch food supplies carefully—just as the people had to "eat bread by weight and in anxious care" prior to Jerusalem's destruction in 607 B.C.E. (Ezekiel 4:16) In John's time, a quart of wheat was reckoned to be the daily ration for a soldier. How much would such a ration cost? One denarius—a whole day's wage! (Matthew 20:2)* What if a man had a family? Well, he could buy three quarts of unpolished barley instead. Even that would feed only a small family. And barley was not viewed as a quality food such as wheat.

23 What is implied by the statement, "Do not harm the olive oil and the wine"? Some have viewed it as meaning that while many would be short of food and even starving, the luxuries of the rich would not be harmed. But in the Middle East, oil and wine are not really luxuries. In Bible times, bread, oil, and wine were viewed as staples. (Compare Genesis 14:18; Psalm 104:14, 15.) Water was not always good, so wine was widely used for drinking and sometimes for medicinal purposes. (1 Timothy 5:23) With regard to oil, in Elijah's day the widow of Zarephath, poor as she was, still had some oil left with which to cook her remaining flour. (1 Kings 17:12) Therefore, the command "do not harm the olive oil and the wine" appears to be advice not to use up these basic commodities too quickly but to be sparing in their use. Otherwise, they will be 'harmed,' that is, they will run out before the famine ends.

---

* See *New World Translation Reference Bible,* footnote.

---

23. What is implied by the statement, "Do not harm the olive oil and the wine"?

24 How happy we can be that the Rider of the white horse will soon rein in that galloping black horse! For it is written concerning His loving provision for the new world: "In his days the righteous one will sprout, and the abundance of peace until the moon is no more. . . . There will come to be plenty of grain on the earth; on the top of the mountains there will be an overflow."—Psalm 72: 7, 16; see also Isaiah 25:6-8.

The Pale Horse and Its Rider

25 The story is not yet completely told. Jesus opens the fourth seal, and John tells us the result: *"And when he opened the fourth seal, I heard the voice of the fourth living creature say: 'Come!'"* (*Revelation 6:7*) This is the voice of the cherub that resembles a flying eagle. Farsighted wisdom is indicated, and truly John, the John class, and all other earthly servants of God have needed to observe and act with insight in view of what is here depicted. So doing, we may find a measure of protection from the scourges that plague the worldly-wise of today's proud, immoral generation.—1 Corinthians 1:20, 21.

26 What new horrors are unleashed, then, as the fourth horseman responds to the call? John tells us: *"And I saw, and, look! a pale horse; and the one seated upon it had the name Death. And Hades was closely following him."* (*Revelation 6:8a*) The rider of the last horse has a name: *Death.* He is the only one of the four horsemen of Apocalypse to reveal his identity so directly. Fittingly, Death rides a horse that is pale, since the word pale (Greek, *khlo·ros'*) is used in Greek literature to describe faces that are blanched, as if by disease. Also fittingly, Death is closely followed in some unexplained manner by Ha-

---

24. Why will the black horse not continue its gallop for much longer?
25. When Jesus opens the fourth seal, whose voice does John hear, and what does this indicate?
26. (a) Who is the fourth horseman, and why is the color of his horse fitting? (b) Who is following the fourth horseman, and what happens to his victims?

REVELATION CLIMAX

des (gravedom), since Hades receives to itself the greater number of those who fall victim to the ravages of the fourth horseman. Happily, for these there will be a resurrection, when 'death and Hades give up those dead in them.' (Revelation 20:13) But how does Death claim those victims?

27 The vision enumerates some of the ways: *"And authority was given them over the fourth part of the earth, to kill with a long sword and with food shortage and with deadly plague and by the wild beasts of the earth."* (*Revelation 6:8b*) Not necessarily a literal fourth of earth's population but a large portion of the earth, whether densely or sparsely inhabited, would be affected by this ride. This horseman reaps the victims of the big sword of the second horseman and the famines and food shortages of the third. He reaps his own harvest, too, from deadly plague and also a harvest from earthquakes, as described at Luke 21:10, 11.

28 Of current importance here is "deadly plague." Following in the wake of the ravages of World War I, the Spanish flu reaped over 20 million human lives in just a few months of 1918-19. The only territory on earth to escape this scourge was the small island of St. Helena. In places where the population was decimated, funeral pyres were lit to burn the piles of bodies. And today there is the frightful incidence of heart disease and cancer, much of which is caused by tobacco pollution. In what has been described as "the ugly decade" of the 1980's, a way of life that is lawless by Bible standards has added the scourge of AIDS to the "deadly plague." At the time of this writing, all who contract this disease die, and it is estimated that in the United States alone 270,000 will

be sick with AIDS by 1991; millions appear to be doomed in Africa. How thankful Jehovah's people are that the wise counsel of his Word keeps them away from fornication and misuse of blood, through which so many diseases are transmitted today!—Acts 15:28, 29; compare 1 Corinthians 6:9-11.

29 John's vision mentions wild beasts as a fourth cause of untimely death. Indeed, the four things featured by the opening of the fourth seal—warfare, famine, disease, and wild beasts—were in ancient times viewed as predominant causes of untimely death. So they would foreshadow all causes of

27. (a) How does the rider Death claim his victims? (b) What is meant by "the fourth part of the earth" over which Death has authority?

28. (a) How has there been a fulfillment of prophecy concerning "deadly plague"? (b) How have Jehovah's people been protected from many diseases today?

29, 30. (a) What application would the "four injurious acts" of Ezekiel 14:21 have today? (b) What may we understand by "the wild beasts" of Revelation 6:8? (c) What appears to be the main point of the prophetic scene?

FOUR HORSEMEN AT THE GALLOP!

97

untimely death today. It is just as Jehovah warned Israel: "So, too, it will be when there will be my four injurious acts of judgment —sword and famine and injurious wild beast and pestilence—that I shall actually send upon Jerusalem in order to cut off from it earthling man and domestic animal."—Ezekiel 14:21.

30 Death by wild beasts has seldom made headlines in modern times, though in tropical countries wild animals have steadily claimed victims throughout the 20th century. In the future, they may claim even more if lands become desolated because of warfare or people become too emaciated by famine to fight off hungry animals. Additionally, there are many humans today who, like unreasoning animals, display beastly dispositions quite contrary to those described at Isaiah 11:6-9. These people are largely responsible for the global expansion of sex-related crimes, murder, terrorism, and bombings in the modern world. (Compare Ezekiel 21:31; Romans 1: 28-31; 2 Peter 2:12.) The fourth horseman reaps *their* victims, too. Indeed, the main point of this prophetic scene appears to be that the rider of the pale horse harvests untimely death of mankind in many ways.

31 The information revealed by the opening of the first four seals reassures us because it teaches us not to despair at the warfare,

31. Despite the ravages caused by the riders of the red, black, and pale horses, why may we be encouraged?

The Framework of the Book of Revelation

Having progressed thus far in our discussion of the book of Revelation, we begin to see more clearly the book's framework. After its rousing introduction (Revelation 1:1-9), Revelation can be viewed as divided into 16 visions as follows:

1 ST VISION (1:10–3:22): John sees by inspiration the glorified Jesus, who sends warm messages of counsel to the seven congregations.

2 ND VISION (4:1–5:14): A magnificent view of the heavenly throne of Jehovah God. This One hands a scroll to the Lamb.

3 RD VISION (6:1-17): Breaking open the first six seals of the scroll, the Lamb progressively reveals a composite vision of events due to happen in the Lord's day. The four horsemen of Apocalypse ride forth, God's martyred slaves receive white robes, and the great day of wrath is described.

4 TH VISION (7:1-17): Angels hold back the winds of destruction until the 144,000 of spiritual Israel are sealed. A great crowd out of all nations attribute salvation to God and Christ and are gathered for survival through the great tribulation.

5 TH VISION (8:1–9:21): At the opening of the seventh seal, there are seven trumpet blasts, the first six of which comprise the fifth vision. These six trumpet blasts herald expressions of Jehovah's judgment on mankind. The fifth and sixth trumpets also introduce the first and second woes.

6 TH VISION (10:1–11:19): A strong angel gives John a little scroll, the temple is measured, and we learn the experiences of the two witnesses. It climaxes with the blowing of the seventh trumpet, which heralds the third woe for God's enemies—the incoming Kingdom of Jehovah and of his Christ.

7 TH VISION (12:1-17): This describes the birth of the Kingdom, resulting in Michael's hurling the Serpent, Satan, down to the earth.

REVELATION CLIMAX

hunger, disease, and other causes of untimely death that are so rampant today; neither should we lose hope because human leaders have failed to solve current problems. If world conditions make it evident that the riders of the red, black, and pale horses are abroad, do not forget that the Rider of the white horse was first to begin his ride. Jesus has become King, and he has already conquered to the extent of casting Satan out of the heavens. His further conquests have included his gathering out the remaining ones of the sons of spiritual Israel and the international great crowd, numbering into the millions, for survival through the great tribulation. (Revelation 7:4, 9, 14) His ride must continue until he completes his conquest.

32 The opening of each of the first four seals has been followed by the summons: "Come!" Each time, a horse and its rider came charging forth. Starting with the fifth seal, we no longer hear such a summons. But those horsemen are still riding, and they will continue at the gallop throughout the conclusion of the system of things. (Compare Matthew 28:20.) What other momentous events does Jesus reveal as he opens the remaining three seals? Some of the happenings are invisible to human eyes. Others, though visible, are yet future. Nevertheless, their fulfillment is certain. Let us see what they are.

32. What characterizes the opening of each of the first four seals?

8TH VISION (13:1-18): The powerful wild beast comes out of the sea, and the beast with two horns like a lamb urges mankind to worship it.

9TH VISION (14:1-20): A splendid foreview of the 144,000 on Mount Zion. Angelic messages are heard around the earth, the vine of the earth is reaped, and the winepress of God's anger is trodden.

10TH VISION (15:1–16:21): Another glimpse of the heavenly court, followed by the pouring out of the seven bowls of Jehovah's anger into the earth. This section, too, ends with a prophetic description of the end of Satan's system.

11TH VISION (17:1-18): The great harlot, Babylon the Great, rides a scarlet-colored wild beast, which goes briefly into the abyss but comes forth again and devastates her.

12TH VISION (18:1–19:10): The fall and final destruction of Babylon the Great are announced. After her execution, some mourn, others praise Jehovah; the marriage of the Lamb is announced.

13TH VISION (19:11-21): Jesus leads the armies of heaven to execute God's wrathful judgment on Satan's system, its armies, and its supporters; carrion birds feast on their corpses.

14TH VISION (20:1-10): The abyssing of Satan the Devil, the Thousand Year Reign of Christ and his fellow kings, mankind's final test, and the destruction of Satan and his demons.

15TH VISION (20:11–21:8): The general resurrection and the great Judgment Day; a new heaven and a new earth appear, with eternal blessings for righteous mankind.

16TH VISION (21:9–22:5): Revelation is climaxed with a glorious vision of New Jerusalem, the Lamb's wife. God's provision of healing and life for mankind flows from that city.

> **Revelation** concludes with warm words of greeting and counsel from Jehovah, Jesus, the angel, and John himself. The invitation to everyone is "Come!"—Revelation 22:6-21.

SEPT· 4,89 ## 'Slaughtered Souls' Rewarded

GOD'S Kingdom rules! The Rider of the white horse is about to complete his conquest! The red horse, the black horse, and the pale horse are galloping through the earth! Indisputably, Jesus' own prophecies concerning his royal presence are being fulfilled. (Matthew, chapters 24, 25; Mark, chapter 13; Luke, chapter 21) Yes, we are living in the last days of this system of things. (2 Timothy 3:1-5) That being so, let us pay close attention as the Lamb, Jesus Christ, breaks open the fifth seal of that scroll. In what further revelation are we now to share?

2 John describes a moving scene: *"And when he opened the fifth seal, I saw underneath the altar the souls of those slaughtered because of the word of God and because of the witness work that they used to have." (Revelation 6:9)* What is that? A sacrificial altar up in heaven? Yes! It is the first time that John mentions an altar. Already, though, he has described Jehovah on His throne, the surrounding cherubs, the glassy sea, the lamps, and the 24 elders carrying incense—all of these resembling features of the earthly tabernacle, Jehovah's sanctuary in Israel. (Exodus 25: 17, 18; 40:24-27, 30-32; 1 Chronicles 23:4) Should it, then, surprise us to find a symbolic altar of sacrifice also in heaven?—Exodus 40:29.

3 Underneath this altar are "the souls of those slaughtered because of the word of God and because of the witness work that they used to have." What does this mean? These could not be disembodied souls—like those believed in by the pagan Greeks. (Genesis 2:7; Ezekiel 18:4) Rather, John knows that the soul, or life, is symbolized by the blood, and when the priests at the ancient Jewish tabernacle slaughtered a sacrificial animal, they sprinkled the blood "round about upon the altar" or poured it "at the base of the altar of burnt offering." (Leviticus 3:2, 8, 13; 4:7; 17:6, 11, 12) Hence, the animal's soul was closely identified with the altar of sacrifice. But why would the souls, or blood, of these particular servants of God be seen underneath a symbolic altar in heaven? Because their deaths are viewed as sacrificial.

4 Indeed, all those who are begotten as spirit sons of God die a sacrificial death. Because of the role they are to play in Jehovah's heavenly Kingdom, it is God's will that they renounce and sacrifice any hope of life everlasting on earth. In this respect, they submit to a sacrificial death in behalf of Jehovah's sovereignty. (Philippians 3:8-11; compare 2:17.) This is true in a very real sense of those whom John saw under the altar. They are anointed ones who in their day were martyred for their zealous ministry in upholding Jehovah's Word and sovereignty. Their "souls [were] slaughtered because of the word of God and because of the witness work [*mar·ty·ri'an*] that they used to have."

---

1. In what period of time are we living, and what evidence is there for this?
2. (a) What did John see when the fifth seal was opened? (b) Why should we not be surprised to read of a symbolic altar of sacrifice in heaven?
3. (a) At the ancient Jewish tabernacle, how were souls poured "at the base of the altar"? (b) Why did John see the souls of slaughtered witnesses underneath a symbolic altar in heaven?

---

4. In what way is the death of spirit-begotten Christians sacrificial?

5 The scenario continues to unfold: *"And they cried with a loud voice, saying: 'Until when, Sovereign Lord holy and true, are you refraining from judging and avenging our blood upon those who dwell on the earth?'"* (*Revelation 6:10*) How can their souls, or blood, cry out for vengeance, since the Bible shows that the dead are unconscious? (Ecclesiastes 9:5) Well, did not righteous Abel's blood cry out after Cain murdered him? Jehovah then said to Cain: "What have you done? Listen! Your brother's blood is crying out to me from the ground." (Genesis 4:10, 11; Hebrews 12:24) It was not that Abel's blood was literally uttering words. Rather, Abel had died as an innocent victim, and justice called out for his murderer to be punished. Similarly, those Christian martyrs are innocent, and in justice they must be avenged. (Luke 18:7, 8) The cry for vengeance is loud because many thousands have thus died. —Compare Jeremiah 15:15, 16.

6 The situation may also be likened to that in apostate Judah when King Manasseh came to the throne in 716 B.C.E. He shed much innocent blood, probably 'sawing asunder' the prophet Isaiah. (Hebrews 11:37; 2 Kings 21:16) Although Manasseh later repented and reformed, that bloodguilt remained. In 607 B.C.E., when the Babylonians desolated the kingdom of Judah, "it was only by the order of Jehovah that it took place against Judah, to remove it from his sight for the sins of Manasseh, according to all that he had done; and also for the innocent blood that he had shed, so that he filled Jerusalem with innocent blood, and Jehovah did not consent to grant forgiveness."—2 Kings 24:3, 4.

7 As in Bible times, so today many of the individuals who killed God's witnesses may be long dead. But the organization that caused their martyrdom is still very much alive and bloodguilty. It is Satan's earthly organization, his earthly seed. Prominent therein is Babylon the Great, the world empire of false religion.* She is described as being "drunk with the blood of the holy ones and with the blood of the witnesses of Jesus." Yes, "in her was found the blood of prophets and of holy ones and of all those who have been slaughtered on the earth." (Revelation 17:5, 6; 18:24; Ephesians 4:11; 1 Corinthians 12:28) What a load of bloodguiltiness! As long as Babylon the Great exists, the blood of her victims will cry out for justice.—Revelation 19:1, 2.

8 John himself witnessed martyrdom in the first century as the cruel Serpent and his earthly seed waged war on the growing congregation of anointed Christians. John had seen our Lord impaled and had survived through the slayings of Stephen, of his own brother James, and of Peter, Paul, and other close associates. (John 19:26, 27; 21:15, 18, 19; Acts 7:59, 60; 8:2; 12:2; 2 Timothy 1:1; 4:6, 7) In 64 C.E., Roman emperor Nero had made a scapegoat of the Christians, accusing them of burning the city, to counteract a rumor that he was the guilty one. The historian Tacitus reports: "They [Christians] died by methods of mockery; some were covered with the skins of wild beasts and then torn by dogs, some were [impaled],# some were burned as torches to light at night." A further wave of persecution under Emperor Domitian (81-96 C.E.) had resulted in John's being exiled to the island of Patmos. As Jesus said: "If they have persecuted me, they will persecute you also."—John 15:20; Matthew 10:22.

---

* The identity of Babylon the Great is discussed in detail in Chapter 33.
# Compare *New World Translation Reference Bible*, page 1577, appendix 5C, "Torture Stake."

---

5. How is it that the souls of faithful ones, although dead, are crying out for vengeance?
6. What shedding of innocent blood was avenged in 607 B.C.E.?
7. Who is primarily guilty of shedding "the blood of the holy ones"?

8. (a) What instances of martyrdom had taken place during John's lifetime? (b) What persecutions were instigated by Roman emperors?

9 By the fourth century C.E., that old Serpent, Satan the Devil, had brought forth his masterpiece of deception, the apostate religion of Christendom—a Babylonish system hidden under a "Christian" veneer. It is the principal part of the seed of the Serpent and has developed into a multitude of conflicting sects. Like unfaithful Judah of old, Christendom carries a heavy bloodguilt, having been deeply involved on both sides in World Wars I and II. Some political rulers in Christendom even used these wars as a pretext for slaughtering anointed servants of God. Reporting on Hitler's persecution of Jehovah's Witnesses, a review of Friedrich Zipfel's book *Kirchenkampf in Deutschland* (Fight of the Churches in Germany) stated: "One third of them [the Witnesses] were killed, either by execution, other violent acts, hunger, sickness or slave labor. The severity of this subjection was without precedent and was the result of uncompromising faith that could not be harmonized with National Socialistic

---

9. (a) What masterpiece of deception did Satan bring forth by the fourth century C.E., and of what is it the main part? (b) How did some rulers in Christendom treat Jehovah's Witnesses during World Wars I and II?

'Slaughtered souls'

McClintock and Strong's *Cyclopedia* quotes John Jortin, an 18th-century English Protestant, born of French Huguenot parents, as saying: "Where persecution begins, Christianity ends . . . It was after Christianity had been established as the religion of the [Roman] empire, and after wealth and honor had been conferred on its ministers, that the monstrous evil of persecution acquired gigantic strength, and threw its blasting influence over the religion of the Gospel."

---

ideology." Truly, it can be said of Christendom, including its priesthood: "In your skirts there have been found the blood marks of the souls of the innocent poor ones."—Jeremiah 2:34.*

10 Since 1935 faithful young men of the great crowd have borne the brunt of persecution in many lands. (Revelation 7:9) Even as World War II ended in Europe, in just one town 14 young witnesses of Jehovah were executed by hanging. Their crime? Refusal to "learn war anymore." (Isaiah 2:4) More recently, young men in the Orient and in Africa have been beaten to death or executed by firing squad over the same issue. These youthful martyrs, worthy supporters of Jesus' anointed brothers, will surely have a resurrection into the promised new earth. —2 Peter 3:13; compare Psalm 110:3; Matthew 25:34-40; Luke 20:37, 38.

A White Robe

11 After documenting the faith of integrity keepers of ancient times, the apostle Paul said: "And yet all these, although they had witness borne to them through their faith, did not get the fulfillment of the promise, as God foresaw something better for us, in order that they might not be made perfect apart from us." (Hebrews 11:39, 40) What is that "something better" that Paul and other anointed Christians anticipate? John sees it here in vision: *"And a white robe was given to each of them; and they were told to rest a little while longer, until the number was filled also of their fellow slaves and their brothers who were about to be killed as they also had been."* (*Revelation 6:11*) Their receiving "a white robe" has to do with their resurrection to be immortal spirit creatures. No longer do they

---

* Proof of religion's bloodguilt is given in more detail in chapter 36.

---

10. What persecutions have young men of the great crowd suffered in many lands?
11. In what sense do martyred anointed Christians receive "a white robe"?

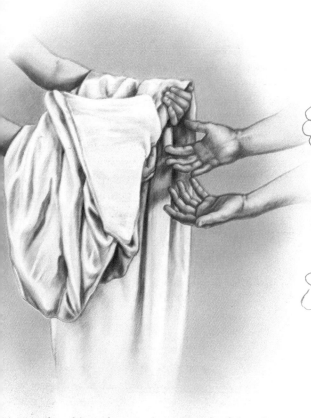

enthronement in 1914 and his riding forth to start his kingly conquest by cleansing the heavens of Satan and his demons. Yet, those resurrected anointed ones are told that they must "rest a little while longer, until the number . . . also of their fellow slaves" is filled. Those of the John class still on earth must prove their integrity under trial and persecution, and some of these may yet be killed. Finally, though, all the righteous blood shed by Babylon the Great and her political paramours will be avenged. In the meantime, resurrected ones are doubtless busy with heavenly duties. They rest, not by relaxing in blissful inactivity, but in that they patiently await the day of Jehovah's vengeance. (Isaiah 34:8; Romans 12:19) Their rest will end when they witness the destruction of false religion and, as "called and chosen and faithful" ones, they accompany the Lord Jesus Christ in executing judgment on all other parts of Satan's wicked seed here on earth.—Revelation 2:26, 27; 17:14; Romans 16:20.

'Those Who Are Dead Rise First' *Start 9/16/91*

13 The insight granted by the opening of the fifth seal agrees completely with other scriptures that have to do with the heavenly resurrection. For example, the apostle Paul wrote: "For this is what we tell you by Jehovah's word, that we the living who survive to the presence of the Lord shall in no way precede those who have fallen asleep in death; because the Lord himself will descend from heaven with a commanding call, with an archangel's voice and with God's trumpet, and those who are dead in union with Christ will rise first. Afterward we the living who are surviving will, together with them, be caught away in clouds to meet the Lord in the air; and thus we shall always be with the Lord."—1 Thessalonians 4:15-17.

13, 14. (a) According to the apostle Paul, when does the heavenly resurrection begin, and who are resurrected? (b) When are the anointed who survive into the Lord's day resurrected to heaven?

"And a white robe was given to each of them"

lie as slaughtered souls underneath the altar, but they are raised to be part of the group of 24 elders that worship before the heavenly throne of God. There, they themselves have been given thrones, showing that they have entered into royal privileges. And they are "dressed in white outer garments," signifying that they have been adjudged righteous, worthy of an honored place before Jehovah in that heavenly court. This is also in fulfillment of Jesus' promise to faithful anointed Christians in the congregation in Sardis: "He that conquers will thus be arrayed in white outer garments."—Revelation 3:5; 4:4; 1 Peter 1:4.

12 All the evidence indicates that this heavenly resurrection began in 1918, after Jesus'

---

12. In what way do resurrected anointed ones "rest a little while longer," and until when?

¹⁴ What a stirring story these verses tell! Those of Jesus' anointed brothers who survive to Jesus' presence, that is, who are still alive on earth during his presence, are preceded into heaven by those who have already died. Such ones, dead in union with Christ, rise first. Jesus descends, that is, turns his attention to them, and resurrects them to spirit life, giving them "a white robe." Afterward, those who are still alive as humans finish their earthly course, many of them dying violently at the hands of opposers. They do not, however, sleep in death as their predecessors did. Rather, when they die, they are instantly changed—"in the twinkling of an eye"—caught away to the heavens to be with Jesus and fellow members of the body of Christ. (1 Corinthians 15:50-52; compare Revelation 14:13.) Thus, the resurrection of anointed Christians starts soon after the four horsemen of Apocalypse begin their ride.

¹⁵ The opening of this fifth seal of the scroll has provided good news concerning anointed integrity keepers who have conquered, faithful to the death. But it provides no good news for Satan and his seed. The ride of the Conqueror on the white horse continues irresistibly and culminates in a time of reckoning for the world that "is lying in the power of the wicked one." (1 John 5:19) This is made clear when the Lamb opens the sixth seal.

15. (a) What good news has the opening of the fifth seal provided? (b) How does the ride of the Conqueror on the white horse culminate?

Earthquakes in the Lord's Day

HAVE you ever lived through a severe earthquake? It is not a pleasant experience. A big temblor may start with a sickening roll and a rumbling noise. The swaying may worsen by fits and starts while you dash for safety—perhaps under a desk. Or it may come as a sudden, shattering jolt, followed by the crashing of crockery, furnishings, even buildings. Damage may be catastrophic, with frequent aftershocks inflicting further damage and adding to the misery.

² Having this in mind, consider what John describes at the opening of the sixth seal: *"And I saw when he opened the sixth seal, and a great earthquake occurred."* (*Revelation 6:* 12a*) This must fall within the same time frame as the opening of the other seals. Just when in the Lord's day does this earthquake occur, and what kind of quake is it?—Revelation 1:10.

³ Literal and figurative quakings of the earth are mentioned a number of times in the Bible. In his great prophecy about the sign of his presence in Kingdom power, Jesus forecast "earthquakes in one place after another." These would be part of "a beginning of pangs of distress." Since 1914, with earth's population exploding into the thousands of millions, literal temblors have con-

1, 2. (a) What is it like to live through a severe earthquake? (b) What does John describe when the sixth seal is opened?

3. (a) What occurrences did Jesus foretell in the prophecy about the sign of his presence? (b) How do the literal earthquakes relate to the great symbolic earthquake of Revelation 6:12?

1914 Foreseen

"**It was in B.C. 606,** that God's kingdom ended, the diadem was removed, and all the earth given up to the Gentiles. 2520 years from B.C. 606, will end in A.D. 1914."*—*The Three Worlds,* published in 1877, page 83.

"**The Bible evidence** is clear and strong that the 'Times of the Gentiles' is a period of 2520 years, from the year B.C. 606 to and including A.D. 1914."—*Studies in the Scriptures,* Volume 2, written by C. T. Russell and published in 1889, page 79.

Charles Taze Russell and his fellow Bible students realized decades earlier that 1914 would mark the end of the Gentile Times, or the appointed times of the nations. (Luke 21:24) While they did not in those early days fully understand what this would mean, they were convinced that 1914 was going to be a pivotal date in world history, and they were right. Notice the following newspaper quotation:

"**The terrific war outbreak** in Europe has fulfilled an extraordinary prophecy. For a quarter of a century past, through preachers and through press, the 'International Bible Students,' best known as 'Millennial Dawners,' have been proclaiming to the world that the Day of Wrath prophesied in the Bible would dawn in 1914. 'Look out for 1914!' has been the cry of the hundreds of traveling evangelists."—*The World,* a New York newspaper, August 30, 1914.

---

* Providentially, those Bible Students had not realized that there is no zero year between "B.C." and "A.D." Later, when research made it necessary to adjust B.C. 606 to 607 B.C.E., the zero year was also eliminated, so that the prediction held good at "A.D. 1914."—See *"The Truth Shall Make You Free,"* published by the Watch Tower Society in 1943, page 239.

---

tributed significantly to the distresses of our times. (Matthew 24:3, 7, 8) Nevertheless, even though they fulfill prophecy, those earthquakes have been natural, physical disasters. They are preliminary to the great symbolic earthquake of Revelation 6:12. This, indeed, comes as the devastating *finale* to a series of advance tremors that shake Satan's human earthly system of things to its foundations.*

Tremors in Human Society

4 From the mid-1870's, Jehovah's people had been anticipating that catastrophic events would start in 1914 and would mark the end of the Gentile Times. This is the period of "seven times" (2,520 years) run-

---

* Literal earthquakes are often preceded by seismic disturbances that cause dogs to bark or act skittishly and excite other animals and fish, though humans may be unsuspecting until the actual quake strikes.—See *Awake!,* July 8, 1982, page 14.

---

4. (a) Since when had Jehovah's people been anticipating that catastrophic events would begin in 1914? (b) Of what period of time would 1914 mark the end?

ning from the overthrow of the Davidic kingdom in Jerusalem in 607 B.C.E. to Jesus' enthronement in heavenly Jerusalem in 1914 C.E.—Daniel 4:24, 25; Luke 21:24, *King James Version.**

5 Thus, when C. T. Russell, first president of the Watch Tower Society, appeared for morning worship with the Brooklyn, New York, Bethel family on the morning of October 2, 1914, he made the dramatic announcement: "The Gentile Times have ended; their kings have had their day." Indeed, the worldwide upheaval that began in 1914 was so far-reaching that many long-standing monarchies disappeared. The overthrow of czardom in the Bolshevik revolution of 1917 led to the current confrontation between Marxism and capitalism. Tremors of political change continue to disturb human society

---

* For a detailed explanation, see pages 22, 24.

---

5. (a) What announcement did the Society's first president make on October 2, 1914? (b) What political upheavals have taken place since 1914?

earth wide. Today, many governments fail to survive more than a year or two. Lack of stability in the political world is illustrated in the case of Italy, which had 47 new governments in just 42 years following World War II. But such advance tremors are only preliminary to a climactic governmental upheaval. The result? God's Kingdom will take over sole rulership of the earth.—Isaiah 9: 6, 7.

⁶ Historians, philosophers, and political leaders have pointed to the year 1914 as the start of a new and momentous epoch. Seventeen years into that epoch, historian H. G. Wells commented: "Gladly would the prophet prophesy pleasant things. But his duty is to tell what he sees. He sees a world still firmly controlled by soldiers, patriots, usurers, and financial adventurers; a world surrendered to suspicion and hatred, losing what is left of private liberties very rapidly, blundering toward bitter class conflicts, and preparing for new wars." In 1953 philosopher Bertrand Russell wrote: "Ever since 1914, everybody conscious of trends in the world has been deeply troubled by what has seemed like a fated and predetermined march toward ever greater disaster. . . . They see the human race, like the hero of a Greek tragedy, driven on by angry gods and no longer the master of fate." In 1980 statesman Harold Macmillan, reflecting on the peaceful start of our 20th century, said: "Everything would get better and better. This was the world I was born in. . . . Suddenly, unexpectedly, one morning in 1914 the whole thing came to an end."

⁷ World War II brought another wave of upheavals. And smaller wars continue to

---

6. (a) How did H. G. Wells describe the new and momentous epoch? (b) What did a philosopher and a statesman write about the epoch since 1914?

7-9. (a) What upheavals have shaken human society since 1914? (b) How does Jesus' prophecy at Luke chapter 21 describe upheavals in human society and their effect?

1914—A Turning Point

The work *Politikens Verdenshistorie—Historiens Magt og Mening* (*Politiken's* World History —The Power and Meaning of History), published in 1987 in Copenhagen, makes the following observation on page 40:

"**The 19th century's faith** in progress received its fatal blow in 1914. The year before the outbreak of war, Danish historian and politician Peter Munch wrote optimistically: 'All evidence is against the probability of a war between the great European powers. "The danger of war" will also disappear in future, as it has done time after time since 1871.'

"**In contrast,** we read in his later memoirs: 'The outbreak of the war in 1914 is the great turning point of the history of humanity. From a bright epoch of progress, where pursuits could be followed in reasonable security, we entered an age of disaster, horror, and hatred, with insecurity everywhere. No one could tell, and even today no one can tell, whether the darkness that fell upon us at that time will mean the permanent destruction of the entire cultural structure that man has created for himself over millenniums.'"

---

shake the earth as we approach the end of this century. But will the present system make it that far? The fearful threat of a nuclear holocaust has many people wondering. Happily, the answer rests not with man but with his Creator.—Jeremiah 17:5.

⁸ Other things besides wars, though, have shaken human society to its foundations since 1914. One of the most traumatic upheavals was triggered by the U.S. stock-market crash of October 29, 1929. This brought on the Great Depression, which affected all capitalist countries. That depression bottomed out between 1932 and 1934, but we are still feeling its effects. Since 1929 an economically sick world has been patched up by makeshift schemes. Governments indulge in deficit financing. The oil crisis of 1973 and the stock market plunge of 1987 added to the shakings of the financial empire. Meantime, millions of people

buy largely on credit. Countless numbers are victimized by financial gimmicks, pyramid schemes, and lotteries and other gambling subterfuges, many of which are sponsored by governments that should be protecting the people. Even Christendom's television evangelists stretch their hands out for their multimillion-dollar share!—Compare Jeremiah 5:26-31.

⁹ Earlier, economic troubles had opened the way for Mussolini and Hitler to seize power. Babylon the Great lost no time in courting their favors, and the Vatican entered into concordats with Italy in 1929 and Germany in 1933. (Revelation 17:5) The dark days that followed were surely a part of the fulfillment of Jesus' prophecy that the sign of his presence would include "anguish of nations, not knowing the way out . . . while men become faint out of fear and expectation of the things coming upon the inhabited earth." (Luke 21:7-9, 25-31)* Yes, the quakes that began to shake human society in 1914 have continued, with powerful aftershocks.

Jehovah Does Some Shaking

¹⁰ Such tremors in human affairs are the result of man's inability to direct his own step. (Jeremiah 10:23) Moreover, that old Serpent, Satan, "who is misleading the entire inhabited earth," is inflicting woes in his last-ditch effort to turn all mankind away from the worship of Jehovah. Modern technology has caused the earth to shrink into a single neighborhood, where nationalistic and racial hatreds are shaking human society to its foundations, and the United Nations, so-called, can find no effective cure. As never before, man is dominating man to his injury.

---

* For more than 35 years, from 1896 to 1931, the words of Luke 21:25, 28, 31 were quoted on the cover of the *Watchtower* magazine against the backdrop of a lighthouse illuminating stormy skies over raging seas.

---

10. (a) Why are there so many tremors in human affairs? (b) What is Jehovah doing, in preparation for what?

(Revelation 12:9, 12; Ecclesiastes 8:9) Nevertheless, the Sovereign Lord Jehovah, Maker of heaven and earth, has been doing his own kind of shaking over the past 70 years, in preparation for solving earth's problems once and for all. How so?

¹¹ At Haggai 2:6, 7 we read: "For this is what Jehovah of armies has said, 'Yet once —it is a little while—and I am rocking the heavens and the earth and the sea and the dry ground. And I will rock all the nations, and the desirable things of all the nations must come in; and I will fill this house with glory,' Jehovah of armies has said." Since the year 1919 in particular, Jehovah has caused his witnesses to proclaim his judgments among all elements of human society on earth. Satan's world system has been rocked and shaken by this global warning.* As the warning intensifies, God-fearing humans, "the desirable things," have been stirred to separate themselves from the nations. It is not that they are shaken out by the quaking in Satan's organization. But as they discern the situation, they make their own decision to share with the anointed John class in filling Jehovah's house of worship with glory. How is this accomplished? By the zealous work of preaching the good news of God's established Kingdom. (Matthew 24:14) This Kingdom, made up of Jesus and his anointed followers, will ever keep standing to Jehovah's glory as "a kingdom that cannot be shaken."—Hebrews 12:26-29.

¹² Are you one who has started to respond to that preaching? Are you perhaps among the eight million and more who in recent

---

* For example, in a special campaign in 1931, Jehovah's Witnesses personally delivered many thousands of the booklet *The Kingdom, the Hope of the World* to clergymen, politicians, and businessmen throughout the earth.

---

11. (a) What rocking is described at Haggai 2:6, 7? (b) How is Haggai's prophecy being fulfilled?

12. If you have started to respond to the preaching foretold at Matthew 24:14, what should you do before the great earthquake of Revelation 6:12 takes place?

years have attended the Memorial celebration of Jesus' death? If so, keep on progressing in your study of Bible truth. (2 Timothy 2:15; 3:16, 17) Abandon completely the corrupt life-style of Satan's doomed earthly society! Come right on into the Christian new world society and share fully in its activity before the final catastrophic "earthquake" smashes all of Satan's world to pieces. But what is that great earthquake? Let us now see.

The Great Earthquake!

[13] Yes, these critical last days have been a time of earthquakes—literal and figurative. (2 Timothy 3:1) But not one of these quakings is the final great shaking that John sees at the opening of the sixth seal. The time for advance tremors is ended. There now comes a *great* earthquake that is totally new to human experience. It is so great an earthquake that the upheavals and convulsions it causes cannot be measured by the Richter scale or by any other human gauge. This is no mere local shock but a cataclysmic shaking that devastates the entire "earth," that is, all depraved human society.

[14] Others of Jehovah's prophets foretold such an earthquake and its catastrophic consequences. For example, about 820 B.C.E., Joel spoke of "the coming of the great and fear-inspiring day of Jehovah," stating that then "the sun itself will be turned into darkness, and the moon into blood." Later, he adds these words: "Crowds, crowds are in the low plain of the decision, for the day of Jehovah is near in the low plain of the decision. Sun and moon themselves will certainly become dark, and the very stars will actually withdraw their brightness. And out of Zion Jehovah himself will roar, and out of

Jerusalem he will give forth his voice. And heaven and earth certainly will rock; but Jehovah will be a refuge for his people, and a fortress for the sons of Israel." (Joel 2:31; 3:14-16) This rocking could apply only to Jehovah's execution of judgment during the great tribulation. (Matthew 24:21) So the parallel account at Revelation 6:12, 13 would logically have the same application.—See also Jeremiah 10:10; Zephaniah 1:14, 15.

[15] Some 200 years after Joel, the prophet Habakkuk said in prayer to his God: "O Jehovah, I have heard the report about you. I have become afraid, O Jehovah, of your activity. In the midst of the years O bring it to life! In the midst of the years may you make it known. During the agitation, to show mercy may you remember." What would that "agitation" be? Habakkuk goes on to give a graphic description of the great tribulation, saying of Jehovah: "He stood still, that he might shake up the earth. He saw, and then caused nations to leap. . . . With denunciation you went marching through the earth. In anger you went threshing the nations. Yet, as for me, I will exult in Jehovah himself; I will be joyful in the God of my salvation." (Habakkuk 3:1, 2, 6, 12, 18) What a mighty shaking Jehovah will cause in all the earth when he threshes the nations!

[16] Ezekiel too foretold that when Gog of Magog (the debased Satan) makes his final attack upon God's people, Jehovah will cause "a great quaking" to occur "in the soil of Israel." (Ezekiel 38:18, 19) Though literal earthquakes may be involved, we should remember that Revelation is presented in signs. This prophecy and the other prophecies cited are highly symbolic. Hence, the opening of the sixth seal appears to disclose the cul-

---

13. In what way is the great earthquake totally new to human experience?
14. (a) What prophecy foretells a great earthquake and its consequences? (b) To what must Joel's prophecy and Revelation 6:12, 13 refer?

15. What mighty shaking did the prophet Habakkuk foretell?
16. (a) What is foretold by the prophet Ezekiel for the time when Satan makes his final attack upon God's people? (b) What results from the great earthquake of Revelation 6:12?

mination of all shakings of this earthly system of things—the great earthquake in which all humans opposed to Jehovah God's sovereignty are destroyed.

✗ A Time of Darkness

17 As John goes on to show, the great earthquake is accompanied by terrifying events that involve even the heavens. He says: *"And the sun became black as sackcloth of hair, and the entire moon became as blood, and the stars of heaven fell to the earth, as when a fig tree shaken by a high wind casts its unripe figs."* (*Revelation 6:12b, 13*) What a striking phenomenon! It represents the culmination of the catastrophic situation that Jesus had earlier prophesied about at Matthew 24:29. Can you imagine the frightening darkness that would result if the prophecy were fulfilled literally? No more warm, comforting sunlight by day! No more friendly, silvery moonlight by night! And the myriad stars would no longer twinkle against the velvety backdrop of the sky. Instead, there would be cold, relentless blackness.

18 In a spiritual sense, such a darkness was prophesied for ancient Israel. Jeremiah warned: "A desolate waste is what the whole land will become, and shall I not carry out a sheer extermination? On this account the land will mourn, and the heavens above will certainly become dark." (Jeremiah 4:27, 28) In 607 B.C.E. when that prophecy was fulfilled, things were dark indeed for Jehovah's people. Their capital city, Jerusalem, fell to the Babylonians. Their temple was destroyed, and their land was abandoned. For them, there was no comforting light from heaven. Rather, it was as Jeremiah mournfully said to Jehovah: "You have killed; you have shown no compassion. You have blocked approach to yourself with a cloud mass, that prayer may not pass through." (Lamentations 3:43, 44) For Jerusalem, that celestial darkness meant death and destruction.

19 Later, a similar darkness in the heavens signified disaster for ancient Babylon. Of this, God's prophet was inspired to write: "Look! The day of Jehovah itself is coming, cruel both with fury and with burning anger, in order to make the land an object of astonishment, and that it may annihilate the land's sinners out of it. For the very stars of the heavens and their constellations of Kesil will not flash forth their light; the sun will actually grow dark at its going forth, and the moon itself will not cause its light to shine. And I shall certainly bring home its own badness upon the productive land, and their

---

17. How does the great earthquake affect the sun, the moon, and the stars?
18. In what way did 'the heavens become dark' for Jerusalem in 607 B.C.E.?

19. (a) How does God's prophet Isaiah describe a darkness in the heavens with regard to ancient Babylon? (b) When and how was Isaiah's prophecy fulfilled?

'Every mountain removed from its place'

Rev. 12:3

own error upon the wicked themselves."
(Isaiah 13:9-11) This prophecy was fulfilled
in 539 B.C.E. when Babylon fell to the Medes
and the Persians. It well describes the blackness, the hopelessness, the lack of any comforting light for Babylon as she fell forever
from her position as premier world power.

[20] In a similar way, when the great earthquake strikes, this entire world system will
be engulfed in the despair of total darkness. The bright, shining luminaries of Satan's earthly system will send forth no ray of
hope. Already today, earth's political leaders,
especially in Christendom, are notorious for
their corruption, lying, and immoral life-
style. (Isaiah 28:14-19) No longer can they be
trusted. Their flickering light will go into
total eclipse when Jehovah executes judgment. Their moonlike influence on earth's
affairs will be exposed as bloodied, death
dealing. Their worldly superstars will be extinguished like plunging meteorites and scattered like unripe figs in a howling windstorm. Our entire globe will quake under a
"great tribulation such as has not occurred
since the world's beginning until now, no,
nor will occur again." (Matthew 24:21) What
a fearful prospect!

---

20. What fearful outcome awaits this system of
things when the great earthquake strikes?

"The Heaven" Departs

START

[21] John's vision continues: **"And the heaven
departed as a scroll that is being rolled up, and
every mountain and every island were removed
from their places."** (*Revelation 6:14*) Clearly,
these are not the literal heavens or the literal
mountains and islands. But what do they
symbolize?

[22] Regarding "the heaven," we are helped
in our understanding by a similar prophecy
that tells of Jehovah's rage against all the
nations: "And all those of the army of the
heavens must rot away. And the heavens
must be rolled up, just like a book scroll."
(Isaiah 34:4) Edom in particular must suffer.
How? She was overrun by the Babylonians
soon after the destruction of Jerusalem in
607 B.C.E. At that time, there were no outstanding events recorded as happening in
the literal heavens. But there were catastrophic events in Edom's "heavens."* Her

---

* In a similar use of the word "heavens," the prophecy
of the "new heavens" in Isaiah 65:17, 18 had its first fulfillment in the new governmental system, involving Governor Zerubbabel and High Priest Jeshua, that was established in the Promised Land after the return of the Jews
from Babylonian exile.—2 Chronicles 36:23; Ezra 5:1, 2;
Isaiah 44:28.

---

21. In his vision, what does John see regarding "the
heaven" and "every mountain and every island"?
22. In Edom what kind of "heavens" were "rolled up,
just like a book scroll"?

REVELATION CLIMAX

human governmental powers were abased from their elevated, heavenlike position. (Isaiah 34:5) They were "rolled up" and put aside, as it were, like an old scroll that was no longer of any use to anyone.

23 Thus, "the heaven" that is to 'depart as a scroll' refers to the anti-God governments that rule over this earth. They will be removed with finality by the all-conquering Rider of the white horse. (Revelation 19:11-16, 19-21) This is confirmed by what the apostle Peter said when he looked forward to the events signified by the opening of the sixth seal: "The heavens and the earth that are now are stored up for fire and are being reserved to the day of judgment and *of destruction of the ungodly men.*" (2 Peter 3:7) But what about the expression, "every mountain and every island were removed from their places"?

24 In Bible prophecy, mountains and islands are said to rock or be otherwise de-

stabilized at times of great political upheaval. For example, when foretelling Jehovah's judgments against Nineveh, the prophet Nahum wrote: "Mountains themselves have rocked because of him, and the very hills found themselves melting. And the earth will be upheaved because of his face." (Nahum 1:5) There is no record of any breaking up of literal mountains when Nineveh actually fell in 632 B.C.E. But a world power that previously had seemed mountainlike in its strength suddenly collapsed.—Compare Jeremiah 4:24.

25 Therefore, "every mountain and every island" as referred to at the opening of the sixth seal would logically be political governments and dependent organizations of this world that have seemed so stable to many of mankind. They will be rocked right out of place, to the consternation and horror of those who have previously trusted in them. As the prophecy goes on to relate, there will be no question that the great day of the wrath of Jehovah and his Son—the

---

23. What is "the heaven" that will 'depart as a scroll,' and how do Peter's words confirm this understanding?

24. (a) When, in Bible prophecy, is it that mountains and islands are said to rock or be destabilized? (b) How did 'mountains rock' when Nineveh fell?

25. At the coming end of this system of things, how will "every mountain and every island" be removed from their places?

They hid themselves in the caves

final quaking that removes all of Satan's organization—has come with a vengeance!

"Fall Over Us and Hide Us"

26 John's words continue: *"And the kings of the earth and the top-ranking ones and the military commanders and the rich and the strong ones and every slave and every free person hid themselves in the caves and in the rock-masses of the mountains. And they keep saying to the mountains and to the rock-masses: 'Fall over us and hide us from the face of the One seated on the throne and from the wrath of the Lamb, because the great day of their wrath has come, and who is able to stand?'"* —Revelation 6:15-17.

27 When Hosea was pronouncing Jehovah's judgment on Samaria, the capital of the northern kingdom of Israel, he said: "The high places of Beth-aven, the sin of Israel, will actually be annihilated. Thorns and thistles themselves will come up upon their altars. And people will in fact say to the mountains, 'Cover us!' and to the hills, 'Fall over us!'" (Hosea 10:8) How were these words fulfilled? Well, when Samaria fell to the cruel Assyrians in 740 B.C.E., there was nowhere for the Israelites to run. The words of Hosea express the feeling of helplessness, abject terror, and abandonment that the conquered people felt. Neither the literal hills nor the mountainlike institutions of Samaria could protect them, even though they had seemed so permanent in the past.

28 Similarly, when Jesus was being led to his death by the Roman soldiers, he addressed the women of Jerusalem and said: "Days are coming in which people will say, 'Happy are the barren women, and the wombs that did not give birth and the breasts that did not nurse!' Then they will start to say to the mountains, 'Fall over us!' and to the hills, 'Cover us over!'" (Luke 23: 29, 30) The destruction of Jerusalem by the Romans in 70 C.E. is well documented, and it is evident that Jesus' words had an import similar to that of Hosea's. There was no hiding place then for the Jews who remained in Judea. Wherever they tried to hide in Jerusalem, or even when they fled to the mountaintop citadel of Masada, they were unable to escape the violent expression of Jehovah's judgment.

29 Now, the opening of the sixth seal has shown that something similar will happen during the coming day of Jehovah's wrath. At the final shaking of this earthly system of things, those committed to supporting it will desperately seek for a hiding place, but they will not find one. False religion, Babylon the Great, has already failed them miserably. Neither caves in the literal mountains nor symbolic mountainlike political and commercial organizations will provide financial security or any other kind of help. Nothing will shelter them from Jehovah's wrath. Their terror is well described by Jesus: "Then the sign of the Son of man will appear in heaven, and then all the tribes of the earth will beat themselves in lamentation, and they will see the Son of man coming on the clouds of heaven with power and great glory."—Matthew 24:30.

30 Yes, those who have refused to recognize the authority of the victorious Rider of the white horse will be forced to admit their error. Humans who have willingly been part of the seed of the Serpent will be faced with

---

26. How will humans who oppose God's sovereignty act in their terror, and what expression of horror will they utter?
27. What cries were uttered by the unfaithful Israelites of Samaria, and how were those words fulfilled?
28. (a) What warning did Jesus give the women of Jerusalem? (b) How was Jesus' warning fulfilled?

29. (a) When Jehovah's day of wrath comes, what will be the plight of those committed to supporting this system of things? (b) What prophecy of Jesus will be fulfilled when Jehovah expresses His wrath?
30. (a) What is implied by the question: "Who is able to stand?" (b) Will any be able to stand at the time of Jehovah's judgment?

destruction when Satan's world passes away. (Genesis 3:15; 1 John 2:17) The world situation at that time will be such that many will, in effect, ask: "Who is able to stand?" They will apparently assume that no one at all can stand approved before Jehovah in that day of his judgment. But they will be wrong, as the book of Revelation goes on to show.

Chapter 19

Sealing the Israel of God

10/7/91

"**W**HO is able to stand?" (Revelation 6:17) Yes, who indeed? When the great day of divine wrath devastates Satan's system, rulers and peoples of the world may well ask that question. To them it will appear that the impending cataclysm will snuff out all human life. But will it? Happily, God's prophet assures us: "Everyone who calls on the name of Jehovah will get away safe." (Joel 2:32) The apostles Peter and Paul confirm that fact. (Acts 2:19-21; Romans 10:13) Yes, those who call on the name of Jehovah will be survivors. Who are these ones? As the next vision unfolds, we shall see.

² It is truly remarkable that anyone should come through Jehovah's day of judgment alive, for another of God's prophets describes it in these words: "Look! A windstorm of Jehovah, rage itself, has gone forth, an onward-sweeping tempest. Upon the head of the wicked ones it will whirl. The burning anger of Jehovah will not turn back until he will have executed and until he will have carried out the ideas of his heart." (Jeremiah 30:23, 24) It is urgent that we take steps to weather that storm!—Proverbs 2:22; Isaiah 55:6, 7; Zephaniah 2:2, 3.

The Four Winds

³ Before Jehovah unleashes this fury, heavenly angels perform a special service. John now beholds this in vision: "*After this I saw four angels standing upon the four corners of the earth, holding tight the four winds of the earth, that no wind might blow upon the earth or upon the sea or upon any tree.*" (*Revelation 7:1*) What does this mean for us today? These "four winds" are a vivid symbol of destructive judgment about to be let loose on a wicked earthly society, on the surging "sea" of lawless humanity, and on lofty treelike rulers that draw support and sustenance from the people of the earth. —Isaiah 57:20; Psalm 37:35, 36.

---

1. "Who is able to stand" during the great day of divine wrath?
2. Why is it remarkable that there will be survivors of Jehovah's day of judgment?

---

3. (a) What special service performed by angels does John see? (b) What is symbolized by "the four winds"?

Vision _____ *4*

Revelation 7:1-17

Subject: The 144,000 are sealed, and a great crowd is observed standing before Jehovah's throne and before the Lamb

Time of fulfillment: From the enthronement of Christ Jesus in 1914 on into his Millennial Reign

113

[4] No doubt, these four angels represent four angelic groups, whom Jehovah uses to hold back the execution of judgment until the appointed time. When the angels release those winds of divine wrath to whirl at one time from north, south, east, and west, the devastation will be tremendous. It will resemble, but on a stupendous scale, Jehovah's use of the four winds to scatter the ancient Elamites, shattering and exterminating them. (Jeremiah 49:36-38) It will be a gigantic storm wind far more devastating than the "tempest" by which Jehovah annihilated the nation of Ammon. (Amos 1:13-15) No part of Satan's organization on earth will be able to stand in the day of Jehovah's fury, when he vindicates his sovereignty for all eternity to come.—Psalm 83:15, 18; Isaiah 29:5, 6.

[5] Can we be sure that God's judgments will ravage the entire earth? Listen again to his prophet Jeremiah: "Look! A calamity is going forth from nation to nation, and a great tempest itself will be roused up from the remotest parts of the earth. And those slain by Jehovah will certainly come to be in that day from one end of the earth clear to the other end of the earth." (Jeremiah 25:32, 33) It is during this tempestuous storm that darkness will engulf this world. Its ruling agencies will be shaken into oblivion. (Revelation 6:12-14) But the future will not be dark for everyone. For whose sake, then, are the four winds held back?

The Sealing of God's Slaves

[6] John goes on to describe how some will be marked for survival, saying: *"And I saw another angel ascending from the sunrising, having a seal of the living God; and he cried*

with a loud voice to the four angels to whom it was granted to harm the earth and the sea, saying: 'Do not harm the earth or the sea or the trees, until after we have sealed the slaves of our God in their foreheads.'"—Revelation 7:2, 3.

[7] Though this fifth angel is not named, all the evidence indicates that he must be the glorified Lord Jesus. In line with Jesus' being the Archangel, he is here shown to have authority over the other angels. (1 Thessalonians 4:16; Jude 9) He ascends from the east, like "the kings from the rising of the sun" —Jehovah and his Christ—who come to execute judgment, as did kings Darius and Cyrus when they humbled ancient Babylon. (Revelation 16:12; Isaiah 45:1; Jeremiah 51:11; Daniel 5:31) This angel also resembles Jesus in that he is entrusted with sealing anointed Christians. (Ephesians 1:13, 14) Further, when the winds are unleashed, it is Jesus who leads the heavenly armies in executing judgment on the nations. (Revelation 19:11-16) Logically, then, Jesus would be the one to command that destruction of Satan's earthly organization be held back until God's slaves are sealed.

[8] What is this sealing, and who are these slaves of God? The sealing began at Pentecost 33 C.E. when the first Jewish Christians were anointed with holy spirit. Later, God proceeded to call out and anoint "people of the nations." (Romans 3:29; Acts 2:1-4, 14, 32, 33; 15:14) The apostle Paul wrote about anointed Christians' having a guarantee that they "belong to Christ" and added that God "has also put his seal upon us and has given us the token of what is to come, that is, the spirit, in our hearts." (2 Corinthians 1:21, 22; compare Revelation 14:1.) Thus, when these slaves are adopted as God's spiritual sons, they receive a token in advance of their heavenly inheritance—a seal, or pledge.

---

4. (a) What do the four angels represent? (b) What will be the effect on Satan's earthly organization when the four winds are released?

5. How does Jeremiah's prophecy help us understand that God's judgments will embrace the entire earth?

6. Who tells the angels to hold back the four winds, and for what does this allow time?

---

7. Who really is the fifth angel, and what evidence helps us establish his identity?

8. What is the sealing, and when did it begin?

(2 Corinthians 5:1, 5; Ephesians 1:10, 11) They can then say: "The spirit itself bears witness with our spirit that we are God's children. If, then, we are children, we are also heirs: heirs indeed of God, but joint heirs with Christ, provided we suffer together that we may also be glorified together."—Romans 8:15-17.

9 "Provided we suffer together"—what does that mean? In order to receive the crown of life, anointed Christians must endure, faithful even to death. (Revelation 2:10) It is not a matter of 'once saved, always saved.' (Matthew 10:22; Luke 13:24) Rather, they are admonished: "Do your utmost to make the calling and choosing of you sure for yourselves." Like the apostle Paul, ultimately they must be able to say: "I have fought the fine fight, I have run the course to the finish, I have observed the faith." (2 Peter 1:10, 11; 2 Timothy 4:7, 8) So here on earth the testing and sifting of the remaining spirit-begotten sons of God must go on until Jesus and his accompanying angels will have firmly implanted the seal 'in

the forehead' of all of these, identifying them conclusively, irrevocably, as tried and faithful "slaves of our God." That seal then becomes a permanent mark. Evidently, when the four winds of tribulation are unleashed, all of spiritual Israel will have been sealed in finality, even though a few will still be alive in the flesh. (Matthew 24:13; Revelation 19:7) The entire membership will be complete!—Romans 11:25, 26.

How Many Are Sealed?

10 Jesus said to those in line for this sealing: "Have no fear, little flock, because your Father has approved of giving you the kingdom." (Luke 12:32) Other scriptures, such as Revelation 6:11 and Romans 11:25, indicate that the number of this little flock is indeed limited and, in fact, predetermined. John's next words confirm this: *"And I heard the number of those who were sealed, a hundred and forty-four thousand, sealed out of every tribe of the sons of Israel: Out of the tribe of Judah twelve thousand sealed; out of the tribe of Reuben twelve thousand; out of the tribe of*

9. (a) What endurance on the part of the remaining spirit-begotten sons of God is required? (b) For how long will the testing of the anointed go on?

10. (a) What scriptures indicate that the number of the sealed ones is limited? (b) What is the total number sealed, and how are they listed?

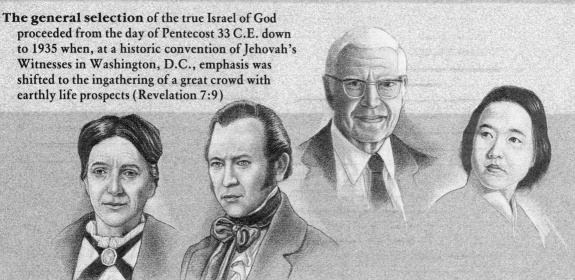

The general selection of the true Israel of God proceeded from the day of Pentecost 33 C.E. down to 1935 when, at a historic convention of Jehovah's Witnesses in Washington, D.C., emphasis was shifted to the ingathering of a great crowd with earthly life prospects (Revelation 7:9)

NOT THE ORIGINAL 12 TRIBE (handwritten)

Gad twelve thousand; out of the tribe of Asher twelve thousand; out of the tribe of Naphtali twelve thousand; out of the tribe of Manasseh twelve thousand; out of the tribe of Simeon twelve thousand; out of the tribe of Levi twelve thousand; out of the tribe of Issachar twelve thousand; out of the tribe of Zebulun twelve thousand; out of the tribe of Joseph twelve thousand; out of the tribe of Benjamin twelve thousand sealed."—Revelation 7:4-8.

[11] Could this not be a reference to literal, fleshly Israel? No, for Revelation 7:4-8 diverges from the usual tribal listing. (Numbers 1:17, 47) Obviously, the listing here is not for the purpose of identifying fleshly Jews by their tribes but to show a similar organizational structure for spiritual Israel. This is balanced. There are to be exactly 144,000 members of this new nation—12,000 from each of 12 tribes. No tribe in this Israel of God is exclusively royal or priestly. The whole nation is to rule as kings, and the whole nation is to serve as priests.—Galatians 6:16; Revelation 20:4, 6.

---

11. (a) Why could the reference to the 12 tribes not apply to literal, fleshly Israel? (b) Why does Revelation list the 12 tribes? (c) Why is there no exclusively royal or priestly tribe in the Israel of God?

[12] Although the natural Jews and Jewish proselytes were given the first opportunity to be chosen for spiritual Israel, only a minority of that nation responded. Jehovah therefore extended the invitation to the Gentiles. (John 1:10-13; Acts 2:4, 7-11; Romans 11:7) As in the case of the Ephesians, who previously had been "alienated from the state of Israel," now non-Jews could be sealed with God's spirit and become part of the congregation of anointed Christians. (Ephesians 2:11-13; 3:5, 6; Acts 15:14) It is appropriate, then, for the 24 elders to sing before the Lamb: "With your blood you bought persons for God out of every tribe and tongue and people and nation, and you made them to be a kingdom and priests to our God, and they are to rule as kings over the earth."—Revelation 5:9, 10.

[13] The Christian congregation is "a chosen race, a royal priesthood, a holy nation." (1 Peter 2:9) Replacing natural Israel as God's nation, it becomes a new Israel that is

---

12. Why is it appropriate that the 24 elders sing before the Lamb the words of Revelation 5:9, 10?
13. Why could Jesus' half brother James properly address his letter "to the twelve tribes that are scattered about"?

"really 'Israel.'" (Romans 9:6-8; Matthew 21: 43)* For this reason, it was quite proper for Jesus' half brother James to address his pastoral letter "to the twelve tribes that are scattered about," that is, to the worldwide congregation of anointed Christians that in time would number 144,000.—James 1:1.

The Israel of God Today

14 Interestingly, the first president of the Watch Tower Society, Charles T. Russell, recognized the 144,000 to be a literal number of individuals making up a spiritual Israel. In *The New Creation,* Volume VI of his *Studies in the Scriptures,* published in 1904, he wrote: "We have every reason to believe that the definite, fixed number of the elect [chosen anointed ones] is that several times stated in Revelation (7:4; 14:1); namely, 144,000 'redeemed *from amongst* men.'" In *Light,* Book One, published in 1930 by the Watch Tower Society's second president, J. F. Rutherford, it was likewise stated: "The 144,000 members of the body of Christ are thus in the assembly shown as selected and anointed, or sealed," Jehovah's Witnesses have consistently held to the view that literally 144,000 anointed Christians make up spiritual Israel.

15 Nevertheless, does not natural Israel today merit *some* special favor? In the period just prior to the Lord's day, when sincere Bible students were rediscovering many of the basic truths of God's Word, it was thought that with the ending of the Gentile Times the Jews would again enjoy a privileged standing before God. Thus, C. T. Russell's book *The Time Is at Hand* (Volume II

of *Studies in the Scriptures*), published in 1889, applied Jeremiah 31:29-34 to the natural Jews, and commented: "The world is witness to the fact that Israel's punishment under the dominion of the Gentiles has been continuous since B.C. [607], that it still continues, and that there is no reason to expect their national re-organization sooner than A.D. 1914, the limit of their 'seven times'—2520 years." It seemed that the Jews would then experience a national restoration, and this prospect apparently brightened in 1917, when the Balfour Declaration pledged British support for making Palestine a national home for the Jews.

16 Following the first world war, Palestine became a mandated territory under Great Britain, and the way opened for many Jews to return to that land. In 1948 the political State of Israel was brought forth. Did this not indicate that the Jews were in line for divine blessings? For many years, Jehovah's Witnesses believed that this was so. Thus, in 1925 they published a 128-page book, *Comfort for the Jews.* In 1929 they released an attractive 360-page volume, *Life,* designed to appeal to the Jews and dealing also with the Bible book of Job. Great efforts were made, especially in New York City, to reach the Jews with this Messianic message. Happily, a few individuals responded, but the Jews by and large, like their forefathers of the first century, rejected the evidence of Messiah's presence.

17 It was obvious that Jewry, as a people and as a nation, was not the Israel described in Revelation 7:4-8 or other Bible prophecies related to the Lord's day. Following tradition, the Jews continued to avoid using the divine name. (Matthew 15:1-3, 7-9) In discussing Jeremiah 31:31-34, the book *Jehovah,*

---

* Fittingly, the name Israel means "God Contends; Contender (Perseverer) With God."—Genesis 32:28, *New World Translation Reference Bible,* footnote.

14. What shows that Jehovah's Witnesses have consistently held that the 144,000 is the literal number of those making up spiritual Israel?

15. Just prior to the Lord's day, what did sincere Bible students think the natural Jews would enjoy after the ending of the Gentile Times?

16. What efforts were made by Jehovah's Witnesses to reach the natural Jews with the Christian message, and with what result?

17, 18. What did God's slaves on earth come to understand regarding the new covenant and the Bible's restoration prophecies?

published by the Watch Tower Society in 1934, stated conclusively: "The new covenant has nothing to do with the natural descendants of Israel and with mankind in general, but . . . is limited to spiritual Israel." The Bible's restoration prophecies relate neither to the natural Jews nor to political Israel, which is a member of the United Nations and a part of the world that Jesus spoke of at John 14:19, 30 and 18:36.

[18] In 1931 God's slaves on earth had received, with great joy, the name Jehovah's Witnesses. They could subscribe wholeheartedly to the words of Psalm 97:11: "Light itself has flashed up for the righteous one, and rejoicing even for the ones upright in heart." They could clearly discern that *spiritual* Israel alone had been brought into the new covenant. (Hebrews 9:15; 12:22, 24) Unresponsive natural Israel had no part therein, nor did mankind in general. This understanding cleared the way for a brilliant flash of divine light, outstanding in the annals of theocratic history. This would reveal how abundantly Jehovah extends his mercy, loving-kindness, and truth to all humans who draw close to him. (Exodus 34:6; James 4:8) Yes, others besides the Israel of God would benefit by the angels' holding back the four winds of destruction. Who might these be? Could you be one of them? Let us now see.

Chapter 20

A Multitudinous Great Crowd

HAVING described the sealing of the 144,-000, John goes on to report one of the most exciting revelations in all Scripture. His heart must have leaped with joy as he reported it, saying: *"After these things I saw, and, look! a great crowd, which no man was able to number, out of all nations and tribes and peoples and tongues, standing before the throne and before the Lamb, dressed in white robes; and there were palm branches in their hands."* (Revelation 7:9) Yes, the holding back of the four winds allows for the salvation of another group besides the 144,000 members of spiritual Israel: a multilanguage, international great crowd.*—Revelation 7:1.

1. After describing the sealing of the 144,000, what other group does John see?

* See *New World Translation Reference Bible*, footnote.

Interpretations Belong to God

For many decades the John class inquired as to the identity of the great crowd but without finding a satisfactory explanation. Why? We find the answer in the words of faithful Joseph, when he said: "Do not interpretations belong to God?" (Genesis 40:8) When and how does God interpret the fulfillment of his prophecies? Usually, it is when they are due to be fulfilled or are in course of fulfillment so that their message can be clearly discerned by his searching servants. This understanding is given "for our instruction, that through our endurance and through the comfort from the Scriptures we might have hope."—Romans 15:4.

[2] Worldly commentators have interpreted this great crowd to be fleshly non-Jews converted to Christianity or to be heaven-bound Christian martyrs. Even the Bible Students in the past regarded them as a secondary heavenly class, as noted in 1886 in Volume I of *Studies in the Scriptures, The Divine Plan of the Ages:* "They lose the prize of the throne and the divine nature, but will finally reach birth as spirit beings of an order lower than the divine nature. Though these are truly consecrated, they are overcome by the worldly spirit to such an extent that they fail to render their lives in sacrifice." And as late as 1930, the thought was expressed in *Light, Book One:* "Those who make up this great crowd fail to respond to the invitation to become the zealous witnesses for the Lord." They were described as a self-righteous group that had a knowledge of the truth but did little about preaching it. They were to get to heaven as a secondary class that would not share in reigning with Christ.

[3] There were, however, other associates of the anointed Christians who later became most zealous in the preaching work. They had no aspirations of going to heaven. Indeed, their hope was in line with the title of a public talk featured by Jehovah's people from 1918 to 1922. Originally, this was "The World Has Ended—Millions Now Living Will Never Die."* Soon thereafter, the *Watch Tower* magazine of October 15, 1923, explained Jesus' parable of the sheep and the goats (Matthew 25:31-46), stating: "Sheep represent all the peoples of the nations, not spirit-begotten but disposed toward righteousness, who *mentally acknowledge Jesus Christ* as the Lord and who are looking for and hoping for a better time under his reign."

[4] Some years later, in 1931, *Vindication, Book One,* discussed Ezekiel chapter 9, identifying those persons marked on the forehead for preservation at the world's end as the sheep of the above parable. *Vindication, Book Three,* released in 1932, described the upright heart attitude of the non-Israelite man Jehonadab, who joined Israel's anointed King Jehu in his chariot and went along to see Jehu's zeal in executing false religionists. (2 Kings 10:15-17) The book commented: "Jehonadab represented or foreshadowed that class of people now on the earth during the time that the Jehu work [of declaring Jehovah's judgments] is in progress who are of good will, are out of harmony with Satan's organization, who take their stand on the side of righteousness, and are the ones whom the Lord will preserve during the time of Armageddon, take them through that trouble, and give them everlasting life on the earth. These constitute the 'sheep' class." In 1934 *The Watchtower* made it clear that these Christians with earthly hopes should make a dedication to Jehovah and be baptized. The light regarding this earthly class was shining ever brighter.—Proverbs 4:18.

[5] The understanding of Revelation 7:9-17 was now about to burst forth in all its sparkling brilliance! (Psalm 97:11) The *Watchtower* magazine had repeatedly expressed the hope that a convention scheduled for May 30 to June 3, 1935, in Washington, D.C., U.S.A., would be "a real comfort and benefit" to those pictured by Jehonadab. That it proved to be! In a stirring talk on "The Great Multitude," delivered to about 20,000 conventioners, J. F. Rutherford, president of the

---

* *The Watch Tower,* April 1, 1918, page 98.

---

2. How have worldly commentators explained the great crowd, and how did even the Bible Students in the past view this group?

3. (a) What hope was held out to certain righthearted ones who later became zealous in the preaching work? (b) How did *The Watch Tower* in 1923 explain the parable of the sheep and the goats?

4. How did the light regarding the earthly class become brighter in 1931? in 1932? in 1934?

5. (a) What identification of the great crowd was made in 1935? (b) When J. F. Rutherford in 1935 asked conventioners who had the hope of living forever on earth to stand up, what happened?

Watch Tower Society, gave Scriptural proof that the modern-day other sheep are identical with that great crowd of Revelation 7:9. At the climax of this talk, the speaker asked: "Will all those who have the hope of living forever on the earth please stand?" As a large part of the audience stood up, the president declared: "Behold! The great multitude!" There was a hush, followed by thunderous cheering. How elated was the John class—and also the Jehonadab group! On the following day, 840 new Witnesses were baptized, most of these professing to be of that great crowd.

Confirming the Identity of the Great Crowd

⁶ How can we state so positively that the great crowd is this modern-day group of dedicated Christians who hope to live forever on God's earth? Previously, John had seen in vision the heavenly group "bought . . . for God out of every tribe and tongue and people and nation." (Revelation 5:9, 10) The great crowd have a similar origin but a different destiny. Unlike the Israel of God, their number is not predetermined. No man can tell in advance how many there will be. Their robes are washed white in the blood of the Lamb, symbolizing that they have a righteous standing before Jehovah by virtue of their faith in Jesus' sacrifice. (Revelation 7:14) And they are waving palm branches, hailing Messiah as their King.

⁷ As he looks on in this vision, John's thoughts must be taking him back more than 60 years to Jesus' last week on earth. On Nisan 9, 33 C.E., when the crowds flocked to welcome Jesus into Jerusalem, they "took the branches of palm trees and went out to meet him. And they began to shout: 'Save, we pray you! Blessed is he that comes in Jehovah's name, even the king of Israel!'" (John 12:12, 13) In like fashion, the waving of palm branches and crying out on the part of the great crowd shows their unbridled joy in accepting Jesus as Jehovah's appointed King.

⁸ Doubtless, the palm branches and exulting cries also remind John of the ancient Israelite Festival of Booths. For this festival Jehovah commanded: "And you must take for yourselves on the first day the fruit of splendid trees, the fronds of palm trees and the boughs of branchy trees and poplars of the torrent valley, and you must rejoice before Jehovah your God seven days." The palm branches were used as a mark of rejoicing. The temporary booths were a reminder that Jehovah had saved his people out of Egypt, to live in tents in the wilderness. "The alien resident and the fatherless boy and the widow" shared in this festival. All Israel were to "become nothing but joyful."—Leviticus 23:40; Deuteronomy 16:13-15.

⁹ It is fitting, then, that the great crowd, though no part of spiritual Israel, should wave palm branches, since they joyfully and gratefully ascribe the victory and salvation to God and to the Lamb, as John here observes: *"And they keep on crying with a loud voice, saying: 'Salvation we owe to our God, who is seated on the throne, and to the Lamb.'"* (Revelation 7:10) Although they have been separated out of all ethnic groups, the great crowd cry out with just that one "loud voice." How can they do this, despite their diversity of nations and languages?

¹⁰ This great crowd is part of the only truly united multinational organization on earth

---

6. (a) Why can we clearly understand that the great crowd is the modern-day group of dedicated Christians who hope to live forever on earth? (b) What do the white robes of the great crowd symbolize?
7, 8. (a) The waving of palm branches doubtless reminded the apostle John of what events? (b) What is the significance of the fact that those of the great crowd are waving palm branches?

9. In what joyful cry do the great crowd join?
10. How can the great crowd cry out unitedly with one "loud voice" despite the diversity of nations and languages?

today. They do not have different standards for different countries but apply the Bible's right principles consistently wherever they live. They are not involved in nationalistic, revolutionary movements but have truly 'beaten swords into plowshares.' (Isaiah 2:4) They are not divided into sects or denominations, so that they shout confused or mutually contradictory messages as do the religions of Christendom; nor do they leave it to a professional clergy class to do their praising for them. They do not cry out that they owe salvation to the holy spirit, for they are not servants of a trinitarian god. In some 200 geographical territories around the earth, they are at one in calling upon the name of Jehovah as they speak the one pure language of truth. (Zephaniah 3:9) Properly, they publicly acknowledge that their salvation comes from Jehovah, the God of salvation, through Jesus Christ, His Chief Agent of salvation. —Psalm 3:8; Hebrews 2:10.

11 Modern technology has helped to make the loud voice of the united great crowd sound even louder. No other religious group on earth has need of publishing Bible study aids in more than 200 languages, since no other group is interested in reaching all peoples of earth with one united message. As a further aid in this, under the supervision of the anointed Governing Body of Jehovah's Witnesses, a Multilanguage Electronic Phototypesetting System (MEPS) was developed. At the time of this writing, various forms of MEPS are used in more than 60 of the Watch Tower Society's branches around the earth, and this has helped to make possible publication of their principal semimonthly journal, *The Watchtower,* in 39 languages simultaneously. Jehovah's people also simultaneously publish books, such as this one, in a number of languages. Thus, Jehovah's Witnesses, of whom the great crowd make up the vast majority, are able yearly to distribute hundreds of millions of publications in all the better-known languages, enabling additional throngs out of all tribes and tongues to study God's Word and join their voices to the loud voice of the great crowd. —Isaiah 42:10, 12.

In Heaven or on Earth?

12 How do we know that "standing before the throne" does not mean that the great crowd is in heaven? There is much clear evidence on this point. For example, the Greek word here translated "before" (e·no'pi·on) literally means "in [the] sight [of]" and is used several times of humans on earth who are "before" or "in the sight of" Jehovah. (1 Timothy 5:21; 2 Timothy 2:14; Romans 14:22; Galatians 1:20) On one occasion when the Israelites were in the wilderness, Moses said to Aaron: "Say to the entire assembly of the sons of Israel, 'Come near before Jehovah, because he has heard your murmurings.'" (Exodus 16:9) The Israelites did not have to be transported to heaven in order to stand before Jehovah on that occasion. (Compare Leviticus 24:8.) Rather, right there in the wilderness they stood in Jehovah's view, and his attention was on them.

13 Additionally, we read: "When the Son of man arrives in his glory . . . all the nations will be gathered before him."* The whole human race is not in heaven when this prophecy is fulfilled. Certainly, those who "depart into everlasting cutting-off" are not in heaven. (Matthew 25:31-33, 41, 46) Instead, mankind stands on earth in Jesus' view, and he turns his attention to judging them. Similarly, the great crowd is "before the throne and before the Lamb" in that it

* Literally, "in front of him," *The Kingdom Interlinear Translation of the Greek Scriptures.*

---

11. How has modern technology helped those of the great crowd to render their loud voice even louder?

12, 13. In what way is the great crowd "standing before the throne and before the Lamb"?

stands in the view of Jehovah and his King, Christ Jesus, from whom it receives a favorable judgment.

14 The 24 elders and the anointed group of 144,000 are described as being "round about the throne" of Jehovah and "upon the [heavenly] Mount Zion." (Revelation 4:4; 14:1) The great crowd is not a priestly class and does not attain to that exalted position. True, it is later described at Revelation 7:15 as serving God "in his temple." But this temple does not refer to the inner sanctuary, the Most Holy. Rather, it is the earthly courtyard of God's spiritual temple. The Greek word *na·os'*, here translated "temple," often conveys the broad sense of the entire edifice erected for Jehovah's worship. Today, this is a spiritual structure that embraces both heaven and earth. —Compare Matthew 26:61; 27:5, 39, 40; Mark 15:29, 30; John 2:19-21, *New World Translation Reference Bible,* footnote.

14. (a) Who are described as being "round about the throne" and "upon the [heavenly] Mount Zion"? (b) Though the great crowd serve God "in his temple," why does this not make them a priestly class?

Members of the great crowd

- come out of all nations and tribes and peoples and tongues
- stand before Jehovah's throne
- have washed their robes white in the blood of the Lamb
- ascribe salvation to Jehovah and to Jesus
- come out of the great tribulation
- serve Jehovah in his temple day and night
- receive Jehovah's loving protection and care
- are shepherded by Jesus to fountains of waters of life

A Universal Shout of Praise

15 The great crowd is praising Jehovah, but others are also singing his praises. John reports: *"And all the angels were standing around the throne and the elders and the four living creatures, and they fell upon their faces before the throne and worshiped God, saying: 'Amen! The blessing and the glory and the wisdom and the thanksgiving and the honor and the power and the strength be to our God forever and ever. Amen.'"—Revelation 7:11, 12.*

16 When Jehovah created the earth, all of his holy angels "joyfully cried out together, and all the sons of God began shouting in applause." (Job 38:7) Each new revelation of Jehovah's purpose must have evoked similar angelic shouts of praise. When the 24 elders —the 144,000 in their heavenly glory—cry aloud in recognition of the Lamb, all others of God's heavenly creatures chime in with praises for Jesus and for Jehovah God. (Revelation 5:9-14) Already, these creatures have been overjoyed to observe the fulfillment of Jehovah's purpose in his resurrecting faithful anointed humans to a glorious place in the spirit realm. Now, all of Jehovah's faithful heavenly creatures burst into melodious praise as the great crowd appears. Truly, for all of Jehovah's servants, the Lord's day is a thrilling time in which to be living. (Revelation 1:10) Here on earth, how privileged we are to share in the song of praise by witnessing to Jehovah's Kingdom!

The Great Crowd Makes Its Appearance

17 From the time of the apostle John and on into the Lord's day, anointed Christians

15, 16. (a) What is the reaction in heaven to the appearance of the great crowd? (b) How does Jehovah's spirit creation react to each new revelation of his purpose? (c) How can we on earth join in the song of praise?
17. (a) What question is raised by one of the 24 elders, and the fact that the elder could locate the answer suggests what? (b) When was the elder's question answered?

were puzzled as to the identity of the great crowd. It is fitting, then, that one of the 24 elders, representing anointed ones already in heaven, should stir John's thinking by raising a pertinent question. *"And in response one of the elders said to me: 'These who are dressed in the white robes, who are they and where did they come from?' So right away I said to him: 'My lord, you are the one that knows.'"* (Revelation 7:13, 14a) Yes, that elder could locate the answer and give it to John. This suggests that resurrected ones of the 24-elders group may be involved in the communicating of divine truths today. For their part, those of the John class on earth got to learn the identity of the great crowd by closely observing what Jehovah was performing in their midst. They were quick to appreciate the dazzling flash of divine light that emblazoned the theocratic firmament in 1935, at Jehovah's due time.

[18] During the 1920's and early 1930's, the John class had stressed the heavenly hope, both in the publications and in the preaching work. Apparently, the full number of the 144,000 had yet to be filled. But increasing numbers of those who heeded the message and who showed zeal in the witness work came to profess an interest in living forever on the Paradise earth. They had no desire to go to heaven. That was not their calling. They were no part of the little flock but rather of the other sheep. (Luke 12:32; John 10:16) Their being identified in 1935 as the great crowd of other sheep was an indication that the choosing of the 144,000 was then about complete.

[19] Do statistics support this conclusion? Yes, they do. In 1938, worldwide, 59,047 witnesses of Jehovah shared in the ministry.

Of these, 36,732 partook of the emblems at the annual celebration of the Memorial of Jesus' death, thus indicating that they had a heavenly calling. In the years since then, the number of these partakers has progressively decreased, principally because faithful witnesses of Jehovah finished their earthly life course in death. In 1987 only 8,808 partook of the Memorial emblems—just 0.1 percent of the 8,965,221 attending that global observance.

[20] When the second world war broke out, Satan put forth bitter efforts to stop the harvesting of the great crowd. Jehovah's work was restricted in many countries. During those dark days, and shortly before his death in January 1942, J. F. Rutherford, president of the Watch Tower Society, was heard to say: "Well . . . it looks as though the great multitude is not going to be so great after all." But divine blessing directed otherwise! By 1946 the number of Witnesses ministering worldwide had jumped to 176,456 —most of these being of the great crowd. In 1987 there were 3,395,612 Witnesses who were serving Jehovah faithfully in 210 different lands—truly A GREAT CROWD! And the number keeps on increasing.

[21] The harvesting of God's people during the Lord's day has thus been in full harmony with John's vision: first the work of gathering the remaining ones of the 144,000; then the gathering of the great crowd. As Isaiah prophesied, now "in the final part of the days," people of all nations are streaming to share in Jehovah's pure worship. And, indeed, we exult in appreciation of Jehovah's creation of "new heavens and a new earth." (Isaiah 2:2-4; 65:17, 18) God is gathering "all

18, 19. (a) What hope was stressed by the John class during the 1920's and 1930's, but who responded to the message in increasing numbers? (b) The identification of the great crowd in 1935 indicated what with regard to the 144,000? (c) What do Memorial statistics reveal?

20. (a) During World War II, what comment did the Society's president privately make about the great crowd? (b) What facts now show that the great crowd is indeed a great one?
21. (a) How has the harvesting of God's people during the Lord's day been in full harmony with John's vision? (b) How did certain important prophecies begin to be fulfilled?

things together again in the Christ, the things in the heavens and the things on the earth." (Ephesians 1:10) The anointed heirs of the heavenly Kingdom—chosen over the centuries since Jesus' day—are "the things in the heavens." And now, the great crowd of the other sheep appear as initial ones of "the things on the earth." Your serving in harmony with that arrangement can mean eternal happiness for you.

The Blessings of the Great Crowd

22 Through the divine channel, John receives further information regarding this great crowd: *"And he* [the elder] *said to me: 'These are the ones that come out of the great tribulation, and they have washed their robes and made them white in the blood of the Lamb. That is why they are before the throne of God; and they are rendering him sacred service day and night in his temple; and the One seated on the throne will spread his tent over them.'"* —*Revelation 7:14b, 15.*

23 On an earlier occasion, Jesus had said that his presence in Kingdom glory would culminate in "great tribulation such as has not occurred since the world's beginning until now, no, nor will occur again." (Matthew 24:21, 22) In fulfillment of that prophecy, the angels will unleash the four winds of the earth to devastate Satan's world system. First to go will be Babylon the Great, the world empire of false religion. Then, at the peak of the tribulation, Jesus will deliver the remaining ones of the 144,000 on earth, together with the multitudinous great crowd.—Revelation 7:1; 18:2.

24 How do individuals of the great crowd qualify for survival? The elder tells John that they have "washed their robes and made

them white in the blood of the Lamb." In other words, they have exercised faith in Jesus as their Ransomer, have made a dedication to Jehovah, have symbolized their dedication by water baptism, and "hold a good conscience" by their upright conduct. (1 Peter 3:16, 21; Matthew 20:28) Thus, they are clean and righteous in Jehovah's eyes. And they keep themselves "without spot from the world."—James 1:27.

25 Further, they have become zealous witnesses of Jehovah—"rendering him sacred service day and night in his temple." Are you one of this dedicated great crowd? If so, it is your privilege to serve Jehovah without letup in the earthly courtyard of his great spiritual temple. Today, under the direction of the anointed ones, the great crowd is performing by far the greater part of the witness work. Despite secular responsibilities, hundreds of thousands of them have made room for the full-time ministry as pioneers. But whether you are in that group or not, as a dedicated member of the great crowd, you can rejoice that because of your faith and works you are declared righteous as a friend of God and are welcomed as a guest in his tent. (Psalm 15:1-5; James 2:21-26) Jehovah thus 'spreads his tent' over those who love him and, as a good host, protects them. —Proverbs 18:10.

26 The elder continues: *"They will hunger no more nor thirst anymore, neither will the sun beat down upon them nor any scorching heat, because the Lamb, who is in the midst of the throne, will shepherd them, and will guide them to fountains of waters of life. And God will wipe out every tear from their eyes."* (*Revelation 7:16, 17*) Yes, Jehovah is truly hospitable! But what depth of meaning is there to these words?

---

22. What further information does John receive regarding the great crowd?
23. What is the great tribulation from which the great crowd "come out"?
24. How do individuals of the great crowd qualify for survival?

---

25. (a) How is the great crowd rendering Jehovah "sacred service day and night in his temple"? (b) How does Jehovah "spread his tent" over the great crowd?
26. What other blessings will the great crowd enjoy?

REVELATION CLIMAX

The great crowd owes salvation to God and to the Lamb

²⁷ Let us consider a similarly worded prophecy: "This is what Jehovah has said: 'In a time of goodwill I have answered you, and in a day of salvation I have helped you . . . They will not go hungry, neither will they go thirsty, nor will parching heat or sun strike them. For the One who is having pity upon them will lead them, and by the springs of water he will conduct them.'" (Isaiah 49:8, 10; see also Psalm 121:5, 6.) The apostle Paul quoted part of this prophecy and applied it to the "day of salvation" that began at Pentecost 33 C.E. He wrote: "For he [Jehovah] says: 'In an acceptable time I heard you, and in a day of salvation I helped you.' Look! Now is the especially acceptable time. Look! Now is the day of salvation."—2 Corinthians 6:2.

²⁸ What application did the promise about

not getting hungry or thirsty or suffering parching heat have back then? Certainly, Christians in the first century did suffer literal hunger and thirst at times. (2 Corinthians 11:23-27) In a spiritual way, though, they had an abundance. They were richly provided for, so that they did not go hungry or thirsty for spiritual things. Moreover, Jehovah did not cause the heat of his anger to blaze against them when he destroyed the Jewish system of things in 70 C.E. The words of Revelation 7:16 have a similar spiritual fulfillment for the great crowd today. Along with the anointed Christians, they enjoy bounteous spiritual provisions.—Isaiah 65:13; Nahum 1:6, 7.

²⁹ If you are one of that great crowd, your good condition of heart will make you "cry out joyfully," no matter what you have to endure in the way of privations and pressures during the twilight years of Satan's system. (Isaiah 65:14) In that sense, even now, the Lamb can 'wipe out every tear from your eyes.' No longer does God's torrid "sun" of adverse judgment threaten you, and when the four winds of destruction are unleashed, you may be spared the "scorching heat" of Jehovah's displeasure. After that destruction

---

27. (a) How did Isaiah prophesy something similar to the words of the elder? (b) What shows that Isaiah's prophecy began to be fulfilled on the Christian congregation in Paul's day?

28, 29. (a) How were Isaiah's words fulfilled in the first century? (b) How are the words of Revelation 7:16 fulfilled with regard to the great crowd? (c) What will result from the great crowd's being guided to "fountains of waters of life"? (d) Why will the great crowd be unique among mankind?

The Lamb will guide the great crowd to fountains of waters of life

is over, the Lamb will guide you to benefit fully from the revitalizing "fountains of waters of life," these representing all the provisions that Jehovah makes for your gaining everlasting life. Your faith in the blood of the Lamb will be vindicated in that you will gradually be raised to human perfection. You of the great crowd will be unique among mankind as the "millions" that did not even have to die! In the fullest sense, every tear will have been wiped from your eyes.—Revelation 21:4.

Making the Calling Sure

START

11/5/91

30 What a magnificent vista these words open up to us! Jehovah himself is on his throne, and all his servants, heavenly and earthly, unite in praising him. His earthly servants appreciate what an awesome privilege it is to share in this swelling chorus of praise. Very soon, Jehovah and Christ Jesus will execute judgment, and the cry will be heard: "The great day of their wrath has

come, and who is able to stand?" (Revelation 6:17) The answer? Only a minority of mankind, including those of the sealed 144,000 still remaining in the flesh and a great crowd of other sheep who will "stand," that is, survive with them.—Compare Jeremiah 35: 19; 1 Corinthians 16:13.

31 In view of this fact, anointed Christians of the John class exert themselves vigorously in "pursuing down toward the goal for the prize of the upward call of God by means of Christ Jesus." (Philippians 3:14) They are fully aware that events during these days call for special endurance on their part. (Revelation 13:10) After loyally serving Jehovah for so many years, they hold fast to the faith, rejoicing that their names are "inscribed in the heavens." (Luke 10:20; Revelation 3:5) Those of the great crowd too know that only "he that has endured to the end is the one that will be saved." (Matthew 24:13) While the great crowd as a group is marked to come out of the great tribulation, individuals thereof must exert themselves to remain clean and active.

---

30. What magnificent vista opens up to us in John's vision, and who will be able to "stand"?

31. How should the fulfillment of John's vision affect Christians, both of the anointed and of the great crowd?

32 There is no evidence that any apart from these two groups will "stand" in the day of Jehovah's wrath. What does this mean for the millions who each year show a certain respect for Jesus' sacrifice by attending the celebration of the Memorial of his death but who have not yet exercised faith in Jesus' sacrifice to the point of becoming dedicated, baptized servants of Jehovah, active in his service? Further, what about those who were once active but who have allowed their hearts to "become weighed down with . . . anxieties of life"? May all of such awaken, and stay awake, in order to "succeed in escaping all these things that are destined to occur, and in standing before the Son of man" —Jesus Christ. The time is short!—Luke 21: 34-36.

---

32. What urgent situation is highlighted by the fact that only two groups will "stand" in the day of Jehovah's wrath?

Chapter 21

Oct. 16, 1989

Jehovah's Plagues on Christendom

"THE four winds" have been held back until the 144,000 of spiritual Israel are sealed and the great crowd is approved for survival. (Revelation 7:1-4, 9) However, before that tempestuous storm breaks over the earth, Jehovah's adverse judgments against Satan's world must also be made known! As the Lamb proceeds to open the seventh and final seal, John must be watching keenly to see what will unfold. Now he shares his experience with us: "*And when he* [the Lamb] *opened the seventh seal, a silence occurred in heaven for about a half hour. And I saw the seven angels that stand before God, and seven trumpets were given them.*"—*Revelation 8:1, 2.*

A Time for Fervent Prayer

2 A significant silence this! Half an hour can seem a long time when you are waiting for something to happen. Now, even the constant heavenly chorus of praise is no longer heard. (Revelation 4:8) Why? John sees the reason in vision: "*And another angel arrived and stood at the altar, having a golden incense vessel; and a large quantity of incense was given him to offer it with the prayers of all the holy ones upon the golden altar that was before the throne. And the smoke of the incense ascended from the hand of the angel with the prayers of the holy ones before God.*"—*Revelation 8:3, 4.*

---

1. What happens when the Lamb opens the seventh seal?

2. What takes place during the symbolic half hour of silence in heaven?

Vision	*5*

Revelation 8:1–9:21

Subject: The sounding of six of the seven trumpets

Time of fulfillment: From the enthronement of Christ Jesus in 1914 to the great tribulation

---

129

³ This reminds us that under the Jewish system of things, incense was burned daily at the tabernacle and, in later years, at the temple in Jerusalem. (Exodus 30:1-8) During such incense burning, the nonpriestly Israelites waited outside the sacred area, praying —no doubt silently in their hearts—to the One to whom the incense smoke was ascending. (Luke 1:10) John now sees something similar happening in heaven. The incense offered by the angel is associated with "the prayers of the holy ones." In fact, in an earlier vision, incense is said to represent such prayers. (Revelation 5:8; Psalm 141:1, 2) Evidently, then, the symbolic silence in heaven is to allow the prayers of the holy ones on earth to be heard.

⁴ Can we determine when this happened? Yes, we can, by examining the context, together with historical developments early in the Lord's day. (Revelation 1:10) During 1918 and 1919, events on earth harmonized remarkably with the scenario described at Revelation 8:1-4. For 40 years before 1914, the Bible Students—as Jehovah's Witnesses were then called—had been announcing boldly

---

3. (a) Of what does incense burning remind us? (b) What is the purpose of the half hour of silence in heaven?
4, 5. What historical developments help us determine the time period corresponding to the symbolic half hour of silence?

that the times of the Gentiles would end in that year. The distressful events of 1914 proved them correct. (Luke 21:24, *King James Version;* Matthew 24:3, 7, 8) But many of them also believed that in 1914 they would be taken from this earth to their heavenly inheritance. That did not happen. Instead, during the first world war, they endured a time of severe persecution. On October 31, 1916, the first president of the Watch Tower Society, Charles T. Russell, died. Then, on July 4, 1918, the new president, Joseph F. Rutherford, and seven other representatives of the Society were transported to the Atlanta, Georgia, penitentiary, wrongly sentenced to long years in prison.

⁵ The sincere Christians of the John class

were perplexed. What did God want them to do next? When would they be taken up to heaven? An article entitled "The Harvest Ended—What Shall Follow?" appeared in the May 1, 1919, issue of *The Watch Tower*. It reflected this state of uncertainty and encouraged the faithful to continued endurance, adding: "We believe it is now a true saying that the harvest of the kingdom class is an accomplished fact, that all such are duly sealed and that the door is closed." During this difficult period, the fervent prayers of the John class were ascending, as though in the smoke of a large quantity of incense. And their prayers were being heard!

Hurling Fire to the Earth

6 John tells us: *"But right away the angel took the incense vessel, and he filled it with some of the fire of the altar and hurled it to the earth. And thunders occurred and voices and lightnings and an earthquake."* (*Revelation 8:5*) After the silence, there is sudden dramatic activity! This is evidently in response to the prayers of the holy ones, since it is triggered by fire taken from the incense altar. Back in 1513 B.C.E., at Mount Sinai, thunders and lightnings, a loud noise, fire, and a quaking of the mountain signaled Jehovah's turning his attention to his people. (Exodus 19: 16-20) The similar manifestations reported by John likewise indicate Jehovah's giving attention to his servants on earth. But what John observes is presented in signs. (Revelation 1:1) So how are the symbolic fire, thunders, voices, lightnings, and earthquake to be interpreted today?

7 On one occasion, Jesus told his disciples: "I came to start a fire on the earth." (Luke 12:49) Truly, he did ignite a fire. By his zealous preaching, Jesus made God's Kingdom

the paramount issue before the Jewish people, and this sparked heated controversy throughout that nation. (Matthew 4:17, 25; 10:5-7, 17, 18) In 1919 Jesus' spiritual brothers on earth, the small band of anointed Christians who had survived the trialsome days of World War I, set light to a similar fire in Christendom. In September of that year, Jehovah's spirit was remarkably in evidence as his loyal Witnesses assembled from near and far at Cedar Point, Ohio, U.S.A. Joseph F. Rutherford, recently released from prison and soon to be completely exonerated, boldly addressed that convention, saying: "Obedient to the command of our Master, and recognizing our privilege and duty to make war against the strongholds of error which have so long held the people in bondage, our vocation was and is to announce the incoming glorious kingdom of Messiah." That is the primary issue—God's Kingdom!

8 Referring to the recent hard experiences of God's people, the speaker said: "So pitiless was the onslaught of the enemy that many of the Lord's dear flock were stunned and stood still in amazement, praying and waiting for the Lord to indicate his will. . . . But notwithstanding the momentary discouragement, there was a burning desire to proclaim the message of the kingdom."—See the September 15, 1919, issue of *The Watch Tower*, page 280.

9 In 1919 that desire was satisfied. This small but active group of Christians was set on fire, spiritually speaking, to begin a worldwide preaching campaign. (Compare 1 Thessalonians 5:19.) Fire was hurled to the earth in that God's Kingdom was made the burning issue, and so it continues to be! Strong voices replaced silence, sounding out the Kingdom message with clarity. Thunderous

---

6. What happens after the silence in heaven, and this in response to what?

7. (a) What symbolic fire did Jesus ignite on earth during his ministry? (b) How did Jesus' spiritual brothers set light to a fire in Christendom?

8, 9. (a) How did the Society's president describe the attitude and desire of God's people during the difficult war years? (b) How was it that fire was hurled to the earth? (c) How have thunders, voices, lightnings, and an earthquake occurred?

The opening of the seven seals leads to √
the sounding of seven trumpets

storm warnings from the Bible pealed forth. Like flashes of lightning, brilliant beams of truth shone from Jehovah's prophetic Word, and, as if by a mighty earthquake, the religious realm was shaken to its foundations. The John class saw that there was work to be done. And to this day, that work continues to expand gloriously throughout the entire inhabited earth!—Romans 10:18.

Preparing for the Blasts of the Trumpets

11/12/91

10 John goes on to say: *"And the seven angels with the seven trumpets prepared to blow them."* (*Revelation 8:6*) What does the blowing of those trumpets mean? In the days of Israel, trumpet blasts were used to signal important days or noteworthy events. (Leviticus 23:24; 2 Kings 11:14) Similarly, the blasts of the trumpets that John is to hear will call attention to matters of life-and-death importance.

---

10. What do the seven angels prepare to do, and why?

11 As the angels got ready to blow those trumpets, no doubt they were also giving direction to a preparatory work on earth. From 1919 to 1922, the revitalized John class was busy in reorganizing the public ministry and building up publishing facilities. In 1919 the magazine *The Golden Age,* known today as *Awake!,* had been brought forth as "A Journal of Fact, Hope, and Conviction"—a trumpetlike instrument that would play a key role in exposing false religion's political involvements.

12 As we shall now see, each of the trumpet blasts heralds a dramatic scene in which terrible plagues affect portions of the earth. Some of these remind us of the plagues that Jehovah sent to punish the Egyptians in Moses' day. (Exodus 7:19–12:32) These were expressions of Jehovah's judgment on that na-

---

11. In what preparatory work on earth was the John class busily engaged from 1919 to 1922?
12. What is heralded by each trumpet blast, reminding us of what in Moses' day?

tion, and they opened the way for God's people to escape from slavery. The plagues seen by John accomplish something similar. However, they are not literal plagues. They are signs that symbolize Jehovah's righteous judgments.—Revelation 1:1.

Identifying the "Third"

13 As we shall see, when the first four trumpets are blown, plagues are inflicted on "a third" of the earth, of the sea, of the rivers and fountains of waters, and of the earth's sources of light. (Revelation 8:7-12) A third is a considerable part of something but not the whole. (Compare Isaiah 19:24; Ezekiel 5:2; Zechariah 13:8, 9.) So which "third" would be most deserving of these plagues? The vast majority of mankind has been blinded and corrupted by Satan and his seed. (Genesis 3:15; 2 Corinthians 4:4) The situation is as described by David: "They have all turned aside, they are all alike corrupt; there is no one doing good, not even one." (Psalm 14:3) Yes, the whole of mankind is in danger of receiving an adverse judgment. But one section thereof is particularly guilty. One part —"a third"—should have known better! What is that "third"?

14 It is Christendom! In the 1920's, her realm embraced about one third of mankind. Her religion is the fruit of the great apostasy from true Christianity—the apostasy that Jesus and his disciples foretold. (Matthew 13: 24-30; Acts 20:29, 30; 2 Thessalonians 2:3; 2 Peter 2:1-3) The clergy of Christendom claim to be in God's temple and have represented themselves as teachers of Christianity. But their doctrines are far removed from Bible truth, and they continually bring God's name into disrepute. Aptly represented by the symbolic third, Christendom receives potent, plaguing messages from Jehovah. That

third of mankind merits no divine favor whatsoever!

15 In line with there being a sequence of trumpet blasts, special resolutions were featured at seven conventions from 1922 to 1928. But the trumpeting has not been confined to those years. The powerful exposing of Christendom's wicked ways has been continuous, ongoing, as the Lord's day progresses. Jehovah's judgments must be proclaimed universally, to all nations, despite international hatred and persecutions. Only then does the end of Satan's system come. (Mark 13:10, 13) Happily, the great crowd has now added its voice to that of the John class in making those thunderous pronouncements of worldwide importance.

A Third of the Earth Burned Up

16 Reporting on the angels, John writes: *"And the first one blew his trumpet. And there occurred a hail and fire mingled with blood, and it was hurled to the earth; and a third of the earth was burned up, and a third of the trees was burned up, and all the green vegetation was burned up."* (Revelation 8:7) This is similar to the seventh plague on Egypt, but what does it mean for our 20th century?—Exodus 9:24.

17 In the Bible, the word "earth" often refers to mankind. (Genesis 11:1; Psalm 96:1) Since the second plague is on the sea, which also has to do with mankind, "the earth" must refer to the seemingly stable human society that Satan has built up and that is due to be destroyed. (2 Peter 3:7; Revelation 21:1) The plague scenario reveals that Christendom's third of the earth is scorched by the searing heat of Jehovah's disapproval. Her

13. What happens when the first four trumpets are blown, and what question does this raise?
14. What is the symbolic third that receives the plaguing messages from Jehovah?

15. (a) Is each of the trumpet blasts confined to a particular year? Explain. (b) Whose voice has been added to that of the John class in proclaiming Jehovah's judgments?
16. What follows when the first angel blows his trumpet?
17. (a) What is represented by the word "earth" at Revelation 8:7? (b) How is Christendom's third of the earth burned up?

prominent ones—standing like trees in the midst of her—are burned up by the proclaiming of Jehovah's adverse judgment. All her hundreds of millions of church members, if they continue to support Christendom's religion, become like scorched blades of grass, spiritually wilted in God's eyes. —Compare Psalm 37:1, 2.*

18 How is this judgment message delivered? Generally, not by the world's news media, which are part of the world and often reproachful of God's "slave." (Matthew 24: 45) It was proclaimed in a notable way at the second historic gathering of God's people at Cedar Point, Ohio, September 10, 1922. These unanimously and enthusiastically adopted a resolution entitled "A Challenge to World Leaders." In outspoken terms, it put the modern-day symbolic earth on notice, as follows: "We therefore call upon the nations of earth, their rulers and leaders, and upon all the clergymen of all the denominational churches of earth, their followers and allies, big business and big politicians, to bring forth their proof in justification of the position taken by them that they can establish peace and prosperity on earth and bring happiness to the people; and their failing in this, we call upon them to give ear to the testimony that we offer as witnesses for the Lord, and then let them say whether or not our testimony is true."

19 What testimony did these Christians offer? This: "We hold and declare that Messiah's kingdom is the complete panacea for all the ills of humankind and will bring peace on earth and good will to men, the desire of all nations; that those who yield themselves willingly to his righteous reign now begun will be blessed with lasting peace, life, liberty and endless happiness." In these corrupt times, when man-made governments, especially those in Christendom, are failing utterly to solve the world's problems, that trumpeting challenge rings out with even greater force than in 1922. How true that God's Kingdom in the hands of his conquering Christ is mankind's one and only hope!

20 Through resolutions, tracts, booklets, books, magazines, and discourses, this and later proclamations were trumpeted forth by means of the congregation of anointed Christians. The first trumpet blast resulted in Christendom's being beaten as with the hardened water of a pounding hail. Her bloodguilt, due to her share in the wars of this 20th century, has been laid bare, and she has been shown to be deserving of the fiery expression of Jehovah's wrath. The John class, with later support from the great crowd, has continued to echo the first trumpet blast, drawing attention to Jehovah's view of Christendom, as being fit for destruction.—Revelation 7:9, 15.

Like a Burning Mountain

21 "And the second angel blew his trumpet. And something like a great mountain burning with fire was hurled into the sea. And a third of the sea became blood; and a third of the creatures that are in the sea which have souls died, and a third of the boats were wrecked." (Revelation 8:8, 9) What does this frightful scene picture?

22 We may best understand it against the background of the convention of Jehovah's people held in Los Angeles, California, U.S.A.,

---

* In contrast, Revelation 7:16 shows that the great crowd do not experience the scorching heat of Jehovah's disapproval.

---

18. How was Jehovah's judgment message proclaimed at the 1922 Cedar Point convention?
19. What testimony did God's people deliver to Christendom regarding God's Kingdom?

20. (a) By what means have judgment messages in 1922 and thereafter been trumpeted forth by the congregation of anointed Christians? (b) What resulted in Christendom from the first trumpet blast?
21. What happens when the second angel blows his trumpet?
22, 23. (a) What resolution doubtless came as a result of the sounding of the second trumpet? (b) What is represented by "a third of the sea"?

REVELATION CLIMAX

on August 18-26, 1923. The featured Saturday afternoon talk by the Watch Tower Society's president was on the topic "Sheep and Goats." The "sheep" were clearly identified as those righteously disposed persons who would inherit the earthly realm of God's Kingdom. A resolution that followed drew attention to the hypocrisy of "apostate clergymen and 'the principal of their flocks,' who are worldly men of strong financial and political influence." It called on the "multitude of the peace and order loving ones in the denominational churches . . . to withdraw themselves from the unrighteous ecclesiastical systems designated by the Lord as 'Babylon'" and to ready themselves "to receive the blessings of God's kingdom."

23 Doubtless, this resolution came as a result of the sounding of the second trumpet. Those who would in due course respond to that message would separate from the goatlike group that Isaiah described in these words: "But the wicked are like the sea that is being tossed, when it is unable to calm down, the waters of which keep tossing up seaweed and mire." (Isaiah 57:20; 17:12, 13) Thus, "the sea" well pictures restless, unsettled, and rebellious humanity that churns up unrest and revolution. (Compare Revelation 13:1.) The time will come when that "sea" will be no more. (Revelation 21:1) Meantime, with the blast of the second trumpet, Jehovah pronounces judgment against a third of it—the unruly part that is in the realm of Christendom herself. *JER. 5:22*

24 A great mountainlike mass burning with fire is hurled into this "sea." In the Bible, mountains very often symbolize governments. For example, God's Kingdom is portrayed as a mountain. (Daniel 2:35, 44) Ruinous Babylon became a "burnt-out mountain." (Jeremiah 51:25) But the mountainous mass that John sees is still burning. Its being hurled into the sea well represents how, during and after the first world war, the question of government became a burning issue among mankind, especially in the lands of Christendom. In Italy, Mussolini introduced Fascism. Germany embraced Hitler's Nazism, while other countries tried different forms of socialism. A radical change occurred in Russia, where the Bolshevik revolution produced the first communist state, with the result that religious leaders of

24. What is pictured by the burning mountainous mass that was hurled into the sea?

Christendom lost power and influence in what was formerly one of their strongholds.

25 The Fascist and Nazi experiments were snuffed out by the second world war, but government continued to be a fiery issue, and the human sea continued to churn and throw up new revolutionary governments. In the decades since 1945, these have been installed in many places, such as China, Vietnam, Cuba, and Nicaragua. In Greece an experiment in military dictatorship failed. In Kampuchea (Cambodia) an excursion into fundamentalist communism resulted in a reported two million and more deaths.

26 That "mountain burning with fire" continues to make waves in the sea of mankind. Ongoing struggles over government are reported in Africa, the Americas, Asia, and the Pacific islands. Many of these struggles are taking place in lands of Christendom or where Christendom's missionaries have become activists. Roman Catholic priests have even joined up with and fought as members of communist guerrilla bands. At the same time, Protestant evangelical groups have worked in Central America to counter what they call the communists' "vicious and relentless thirst for power." But none of these convulsions in the sea of mankind can bring peace and security.—Compare Isaiah 25:10-12; 1 Thessalonians 5:3.

27 The second trumpet blast reveals that those of mankind who got involved in revolutionary conflicts over government rather than submit to God's Kingdom are bloodguilty. Particularly Christendom's "third of the sea" has become as blood. All living things therein are dead in God's eyes. None of the radical organizations floating like boats in that third of the sea can avoid ulti-

mate shipwreck. How happy we are that millions of sheeplike people have now heeded the trumpetlike call to separate from those who are still wallowing in the narrow nationalism and bloodguilt of that sea!

A Star Falls From Heaven

28 "And the third angel blew his trumpet. And a great star burning as a lamp fell from heaven, and it fell upon a third of the rivers and upon the fountains of waters. And the name of the star is called Wormwood. And a third of the waters turned into wormwood, and many of the men died from the waters, because these had been made bitter." (Revelation 8:10, 11) Once again, other parts of the Bible help us to see how this scripture applies in the Lord's day.

29 We have already met the symbolism of a star in Jesus' messages to the seven congregations, in which the seven stars symbolize the elders in the congregations.* (Revelation 1:20) Anointed "stars," along with all others of the anointed, inhabit heavenly places in a spiritual sense from the time that they are sealed with the holy spirit as a token of their heavenly inheritance. (Ephesians 2:6, 7) However, the apostle Paul warned that from among such starlike ones would come apostates, sectarians, who would mislead the flock. (Acts 20:29, 30) Such unfaithfulness would result in a great apostasy, and these fallen elders would come to make up a composite man of lawlessness that would elevate himself to a godlike position among mankind. (2 Thessalonians 2:3, 4) Paul's warnings were fulfilled when the clergy

---

* While the seven stars in Jesus' right hand picture the anointed overseers in the Christian congregation, the elders in most of the 55,000-and-more congregations in the world today are of the great crowd. (Revelation 1:16; 7:9) What is their position? Since they receive their appointment by holy spirit through the anointed faithful and discreet slave class, these can be said to be under Jesus' right hand of control, for they are also his undershepherds. (Isaiah 61:5, 6; Acts 20:28) They support the "seven stars" in that they serve where qualified anointed brothers are not available.

---

25. How did government continue to be a burning issue after World War II?
26. How has the "mountain burning with fire" continued to make waves in the sea of mankind?
27. (a) How has "a third of the sea" become as blood? (b) How have 'a third of the creatures in the sea' died and how are "a third of the boats" to fare?

28. What happens when the third angel blows his trumpet?
29. What fulfills the symbolism of "a great star burning as a lamp," and why?

king help us to understand. Speaking to the king of Babylon, Isaiah said: "O how you have fallen from heaven, you shining one, son of the dawn! How you have been cut down to the earth, you who were disabling the nations!" (Isaiah 14:12) This prophecy was fulfilled when Babylon was overthrown by the armies of Cyrus, and its king made an abrupt descent from world rulership to shameful defeat. Thus, a fall from heaven can refer to losing a high position and falling into ignominy.

31 When the clergy of Christendom apostatized from true Christianity, they fell from the lofty "heavenly" position described by Paul at Ephesians 2:6, 7. Instead of offering fresh waters of truth, they served up "wormwood," bitter lies such as hellfire, purgatory, the Trinity, and predestination; also, they led the nations into war, failing to build them up as moral servants of God. The result? Spiritual poisoning of those who believed the lies. Their case was similar to that of the unfaithful Israelites of Jeremiah's day, to whom Jehovah said: "Here I am making them eat wormwood, and I will give them poisoned water to drink. For from the prophets of Jerusalem apostasy has gone forth to all the land."—Jeremiah 9:15; 23:15.

32 This fall from the spiritual heavens became apparent in the year 1919 when, rather than Christendom's clergy, the small remnant of anointed Christians was appointed over the Kingdom interests. (Matthew 24:45-47) And from 1922 that fall was dramatized when this group of Christians renewed their campaign of frankly exposing the failings of the clergy of Christendom.

33 Outstanding in this connection was the

of Christendom appeared on the world scene. This group is well represented by the symbol of "a great star burning as a lamp."

30 John sees this particular star falling from heaven. How? The experiences of an ancient

---

30. (a) When the king of Babylon was spoken to as one fallen from heaven, what was meant? (b) To what can a fall from heaven refer?

---

31. (a) When did the clergy of Christendom fall from a "heavenly" position? (b) How have the waters served up by the clergy turned into "wormwood," and with what result to many?
32. When did Christendom's fall from the spiritual heavens become apparent, and how was it dramatized?
33. What exposé of the clergy of Christendom was made at the 1924 convention in Columbus, Ohio, U.S.A.?

proclamation made at what *The Golden Age* magazine described as "the greatest convention of Bible Students held during the ages." This convention assembled in Columbus, Ohio, July 20-27, 1924. No doubt at the direction of the angel that sounded the third trumpet, a forceful resolution was there adopted and later 50 million copies were distributed as a tract. It was published under the title *Ecclesiastics Indicted*. A subheading presented the issue: "The Seed of Promise Versus the Seed of the Serpent." The Indictment itself roundly exposed Christendom's clergy on matters such as their taking of high-sounding religious titles, their making commercial giants and professional politicians the principal ones of their flocks, their desiring to shine before men, and their refusing to preach to the people the message of Messiah's Kingdom. It emphasized that every dedicated Christian is commissioned by God to proclaim "the day of vengeance of our God; to comfort all that mourn."—Isaiah 61:2, *KJ.*

[34] Since the third angel started to blow his trumpet, the clergy's position of dominance among mankind has been slipping until, in this day and age, very few of them retain the godlike powers they enjoyed in former centuries. Because of the preaching of Jehovah's Witnesses, great numbers of people have come to realize that many doctrines taught by the clergy are spiritual poison—"wormwood." Furthermore, the clergy's power in northern Europe is almost spent, while in most Eastern European lands, as well as in China, the government strictly curtails their influence. In Catholic parts of Europe and in the Americas, the clergy's scandalous behavior in financial, political, and moral affairs has sullied their reputation. From now on, their position can only get worse, since soon they will suffer the same fate as all other false religionists.—Revelation 18:21; 19:2.

[35] Jehovah's plaguing of Christendom is not yet finished. Consider what happens after the fourth trumpet blast.

Darkness!

[36] *"And the fourth angel blew his trumpet. And a third of the sun was smitten and a third of the moon and a third of the stars, in order that a third of them might be darkened and the day might not*

34, 35. (a) What has happened to the clergy's power and influence since the third angel started to blow his trumpet? (b) What does the future hold for Christendom's clergy?

36. What happens after the fourth angel blows his trumpet?

REVELATION CLIMAX

Christendom's
Waters Revealed to Be Wormwood

Beliefs and Attitudes of Christendom	What the Bible Really Says
God's personal name is unimportant: "The use of any proper name for the one and only God . . . is entirely inappropriate for the universal faith of the Christian Church." (Preface to the *Revised Standard Version*)	**Jesus prayed that God's name be sanctified.** Peter said: "Everyone who calls on the name of Jehovah will be saved." (Acts 2:21; Joel 2:32; Matthew 6:9; Exodus 6:3; Revelation 4:11; 15:3; 19:6)
God is a Trinity: "The Father is God, the Son is God, and the Holy Spirit is God, and yet there are not three Gods but one God." (*The Catholic Encyclopedia*, 1912 edition)	**The Bible says that Jehovah** is greater than Jesus and is the God and head of Christ. (John 14:28; 20:17; 1 Corinthians 11:3) The holy spirit is God's active force. (Matthew 3:11; Luke 1:41; Acts 2:4)
The human soul is immortal: "When man dies his soul and body are disunited. His body . . . decays . . . The human soul, however, does not die." (*What Happens After Death*, a Roman Catholic publication)	**Man *is* a soul.** At death the soul ceases to think or feel and returns to the dust from which it was made. (Genesis 2:7; 3:19; Psalm 146:3, 4; Ecclesiastes 3:19, 20; 9:5, 10; Ezekiel 18:4, 20)
The wicked are punished after death in hell: "According to traditional Christian belief, hell is a place of unending anguish and pain." (*The World Book Encyclopedia*, 1987 edition)	**The wages of sin is death,** not life in torment. (Romans 6:23) The dead rest unconscious in hell (Hades, Sheol), awaiting a resurrection. (Psalm 89: 48; John 5:28, 29; 11:24, 25; Revelation 20:13, 14)
"The title Mediatrix [female mediator] is applied to Our Lady." (*New Catholic Encyclopedia*, 1967 edition)	**The only mediator** between God and men is Jesus. (John 14:6; 1 Timothy 2:5; Hebrews 9:15; 12:24)
Infants should be baptized: "From the very beginning the Church has administered the Sacrament of Baptism to infants. Not only was this practice considered lawful, but it was also taught to be absolutely necessary for salvation." (*New Catholic Encyclopedia*, 1967 edition)	**Baptism is for those** who have been made disciples and taught to obey Jesus' commandments. To qualify for baptism, a person must understand God's Word and exercise faith. (Matthew 28:19, 20; Luke 3:21-23; Acts 8:35, 36)
Most churches are divided into a laity class and a clergy class, which ministers to the laity. The clergy are usually given a salary in exchange for their ministry and are exalted over the laity by titles such as "Reverend," "Father," or "His Eminence."	**All first-century Christians were ministers** and shared in preaching the good news. (Acts 2: 17, 18; Romans 10:10-13; 16:1) A Christian should "give free," not for a salary. (Matthew 10:7, 8) Jesus strictly forbade the use of religious titles. (Matthew 6:2; 23:2-12; 1 Peter 5:1-3)
Images, icons, and crosses are used in worship: "The images . . . of Christ, of the Virgin Mother of God, and of the other saints, are to be . . . kept in churches and due reverence and honor be paid to them." (Declaration of the Council of Trent [1545-63])	**Christians must flee** from every sort of idolatry, including so-called relative worship. (Exodus 20:4, 5; 1 Corinthians 10:14; 1 John 5:21) They worship God not by sight but with spirit and truth. (John 4:23, 24; 2 Corinthians 5:7)
Church members are taught that God's purposes will be accomplished through politics. The late Cardinal Spellman stated: "There is only one road to peace . . . , the highroad of democracy." News items report religion's involvement in the world's politics (even in insurrections) and her support of the UN as "the last hope of concord and peace."	**Jesus preached God's Kingdom,** not some political system, as the hope for mankind. (Matthew 4:23; 6:9, 10) He refused to get involved in politics. (John 6:14, 15) His Kingdom was no part of this world; hence, his followers were to be no part of the world. (John 18:36; 17:16) James warned against friendship with the world. (James 4:4)

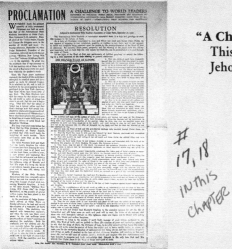

"A Challenge to World Leaders." (1922)
This resolution helped to publicize
Jehovah's plague against "the earth"

 # 17, 18 in this chapter

to believe in God and who say they accept Jesus as their Savior?

38 Jesus said that true Christians would be recognized by their fruits and that many claiming to be his followers would be "workers of lawlessness." (Matthew 7:15-23) No one looking at the fruits of the third of the world occupied by Christendom can deny that she is groping in gross spiritual darkness. (2 Corinthians 4:4) She is most blameworthy, for she claims to be Christian. Hence, it is only proper that the fourth angel should trumpet the fact that Christendom's "light" is, in fact, darkness, and her sources of "light" are Babylonish—non-Christian.—Mark 13:22, 23; 2 Timothy 4:3, 4.

39 In line with that heavenly proclamation, a capacity crowd of God's people assembled in convention in Indianapolis, Indiana, U.S.A., on August 29, 1925, and adopted for publication a forthright resolution entitled "Message of Hope." Again, some 50 million copies were distributed in a number of languages. It described the false light held out by the combine of commercial profiteers, political leaders, and the religious clergy, as a result of which "the peoples have fallen into darkness." And it pointed to God's Kingdom as the real hope for receiving "the blessings of peace, prosperity, health, life, liberty and eternal happiness." It took courage for the small band of anointed Christians to proclaim such messages against the giant organization of Christendom. But

have illumination for a third of it, and the night likewise." (*Revelation 8:12*) The ninth plague on Egypt was a plague of literal darkness. (Exodus 10:21-29) But what is this symbolic darkness that comes to plague men in our 20th century?

37 The apostle Peter told fellow believers that they had been in darkness, spiritually speaking, before they became Christians. (1 Peter 2:9) Paul too used the word "darkness" to describe the spiritual state of those outside the Christian congregation. (Ephesians 5:8; 6:12; Colossians 1:13; 1 Thessalonians 5:4, 5) But what about those in Christendom who claim

---

37. How did the apostles Peter and Paul describe the spiritual estate of those outside the Christian congregation?

---

38. The fourth angel trumpets what fact about Christendom's "light"?
39. (a) How did the resolution adopted at the convention in 1925 describe Christendom's false light? (b) What further exposé was made in 1955?

 # 23

"A Warning to All Christians." (1923)
Jehovah's adverse judgment against "a third of the sea" was proclaimed abroad by this resolution

"Ecclesiastics Indicted." (1924)
The wide circulation of this tract helped to put people on notice that the "star" of Christendom's clergy had fallen

#33

consistently, from the early 1920's until now, they have done so. In more recent times, in 1955, a further exposé of the clergy class was made by the worldwide distribution in many languages of a booklet entitled *Christendom or Christianity—Which One Is "the Light of the World"?* Today, Christendom's hypocrisy has become so evident that many in the world can see it for themselves. But Jehovah's people have not let up in exposing her for what she is: a kingdom of darkness.

A Flying Eagle

40 These first four trumpet blasts truly resulted in uncovering the desolate and death-dealing condition of Christendom. Her part of "the earth" was exposed as deserving of Jehovah's judgment. Revolutionary governments springing up in her lands and elsewhere were shown to be inimical to spiritual life. The fallen condition of her clergy was laid bare, and the general darkness of her spiritual condition was exposed for all to see. Christendom is truly the most reprehensible part of Satan's system of things.

41 What more is there to reveal? Before we find the answer to this question, there is a brief pause in the series of trumpet blasts. John describes what he next sees: *"And I saw, and I heard an eagle flying in midheaven say with a loud voice: 'Woe, woe, woe to those dwelling on the earth because of the rest of the trumpet blasts of*

---

40. What did the four trumpet blasts show Christendom to be?
41. During a pause in the series of trumpet blasts, what does John see and hear?

"Message of Hope" (1925)
This forthright resolution was used to expose Christendom's supposed light sources as being in truth sources of darkness

the three angels who are about to blow their trumpets!'"—Revelation 8:13.

42 An eagle flies high in the sky, so that people in a wide area can see it. It has exceptionally keen sight and can see a long way ahead of itself. (Job 39:29) One of the four cherubic living creatures around God's throne was pictured as a flying eagle. (Revelation 4: 6, 7) Whether it is this cherub or another farsighted servant of God, it loudly proclaims a dynamic message: "Woe, woe, woe"! Let earth's inhabitants take note, as the three remaining trumpet blasts are heard, each of them linked to one of these woes.

---

42. What may be signified by the flying eagle, and what is its message?

141

The First Woe—Locusts

THE fifth angel prepares to blow his trumpet. Four heavenly trumpets have already sounded, and four plagues have been directed to the third of the earth that Jehovah regards as most reprehensible—Christendom. Her deathly sick condition has been uncovered. While angels sound the trumpet blasts, human heralds follow through on earth. Now the fifth angelic trumpet is about to announce the first woe, more fearsome even than what has gone before. It is related to a terrifying locust plague. First, though, let us examine other scriptures that will help us to understand this plague better.

² The Bible book of Joel, written during the ninth century B.C.E., describes a plague of insects, including locusts, that is similar to the one that John sees. (Joel 2:1-11, 25)* It was to cause much discomfort for apostate Israel but would also result in individual Jews' repenting and returning to Jehovah's favor. (Joel 2: 6, 12-14) When that time arrived, Jehovah would pour out his spirit upon "every sort of flesh," while fearful signs and alarming portents would precede "the coming of the great and fear-inspiring day of Jehovah."—Joel 2: 11, 28-32.

---

* Compare Joel 2:4, 5, 7 (where the insects are described as horses, people, and men, and as making a sound like a chariot) with Revelation 9:7-9; also, compare Joel 2:6, 10 (describing the painful effect of the insect plague) with Revelation 9:2, 5.

---

1. Who follow through when the angels sound the trumpet blasts, and what does the fifth trumpet blast announce?
2. What Bible book describes a plague of locusts similar to the one that John sees, and what was the effect of it on ancient Israel?

A First-Century Plague

³ There was a fulfillment of Joel chapter 2 in the first century. It was then, at Pentecost 33 C.E., that holy spirit was poured out, anointing the first Christians and empowering them to speak "the magnificent things of God" in many tongues. As a result, a large crowd assembled. The apostle Peter addressed those astonished onlookers, quoting Joel 2:28, 29 and explaining that they were witnessing its fulfillment. (Acts 2:1-21) But there is no record of a literal insect plague at that time, causing discomfort to some and leading others to repentance.

⁴ Was there a figurative plague during those days? Yes, indeed! It came as a result of the relentless preaching of the newly anointed Christians.* Through them, Jehovah invited those Jews who would listen to repent and enjoy blessings from him. (Acts 2:38-40; 3:19) The individuals who responded received his favor to a remarkable degree. But to the ones who refused the invitation, the first-century Christians became like a devastating swarm of locusts. Starting in Jerusalem, they spread through all Judea and Samaria. Soon they were everywhere, tormenting the unbelieving Jews by publicly proclaiming Jesus' resurrection, with all that this implied. (Acts 1:8; 4:18-20; 5:17-21, 28, 29, 40-42; 17:5, 6; 21:

---

* See the article "United Against Nations in the Valley of Decision" in the December 1, 1961, issue of The Watchtower.

3, 4. (a) When was there a fulfillment of Joel chapter 2, and how? (b) How was there a plague like a swarm of locusts in the first century C.E., and how long did the plaguing continue?

The blowing of the fifth trumpet introduces the first of three woes

27-30) That plaguing continued until the "fear-inspiring day," in 70 C.E., when Jehovah brought the Roman armies against Jerusalem to destroy it. Only those Christians who in faith called on the name of Jehovah were saved.—Joel 2:32; Acts 2:20, 21; Proverbs 18:10.

The 20th-Century Plague

5 Reasonably, we could expect Joel's prophecy to have a final fulfillment in the time of the end. How true this has proved to be! At the Bible Students' convention at Cedar Point, Ohio, U.S.A., September 1-8, 1919, a notable outpouring of Jehovah's spirit activated his people to organize a global campaign of preaching. Of all professed Christians, they alone, recognizing that Jesus had been enthroned as heavenly King, spared no effort in publishing abroad that good news. Their relentless witnessing, in fulfillment of prophecy, became as a tormenting plague to apostate Christendom.—Matthew 24:3-8, 14; Acts 1:8.

6 Revelation, written some 26 years after Jerusalem's destruction, also describes that plague. What does it add to Joel's description? Let us take up the record, as reported by

John: *"And the fifth angel blew his trumpet. And I saw a star that had fallen from heaven to the earth, and the key of the pit of the abyss was given him."* (Revelation 9:1) This "star" is different from that at Revelation 8:10 that John saw in the act of falling. He sees "a star that had fallen from heaven" and that now has an assignment with respect to this earth. Is this a spirit or a fleshly person? The holder of this "key of the pit of the abyss" is later described as hurling Satan into "the abyss." (Revelation 20:1-3) So he must be a mighty spirit person. At Revelation 9:11, John tells us that the locusts have "a king, the angel of the abyss." Both verses must refer to the same individual, since the angel holding the key of the abyss would logically be the angel of the abyss. And the star must symbolize Jehovah's appointed King, since anointed Christians acknowledge only the one angelic King, Jesus Christ.—Colossians 1:13; 1 Corinthians 15:25.

7 The account continues: *"And he opened the pit of the abyss, and smoke ascended out of the pit as the smoke of a great furnace, and the sun was darkened, also the air, by the smoke of the pit. And out of the smoke locusts came forth upon the earth; and authority was given them, the same authority as the scorpions of the earth have."* (Revelation 9:2, 3) Scripturally, "the abyss" is a place of inactivity, even of death. (Compare Romans 10:7; Revelation 17:8; 20:1, 3.) The small band of Jesus' brothers spent a short time in such an "abyss" of relative inactivity at the end of the first world war (1918-19). But when Jehovah poured his spirit upon his repentant servants in 1919, they swarmed forth to meet the challenge of the work that lay ahead.

8 As John observes, the release of the locusts is accompanied by much smoke, like

---

5. How has Joel's prophecy had a fulfillment since 1919?
6. (a) What did John see when the fifth angel blew his trumpet? (b) Whom does this "star" symbolize, and why?

7. (a) What happens when "the pit of the abyss" is opened? (b) What is "the abyss," and who spent a short time in it?
8. How is it that the release of the locusts is accompanied by much "smoke"?

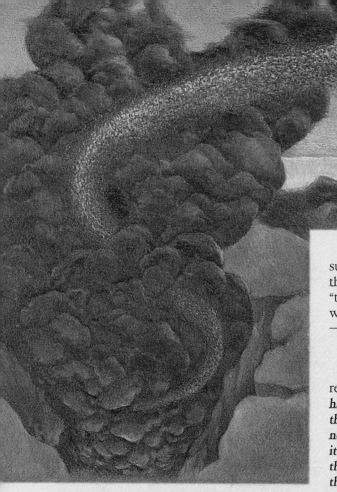

suffered an eclipse, and "the air" became thick with declarations of divine judgment as "the ruler of the authority of the air" of this world was shown to be Christendom's god. —Ephesians 2:2; John 12:31; 1 John 5:19.

Those Tormenting Locusts!

9 What battle instructions did those locusts receive? John reports: *"And they were told to harm no vegetation of the earth nor any green thing nor any tree, but only those men who do not have the seal of God on their foreheads. And it was granted the locusts, not to kill them, but that these should be tormented five months, and the torment upon them was as torment by a scorpion when it strikes a man. And in those days the men will seek death but will by no means find it, and they will desire to die but death keeps fleeing from them."—Revelation 9: 4-6.*

10 Notice that this plague is not directed first against the people or prominent ones among them—the 'vegetation and trees of the earth.' (Compare Revelation 8:7.) The locusts are to harm only those men who do not have the seal of God on their foreheads, those in Christendom who claim to be sealed but whose record belies that claim. (Ephesians 1:13, 14) Thus, the tormenting utterances of

"the smoke of a great furnace."* That is how it proved to be in 1919. The situation darkened for Christendom and for the world in general. (Compare Joel 2:30, 31.) The release of those locusts, the John class, was actually a defeat for Christendom's clergy, who had schemed and plotted to kill the Kingdom work for good and who now rejected God's Kingdom. Evidence of a smokelike pall started to spread over apostate Christendom as that locust band was given divine authority and began to exercise it in proclaiming powerful judgment messages. Christendom's "sun"—her appearance of enlightenment—

---

* Notice that this scripture cannot be used to prove that there was a fire in the abyss, as if the abyss were some kind of hellfire. John says he saw thick smoke that was "*as,*" or like, the smoke of a great furnace. (Revelation 9:2) He does not report seeing actual flames in the abyss.

---

9. What battle instructions did the locusts receive?
10. (a) Against whom primarily is the plague directed, and with what effect on them? (b) What kind of torment is involved? (See also footnote.)

144

these modern-day locusts were directed first against the religious leaders of Christendom. How these self-assuming men must have been tormented at hearing it publicly announced that not only were they failing to lead their flocks to heaven but they themselves would not get there!* Truly, it has been a case of 'the blind leading the blind'!—Matthew 15:14.

11 The torment lasts for five months. Is that a relatively short time? Not from the point of view of a literal locust. Five months describes the normal life span of one of these insects. Therefore, it is for as long as they live that the modern-day locusts keep stinging God's enemies. Moreover, the torment is so severe that men seek to die. True, we have no record that any of those who were stung by the locusts actually tried to kill themselves. But the expression helps us to picture the intensity of the torment—as though by the relentless assault of scorpions. It is like the suffering

---

* The Greek word used here comes from the root ba·sa·ni′zo, which is sometimes used of literal torture; however, it can also be used of mental torment. For example, at 2 Peter 2:8 we read that Lot "was tormenting his righteous soul" because of the evil that he saw in Sodom. The religious leaders of the apostolic era experienced mental torment although, of course, for a very different reason.

---

11. (a) How long are the locusts authorized to torment God's enemies, and why is that not really a short time? (b) How severe is the torment?

foreseen by Jeremiah for those unfaithful Israelites who would be scattered by the Babylonian conquerors and for whom death would be preferable to life.—Jeremiah 8:3; see also Ecclesiastes 4:2, 3.

12 Why is it granted to torment these ones, in a spiritual sense, and not to kill them? This is an initial woe in the exposing of the lies of Christendom and her failures, but only later, as the Lord's day progresses, will her death-like spiritual state be fully publicized. It will be during a second woe that a third of the men are killed.—Revelation 1:10; 9:12, 18; 11:14.

Locusts Equipped for Battle

13 What a remarkable appearance those locusts have! John describes it: *"And the likenesses of the locusts resembled horses prepared for battle; and upon their heads were what seemed to be crowns like gold, and their faces were as men's faces, but they had hair as women's hair. And their teeth were as those of lions; and they had breastplates like iron breastplates. And the sound of their wings was as the sound of chariots of many horses running into battle."*—Revelation 9:7-9.

---

12. Why are the locusts granted to torment the religious leaders of Christendom, in a spiritual sense, but not to kill them?

13. What appearance do the locusts have?

¹⁴ This well illustrates the loyal group of revived Christians in 1919. Like horses, they were ready for battle, eager to fight for the truth in the way described by the apostle Paul. (Ephesians 6:11-13; 2 Corinthians 10:4) On their heads John sees what *seem* to be crowns as of gold. It would not be proper for them to have actual crowns because they do not begin ruling while they are still on earth. (1 Corinthians 4:8; Revelation 20:4) But in 1919 they already had a royal appearance. They were brothers of the King, and their heavenly crowns were reserved for them provided they continued faithful to the end. —2 Timothy 4:8; 1 Peter 5:4.

¹⁵ In the vision, the locusts have iron breastplates, symbolizing unbreakable righteousness. (Ephesians 6:14-18) They also have men's faces, this feature pointing to the quality of love, since man was made in the image of God, who is love. (Genesis 1:26; 1 John 4:16). Their hair is long like a woman's, which well pictures subjection to their King, the angel of the abyss. And their teeth resemble a lion's teeth. A lion uses its teeth to tear meat. From 1919 onward, the John class has again been able to take in solid spiritual food, particularly the truths about God's Kingdom ruled by "the Lion that is of the tribe of Judah," Jesus Christ. Just as the lion symbolizes courage, so great courage has been needed to digest this hard-hitting message, to bring it forth in publications, and to distribute it around the globe. Those figurative locusts have made a lot of noise, like "the sound of chariots of many horses running into battle." After the example of first-century Christians, they do not intend to stay quiet. —1 Corinthians 11:7-15; Revelation 5:5.

¹⁶ This preaching involves more than the

Thine arrows are sharp in the heart of the King's enemies. (Psalm 45:5) Appearing with this caption, the above cartoon is typical of many published in the 1930's that stung "those men who do not have the seal of God"

spoken word! *"Also, they have tails and stings like scorpions; and in their tails is their authority to hurt the men five months."* (Revelation 9:10) What could this mean? As they go about their Kingdom work, Jehovah's Witnesses leave behind them publications—books, magazines, brochures, timely tracts. These contain authoritative statements, based on God's Word, for the people to read in their homes, and they have a scorpionlike sting because they warn of Jehovah's approaching day of vengeance. (Isaiah 61:2) Before the present generation of spiritual locusts lives out its life span, its divinely ordained work of declaring Jehovah's judgments will be completed—to the hurt of all stiff-necked blasphemers.

¹⁷ That locust band was overjoyed when a new magazine, *The Golden Age,* was announced at their 1919 convention. It was a biweekly magazine, designed to intensify the

---

14. Why did John's description of the locusts fit the group of revived Christians in 1919?
15. What is denoted by the locusts' (a) iron breastplates? (b) faces like men's? (c) hair like a woman's? (d) teeth as those of lions? (e) making a lot of noise?
16. What is the significance in the locusts' having "tails and stings like scorpions"?

17. (a) What was announced at the 1919 convention of the Bible Students that would intensify the sting of their witnessing? (b) How have the clergy been tormented, and how did they act in response?

sting of their witnessing.* Its issue No. 27, of September 29, 1920, exposed the clergy's duplicity in persecuting the Bible Students in the United States during the 1918-19 period. Through the 1920's and 1930's, *The Golden Age* tormented the clergy with further stinging articles and cartoons that exposed their crafty dabbling in politics, and especially the Catholic hierarchy's accords made with the Fascist and Nazi dictators. In response, the clergy 'framed mischief by law' and organized mob violence against God's people. —Psalm 94:20, *King James Version.*

World Rulers Put on Notice

¹⁸ The modern-day locusts had a job to do. The Kingdom good news had to be preached. Errors had to be exposed. Lost sheep had to be found. As the locusts went about these tasks, the world was forced to sit up and take notice. In obedience to the angels' trumpet blasts, the John class has continued to expose Christendom as deserving of Jehovah's adverse judgments. In response to the fifth trumpet, a particular aspect of these judgments was emphasized at a convention of the Bible Students in London, England, May 25-31, 1926. This featured a resolution, "A Testimony to the Rulers of the World," and a

---

* This magazine, now published semimonthly, was renamed *Consolation* in 1937 and *Awake!* in 1946.

---

18. What job did the locusts have to do, and what occurred in response to the fifth trumpet blast?

public talk at the Royal Albert Hall on "Why World Powers Are Tottering—The Remedy," the complete text of both of these being printed in a leading London newspaper the following day. Later, the locust band distributed worldwide, as a tract, 50 million copies of that resolution—a torment indeed to the clergy! Years later, people in England still spoke of this stinging exposé.

¹⁹ At this convention, the symbolic locusts received further fighting equipment, notably a new book entitled *Deliverance.* It included a Scriptural discussion of the sign proving that the 'man child' government, Christ's heavenly Kingdom, had been born in 1914. (Matthew 24:3-14; Luke 21:24-26; Revelation 12:1-10) Thereafter, it quoted the manifesto published in London in 1918 and signed by eight clergymen, who were described as being "among the world's greatest preachers." They represented the leading Protestant denominations—Baptist, Congregational, Presbyterian, Episcopalian, and Methodist. This manifesto proclaimed that "the present crisis points toward the close of the times of the Gentiles" and that "the revelation of the Lord may be expected at any moment." Yes, those clergymen had recognized the sign of Jesus' presence! But did they want to do anything about it? The book *Deliverance* informs us: "The most remarkable part of the affair is that

19. What further fighting equipment did the symbolic locusts receive, and what did it have to say about the London manifesto?

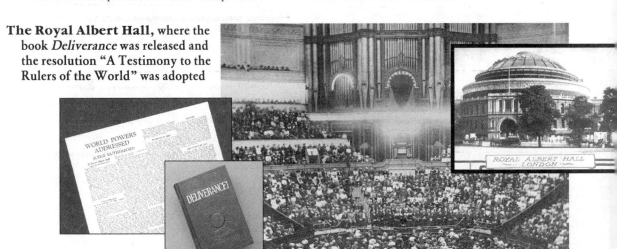

The Royal Albert Hall, where the book *Deliverance* was released and the resolution "A Testimony to the Rulers of the World" was adopted the very men who signed the manifesto subsequently repudiated it and rejected the evidence which proves that we are at the end of the world and in the day of the Lord's second presence."

[20] Rather than announce the incoming Kingdom of God, Christendom's clergy have

---

20. (a) What choice have the clergy made with regard to the locust band and their King? (b) Who does John say is over the locust band, and what is his name?

chosen to remain with Satan's world. They want no part with the locust band and their King, concerning whom John now observes: *"They have over them a king, the angel of the abyss. In Hebrew his name is Abaddon* [meaning "Destruction"], *but in Greek he has the name Apollyon* [meaning "Destroyer"]. *"* (*Revelation 9:11*) As "angel of the abyss" and "Destroyer," Jesus had truly released a plaguing woe on Christendom. But more is to follow!

The Second Woe —Armies of Cavalry

FROM 1919 onward, the symbolic locusts' invasion of Christendom has caused the clergy much discomfort. They have tried to stamp out the locusts, but these have kept coming on stronger than ever. (Revelation 9:7) And that is not all! John writes: *"The one woe is past. Look! Two more woes are coming after these things."* (*Revelation 9:12*) Further tormenting plagues are in store for Christendom.

[2] What is the source of the second woe? John writes: *"And the sixth angel blew his trumpet. And I heard one voice out of the horns of the golden altar that is before God say to the sixth angel, who had the trumpet: 'Untie the four angels that are bound at the great river*

---

1. Despite clergy efforts to stamp out the locusts, what has happened, and what does the coming of two more woes indicate?
2. (a) What happens when the sixth angel blows his trumpet? (b) What does the "one voice out of the horns of the golden altar" represent? (c) Why are four angels mentioned?

Euphrates.'" (*Revelation 9:13, 14*) The angels' release is in answer to the voice that comes from the horns of the golden altar. This is the golden incense altar, and twice previously the incense of the golden bowls from this altar has been associated with the prayers of the holy ones. (Revelation 5:8; 8:3, 4) Therefore, this one voice represents the united prayers of the holy ones on earth. They petition that they themselves be delivered for further energetic service as Jehovah's "messengers," this being the basic meaning of the Greek word here translated "angels." Why are there four angels? This symbolic number seems to indicate that they would be so organized as to cover the earth in its entirety.—Compare Revelation 7:1; 20:8.

[3] How had those angels been "bound at the great river Euphrates"? The river Euphrates in ancient times was the northeastern border of

---

3. How had the four angels been "bound at the great river Euphrates"?

The blowing of the sixth trumpet introduces the second woe

the land that Jehovah promised to Abraham. (Genesis 15:18; Deuteronomy 11:24) Apparently, the angels had been restrained at the border of their God-given land, or earthly realm of activity, held back from entering fully into the service that Jehovah had prepared for them. The Euphrates was also prominently associated with the city of Babylon, and after the fall of Jerusalem in 607 B.C.E., fleshly Israelites spent 70 years there in captivity, "bound at the great river Euphrates." (Psalm 137:1) The year 1919 found the spiritual Israelites bound in a similar restraint, disconsolate and asking Jehovah for guidance.

⁴ Happily, John can report: **"And the four angels were untied, who have been prepared for the hour and day and month and year, to kill a third of the men."** (Revelation 9:15) Jehovah is a precise Timekeeper. He has a timetable and is keeping to it. Hence, these messengers are released exactly on schedule and in time to accomplish what they have to do. Imagine their joy on coming forth from bondage in 1919, ready for work! They have a commission not only to torment but finally "to kill a third of the men." This is related to the plagues heralded by the first four trumpet blasts, which afflicted a third of the earth, the sea, the creatures in the sea, the fountains and rivers, and the heavenly light sources. (Reve-

lation 8:7-12) The four angels go further. They "kill," exposing to a completion Christendom's spiritually dead condition. Trumpeted pronouncements, made from 1922 onward and continuing to the present time, have accomplished this.

⁵ Remember, the heavenly angel has just sounded the sixth trumpet. Responding thereto, the sixth of the series of Bible Students' annual international conventions was held in Toronto, Ontario, Canada. The program there on Sunday, July 24, 1927, was aired through a chain of 53 radio stations, the most extensive broadcast network up to that time. That spoken message went out to an audience of possibly many millions. First, a forceful resolution exposed Christendom as spiritually dead and extended the invitation: "In this hour of perplexity Jehovah God bids the peoples to abandon and for ever forsake 'Christendom' or 'organized Christianity' and to turn completely away from it . . . ; [let] the peoples give their heart's devotion and allegiance wholly to Jehovah God and to his King and kingdom." "Freedom for the Peoples" was the title of the public talk that followed. J. F. Rutherford, president of the Watch Tower Society, delivered this in his usual dynamic style, appropriate to "the fire and the smoke and the sulphur" that John next observes in vision.

⁶ **"And the number of the armies of cavalry was two myriads of myriads: I heard the number of them. And this is how I saw the horses in the vision, and those seated on them: they had fire-red and hyacinth-blue and sulphur-yellow breastplates; and the heads of the horses were as heads of lions, and out of their mouths fire and smoke and sulphur issued forth. By these three plagues a third of the men were killed, from the fire and the smoke and the sulphur which issued forth from their mouths."—Revelation 9:16-18.**

---

4. What commission do the four angels have, and how has it been accomplished?

5. With regard to Christendom, how was the sound of the sixth trumpet blast echoed in 1927?
6. How does John describe the armies of cavalry that he next sees?

The four angels direct the greatest cavalry charge in history

⁷ Apparently, this cavalry thunders forth under the guiding direction of the four angels. What a fearsome spectacle! Imagine your reaction if you were to be the target of such a cavalry charge! Its very appearance would strike terror into your heart. Did you notice, though, how similar this cavalry is to the locusts that preceded it? The locusts were *like* horses; in the cavalry there *are* horses. Both, then, are involved in theocratic warfare. (Proverbs 21:31) The locusts had teeth like lions; the horses of the cavalry have heads like lions. Both are therefore tied in with the courageous Lion of the tribe of Judah, Jesus Christ, who is their Leader, Commander, and Exemplar.—Revelation 5:5; Proverbs 28:1.

⁸ Both the locusts and the cavalry share in Jehovah's work of judgment. The locusts emerged from smoke that portended woe and destructive fire for Christendom; from the mouths of the horses, there issue forth fire, smoke, and sulfur. The locusts had breastplates of iron, signifying that their hearts were protected by unbending devotion to righteousness; the cavalry wear breastplates colored red, blue, and yellow, reflecting the fire, smoke, and sulfur of the lethal judgment messages that gush from the mouths of the horses. (Compare Genesis 19:24, 28; Luke 17:29, 30.) The locusts had tails like scorpions for tormenting; the horses have tails like serpents for killing! It seems that what was started by the locusts is to be pursued by the cavalry with greater intensity to a completion.

⁹ So, what does this cavalry symbolize? Just as the anointed John class started the trumpetlike proclamation of Jehovah's judgment of divine vengeance against Christendom, with authority to 'sting and hurt,' so we would expect the same living group to be used in the 'killing,' that is, in making known that Christendom and its clergy are completely dead spiritually, cast off by Jehovah and

7, 8. (a) Under whose guiding direction does the cavalry thunder forth? (b) In what ways is the cavalry similar to the locusts that preceded it?

9. What does the cavalry symbolize?

ready for "the fiery furnace" of everlasting destruction. Indeed, all of Babylon the Great must perish. (Revelation 9:5, 10; 18:2, 8; Matthew 13:41-43) Preliminary to her destruction, however, the John class uses "the sword of the spirit, that is, God's word," in exposing Christendom's deathlike condition. The four angels and the riders of the horses give direction to this figurative killing of "a third of the men." (Ephesians 6:17; Revelation 9:15, 18) This indicates proper organization and theocratic direction under the oversight of the Lord Jesus Christ as the awesome band of Kingdom proclaimers charges forth to the battle.

Two Myriads of Myriads

[10] How can there be two myriads of myriads of this cavalry? A myriad is literally 10,-000. So two myriads of myriads would come to 200 million.* Happily, there are now millions of Kingdom proclaimers, but their number is far short of hundreds of millions! Re-

* Commentary on Revelation, by Henry Barclay Swete, notes regarding the number "two myriads of myriads": "These vast numbers forbid us to seek a literal fulfilment, and the description which follows supports this conclusion."

10. In what sense are there two myriads of myriads of cavalry?

member, though, Moses' words at Numbers 10:36: "Do return, O Jehovah, to the myriads of thousands of Israel." (Compare Genesis 24:60.) That would mean, literally, 'Do return to the tens of millions of Israel.' Israel, however, numbered only about two to three million in Moses' day. What, then, was Moses saying? No doubt he had in mind that the Israelites should be unnumbered as "the stars of the heavens and like the grains of sand that are on the seashore," rather than be counted. (Genesis 22:17; 1 Chronicles 27:23) So he used the word for "myriad" to indicate a large but unspecified number. Thus, The New English Bible renders this verse: "Rest, LORD of the countless thousands of Israel." This agrees with a second definition of the word for "myriad" found in Greek and Hebrew dictionaries: "an innumerable multitude," a "multitude."—The New Thayer's Greek-English Lexicon of the New Testament; Gesenius' A Hebrew and English Lexicon of the Old Testament, translated by Edward Robinson.

[11] Nevertheless, those of the John class still remaining on earth number fewer than

11. For the John class to become myriads even in a symbolic sense, what would be needed?

10,000—less than one literal myriad. How could they be likened to countless thousands of cavalry? To become myriads even in a symbolic sense, would they not need reinforcements? That is what they have needed, and by Jehovah's undeserved kindness, that is what they have received! From where have these come?

¹² From 1918 to 1922, the John class began to hold out to distressed humanity the happy prospect that "millions now living will never die." In 1923 it was also made known that the sheep of Matthew 25:31-34 would inherit life on earth under God's Kingdom. A similar hope was held out in the booklet *Freedom for the Peoples,* released at the international convention in 1927. In the early 1930's the upright Jehonadab class and the 'men sighing and groaning' over Christendom's sorry spiritual condition were shown to be identical with the symbolic sheep having earthly life prospects. (Ezekiel 9:4; 2 Kings 10:15, 16) Directing such ones to the modern-day "cities of refuge," *The Watchtower* of August 15, 1934, stated: "Those of the Jonadab class have heard the sound of God's trumpet and have heeded the warning by fleeing to God's organization and associating with God's people, and there they must abide."—Numbers 35:6.

¹³ In 1935 those of this Jonadab class were specially invited to attend the convention of Jehovah's Witnesses in Washington, D.C., U.S.A. There, on Friday, May 31, J. F. Rutherford gave his famous talk "The Great Multitude," in which he clearly showed that this group of Revelation 7:9 (*King James Version*) was the same as the sheep of Matthew 25:33 —a dedicated group with earthly hopes. As a harbinger of things to come, at that convention 840 new Witnesses were baptized, most of them being of the great crowd.*

---

* See the preceding pages 119-26; also *Vindication,* Book Three, published in 1932 by the Watch Tower Bible and Tract Society, pages 83-4.

12, 13. What historical developments from 1918 to 1935 indicated the source of the reinforcements?

¹⁴ Has this great crowd had a part in the cavalry charge that got under way in 1922 and that received particular emphasis at the Toronto convention in 1927? Under the direction of the four angels, the anointed John class, it certainly has! At the world-circling "Everlasting Good News" Assembly of 1963, it joined with the John class in a rousing resolution. This declared that the world "faces an earthquake of world trouble the like of which it has never known, and all its political institutions and its modern religious Babylon will be shaken to bits." The resolve was expressed that "we will continue to declare to all peoples without partiality the 'everlasting good news' concerning God's Messianic kingdom and concerning his judgments, which are like plagues to his enemies but which will be executed for the liberation of all persons who desire to worship God the Creator acceptably with spirit and with truth." This resolution was adopted enthusiastically at 24 assemblies around the globe by a grand total of 454,977 conventioners, of whom well over 95 percent were of the great crowd.

¹⁵ The great crowd has continued to declare its unqualified unity with the John class in pouring out the plagues on Christendom. In 1988 this great crowd made up more than 99.7 percent of the work force that Jehovah is using in the field. Its members are wholeheartedly in accord with the John class, concerning whom Jesus prayed at John 17:20, 21: "I make request, not concerning these only, but also concerning those putting faith in me through their word; in order that they may all be one, just as you, Father, are in union with me and I am in union with you, that they also may be in union with us, in order

---

14. Would the great crowd have a part in the symbolic cavalry charge, and what resolve was expressed in 1963?
15. (a) In 1988 the great crowd made up what percent of the work force that Jehovah is using in the field? (b) How does Jesus' prayer at John 17:20, 21 express the unity of the great crowd with the John class?

REVELATION CLIMAX

that the world may believe that you sent me forth." As the anointed John class takes the lead under Jesus, the zealous great crowd shares with them in the most devastating cavalry charge of all human history!*

¹⁶ That cavalry needs equipment for the warfare. And how wonderfully Jehovah has provided this! John describes it: *"For the authority of the horses is in their mouths and in their tails; for their tails are like serpents and have heads, and with these they do harm."* (*Revelation 9:19*) Jehovah has ordained his dedicated, baptized ministers for this service. Through the Theocratic Ministry School and other congregation meetings and schools, he has taught them how to preach the word, so that they are able to speak authoritatively with "the tongue of the taught ones." He has put his words in their mouths and sent them forth to make known his judgments "publicly and from house to house." (2 Timothy 4:2; Isaiah 50:4; 61:2; Jeremiah 1:9, 10; Acts 20:20) The John class and the great crowd have left behind a stinging message, corresponding to "tails," in the thousands of millions of Bibles, books, brochures, and magazines distributed over the years. To their opponents, who are advised of the coming "harm" from Jehovah, these armies of cavalry truly seem like two myriads of myriads.—Compare Joel 2:4-6.

¹⁷ A most zealous division of this cavalry is made up of brothers in lands where the work of Jehovah's Witnesses is under ban. Like sheep amidst wolves, these have to be "cautious as serpents and yet innocent as doves."

---

* Unlike the locusts, the armies of cavalry seen by John did not wear "what seemed to be crowns like gold." (Revelation 9:7) This harmonizes with the fact that the great crowd, which today makes up the larger part of the cavalry, does not hope to reign in God's heavenly Kingdom.

16. (a) How does John describe the mouths and tails of the symbolic horses? (b) How have the mouths of Jehovah's people been prepared for service? (c) What corresponds to the fact that "their tails are like serpents"?
17. Do Jehovah's Witnesses have any part in the cavalry charge in lands where literature cannot be distributed because the work is banned? Explain.

THE SECOND WOE—ARMIES OF CAVALRY

The innumerable cavalry has distributed countless millions of Bible-based publications

In obedience to Jehovah, they cannot stop speaking about the things they have seen and heard. (Matthew 10:16; Acts 4:19, 20; 5:28, 29, 32) Since they have little or no printed material to distribute publicly, must we conclude that they have no share in the cavalry charge? Not at all! They have their mouths and authority from Jehovah to use them to express Bible truth. This they do, informally and persuasively, establishing studies in the Bible and "bringing the many to righteousness." (Daniel 12:3) Though they may not sting with their tails in the sense of leaving behind hard-hitting literature, symbolic fire, smoke, and sulfur issue from their mouths as they witness tactfully and with discretion concerning Jehovah's approaching day of vindication.

¹⁸ In other places, the Kingdom literature continues to expose Christendom's Babylonish doctrines and ways, bringing her deserved harm in a figurative way. By using updated printing methods, this numer-

18. In how many languages and to what number has this cavalry distributed the plaguing message in printed form?

The rest of the men did not repent

ous cavalry in the 50 years before 1987 was able to distribute, in upwards of 200 of earth's languages, Bibles, books, magazines, and brochures to the astronomical number of 7,821,-078,415 copies—many times more than a literal two myriads of myriads. What a sting those tails have inflicted!

¹⁹ Jehovah purposed that this plaguing message should "kill a third of the men." Hence, its specific target has been Christendom. But it has reached lands far beyond Christendom, including many where the hypocrisy of Christendom's religions is well known. Have the people of these lands drawn closer to Jehovah as a result of seeing the plaguing of this corrupt religious organization? Many have! There has been a ready response among meek and lovable people who live in areas outside Christendom's immediate sphere of influence. But as for the people in general, John describes their reaction: *"But the rest of the men who were not killed by these plagues did not repent of the works of their hands, so that they should not worship the demons and the idols of gold and silver and copper and stone and wood, which can neither see nor hear nor walk; and they did not repent of their murders nor of their spiritistic practices nor of their fornication nor of their thefts."* (*Revelation 9:20, 21*) There will be no world conversion of such unrepentant ones. All who persist in their wicked ways will have to face adverse judgment from Jehovah in the great day of his vindication. But "everyone who calls on the name of Jehovah will get away safe."—Joel 2:32; Psalm 145:20; Acts 2:20, 21.

²⁰ What we have just discussed is part of the second woe. There is more to come before this woe runs its course, as we shall see in the chapters that follow.

19, 20. (a) Though the specific target of the plaguing messages has been Christendom, how have some in lands far beyond Christendom responded? (b) How does John describe the reaction of the people in general?

A Sweet-and-Bitter Message

THE second woe has been devastating. It has plagued Christendom and her leaders, "a third of the men," who are thus exposed as being spiritually dead. (Revelation 9:15) John must have wondered after that what the third woe could possibly bring. But wait! The second woe is not yet finished—not until we reach the point recorded at Revelation 11:14. Before then, John is to witness a turn of events in which he himself takes an active part. It begins with an awe-inspiring sight:

2 *"And I saw another strong angel descending from heaven, arrayed with a cloud, and a rainbow was upon his head, and his face was as the sun, and his feet were as fiery pillars."*—Revelation 10:1.

3 Who is this "strong angel"? It is evidently the glorified Jesus Christ in another role. He is arrayed with a cloud of invisibility, which reminds us of John's earlier words about Jesus: "Look! He is coming with the clouds, and every eye will see him, and those who pierced him." (Revelation 1:7; compare Matthew 17:2-5.) The rainbow upon his head reminds us of John's earlier vision of Jehovah's throne, with its "rainbow like an emerald in appearance." (Revelation 4:3; compare Ezekiel 1:28.) That rainbow suggested the serenity and peace surrounding God's throne. In the same way, this rainbow on the angel's head would identify him as a special

peace messenger, Jehovah's foretold "Prince of Peace."—Isaiah 9:6, 7.

4 The face of the strong angel was "as the sun." Earlier, in his vision of Jesus at the divine temple, John had noted that Jesus' countenance was "as the sun when it shines in its power." (Revelation 1:16) Jesus, as "the sun of righteousness," shines forth with healing in his wings for the benefit of those who fear Jehovah's name. (Malachi 4:2) Not only the face but also the feet of this angel are glorious, "as fiery pillars." His firm stance is that of the One to whom Jehovah has given "all authority . . . in heaven and on the earth." —Matthew 28:18; Revelation 1:14, 15.

5 John observes further: *"And he had in his hand a little scroll opened. And he set his right*

---

4. What is denoted (a) by the face of the strong angel being "as the sun"? (b) by the angel's feet being "as fiery pillars"?
5. What does John see in the hand of the strong angel?

Vision _____ *6*

Revelation 10:1–11:19

Subject: The vision of the little scroll; temple experiences; the blowing of the seventh trumpet

Time of fulfillment: From the enthronement of Jesus in 1914 to the great tribulation

---

1, 2. (a) In what did the second woe result, and when will this woe be declared over? (b) Whom does John now see descending from heaven?
3. (a) Who is the "strong angel"? (b) What is the significance of the rainbow upon his head?

foot upon the sea, but his left one upon the earth." (*Revelation 10:2*) Another scroll? Yes, but this time it is not sealed. With John, we can expect soon to see further thrilling disclosures. First, though, we are given the setting for what is to follow.

⁶ Let us return to the description of Jesus. His fiery feet are upon the earth and the sea, over which he now exercises full authority. It is just as stated in the prophetic psalm: "You [Jehovah] also proceeded to make him [Jesus] a little less than godlike ones, and with glory and splendor you then crowned him. You make him dominate over the works of your hands; everything you have put under his feet: small cattle and oxen, all of them, and also the beasts of the open field, the birds of heaven and the fish of the sea, anything passing through the paths of the seas." (Psalm 8:5-8; see also Hebrews 2:5-9.) This psalm was completely fulfilled in 1914, when Jesus was installed as King of God's Kingdom and the time of the end began. Thus, what John sees here in vision applies since that year.—Psalm 110:1-6; Acts 2:34-36; Daniel 12:4.

The Seven Thunders

⁷ John's contemplation of this strong angel is interrupted by the angel himself: *"And he [the angel] cried out with a loud voice just as when a lion roars. And when he cried out, the seven thunders uttered their own voices."* (*Revelation 10:3*) Such a powerful shout would catch John's attention, confirming that Jesus is truly "the Lion that is of the tribe of Judah." (Revelation 5:5) John would also be aware that Jehovah, too, is sometimes said to "roar." Jehovah's roaring prophetically heralds the regathering of spiritual Israel and the coming of the destructive "day of Jehovah." (Hosea 11:10; Joel 3:14, 16; Amos 1:2; 3:7, 8) Clearly, then, the lionlike cry of this strong angel forebodes similar great events for the sea and the earth. It calls on the seven thunders to speak.

⁸ John has previously heard thunders proceeding from the very throne of Jehovah. (Revelation 4:5) Back in David's day, literal thunder was at times spoken of as "the voice of Jehovah." (Psalm 29:3) When Jehovah audibly proclaimed his purpose to glorify his own name in the days of Jesus' earthly

---

6. (a) Why is it appropriate that Jesus' feet are upon the earth and the sea? (b) When was Psalm 8:5-8 completely fulfilled?

7. In what manner does the strong angel cry out, and what is the significance of his cry?
8. What are the 'voices of the seven thunders'?

ministry, to many it sounded like thunder. (John 12:28, 29) Therefore, it is reasonable to conclude that the 'voices of the seven thunders' are Jehovah's own expression of his purposes. The fact that there were "seven" thunders suggests the completeness of what John heard.

⁹ But listen! Another voice sounds forth. It brings a command that must seem strange to John: *"Now when the seven thunders spoke, I was at the point of writing; but I heard a voice out of heaven say: 'Seal up the things the seven thunders spoke, and do not write them down.'"* (*Revelation 10:4*) John must have been anxious to hear and record those thunderous messages, just as the John class today has waited eagerly for Jehovah to disclose his divine purposes for publication. Such revelations come only at Jehovah's appointed time. —Luke 12:42; see also Daniel 12:8, 9.

The Finish of the Sacred Secret

¹⁰ Meantime, Jehovah has another commission for John. After the seven thunders have sounded, the strong angel speaks again: *"And the angel that I saw standing on the sea and on the earth raised his right hand to heaven, and by the One who lives forever and ever, who created the heaven and the things in it and the earth and the things in it and the sea and the things in it, he swore: 'There will be no delay any longer.'"* (*Revelation 10:5, 6*) By whom does the strong angel swear? The glorified Jesus swears, not by himself, but by the highest Authority of all, Jehovah, the immortal Creator of the heavens and the earth. (Isaiah 45:12, 18) With this oath, the angel assures John that there will be no further delay on God's part.

¹¹ The Greek word here translated "delay" is *khro′nos,* which literally means "time."

9. What does a voice out of heaven command?
10. By whom does the strong angel swear, and to what pronouncement?
11, 12. (a) What is meant by there being "no delay any longer"? (b) What is brought to a finish?

A SWEET-AND-BITTER MESSAGE

Some have thus felt that this declaration of the angel should be translated: "There will be no more time," as though time as we know it will end. But the word *khro′nos* here is used without a definite article. So it does not mean time in general but, rather, "a time" or "a period of time." In other words, there will be no further period of time (or, delay) by Jehovah. A Greek verb derived from *khro′nos* is used also at Hebrews 10:37, where Paul, quoting from Habakkuk 2:3, 4, writes that "he who is coming . . . will not delay."

¹² "No delay any longer"—how those words appeal to the aging John class today! In what respect is there no delay? John informs us: *"But in the days of the sounding of the seventh angel, when he is about to blow his trumpet, the sacred secret of God according to the good news which he declared to his own slaves the prophets is indeed brought to a finish."* (*Revelation 10:7*) Jehovah's time is here for bringing his sacred secret to its happy climax, with glorious success!

¹³ What is this sacred secret? It involves the

13. What is the sacred secret of God?

seed first promised in Eden, which proved primarily to be Jesus Christ. (Genesis 3:15; 1 Timothy 3:16) It also has to do with the identity of the woman out of whom the Seed comes. (Isaiah 54:1; Galatians 4:26-28) Further, it takes in the secondary members of the seed class and the Kingdom in which the Seed reigns. (Luke 8:10; Ephesians 3:3-9; Colossians 1:26, 27; 2:2; Revelation 1:5, 6) The good news about this unique heavenly Kingdom must be preached in all the earth during the time of the end.—Matthew 24:14.

[14] Surely, this is the very best of news. Yet, at Revelation 11:14, 15, the third woe is linked with the Kingdom. Why? Because for those of mankind who prefer Satan's system of things, the trumpeting forth of the good news that the sacred secret of God is brought to a finish—that is, God's Messianic Kingdom is here—is woeful news. (Compare 2 Corinthians 2:16.) It means that the world arrangement that they like so well is near to being destroyed. The voices of the seven thunders, containing such ominous storm warnings, become clearer and louder with the approach of Jehovah's great day of vengeance. —Zephaniah 1:14-18.

The Opened Scroll

[15] While John is waiting for the blowing of this seventh trumpet and the bringing to a finish of the sacred secret of God, he is given a further assignment: *"And the voice that I heard out of heaven is speaking again with me and saying: 'Go, take the opened scroll that is in the hand of the angel who is standing on the sea and on the earth.' And I went away to the angel and told him to give me the little scroll. And he said to me: 'Take it and eat it up, and it will make your belly bitter, but in your mouth*

it will be sweet as honey.' And I took the little scroll out of the hand of the angel and ate it up, and in my mouth it was sweet as honey; but when I had eaten it up, my belly was made bitter. And they say to me: 'You must prophesy again with regard to peoples and nations and tongues and many kings.'"—Revelation 10: 8-11.*

[16] John's experience is rather similar to that of the prophet Ezekiel during his exile in the land of Babylonia. He too was commanded to eat a scroll that tasted sweet in his mouth. But when it filled his stomach, it made him responsible to foretell bitter things for the rebellious house of Israel. (Ezekiel 2:8–3:15) The opened scroll that the glorified Jesus Christ gives to John is likewise a divine message. John is to preach regarding "peoples and nations and tongues and many kings." To feed upon this scroll is sweet for him because it is from a divine source. (Compare Psalm 119:103; Jeremiah 15:15, 16.) But he finds it bitter to digest because—as previously with Ezekiel—it foretells unsavory things for rebellious humans.—Psalm 145:20.

[17] The ones who tell John to prophesy again are doubtless Jehovah God and Jesus Christ. John, although exiled on the island of Patmos, has already prophesied regarding peoples, nations, tongues, and kings through the information recorded so far in the book of Revelation. The word "again" means that he must write and publish the rest of the information recorded in the book of Revelation. But remember, John is here actually participating in the prophetic vision. What he records is, in fact, a prophecy to be fulfilled after 1914, when the strong angel takes up his position astride the earth and the

---

14. Why is the third woe linked with God's Kingdom?
15. What do the voice out of heaven and the strong angel tell John, and what is the effect on John?

16. (a) How did the prophet Ezekiel have an experience similar to John's? (b) Why did the little scroll taste sweet to John, but why was it bitter to digest?
17. (a) Who are the ones who tell John to prophesy "again," and what does this mean? (b) When was the dramatic portrayal seen by John due to be fulfilled?

REVELATION CLIMAX

sea. What, then, does this dramatic portrayal mean to the John class today?

The Little Scroll Today

18 What John sees foreshadows remarkably the experience of the John class at the beginning of the Lord's day. Their understanding of Jehovah's purposes, including the implication of the seven thunders, was then incomplete. Nevertheless, they had a deep interest in Revelation, and Charles Taze Russell had commented on many parts of it during his lifetime. After his death in 1916, many of his writings were collected and published in a book entitled *The Finished Mystery*. In time, though, this book proved to be unsatisfactory as an explanation of Revelation. The remnant of Christ's brothers had to wait a while longer, until the visions started to be fulfilled, for an accurate understanding of that inspired record.

19 Like John, however, they were used by Jehovah even before the voices of the seven thunders were fully published. They had preached diligently for 40 years before 1914, and they had struggled to stay active during the first world war. They had proved to be the ones who, when the master arrived, were found to be giving the domestics food at the proper time. (Matthew 24:45-47) Thus, in 1919 they were the ones who were given the opened little scroll—that is, an open message to preach to mankind. Like Ezekiel they had a message for an unfaithful organization —Christendom—that claimed to be serving God but, in fact, was not. Like John they had to preach some more regarding "peoples and nations and tongues and many kings."

20 John's eating up the scroll pictured that

18. At the beginning of the Lord's day, what interest did the John class show in the book of Revelation?
19. (a) How was the John class used by Jehovah God even before the voices of the seven thunders were fully published? (b) When was the John class given the opened little scroll, and what did this mean for them?
20. What did John's eating up the scroll picture?

A SWEET-AND-BITTER MESSAGE

Jesus' brothers accepted this assignment. It became a part of them to the extent that they were now identified with this portion of God's inspired Word, drawing nourishment from it. But what they had to preach contained expressions of Jehovah's judgments that were unpalatable to many of mankind. Indeed, it included the plagues foretold in Revelation chapter 8. It was sweet, however, to these sincere Christians to know those judgments and to realize that they were again being used by Jehovah in proclaiming them.—Psalm 19:9, 10.

21 In time, the message of this scroll also became sweet to the "great crowd . . . out of all nations and tribes and peoples and tongues" who were found to be sighing on account of the detestable things they saw being done in Christendom. (Revelation 7:9; Ezekiel 9:4) These, too, vigorously proclaim the good news, using sweet, gracious words to describe Jehovah's marvelous provision for sheeplike Christians. (Psalm 37:11, 29; Colossians 4:6) But to goatlike people, this is bad news. Why? It means that the system in which they trust—and which may even have brought them a transitory satisfaction—must go. For them, the good news spells doom.—Matthew 25:31-34, 41, 46; compare Deuteronomy 28:15; 2 Corinthians 2:15, 16.

21. (a) How has the message of the little scroll become sweet also to the great crowd? (b) Why is the good news bad news for goatlike people?

The John class and their associates proclaim a sweet-and-bitter message to all mankind

Chapter 25

Reviving the Two Witnesses

BEFORE the second woe is finally past, the strong angel calls upon John to take part in another prophetic presentation, this one having to do with the temple. (Revelation 9:12; 10:1) Here is what John reports: *"And a reed like a rod was given me as he said: 'Get up and measure the temple sanctuary of God and the altar and those worshiping in it.'"—Revelation 11:1.*

The Temple Sanctuary

² The temple here mentioned cannot be any literal temple in Jerusalem, since the last of these was destroyed by the Romans in 70 C.E. The apostle Paul, however, showed that even before that destruction, there had appeared another temple sanctuary that would endure right up to our day. This was the great spiritual temple that fulfilled the prophetic types provided by the tabernacle and later by the temples built in Jerusalem. It is "the true tent, which Jehovah put up, and not man," and its High Priest is Jesus, whom Paul describes as having already "sat down at the right hand of the throne of the Majesty in the heavens." Its Most Holy is the location of Jehovah's presence in heaven itself.—Hebrews 8:1, 2; 9:11, 24.

³ The apostle Paul explains that the curtain of the tabernacle, separating the Most Holy from the Holy compartment, pictures Jesus' flesh. When Jesus sacrificed his life, this curtain was rent in two, showing that Jesus' flesh was no longer a barrier to his entry into Jehovah's presence in heaven. On the basis of Jesus' sacrifice, his anointed underpriests who died faithful would, in due course, also pass into the heavens. (Matthew 27:50, 51; Hebrews 9:3; 10:19, 20) Paul points out, too, that the continual sacrifices of animals at the tabernacle pointed forward to Jesus' one sacrifice of his perfect human life. The altar of sacrifice in the courtyard represented Jehovah's provision, according to his will, for accepting Jesus' sacrifice in behalf of the "many"—of the anointed and, later, of the other sheep—who would be "earnestly looking for him for their salvation."—Hebrews 9:28; 10:9, 10; John 10:16.

⁴ From this divinely inspired information, we can conclude that the Holy Place in the tabernacle symbolizes a holy condition enjoyed first by Christ and then by the anointed members of the royal priesthood of the 144,000 while they are still on earth, before entering through "the curtain." (Hebrews 6:19, 20; 1 Peter 2:9) It well represents their having been adopted as spiritual sons of God, even as God acknowledged Jesus to be his Son following Jesus' baptism in the Jordan in 29 C.E. (Luke 3:22; Romans 8:15) And what of the inner courtyard, the only part of the tabernacle visible to nonpriestly Israelites and the place where the sacrifices were made? This pictures the perfect standing of

---

1. What does the strong angel call upon John to do?
2. (a) What temple sanctuary would endure right up to our day? (b) Who is the High Priest of the temple sanctuary, and what is its Most Holy?
3. At the tabernacle, what was pictured by (a) the curtain separating the Most Holy from the Holy? (b) the animal sacrifices? (c) the altar of sacrifice?

---

4. What was symbolized by (a) the Holy Place (b) the inner courtyard?

the man Jesus that qualified him to offer his life for mankind. It also represents the righteous standing as holy ones, imputed on the basis of Jesus' sacrifice, that his anointed followers enjoy while on earth.*—Romans 1:7; 5:1.

Measuring the Temple Sanctuary

5 John is told to "measure the temple sanctuary of God and the altar and those worshiping in it." What does this imply? In the Hebrew Scripture prophecies, such measuring provided a guarantee that justice, tempered with mercy, would be rendered on the basis of Jehovah's perfect standards. In the days of wicked King Manasseh, the prophetic measuring of Jerusalem testified to an unalterable judgment of destruction on that city. (2 Kings 21:13; Lamentations 2:8) Later, however, when Jeremiah saw Jerusalem being measured, this confirmed that the city would be rebuilt. (Jeremiah 31:39; see also Zechariah 2:2-8.) Likewise, the extensive and detailed measuring of the visionary temple witnessed by Ezekiel was a guarantee to the Jewish exiles in Babylon that true worship would be restored in their homeland. It was also a reminder that, in view of their errors, Israel henceforth had to measure up to God's holy standards.—Ezekiel 40:3, 4; 43:10.

6 Therefore, when John is commanded to measure the temple sanctuary and those priests worshiping in it, it is a sign that nothing can prevent the fulfillment of Jehovah's purposes regarding the temple arrangement and those associated with it, and that those purposes are nearing their climax. Now that all things have been placed under the feet of

---

* For a full discussion of this great spiritual temple, see the article "The One True Temple at Which to Worship," in the December 1, 1972, issue of The Watchtower.

5. In Hebrew Scripture prophecies, what was implied by (a) the measuring of Jerusalem? (b) the measuring of Ezekiel's visionary temple?
6. Of what is John's being told to measure the temple sanctuary and the priests worshiping in it a sign? Explain.

Jehovah's strong angel, it is the time for "the mountain of the house of Jehovah" to become "firmly established above the top of the mountains." (Isaiah 2:2-4) Jehovah's pure worship must be exalted, after centuries of Christendom's apostasy. It is also time for those of Jesus' faithful brothers who have died to be resurrected into "the Holy of Holies." (Daniel 9:24; 1 Thessalonians 4:14-16; Revelation 6:11; 14:4) And the last sealed ones on earth of "the slaves of our God" must be measured according to the divine standards in order to qualify for their permanent place in the temple arrangement as spirit-begotten sons of God. The John class today is fully aware of those holy standards and is determined to measure up to them.—Revelation 7: 1-3; Matthew 13:41, 42; Ephesians 1:13, 14; compare Romans 11:20.

The Trampling of the Courtyard

7 Why was John forbidden to measure the courtyard? He tells us in these words: *"But as for the courtyard that is outside the temple sanctuary, cast it clear out and do not measure it, because it has been given to the nations, and they will trample the holy city underfoot for forty-two months." (Revelation 11:2)* We have noted that the inner courtyard pictures the righteous standing on earth of spirit-begotten Christians. As we shall see, the reference here is to the literal 42 months extending from October 1914 into 1918, when all professing Christians were put to a severe test. Would they uphold Jehovah's righteous standards during those war years? Most did not. En bloc, the clergy of Christendom put nationalism ahead of obedience to divine law. On both sides of the war, which was fought mainly in Christendom, the clergy preached the young men into the trenches. Millions

---

7. (a) Why is John told not to measure the courtyard? (b) When was the holy city trampled underfoot for 42 months? (c) How did the clergy of Christendom fail to uphold Jehovah's righteous standards for 42 months?

John measures the spiritual temple
—standards are to be met
by the anointed
priesthood

were slaughtered. By the time that judgment started with the house of God in 1918, the United States had also entered that bloodspilling, and the clergy of all of Christendom had incurred a bloodguilt that still cries out for divine vengeance. (1 Peter 4:17) Their being cast out has become permanent, irreversible.—Isaiah 59:1-3, 7, 8; Jeremiah 19: 3, 4.

[8] What, though, of the small group of Bible Students? Were they to be measured immediately in 1914 by their adherence to divine standards? No. Like the professed Christians of Christendom, they too must be tested. They were 'cast clear out, given to the nations' to be severely tried and persecuted. Many of them realized that they should not go out and kill their fellowman, but as yet they did not fully appreciate Christian neutrality. (Micah 4:3; John 17:14, 16; 1 John 3:15) Under pressure from the nations, some compromised.

[9] How was it, though, that the holy city was trampled underfoot by those nations? Clearly, this does not refer to the Jerusalem that was destroyed over 25 years before Revelation was written. Rather, the holy city is New Jerusalem, described later in Revelation, that is represented now on earth by the remaining anointed Christians in the temple's inner courtyard. In time, these also will become a part of the holy city. So trampling on them is tantamount to trampling on the city itself. —Revelation 21:2, 9-21.

8. During World War I, what did many of the Bible Students realize, but what did they not fully appreciate?

9. What is the holy city that was trampled underfoot by the nations, and on earth, who represents this city?

REVIVING THE TWO WITNESSES

The Two Witnesses

¹⁰ Even while being trampled on, these loyal ones do not cease to be Jehovah's faithful witnesses. Hence, the prophecy continues: *"'And I will cause my two witnesses to prophesy a thousand two hundred and sixty days dressed in sackcloth.' These are symbolized by the two olive trees and the two lampstands and are standing before the Lord of the earth."* —Revelation 11:3, 4.

¹¹ These faithful anointed Christians needed the quality of endurance, for they had to prophesy "in sackcloth." What did this mean? In Bible times sackcloth often symbolized mourning. Wearing it was a sign that the person had been brought low in sorrow or distress. (Genesis 37:34; Job 16:15, 16; Ezekiel 27:31) Sackcloth was associated with the mournful messages of doom or grief that God's prophets had to proclaim. (Isaiah 3:8, 24-26; Jeremiah 48:37; 49:3) The wearing of sackcloth could indicate humility or repentance in view of divine warning. (Jonah 3:5) The sackcloth worn by the two witnesses appears to indicate their humble endurance in announcing Jehovah's judgments. They were witnesses proclaiming his day of vengeance that would bring mourning also to the nations.—Deuteronomy 32:41-43.

¹² The John class had to preach this message for a definitely stated time: 1,260 days, or 42 months, the same length of time that the holy city was to be trampled underfoot. This period seems to be literal, since it is expressed in two different ways, first in months and then in days. Additionally, at the beginning of the Lord's day, there was a marked period of three and a half years when the hard experiences of God's people matched the events

prophesied here—starting from the outbreak of the first world war in the latter part of 1914 and continuing to the early part of 1918. (Revelation 1:10) They preached a "sackcloth" message concerning Jehovah's judgment of Christendom and the world.

¹³ The fact that they were symbolized by two witnesses confirms to us that their message was accurate and well founded. (Compare Deuteronomy 17:6; John 8:17, 18.) John calls them "the two olive trees and the two lampstands," saying that they "are standing before the Lord of the earth." This is an evident reference to the prophecy of Zechariah, who saw a seven-branched lampstand and two olive trees. The olive trees were said to picture "the two anointed ones," that is, Governor Zerubbabel and High Priest Joshua, "standing alongside the Lord of the whole earth."—Zechariah 4:1-3, 14.

¹⁴ Zechariah lived in a time of rebuilding, and his vision of the two olive trees meant that Zerubbabel and Joshua would be blessed with Jehovah's spirit in strengthening the people for the work. The vision of the lampstand reminded Zechariah not to 'despise the day of small things' because Jehovah's purposes would be carried out—"'not by a military force, nor by power, but by my spirit,' Jehovah of armies has said." (Zechariah 4: 6, 10; 8:9) The small band of Christians persistently carrying the light of truth to mankind during the first world war would similarly be used in a rebuilding work. They too would be a source of encouragement and, few as they were, would learn to rely on Jehovah's strength, not despising the day of small beginnings.

---

10. What are Jehovah's faithful witnesses to do while being trampled on?

11. What did it mean for the faithful anointed Christians to prophesy "in sackcloth"?

12. Why does the time period during which the holy city was to be trampled underfoot seem to be literal?

13. (a) What is denoted by the fact that the anointed Christians were symbolized by two witnesses? (b) What prophecy of Zechariah is brought to mind by John's calling the two witnesses "the two olive trees and the two lampstands"?

14. (a) What was indicated by Zechariah's vision of the two olive trees? and the lampstand? (b) What would the anointed Christians experience during the first world war?

The rebuilding work by Zerubbabel and Joshua indicated that in the Lord's day small beginnings would be followed by great increase among Jehovah's Witnesses. Printing facilities such as the ones shown above, which are in Brooklyn, New York, have had to be greatly expanded in order to help meet their needs

¹⁵ The fact that they were described as two witnesses also reminds us of the transfiguration. In that vision, three of Jesus' apostles saw him in Kingdom glory, accompanied by Moses and Elijah. This foreshadowed Jesus' sitting down on his glorious throne in 1914 to accomplish a work prefigured by those two prophets. (Matthew 17:1-3; 25:31) Fittingly, the two witnesses are now seen to perform signs reminiscent of those of Moses and Elijah. For example, John says of them: **"And if anyone wants to harm them, fire issues forth from their mouths and devours their enemies; and if anyone should want to harm them, in this manner he must be killed. These have the authority to shut up heaven that no rain should fall during the days of their prophesying."**—Revelation 11:5, 6a.

¹⁶ This reminds us of the time when Moses' authority was challenged in Israel. That prophet uttered fiery words of judgment, and Jehovah destroyed the rebels, consuming 250 of them by literal fire from heaven. (Numbers 16:1-7, 28-35) Similarly, Christendom's leaders defied the Bible Students, saying that these had never graduated from theological colleges. But God's witnesses had higher credentials as ministers: those meek persons who heeded their Scriptural message. (2 Corinthians 3:2, 3) In 1917 the Bible Students published *The Finished Mystery,* a powerful commentary on Revelation and Ezekiel. This was followed by the distribution of 10,000,-000 copies of the four-page tract *The Bible Students Monthly* with the feature article entitled "The Fall of Babylon—Why Christendom Must Now Suffer—the Final Outcome." In the United States, the irate clergy used the war hysteria as an excuse to get the book banned. In other countries the book was censored. Nevertheless, God's servants

---

15. (a) The fact that the anointed Christians were described as two witnesses also reminds us of what? Explain. (b) What kind of signs are the two witnesses authorized to perform?

---

16. (a) How does the sign involving fire remind us of the time when Moses' authority was challenged in Israel? (b) How did Christendom's clergy defy the Bible Students and stir up trouble for them during the first world war, and how did these fight back?

REVIVING THE TWO WITNESSES

Fiery judgment messages proclaimed by the two witnesses were foreshadowed by the prophetic work of Moses and Elijah

kept fighting back with fiery issues of the four-page tract entitled *Kingdom News*. As the Lord's day proceeded, other publications would make clear Christendom's spiritually defunct condition.—Compare Jeremiah 5:14.

17 What of Elijah? In the days of the kings of Israel, this prophet proclaimed a drought as an expression of Jehovah's indignation on the Baal-worshiping Israelites. It lasted three and a half years. (1 Kings 17:1; 18:41-45; Luke 4:25; James 5:17) Later, when unfaithful King Ahaziah sent soldiers to force Elijah to come

into his royal presence, the prophet called down fire from heaven to consume the soldiers. Only when a military commander showed proper respect for his position as a prophet did Elijah consent to accompany him to the king. (2 Kings 1:5-16) Likewise, between 1914 and 1918, the anointed remnant boldly drew attention to the spiritual drought in Christendom and warned of fiery judgment at "the coming of the great and fear-inspiring day of Jehovah."—Malachi 4:1, 5; Amos 8:11.

18 John goes on to say of the two witnesses: *"And they have authority over the waters to turn them into blood and to strike the earth with every sort of plague as often as they wish."* (*Revelation 11:6b*) In order to persuade Pha-

---

17. (a) What events in the days of Elijah involved a drought and fire? (b) How did fire issue forth from the mouths of the two witnesses, and what drought was involved?

18. (a) What authority is given the two witnesses, and how was this similar to that given Moses? (b) How did the two witnesses expose Christendom?

raoh to let Israel go free, Jehovah used Moses in striking oppressive Egypt with plagues, including the turning of water into blood. Centuries later, the Philistine enemies of Israel well remembered Jehovah's acts against Egypt, causing them to cry: "Who will save us from the hand of this majestic God? This is the God that was the smiter of Egypt with every sort of slaughter ["plague," *Revised Standard Version*] in the wilderness." (1 Samuel 4:8; Psalm 105:29) Moses portrayed Jesus, who had authority to pronounce God's judgments on the religious leaders of his day. (Matthew 23:13; 28:18; Acts 3:22) And during the first world war Christ's brothers, the two witnesses, exposed the death-dealing quality of "the waters" that Christendom was serving to her flocks.

The Two Witnesses Are Killed

¹⁹ So severe was this plague on Christendom that after the two witnesses had prophesied for 42 months in sackcloth, Christendom used her worldly influence to have them 'killed.' John writes: *"And when they have finished their witnessing, the wild beast that ascends out of the abyss will make war with them and conquer them and kill them. And their corpses will be on the broad way of the great city which is in a spiritual sense called Sodom and Egypt, where their Lord was also impaled. And those of the peoples and tribes and tongues and nations will look at their corpses for three and a half days, and they do not let their corpses be laid in a tomb. And those dwelling on the earth rejoice over them and enjoy themselves, and they will send gifts to one another, because these two prophets tormented those dwelling on the earth."*—Revelation 11:7-10.

²⁰ This is the first of 37 references in Revelation to a wild beast. In due course we will examine this and other beasts in detail. Suffice it to say for now that "the wild beast that ascends out of the abyss" is of Satan's design, a living political system of things.*—Compare Revelation 13:1; Daniel 7:2, 3, 17.

²¹ From 1914 to 1918 the nations were occupied with the first world war. Nationalistic feelings ran high, and in the spring of 1918, the religious enemies of the two witnesses took advantage of the situation. They

---

* The "abyss" (Greek, *a'bys·sos;* Hebrew, *tehohm'*) refers symbolically to a place of inactivity. (See Revelation 9:2.) In a literal sense, however, it can also refer to the vast sea. The Hebrew word is often translated "watery deep." (Psalm 71:20; 106:9; Jonah 2:5) Thus, "the wild beast that ascends out of the abyss" can be identified with the "wild beast ascending out of the sea."—Revelation 11:7; 13:1.

---

19. According to the Revelation account, what takes place when the two witnesses finish their witnessing?

20. What is "the wild beast that ascends out of the abyss"?

21. (a) How did the religious enemies of the two witnesses take advantage of the war situation? (b) The fact that the corpses of the two witnesses were left unburied indicated what? (c) How is the time period of three and a half days to be viewed? (See footnote.)

maneuvered the State's legal apparatus so that responsible ministers of the Watch Tower Bible and Tract Society were imprisoned on false charges of sedition. Faithful coworkers were stunned. Kingdom activity almost ceased. It was as though the preaching work were dead. In Bible times it was a terrible indignity not to be interred in a memorial tomb. (Psalm 79:1-3; 1 Kings 13:21, 22) Therefore, great reproach would attach to leaving the two witnesses unburied, In the hot Palestinian climate, a corpse in the open street would really start to smell after three and a half literal days.* (Compare John 11: 39.) This detail in the prophecy thus indicates the shame that the two witnesses had to endure. Those mentioned above who were imprisoned were even denied bail while their

cases were on appeal. They were exposed publicly long enough to become a stench to the inhabitants of "the great city." But what was this "great city"?

22 John gives us some clues. He says that Jesus was impaled there. So we immediately think of Jerusalem. But he also says that the great city is called Sodom and Egypt. Well, literal Jerusalem was once called Sodom because of her unclean practices. (Isaiah 1:8-10; compare Ezekiel 16:49, 53-58.) And Egypt, the first world power, sometimes appears as a picture of this world system of things. (Isaiah 19:1, 19; Joel 3:19) Hence, this great city pictures a defiled "Jerusalem" that claims to worship God but that has become unclean and sinful, like Sodom, and a part of this satanic world system of things, like Egypt. It pictures Christendom, the modern equivalent of unfaithful Jerusalem, the organization whose members had so much reason to rejoice

---

* Notice that in examining the experiences of God's people at this time, it appears that while the 42 months represent a literal three and a half years, the three and a half days do not represent a literal period of 84 hours. Likely, the specific period of three and a half days is mentioned twice (in verses 9 and 11) to highlight that it would be only a short period compared with the actual three and a half years of activity that precede it.

22. (a) What is the great city? (b) How did the public press join in with the clergy in rejoicing over the silencing of the two witnesses? (See box.)

The Rejoicing of Revelation 11:10

In his book *Preachers Present Arms*, published in 1933, Ray H. Abrams refers to the clergy's bitter opposition to the Watch Tower Society's book *The Finished Mystery*. He reviews the clergy's endeavors to rid themselves of the Bible Students and their "pestilential persuasion." This led to the court case that resulted in sentencing of J. F. Rutherford and seven companions to long years of imprisonment. Dr. Abrams adds: "An analysis of the whole case leads to the conclusion that the churches and the clergy were originally behind the movement to stamp out the Russellites. In Canada, in February, 1918, the ministers began a systematic campaign against them and their publications, particularly *The Finished Mystery*. According to the Winnipeg *Tribune*, . . . the suppression of their book was believed to have been directly brought about by the 'representations of the clergy.'"

Dr. Abrams continues: "When the news of the twenty-year sentences reached the editors of the religious press, practically every one of these publications, great and small, rejoiced over the event. I have been unable to discover any words of sympathy in any of the orthodox religious journals. 'There can be no question,' concluded Upton Sinclair, that 'the persecution . . . sprang in part from the fact that they had won the hatred of "orthodox" religious bodies.' What the combined efforts of the churches had failed to do the government now seemed to have succeeded in accomplishing for them." After quoting the derogatory comments of a number of religious publications, the writer referred to the reversal of the decision in the Court of Appeals and remarked: "This verdict was greeted with silence in the churches."

Like the dry bones of Ezekiel chapter 37, the two witnesses are reactivated for the modern-day preaching work

when they silenced the disturbing preaching of the two witnesses.

Raised Again!

23 The public press joined the clergy in vilifying God's people, one paper saying: "The finis of *The Finished Mystery* has been given." Nothing, though, could have been further from the truth! The two witnesses did not stay dead. We read: *"And after the three and a half days spirit of life from God entered into them, and they stood upon their feet, and great fear fell upon those beholding them. And they heard a loud voice out of heaven say to them: 'Come on up here.' And they went up into heaven in the cloud, and their enemies beheld them."* (*Revelation 11:11, 12*) Thus, they had an experience similar to that of the dry bones in the valley that Ezekiel visited in vision. Jehovah breathed upon those dry bones, and

they came to life, providing a picture of the rebirth of the nation of Israel after 70 years of captivity in Babylon. (Ezekiel 37:1-14) These two prophecies, in Ezekiel and in Revelation, had their striking modern-day fulfillment in 1919, when Jehovah restored his "deceased" witnesses to vibrant life.

24 What a shock for those persecutors! The corpses of the two witnesses were suddenly alive and active again. It was a bitter pill for those clergymen to swallow, the more so since the Christian ministers whom they had schemed to put in prison were free again, later to be fully exonerated. The shock must have been even greater when, in September 1919, the Bible Students held a convention in

23. (a) What happens to the two witnesses after three and a half days, and what is the effect on their enemies? (b) When did Revelation 11:11, 12 and Ezekiel's prophecy of Jehovah's breathing upon a valley of dry bones have a modern-day fulfillment?

24. When the two witnesses came to life, what was the effect on their religious persecutors?

Cedar Point, Ohio, U.S.A. Here the recently released president of the Watch Tower Society, J. F. Rutherford, stirred conventioners with his talk "Announcing the Kingdom," based on Revelation 15:2 and Isaiah 52:7. Those of the John class began once again to "prophesy," or preach publicly. They advanced from strength to strength, fearlessly exposing Christendom's hypocrisy.

25 Christendom tried again and again to repeat her triumph of 1918. She resorted to mob action, legal maneuvering, imprisonment, even executions—all to no avail! After 1919 the spiritual domain of the two witnesses was out of her reach. In that year Jehovah had said to them: "Come on up here," and they had ascended to an elevated spiritual state where their enemies could see them but could not touch them. John describes the shocking effect their restoration had on the great city: **"And in that hour a great earthquake occurred, and a tenth of the city fell; and seven thousand persons were killed by the earthquake, and the rest became frightened and gave glory to the God of heaven."** (*Revelation 11:13*) There were truly great convulsions in the realm of religion. The ground seemed to move under the leaders of the established churches as this body of revivified Christians got to work. One tenth of their city, figuratively 7,000 persons, were so profoundly affected that they are spoken of as being killed.

26 The expression "a tenth of the city" reminds us that Isaiah prophesied regarding ancient Jerusalem that a tenth would survive the destruction of the city as a holy seed. (Isaiah 6:13) Similarly, the number 7,000 reminds us that when Elijah felt that he alone remained faithful in Israel, Jehovah told him

that there were, in fact, still 7,000 who had not bent down to Baal. (1 Kings 19:14, 18) In the first century, the apostle Paul said that these 7,000 pictured the remnant of the Jews who had responded to the good news about the Christ. (Romans 11:1-5) These scriptures help us to understand that the "seven thousand" and the "tenth of the city" in Revelation 11:13 are those who respond to the restored two witnesses and abandon the sinful great city. They die, as it were, to Christendom. Their names are taken off her membership roles. They no longer exist as far as she is concerned.*

27 But how did 'the rest [of Christendom] give glory to the God of heaven'? Certainly not by abandoning their apostate religion and becoming servants of God. Rather, it is as explained in Vincent's *Word Studies in the New Testament,* in discussing the expression "gave glory to the God of heaven." There it is stated: "The phrase signifies not conversion, nor repentance, nor thanksgiving, but *recognition,* which is its usual sense in scripture. Compare Josh. vii. 19 (Sept.). John ix. 24; Acts xii. 23; Rom. iv. 20." To her chagrin, Christendom had to acknowledge that the God of the Bible Students had performed a great act in restoring them to Christian activity.

28 It may be that the clergy gave this acknowledgment only mentally, or to themselves. Certainly, none of them went on record as publicly acknowledging the God of the two witnesses. But Jehovah's prophecy through John helps us to discern what was in their hearts and realize the humiliating shock that they experienced in 1919. From that year onward, as the "seven thousand" left Chris-

---

25. (a) When were the two witnesses told, "Come on up here," and how did that take place? (b) What shocking effect did the restoration of the two witnesses have on the great city?
26. Who are represented by the "tenth of the city" and the "seven thousand" of Revelation 11:13? Explain.

---

* Compare the use of the words "dead," "died," and "living" in such scriptures as Romans 6:2, 10, 11; 7:4, 6, 9; Galatians 2:19; Colossians 2:20; 3:3.

27, 28. (a) How did 'the rest give glory to the God of heaven?' (b) What were Christendom's clergy forced to acknowledge?

tendom despite her determined efforts to hold on to her sheep, the clergy were forced to recognize that the God of the John class was stronger than their god. In later years they would realize this even more clearly, as many more of their flock would depart, echoing the words of the people when Elijah triumphed over the Baal religionists at Mount Carmel: "Jehovah is the true God! Jehovah is the true God!"—1 Kings 18:39.

[29] But listen! John tells us: *"The second woe is past. Look! The third woe is coming quickly."* (*Revelation 11:14*) If Christendom is shaken by what has happened so far, what will she do when the third woe is announced, the seventh angel blows his trumpet, and the sacred secret of God is finally finished?—Revelation 10:7.

29. What does John say is coming quickly, and what further shaking awaits Christendom?

REVELATION CLIMAX

Chapter 26

God's Sacred Secret PG 158 #13 —Its Glorious Climax!

D O YOU recall the sworn declaration by the strong angel recorded at Revelation 10:1, 6, 7? He stated: "There will be no delay any longer; but in the days of the sounding of the seventh angel, when he is about to blow his trumpet, the sacred secret of God according to the good news which he declared to his own slaves the prophets is indeed brought to a finish." Jehovah's due time has arrived for the sounding of that final trumpet! How is it, then, that the sacred secret is brought to a finish? John is truly overjoyed to inform us! He writes: *"And the seventh angel blew his trumpet. And loud voices occurred in heaven, saying: 'The kingdom of the world did become the kingdom of our Lord and of his Christ, and he will rule as king forever and ever.'"* (*Revelation 11:15*) Those angelic hosts have reason

to speak loudly, even in thunderous tones! For this historic announcement is of universal importance. It is of vital concern to all living creation.

[2] The sacred secret comes to its happy climax! Gloriously, magnificently, it is brought to a triumphant finish in 1914 when the Lord Jehovah enthrones his Christ as associate King. Acting for his Father, Jesus Christ takes over active rulership in the midst of an enemy world of mankind. As the promised Seed, he receives Kingdom power in order to bring to nothing the Serpent and his brood and restore paradisaic peace to this earth. (Genesis 3:15; Psalm 72:1, 7) As Messianic King, Jesus will thus fulfill Jehovah's Word and vindicate his Father, "the King of eternity," who must rule as Sovereign Lord "forever and ever."—1 Timothy 1:17.

1. (a) How does John inform us that the sacred secret is brought to a finish? (b) Why do the angelic hosts speak loudly?

2. When and with what event is the sacred secret brought to a triumphant finish?

³ But how did "the kingdom of the world . . . become the kingdom of our Lord," Jehovah? Has not Jehovah God always been King? That is true, for the Levite Asaph sang: "God is my King from long ago." And another psalmist proclaimed: "Jehovah himself has become king! . . . Your throne is firmly established from long ago; you are from time indefinite." (Psalm 74:12; 93:1, 2) In his wisdom, though, Jehovah has allowed other sovereignties to exist on earth. Thus the issue raised in Eden as to whether man can govern himself without God has been fully tested. Man-rule has failed miserably. True, indeed, are the words of God's prophet: "I well know, O Jehovah, that to earthling man his way does not belong. It does not belong to man who is walking even to direct his step." (Jeremiah 10:23) Ever since the defection of our first parents, the entire inhabited earth has been under the domination of "the original serpent," Satan. (Revelation 12:9; Luke 4:6) It is time, now, for a dramatic change! To vindicate his rightful position, Jehovah begins to exercise his sovereignty over the earth in a new way, through his designated Messianic Kingdom.

⁴ When the sounding of the seven trumpets got under way in 1922, the Bible Students' convention at Cedar Point, Ohio, featured a talk by the president of the Watch Tower Society, J. F. Rutherford, based on the scripture "The kingdom of heaven is at hand." (Matthew 4:17, *King James Version*) He concluded with these words: "Then back to the field, O ye sons of the most high God! Gird on your armor! Be sober, be vigilant, be active, be brave. Be faithful and true witnesses for the Lord. Go forward in the fight until every vestige of Babylon lies desolate. Herald the message far and wide. The world must know that Jehovah is God and that Jesus Christ is King of kings and Lord of lords. This

is the day of all days. Behold, the King reigns! You are his publicity agents. Therefore advertise, advertise, advertise, the King and his kingdom." God's Kingdom by Christ Jesus was brought to the fore, and that set off the great surge of Kingdom preaching that has included the judgments heralded by the sounding of all seven of the angelic trumpets.

⁵ The trumpet blast of the seventh angel was reflected in highlights of the Bible Students' convention in Detroit, Michigan, July 30-August 6, 1928. At that time 107 broadcasting stations were tied in to what *The New York Times* described as 'the most extensive and expensive radio hook-up in history.' The convention enthusiastically adopted a powerful "Declaration Against Satan and for Jehovah," pointing to the overthrow, at Armageddon, of Satan and his evil organization and the emancipation of all who love righteousness. Loyal subjects of God's Kingdom were delighted to receive a convention release, the 368-page book *Government*. This supplied the clearest of proofs "that God set his Anointed King upon his throne in 1914."

Jehovah Takes Power

⁶ Christ enthroned in God's Kingdom —what joy this announcement calls forth! John reports: **"And the twenty-four elders who were seated before God upon their thrones fell upon their faces and worshiped God, saying: 'We thank you, Jehovah God, the Almighty, the One who is and who was, because you have taken your great power and begun ruling as king.'"—Revelation 11:16, 17.**

⁷ The ones that offer these thanks to Jehovah God are the 24 elders, symbolizing the anointed brothers of Christ in their heavenly

---

3. Why has Jehovah God, though always King, allowed other sovereignties to exist on earth?

4. When the sounding of the trumpets got under way in 1922, what was brought to the fore? Explain.

5. In 1928, what happened at the Bible Students' convention that highlighted the seventh trumpet blast?

6. How does John report the announcement of Christ's having been enthroned in God's Kingdom?

7. How were thanks given to Jehovah God (a) by the remnant of the symbolic 24 elders on earth? (b) by those of the symbolic 24 elders who had been resurrected to their positions in heaven?

positions. From 1922 onward a remnant on earth of these 144,000 anointed ones got busy in the work that was set in motion by the trumpet blasts. They came to realize the full import of the sign at Matthew 24:3–25:46. Even earlier in the Lord's day, however, their fellow witnesses who had already 'proved faithful even to death' had been resurrected to take their positions in heaven, so that they could now represent the entire group of 144,-000 in falling upon their faces to render homage to Jehovah. (Revelation 1:10; 2:10) How thankful all of these are that their Sovereign Lord has not delayed in bringing his sacred secret to a climactic finish!

⁸ On the other hand, the blowing of the seventh trumpet brings no joy to the nations. The time has come for them to experience Jehovah's wrath. As John relates: *"But the nations became wrathful, and your own wrath came, and the appointed time for the dead to be judged, and to give their reward to your slaves the prophets and to the holy ones and to those fearing your name, the small and the great, and to bring to ruin those ruining the earth."* (*Revelation 11:18*) From 1914 onward the nations of the world have fiercely expressed their wrath against one another, against God's Kingdom, and especially against Jehovah's two witnesses.—Revelation 11:3.

⁹ Throughout history the nations have

8. (a) What effect does the blowing of the seventh trumpet have on the nations? (b) Against whom have the nations expressed their wrath?
9. How have the nations been ruining the earth, and what has God determined to do about it?

Highlights of Jehovah's Trumpetlike Judgment Proclamations

1. **1922 Cedar Point, Ohio:** A challenge to Christendom's leaders in religion, politics, and big business to justify their failure to bring peace, prosperity, and happiness. Messiah's Kingdom is the panacea.

2. **1923 Los Angeles, California:** The public talk, "All Nations Now Marching to Armageddon, but Millions Now Living Will Never Die," called on peace-loving "sheep" to abandon the death-dealing sea of humanity.

3. **1924 Columbus, Ohio:** Ecclesiastics indicted for self-exaltation and refusal to preach Messiah's Kingdom. True Christians must preach God's vengeance and comfort mourning humanity.

4. **1925 Indianapolis, Indiana:** A message of hope contrasting the spiritual darkness in Christendom with the bright Kingdom promise of peace, prosperity, health, life, liberty, and eternal happiness.

5. **1926 London, England:** A locustlike plaguing of Christendom and its clergy, exposing their rejection of God's Kingdom, and hailing the birth of that heavenly government.

6. **1927 Toronto, Canada:** An invitation, carried as by armies of cavalry, calling on people to forsake 'organized Christianity' and give heart allegiance to Jehovah God and to his King and Kingdom.

7. **1928 Detroit, Michigan:** A declaration against Satan and for Jehovah, making plain that God's anointed King, enthroned in 1914, will destroy Satan's evil organization and emancipate mankind.

been ruining the earth by their incessant warfare and bad management. Since 1914, however, this ruination has escalated to an alarming degree. Greed and corruption have resulted in expanding deserts and tremendous loss of productive land. Acid rain and radioactive clouds have damaged large areas. Food sources have been polluted. The air we breathe and the water we drink are contaminated. Industrial wastes threaten life on land and in the sea. And the superpowers threaten complete ruination by way of nuclear annihilation of all humankind. Happily, Jehovah will "bring to ruin those ruining the earth"; he will execute judgment on those proud, godless humans who are responsible for earth's sorry state. (Deuteronomy 32:5, 6; Psalm 14:1-3) Therefore, Jehovah arranges for the third woe, to bring these wrongdoers to account.—Revelation 11:14.

Woe to the Ruinous Ones!

¹⁰ Here, then, is the third woe. It comes quickly! It is Jehovah's means of bringing ruination to those who desecrate his "footstool," this lovely earth on which we live. (Isaiah 66:1) It is set in motion by the Messianic Kingdom—the sacred secret of God.

10. (a) What is the third woe? (b) In what way does the third woe bring more than torment?

God's enemies, and Christendom's leaders in particular, have been tormented by the first two woes—resulting principally from the locust plague and the armies of cavalry; but the third woe, which Jehovah's Kingdom itself administers, brings more than torment. (Revelation 9:3-19) It provides the death stroke in ousting a ruinous human society and its rulers. This will come as the climax of Jehovah's judging at Armageddon. It is just as Daniel prophesied: "And in the days of those kings [rulers who are ruining the earth] the God of heaven will set up a kingdom that will never be brought to ruin. And the kingdom itself will not be passed on to any other people. It will crush and put an end to all these kingdoms, and it itself will stand to times indefinite." Like an imposing mountain, God's Kingdom will rule over an earth made glorious, vindicating Jehovah's sovereignty and bringing eternal joy to mankind.—Daniel 2: 35, 44; Isaiah 11:9; 60:13.

Jehovah will "bring to ruin those ruining the earth"

¹¹ The third woe is accompanied by an ongoing series of happy events that will proceed progressively through the Lord's day. It is the time 'for the dead to be judged, and for God to give their reward to his slaves the prophets and to the holy ones and to those fearing his name.' That means a resurrection from the dead! For the anointed holy ones who had already fallen asleep in death, this takes place early in the Lord's day. (1 Thessalonians 4:15-17) In due course the remaining holy ones join these by an instantaneous resurrection. Others too are to be rewarded, including God's slaves the prophets of ancient times and all others of mankind who come to fear Jehovah's name, whether they are of the great crowd who survive the great tribulation or of "the dead, the great and the small," who are raised to life during Christ's Millennial Reign. Since God's Messianic King has the keys of death and of Hades, his Kingdom rule opens the way for him to dispense everlasting life to all who reach out for that precious provision. (Revelation 1:18; 7:9, 14; 20:12, 13; Romans 6:22; John 5:28, 29) Whether it is immortal life in the heavens or eternal life on earth, this gift of life is an undeserved kindness from Jehovah, for which each recipient may be forever thankful!—Hebrews 2:9.

Behold the Ark of His Covenant!

¹² Jehovah rules! Through his Messianic Kingdom, he is exercising his sovereignty toward mankind in a marvelous way. This is confirmed by what John sees next: *"And the temple sanctuary of God that is in heaven was opened, and the ark of his covenant was seen in his temple sanctuary. And there occurred lightnings and voices and thunders and an earthquake and a great hail."* (Revelation 11:19)

---

11. (a) What ongoing series of happy events does the prophecy describe? (b) What undeserved kindness is realized, how, and by whom?
12. (a) According to Revelation 11:19, what does John see in heaven? (b) Of what had the ark of the covenant been a symbol, and what happened to it after Israel went into captivity to Babylon?

Ruining the Earth

"Every three seconds a portion of original rainforest the size of a football field disappears. . . . The loss of primary forest is destroying thousands of plant and animal species."—*Illustrated Atlas of the World* (Rand McNally).

"In two centuries of settlement, [the Great Lakes] have also become the world's biggest sewer."—*The Globe and Mail* (Canada).

In April 1986 an explosion and fire at a nuclear power plant in Chernobyl, U.S.S.R., "was the most significant nuclear event . . . since the bombings of Hiroshima and Nagasaki," emitting "as much long-term radiation into the world's air, topsoil and water as all the nuclear tests and bombs ever exploded."—*JAMA; The New York Times.*

In Minamata, Japan, a chemical plant discharged methylmercury into the bay. Eating fish and shellfish contaminated with the discharge caused Minamata disease (MD) a "chronic neurological disease. . . . To date [1985], 2578 people throughout Japan have officially been verified to have MD."—*International Journal of Epidemiology.*

This is the only mention in Revelation of the ark of God's covenant. The Ark had been the visible symbol of Jehovah's presence with his people Israel. In the tabernacle, and later in the temple built by Solomon, it was kept in the Most Holy. But when Israel went into captivity in Babylon in 607 B.C.E., Jerusalem was desolated and the ark of the covenant disappeared. That was when representatives of the house of David ceased "to sit upon Jehovah's throne as king."—1 Chronicles 29: 23.*

¹³ Now, after more than 2,500 years, the Ark is seen once more. But in John's vision

---

* Roman historian Tacitus reports that when Jerusalem was captured in 63 B.C.E. and Cneius Pompeius entered the sanctuary of Herod's temple, he found it was empty. There was no ark of the covenant within.—Tacitus *History,* 5.9.

---

13. What is denoted by the fact that the ark of God's covenant is seen in the heavenly sanctuary of God?

this Ark is not in an earthly temple. It appears in the heavenly sanctuary of God. Once again, Jehovah rules by means of a king in the royal line of David. This time, however, the King, Christ Jesus, is enthroned in heavenly Jerusalem—the exalted vantage point from which he executes Jehovah's judgments. (Hebrews 12:22) The following chapters of Revelation will unveil these to us.

14 In ancient earthly Jerusalem, the Ark was not seen by the Israelites in general, nor even by the priests serving in the temple, for it was within the Most Holy that was screened off from the Holy Place by a curtain. (Numbers 4:20; Hebrews 9:2, 3) Only the high priest got to see it when he entered the Most Holy on the annual Day of Atonement. Nevertheless, when the temple sanctuary in the heavens is opened, the symbolic ark is visible not only to Jehovah's High Priest, Jesus Christ, but also to his underpriests, the 144,000, including John.

15 Those first ones who have been resurrected to heaven see this symbolic ark at close range, for they have taken their place as part of the 24 elders around Jehovah's throne.

14, 15. (a) In ancient Jerusalem, who only got to see the ark of the covenant, and why? (b) In the heavenly temple sanctuary of God, who get to see the ark of his covenant?

The weighty pronouncements at Revelation 11:15-19 are a prelude to the visions that follow. Revelation chapter 12 is a flashback that amplifies in detail the grand announcements at Revelation 11: 15, 17. Chapter 13 gives background to 11:18, as it describes the origin and development of Satan's political organization that has brought ruination to the earth. Chapters 14 and 15 detail further Kingdom judgments tied in with the sounding of the seventh trumpet and the third woe.

And the John class on earth have been enlightened by Jehovah's spirit to discern His presence in His spiritual temple. There have also been signs to alert mankind in general to this wonderful development. John's vision speaks of lightnings, voices, thunders, an earthquake, and hail. (Compare Revelation 8:5.) What do these symbolize?

16 Since 1914 there has been a tremendous upheaval in the realm of religion. Happily, though, this "earthquake" has been accompanied by dedicated voices giving a clear message about God's established Kingdom. Thunderous 'storm warnings' from the Bible have been sounded. Like lightning, flashes of insight as to God's prophetic Word have been seen and publicized. A hard pounding "hail" of divine judgments has been unleashed against Christendom and false religion in general. All of this should have caught people's attention. Sadly, though, the majority —like the people of Jerusalem in Jesus' time—have failed to discern the fulfillment of these Revelation signs.—Luke 19:41-44.

17 The seven angels continue to sound their trumpets, signaling historic events here on earth. Dedicated Christians have a great responsibility to continue proclaiming these announcements to the world. How joyfully they are fulfilling that commission! This is indicated in that, during just ten years, from 1978 to 1987, they more than doubled the hours spent yearly in their global ministry—from 307,272,262 to 739,019,286—a 140-percent increase. Truly, "the sacred secret of God according to the good news" is being made known "to the extremities of the inhabited earth."—Revelation 10:7; Romans 10:18.

18 Other visions now await us as God's Kingdom purposes continue to be unveiled.

---

16. How have there been lightnings, voices, thunders, an earthquake, and a great hail?
17, 18. (a) The sounding of the trumpets of the seven angels has brought what responsibility to dedicated Christians? (b) How are Christians fulfilling their commission?

Chapter 27

God's Kingdom Is Born!

THE sacred secret of God has been unlocked. (Revelation 10:7) Jehovah's Kingdom by his Messiah is now a dynamic reality. It rules! Its presence spells doom for Satan and his seed and glorious victory for the Seed of God's heavenly organization. The seventh angel has not finished blowing on his trumpet, however, for he has much more to reveal to us about the third woe. (Revelation 11:14) The signs described in Revelation chapters 12 to 14 will help us to broaden our appreciation of all that is involved in that woe and in bringing God's sacred secret to a finish.

2 John now sees a great sign—one of outstanding interest for God's people. It introduces a thrilling prophetic vision, the meaning of which was first published in the March 1, 1925, issue of *The Watch Tower* in an article entitled "Birth of the Nation" and then again in 1926 in the book *Deliverance.* This brilliant flash of Bible understanding became a historic marker in the advancement of Jehovah's work. So let John describe the drama as it starts to unfold: *"And a great sign was seen in heaven, a woman arrayed with the sun, and the moon was beneath her feet, and on her head was a crown of twelve stars, and she was pregnant. And she cries out in her pains and in her agony to give birth."—Revelation 12:1, 2.*

1. How will an understanding of the signs described in Revelation chapters 12 to 14 help us?
2. (a) What great sign does John see? (b) When was the meaning of the great sign revealed?

3 For the first time, John beholds a woman in heaven. She is, of course, not a literal woman. Rather, she is a sign, or a symbol. (Revelation 1:1) What does she symbolize? In the inspired prophecies, women at times represent organizations "married" to outstanding personalities. In the Hebrew Scriptures, Israel was spoken of as a wife of Jehovah God. (Jeremiah 3:14) In the Greek Scriptures, the congregation of anointed Christians is spoken of as Christ's bride. (Revelation 21:9-14) The woman John here sees is also married to someone, and she is about to give birth. Who is her husband? Well, later her child is "caught away to God and to his throne." (Revelation 12:5) Jehovah thus claims the child as his own. Therefore, the woman that John sees must be Jehovah's symbolic wife.

3. What is the identity of the woman seen in heaven?

Vision 7

Revelation 12:1-17

Subject: The heavenly woman gives birth, Michael battles with Satan and casts him to earth

Time of fulfillment: From the enthronement of Christ Jesus in 1914 up to the great tribulation

⁴ About eight centuries earlier, Jehovah had addressed this symbolic wife, saying: "All your sons will be persons taught by Jehovah." (Isaiah 54:5, 13) Jesus quoted this prophecy and showed that these sons were his faithful followers, who later formed the congregation of anointed Christians. (John 6:44, 45) So members of this congregation, spoken of as God's sons, are also children of God's symbolic wife. (Romans 8:14) The apostle Paul adds the final piece of information when he says: "The Jerusalem above is free, and she is our mother." (Galatians 4:26) The "woman" seen by John, then, is "the Jerusalem above."

⁵ Exactly what, though, is Jerusalem above? Since Paul spoke of her as "above," and John sees her in heaven, she is clearly not an earthly city; neither is she the same as "New Jerusalem," since that organization is the bride of Christ, not Jehovah's wife. (Revelation 21:2) Notice that she is crowned with 12 stars. The number 12 is associated with completeness in an organizational setting.* Hence, these 12 stars seem to indicate that she is an organizational arrangement in heaven, just as ancient Jerusalem was on earth. Jerusalem above is Jehovah's universal organization of spirit creatures that acts as his wife, both in serving him and in producing offspring.

⁶ John sees this woman as being robed with the sun and having the moon beneath her feet. When we add her crown of stars, she

---

* Compare the 12 tribes of fleshly Israel, the 12 apostles, the 12 tribes of spiritual Israel, and the 12 gates, 12 angels, and 12 foundation stones of the New Jerusalem.—Revelation 21:12-14.

---

4. Who are the sons of God's symbolic wife, and what does the apostle Paul call the woman seen by John?
5. Since Jehovah's symbolic wife is crowned with 12 stars, what in reality is the Jerusalem above?
6. (a) What is indicated by the fact that the woman seen by John is robed with the sun, has the moon beneath her feet, and has a crown of stars? (b) What is symbolized by the labor pains of the pregnant woman?

is completely surrounded by heavenly lights. God's favor shines upon her day and night. What a fitting symbol of Jehovah's magnificent heavenly organization! She is also pregnant, enduring labor pains. Her cries for divine help show that her time has come to give birth. In the Bible, labor pains often symbolize the hard work needed to produce an important result. (Compare Psalm 90:2; Proverbs 25:23; Isaiah 66:7, 8.) No doubt labor pains of this kind were experienced as Jehovah's heavenly organization prepared for this historic birth.

A Great Fiery-Colored Dragon

⁷ What does John next observe? *"And another sign was seen in heaven, and, look! a great fiery-colored dragon, with seven heads and ten horns and upon its heads seven diadems; and its tail drags a third of the stars of heaven, and it hurled them down to the earth. And the dragon kept standing before the woman who was about to give birth, that, when she did give birth, it might devour her child."—Revelation 12:3, 4.*

⁸ This dragon is Satan, "the original serpent." (Revelation 12:9; Genesis 3:15) He is a ferocious destroyer—a seven-headed dragon, or devourer, that can completely swallow his prey. How strange he looks! Those seven heads and ten horns indicate that he is the architect of the political wild beast soon to be described in Revelation chapter 13. This beast also has seven heads and ten horns. Since Satan has a diadem on each head—seven in all—we can be sure that the world powers represented in that wild beast have been under his rulership. (John 16:11) The ten horns are a fitting symbol of the completeness of the power that he has exercised in this world.

---

7. What is another sign that John sees in heaven?
8. (a) What is the identity of the great fiery-colored dragon? (b) What is indicated by the dragon's having seven heads, ten horns, and a diadem on each head?

⁹ The dragon has authority also in the spirit realm. With his tail, he "drags a third of the stars of heaven." Stars can represent angels. (Job 38:7) Mention of "a third" would emphasize that a considerable number of angels have been misled by Satan. Once these came under his control, there was no escape for them. They could not return to God's holy organization. They became demons, dragged along, as it were, by Satan their king, or ruler. (Matthew 12:24) Satan also cast them down to the earth. This no doubt refers to Noah's day before the Flood, when Satan induced the disobedient sons of God to go down to earth and cohabit with the daughters of men. As a punishment, these "angels that sinned" have been thrown by God into the prisonlike condition called Tartarus.—Genesis 6:4; 2 Peter 2:4; Jude 6.

¹⁰ Thus, two opposing organizations have come clearly into view—Jehovah's heavenly organization as pictured by the woman and Satan's demonic organization that challenges God's sovereignty. The great issue of sovereignty must be settled. But how? Satan, still dragging the demons along with him, is like a vicious beast of prey eyeing a potential victim. He is waiting for the woman to give birth. He wants to devour this expected infant because he knows that it poses an ominous threat to his continued existence and that of the world over which he exercises rulership.—John 14:30.

A Son, a Male

¹¹ The appointed time for the nations to rule without interruption by God came to an end in 1914. (Luke 21:24) Then, right on time, the woman bears her child: **"And she** gave birth to a son, a male, who is to shepherd all the nations with an iron rod. And her child was caught away to God and to his throne. And the woman fled into the wilderness, where she has a place prepared by God, that they should feed her there a thousand two hundred and sixty days." (Revelation 12:5, 6)** The child is "a son, a male." Why does John use this double expression? He does it to show the child's

---

9. What is indicated by the fact that the dragon's tail "drags a third of the stars of heaven" down to the earth?
10. What opposing organizations come into view, and why does the dragon seek to devour the child when the woman gives birth?
11. How does John describe the birth of the woman's child, and why is the child called "a son, a male"?

suitableness, his competence for ruling the nations with adequate power. It also emphasizes how momentous, how joyous an occasion this birth is! It plays a key role in bringing the sacred secret of God to a finish. Why, this male child will even "shepherd all the nations with an iron rod"!

¹² Now, does that expression sound familiar? Yes, Jehovah promised prophetically regarding Jesus: "You will break them with an iron scepter, as though a potter's vessel you will dash them to pieces." (Psalm 2:9) It was also prophesied regarding him: "The rod of your strength Jehovah will send out of Zion, saying: 'Go subduing in the midst of your enemies.'" (Psalm 110:2) Therefore, the birth seen by John closely involves Jesus Christ. No, it is not Jesus' being born of a virgin back before the first century of our Common Era; nor could it refer to Jesus' being raised again to spirit life in 33 C.E. Furthermore, it is no transmigration. Rather, it is the birth of God's Kingdom in 1914 as a reality, with Jesus —already in heaven for close to 19 centuries—now enthroned as King.—Revelation 12:10.

¹³ Never would Jehovah permit Satan to devour His wife or His newborn son! At birth, the male child is "caught away to God and to his throne." He thus comes completely under the protection of Jehovah, who will take the fullest care of this newborn Kingdom, His instrument for sanctifying His holy name. At the same time, the woman flees to a place that God has prepared for her in the wilderness. More details on that later! As for Satan, the stage is now set for a momentous event that will make it utterly impossible for him ever again to threaten the Kingdom in heaven. What is that event?

War in Heaven!

¹⁴ John tells us: ***"And war broke out in heaven: Michael and his angels battled with the dragon, and the dragon and its angels battled but it did not prevail, neither was a place found for them any longer in heaven. So down the great dragon was hurled, the original serpent, the one called Devil and Satan, who is misleading the entire inhabited earth; he was hurled down to the earth, and his angels were hurled down with him."*** (*Revelation 12:7-9*) So as a dramatic development in bringing the sacred secret of God to a finish, Satan is ejected, pitched out of heaven, and his demons are cast down to the earth with him. The one who has misled the entire inhabited earth to the extent of becoming its god is finally restricted to the vicinity of this planet, where his rebellion first began.—2 Corinthians 4:3, 4.

¹⁵ Who accomplish this great victory in Jehovah's name? The Bible says it is Michael and his angels. But who is Michael? The name

---

12. (a) In the Psalms, what did Jehovah prophetically promise regarding Jesus? (b) What is symbolized by the woman's giving birth to a son "who is to shepherd all the nations with an iron rod"?

13. What is indicated by the male child's being "caught away to God and to his throne"?

---

14. (a) As John tells it, what event makes it impossible for Satan ever again to threaten the Kingdom? (b) To what locality are Satan and his demons restricted?

15, 16. (a) Who is Michael, and how do we know? (b) Why is it fitting that Michael is the one who hurls Satan down from heaven?

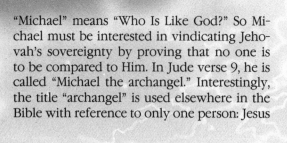

"Michael" means "Who Is Like God?" So Michael must be interested in vindicating Jehovah's sovereignty by proving that no one is to be compared to Him. In Jude verse 9, he is called "Michael the archangel." Interestingly, the title "archangel" is used elsewhere in the Bible with reference to only one person: Jesus Christ.* Paul says of him: "The Lord himself will descend from heaven with a commanding call, with an *archangel's voice* and with God's trumpet." (1 Thessalonians 4:16) The title "archangel" means "chief of the angels." So it is not surprising that Revelation speaks of "Michael and *his* angels." Other places where the Bible mentions angels subject to a righteous servant of God have reference to Jesus. Thus, Paul speaks of "the revelation of the Lord Jesus from heaven with *his* powerful angels."—2 Thessalonians 1:7; see also Matthew 24:30, 31; 25:31.

¹⁶ These and other scriptures lead us to the inescapable conclusion that Michael is no one else but the Lord Jesus Christ in his heavenly position. Now, in the Lord's day, he no longer merely says to Satan: "May Jehovah rebuke you." Since this is a time of judging, Jesus, as Michael, hurls the wicked Satan and his demonic angels down from heaven. (Jude 9; Revelation 1:10) It is most fitting that He should be the One to do this, as He is the newly installed King. Jesus is also the Seed, promised back in Eden, who will ultimately crush the head of that original serpent, thus putting him out of existence for all time. (Genesis 3:15) By ejecting Satan from heaven, Jesus has moved toward that final crushing.

* Notice, however, that Revelation 12:9 speaks of "the great dragon . . . and his angels." So the Devil not only makes a counterfeit god of himself but also tries to become an archangel, though the Bible never gives him that title.

"Be Glad, You Heavens"

[17] John reports a joyous heavenly reaction to this stupendous fall of Satan: *"And I heard a loud voice in heaven say: 'Now have come to pass the salvation and the power and the kingdom of our God and the authority of his Christ, because the accuser of our brothers has been hurled down, who accuses them day and night before our God! And they conquered him because of the blood of the Lamb and because of the word of their witnessing, and they did not love their souls even in the face of death. On this account be glad, you heavens and you who reside in them!'"—Revelation 12:10-12a.*

[18] Whose loud voice is it that John hears? The Bible does not say. But a similar cry reported at Revelation 11:17 came from the resurrected 24 elders in their heavenly positions, where they can now represent the 144,000 holy ones. (Revelation 11:18) And since the persecuted anointed servants of God still on earth are here spoken of as "our brothers," this statement could well come from the same source. No doubt these faithful ones can join their voice, since their resurrection would follow soon after Satan and his demon hordes had been thrown out of heaven.

17, 18. (a) What heavenly reaction does John report as to the fall of Satan from heaven? (b) What is the likely source of the loud voice that John hears?

Woe to the earth

[19] The finishing of the sacred secret of God calls for Jesus to take authority in Jehovah's Kingdom. The way is thus opened for God to carry out his great purpose to deliver faithful mankind. Jesus brings salvation not only to his God-fearing disciples now on earth but also to the countless millions of dead ones who are in God's memory. (Luke 21:27, 28) Satan's being called "the accuser of our brothers" shows that, even though his accusations against Job were proved false, he kept right on challenging the integrity of God's earthly servants. Evidently, he repeated on many occasions the charge that a man will give all he has in exchange for his soul. How dismally Satan has failed!—Job 1:9-11; 2:4, 5.

[20] Anointed Christians, who are counted righteous "because of the blood of the Lamb," are continuing to bear witness to God and to Jesus Christ despite persecutions. For more than a hundred years, this John class has been pointing to the great issues involved with the ending of the Gentile Times in 1914. (Luke 21:24, *King James Version*) And the great crowd are now serving loyally by their side. None of these are "fearful of those who kill the body but cannot kill the soul," as real-life experiences of Jehovah's Witnesses have demonstrated over and over again dur-

---

19. (a) The finishing of the sacred secret of God opens the way for Jesus to do what? (b) What is indicated by Satan's being called "the accuser of our brothers"?

20. How have faithful Christians conquered Satan?

ing this 20th century. By word of mouth and by proper Christian conduct, they have conquered Satan, consistently proving him to be a liar. (Matthew 10:28; Proverbs 27:11; Revelation 7:9) On being resurrected to heaven, how happy anointed Christians must be, since Satan is no longer up there to accuse their brothers! It is the time, indeed, for all the angelic host to respond joyously to the call: "Be glad, you heavens and you who reside in them!"

2/17/92 start

A Rival Woe!

21 Chafing because of the third woe, Satan is now intent on afflicting mankind with his own particular brand of woe. It is: *"Woe for the earth and for the sea, because the Devil has come down to you, having great anger, knowing he has a short period of time."* (*Revelation 12:12b*) Satan's ouster from heaven does indeed mean woe for the literal earth, which is being ruined by selfish humans under his control. (Deuteronomy 32:5) Even more so, Satan's policy of 'rule or ruin' brings woe to the symbolic earth, the structure of human society, as well as to the symbolic sea, the turbulent mass of mankind itself. During the two world wars, Satan's wrath was reflected in the wrath of the nations subject to him, and similar explosions of demonic rage continue to this day—though not for much longer! (Mark 13:7, 8) But terrible as the Devil's devices may be, they will never approach the woeful effect that the third woe—action by God's Kingdom—will produce on Satan's visible organization!

22 Since Satan's catastrophic ouster, Christ's brothers still on the earth have borne the brunt of his wrath. John reports: *"Now when the dragon saw that it was hurled down to the earth, it persecuted the woman that gave birth*

21. How has Satan brought woe to the earth and to the sea?
22, 23. (a) What does John say happens after the dragon has been hurled down to the earth? (b) How is it possible for the dragon to persecute "the woman that gave birth to the male child"?

GOD'S KINGDOM IS BORN!

to the male child. But the two wings of the great eagle were given the woman, that she might fly into the wilderness to her place; there is where she is fed for a time and times and half a time away from the face of the serpent."—Revelation 12:13, 14.

23 Here the vision picks up the thought introduced in verse 6, which tells us that after the birth of her child, the woman flees into the wilderness, away from the dragon. We may wonder how the dragon can persecute the woman, since she is in heaven and the dragon has now been cast down to the earth. Well, remember that the woman has children here on earth, her seed. Later in this vision, we are informed that Satan expresses his rage toward the woman by persecuting her seed. (Revelation 12:17) What happens to the woman's seed here on earth may be regarded as happening to the woman herself. (Compare Matthew 25:40.) And the growing number of companions of the seed here on earth would also experience these persecutions.

A New Nation

24 While the first world war was being fought, Jesus' brothers faithfully kept on with their witnessing to the extent possible. This was done in the face of intensified opposition from Satan and his vicious henchmen. Finally, the Bible Students' public witnessing was

24. What experience did the Bible Students have that was similar to the deliverance of the Israelites from Egypt?

Birth of Kingdom
Birth of new nation
Flood of persecution ▶
1914   1919   1922
Period of recuperation — *is Spiritual*

SEED OF THE WOMAN

183

Satan's Organization

virtually stopped. (Revelation 11:7-10) That was when they had an experience quite similar to that of the Israelites in Egypt who also endured under great oppression. It was then that Jehovah brought them swiftly, as if on wings of eagles, to safety in the desert of Sinai. (Exodus 19:1-4) Likewise, after the bitter persecution of 1918-19, Jehovah delivered his witnesses, as representing his woman, into a spiritual situation that was as safe for them as the desert was for the Israelites. This came as an answer to their prayers.—Compare Psalm 55:6-9.

²⁵ In the wilderness, Jehovah brought forth the Israelites as a nation, providing for them spiritually and physically. Similarly, starting in 1919, Jehovah brought forth the seed of the woman as a spiritual nation. This is not to be confused with the Messianic Kingdom that has been ruling from the heavens since 1914. Rather, this new nation is made up of the remnant of anointed witnesses on earth, who were brought into a glorious spiritual

estate in 1919. Being provided now with "their measure of food supplies at the proper time," these were strengthened for the work that lay ahead.—Luke 12:42; Isaiah 66:8.

²⁶ How long did this respite for the seed of God's woman last? Revelation 12:6 says 1,260 days. Revelation 12:14 calls the period a time, times, and half a time; in other words, three and a half times. In fact, both expressions stand for three and a half years, extending in the Northern Hemisphere from the spring of 1919 to the autumn of 1922. This was a period of refreshing recuperation and reorganization for the restored John class.

²⁷ The dragon did not give up! *"And the serpent disgorged water like a river from its mouth after the woman, to cause her to be drowned by the river."* (Revelation 12:15) What is meant by "water like a river," or "a flood of

---

25. (a) What did Jehovah bring forth in 1919, much as he brought forth the Israelites as a nation in the wilderness? (b) Who make up this nation, and into what have they been brought?

26. (a) How long is the time period mentioned at Revelation 12:6, 14? (b) What was the purpose of the period of three and a half times, when did it start, and when did it finish?

27. (a) According to John's report, what did the dragon do after 1922? (b) What was Satan's purpose in spewing forth a flood of persecution against the Witnesses?

water"? (*The New English Bible*) Ancient King David spoke of the wicked men who opposed him as "flash floods of good-for-nothing men" ["streams of the worthless," *Young*]. (Psalm 18: 4, 5, 16, 17) What Satan now unleashes is likewise persecution by worthless or "good-for-nothing men." After 1922 Satan spewed out a flood of persecution against the Witnesses. (Matthew 24:9-13) This came to include physical violence, "framing trouble by decree," imprisonments, and even executions by hanging, shooting, and beheading. (Psalm 94: 20) The debased Satan, having been denied direct access to God's heavenly woman, set out wrathfully to attack her remaining seed on earth and to destroy them, either directly or by causing them to lose God's favor through breaking their integrity. But their resolve proved to be like that of Job: "Until I expire I shall not take away my integrity from myself!"—Job 27:5.

²⁸ This vicious flood of persecution reached a high point during World War II. In Europe some ten thousand Witnesses were incarcerated in Nazi concentration camps, and thousands died. Under the warlords that ruled Italy, Japan, Korea, and Taiwan, faithful Witnesses suffered similar cruel treatment. Even in so-called democratic lands, the Witnesses were assaulted by Catholic Action groups, tarred and feathered, and run out of town. Christian assemblies were broken up and Witness children were expelled from school.

²⁹ Relief arrived from an unexpected source: *"But the earth came to the woman's help, and the earth opened its mouth and swallowed up the river that the dragon disgorged from its mouth. And the dragon grew wrathful at the woman, and went off to wage war with the remaining ones of her seed, who observe the commandments of God and have the work of bearing witness to Jesus."* (*Revelation 12: 16, 17*) "The earth"—elements within Satan's own system of things—began to swallow up "the river," or "flood." During the 1940's the Witnesses gained a series of favorable

---

"The Earth Opened Its Mouth"

Satan's flash flood of persecution has been unleashed in many lands against anointed Christians and their companions. Often, though, developments within Satan's own system of things have resulted in that flood's being swallowed up.

The flood of mobbings and imprisonments in the United States was largely swallowed up by favorable Supreme Court decisions during the 1940's.

1945: Vicious persecution in lands controlled by Germany and Japan was halted by Allied victories in World War II.

When a ban was imposed on Jehovah's Witnesses in the Dominican Republic, the Witnesses were imprisoned, lashed, and beaten with rifle butts. In 1960 a falling-out between dictator Rafael Trujillo and the Roman Catholic Church led to the lifting of the ban on Jehovah's Witnesses.

The shooting, burning, rape, beating, torture, and killing of Witnesses during a civil war in Nigeria came to a halt in 1970 when government forces conquered the breakaway province where these things were happening.

In Spain homes were invaded and Christians fined and imprisoned for the "crime" of talking about God and holding Christian meetings. This persecution finally ended in 1970, when a change of government led to a lifting of the ban on Jehovah's Witnesses.

In Portugal hundreds of homes were searched without warrant. Witnesses were physically injured and thrown into prison, and their Bibles were confiscated. This terrorism was 'swallowed up' when, in 1974, a military revolution resulted in a change in government and a law was passed granting freedom of assembly.

In Argentina, under a military government, children of Jehovah's Witnesses were expelled from school, and Witnesses around the country were arrested for preaching the good news. This persecution finally ended in 1984 when the then ruling government legally recognized the Association of Jehovah's Witnesses.

---

28. How did the flood of persecution reach a peak during World War II?

29. (a) How does John describe relief arriving from an unexpected source? (b) How is it that "the earth came to the woman's help"? (c) What has the dragon continued to do?

1992 205 lands 4 millions STROUG

decisions in the United States Supreme Court, and from ruling powers in some other lands, that upheld freedom of worship. <u>Finally, the Allied nations swallowed up the Nazi-Fascist juggernaut, to the relief of the Witnesses who had suffered under cruel dictatorships.</u> Persecutions did not stop altogether, for the wrath of the <u>dragon has continued until today, and he keeps up the war against those who "have the work of bearing witness to Jesus."</u> In many lands, loyal Witnesses are still in prison, and some still die because of their integrity. But in some of these lands, the authorities from time to time relax their pressure, and the Witnesses enjoy a greater measure of freedom.* Thus, in fulfillment of the prophe-

---

* The highest courts in a number of lands have granted relief to Jehovah's Witnesses; some of these decisions are cited in the box on page 92.

cy, the earth continues to swallow up the river of persecution.

30 In this way, the earth has provided sufficient relief to allow God's work to spread to more than 200 lands and produce over three million faithful preachers of the good news. Along with the remaining ones of the woman's seed, a great international crowd of new believers is observing the commandments of God as to separateness from the world, clean morals, and love of the brothers, and they are witnessing to the Messianic Kingdom. Their integrity answers Satan's reproachful challenge, so that the death knell is sounded for Satan and his system of things.—Proverbs 27:11.

---

30. (a) The earth has provided sufficient relief for what to take place? (b) The integrity of God's people results in what?

Contending With Two Ferocious Beasts

2/24/92 START

THE great dragon has been cast down to the earth! Our study of Revelation makes it clear that never again will the original Serpent or his demon followers be allowed back into heaven. But we are not yet finished with "the one called Devil and Satan, who is misleading the entire inhabited earth." The account next identifies in greater detail the means used by Satan to fight against 'the woman and her seed.' (Revelation 12:9, 17) John says of that serpentine dragon: *"And it stood still upon the sand of the sea." (Revela-*

1, 2. (a) What does John say about the dragon? (b) How does John, in symbolic language, describe a visible organization used by the dragon?

tion 13:1a) So let us pause to examine the dragon's means of operation.

2 No longer are the holy heavens afflicted by the presence of Satan and his demons. Those wicked spirits have been ousted from heaven and confined to the vicinity of the earth. This no doubt accounts for the tremendous growth of spiritistic practices in this 20th century. The wily Serpent still maintains a corrupt spirit organization. But does he also use a visible organization in order to mislead mankind? John tells us: *"And I saw a wild beast ascending out of the sea, with ten horns and seven heads, and upon its horns ten diadems, but upon its heads blas-*

phemous names. Now the wild beast that I saw was like a leopard, but its feet were as those of a bear, and its mouth was as a lion's mouth. And the dragon gave to the beast its power and its throne and great authority."—Revelation 13: 1b, 2.

3 What is this freakish beast? The Bible itself gives the answer. Before the fall of Babylon in 539 B.C.E., the Jewish prophet Daniel saw visions involving ferocious beasts. At Daniel 7:2-8 he describes four beasts coming out of the sea, the first resembling a lion, the second a bear, the third a leopard, and "see there! a fourth beast, fearsome and terrible and unusually strong . . . and it had ten horns." This is remarkably similar to the wild beast seen by John about the year 96 C.E. That beast also has the characteristics of a lion, a bear, and a leopard, and it has ten horns. What is the identity of the huge beasts seen by Daniel? He informs us: "These huge beasts . . . are four kings that will stand up from the earth." (Daniel 7:17) Yes, those beasts represent "kings," or political powers of the earth.

4 In another vision, Daniel sees a two-horned ram that is struck down by a goat with a great horn. The angel Gabriel explains to him what it means: "The ram . . . stands for the kings of Media and Persia. And the hairy he-goat stands for the king of Greece." Gabriel goes on to prophesy that the great horn of the he-goat would be broken and be succeeded by four horns. This actually happened more than 200 years later when Alexander the Great died and his kingdom was split into four kingdoms ruled over by four of his generals.—Daniel 8:3-8, 20-25.*

5 It is clear, therefore, that the Author of the inspired Bible regards the political powers of the earth as beasts. What kind of beasts? One commentator calls the wild beast of Revelation 13:1, 2 a "brute," and adds: "We accept all the connotations that θηρίον [the·ri′on, the Greek word for "beast"] conveys, such as that of a cruel, destructive, frightful, ravenous, etc., monster."# How well that describes the bloodstained political system by which Satan has dominated mankind! The seven heads of this wild beast stand for six major world powers featured in Bible history up to John's day—Egypt, Assyria, Babylon, Medo-Persia, Greece, and Rome—and a seventh world power prophesied to appear later.—Compare Revelation 17:9, 10.

6 True, there have been other world powers in history besides the seven—just as the wild beast John saw was made up of a body as well as of seven heads and ten horns. But the seven heads represent the seven major powers that have, each in its turn, taken the

---

3. (a) What ferocious beasts did the prophet Daniel see in visions? (b) What did the huge beasts of Daniel 7 represent?
4. (a) In Daniel 8, what did the ram and the he-goat portray? (b) What was indicated when the great horn of the he-goat was broken and it was succeeded by four horns?

---

* For further details, please see pages 166-201 of the book *Your Will Be Done on Earth*, published by the Watchtower Bible and Tract Society of New York, Inc.
# *The Interpretation of St. John's Revelation*, by R. C. H. Lenski, pages 390-1.

5. (a) What connotations does the Greek word for beast convey? (b) What does the wild beast of Revelation 13:1, 2, along with its seven heads, stand for?
6. (a) In what have the seven heads of the wild beast taken the lead? (b) How was Rome used by Jehovah in executing his own judgment on the Jewish system of things, and how did the Christians in Jerusalem fare?

Vision _____ 8

Revelation 13:1-18

Subject: The seven-headed wild beast, the two-horned wild beast, and the image of the wild beast

Time of fulfillment: From Nimrod's day to the great tribulation

---

CONTENDING WITH TWO FEROCIOUS BEASTS

lead in oppressing God's people. In 33 C.E., while Rome was ascendant, Satan used that head of the wild beast to kill the Son of God. At that time, God abandoned the faithless Jewish system of things and later, in 70 C.E., allowed Rome to execute his judgment on that nation. Happily, the true Israel of God, the congregation of anointed Christians, had been forewarned, and those in Jerusalem and Judea had fled to safety beyond the Jordan River.—Matthew 24:15, 16; Galatians 6:16.

7 By the end of the first century C.E., however, many in this early congregation had fallen away from the truth, and the true Christian wheat, "the sons of the kingdom," had been largely choked out by weeds, "the sons of the wicked one." But when the conclusion of the system of things arrived, anointed Christians again appeared as an organized group. During the Lord's day, the righteous ones were due to "shine as brightly as the sun." Hence, the Christian congregation was organized for work. (Matthew 13:24-30, 36-43) By then, the Roman Empire was no more. The huge British Empire, along with the powerful United States of America, held the center of the world stage. This dual world power proved to be the seventh head of the wild beast.

8 Is it not shocking to identify the ruling political powers with a wild beast? That is what some opposers claimed during World War II, when the status of Jehovah's Witnesses, as an organization and as individuals, was being challenged in law courts around the earth. But stop and think! Do not the nations themselves adopt beasts or wild creatures as their national symbols? For example, there are the British lion, the American eagle,

the Chinese dragon, and the Russian bear. So why should anyone object if the divine Author of the Holy Bible also uses beasts to symbolize world powers?

9 Moreover, why should anyone object to the Bible's saying that it is Satan who gives the wild beast its great authority? God is the Source of that statement, and before him 'the nations are as a drop from a bucket and as a film of dust.' Those nations would do better to court God's favor than to take offense at the way his prophetic Word describes them. (Isaiah 40:15, 17; Psalm 2:10-12) Satan is no mythical person assigned to tormenting departed souls in a fiery hell. No such place exists. Rather, Satan is described in Scripture as "an angel of light"—a master of deception who exercises powerful influence in general political affairs.—2 Corinthians 11:3, 14, 15; Ephesians 6:11-18.

10 The wild beast has ten horns on its seven heads. Perhaps four heads had one horn each and three heads two horns each. Moreover, it had ten diadems on its horns. In the book of Daniel, fearsome beasts are described, and the numbering of their horns is to be interpreted literally. For example, the two horns on a ram represented a world empire made up of two partners, Media and Persia, while the four horns on a goat represented the four coexisting empires that grew out of Alexander the Great's Greek empire. (Daniel 8:3, 8, 20-22) On the beast that John saw, however, the numbering of the ten horns appears to be symbolic. (Compare Daniel 7:24; Revelation 17:12.) They represent the completeness of sovereign states making up the entire political organization of Satan. All these horns are violent and aggressive, but as indicated by the seven

7. (a) What was due to take place when the conclusion of the system of things arrived and the Lord's day began? (b) What proved to be the seventh head of the wild beast of Revelation 13:1, 2?
8. Why should it not be shocking that the Anglo-American dual world power is likened to a beast?

9. (a) Why should one not object to the Bible's saying that Satan gives the wild beast its great authority? (b) How is Satan described in the Bible, and how does he influence governments?
10. (a) What is denoted by the fact that on each of the ten horns there was a diadem? (b) What do the ten horns and the ten diadems symbolize?

The one of Pg 241 Does Not

This Beast has Diadems

heads, headship resides in only one world power at a time. Similarly, the ten diadems indicate that all sovereign states would exercise ruling power simultaneously with the dominant state, or world power, of that time.

¹¹ The wild beast has "upon its heads blasphemous names," making claims for itself that show great disrespect for Jehovah God and Christ Jesus. It has used the names of God and Christ as a sham to achieve its political ends; and it has played along with false religion, even allowing the clergy to take part in its political processes. For example, the House of Lords in England includes the bishops. Catholic cardinals have played prominent political roles in France and Italy, and more recently, priests have taken political office in Latin America. Governments print religious slogans, such as "IN GOD WE TRUST," on their bank notes, and on their coins they claim divine approval for their rulers, stating, for example, that these are

appointed "by the grace of God." All of this is actually blasphemous, for it attempts to involve God in the sullied nationalistic political arena.

¹² The wild beast comes out of "the sea," which is a fitting symbol of the turbulent masses from which human government springs. (Isaiah 17:12, 13) This wild beast began to emerge out of the sea of turbulent humanity away back in the days of Nimrod (about the 21st century B.C.E.), when a post-Flood system of things, opposed to Jehovah, first manifested itself. (Genesis 10:8-12; 11:1-9) But only during the Lord's day has the last one of its seven heads fully manifested itself. Notice, too, it is the dragon that "gave to the beast its power and its throne and great authority." (Compare Luke 4:6.) The beast is Satan's political creation among the masses of mankind. Satan is truly "the ruler of this world."—John 12:31.

---

11. What is indicated by the fact that the wild beast has "upon its heads blasphemous names"?

---

12. (a) What is signified by the wild beast's coming out of "the sea," and when did it begin to emerge? (b) What is indicated by the fact that the dragon gives the symbolic beast its great authority?

CONTENDING WITH TWO FEROCIOUS BEASTS

The Death Stroke

START

[13] Early in the Lord's day, calamity strikes the wild beast. John reports: *"And I saw one of its heads as though slaughtered to death, but its death-stroke got healed, and all the earth followed the wild beast with admiration."* (*Revelation 13:3*) This verse says that one head of the wild beast received a death stroke, but verse 12 speaks as though the entire beast suffered. Why is that? Well, the beast's heads are not all in the ascendancy together. Each in its turn has lorded it over mankind, particularly over God's people. (Revelation 17:10) Thus, as the Lord's day begins, there is only one head, the seventh, acting as the dominant world power. A death stroke on that head brings great distress to the entire wild beast.

[14] What was the death stroke? Later, it is called a sword stroke, and a sword is a symbol of warfare. This sword stroke, administered early in the Lord's day, must relate to the first world war, which devastated and drained Satan's political wild beast. (Revelation 6:4, 8; 13:14) Author Maurice Genevoix, who was a military officer during that war, said of it: "Everyone agrees in recognizing that in the whole history of mankind, few dates have had the importance of August 2, 1914. First Europe and soon after almost all humanity found themselves plunged into a dreadful event. Conventions, agreements, moral laws, all the foundations shook; from one day to the next, everything was called into question. The event was to exceed both instinctive forebodings and reasonable anticipations. Enormous, chaotic, monstrous, it still drags us in its wake." —Maurice Genevoix, member of the *Acadé-*

mie Française, quoted in the book *Promise of Greatness* (1968).

[15] For the dominant seventh head of the wild beast, that war was a major disaster. Along with other European nations, Britain lost its young men in traumatic numbers. In one battle alone, the Battle of the River Somme in 1916, 420,000 British soldiers died, along with 200,000 French and 450,000 German—more than 1,000,000 fatalities! Economically, too, Britain—together with the rest of Europe—was shattered. The huge British Empire staggered under the blow and never fully recovered. Indeed, that war, with 28 leading nations participating, sent the entire world reeling as if by a deathblow. On August 4, 1979, just 65 years after the outbreak of World War I, *The Economist,* of London, England, commented: "In 1914 the world lost a coherence which it has not managed to recapture since."

[16] At the same time, the Great War, as it was then called, opened the way for the United States to emerge distinctly as part of the Anglo-American World Power. For the first years of the war, public opinion kept the United States out of the conflict. But as his-

13. (a) What calamity assails the wild beast early in the Lord's day? (b) How is it that the entire wild beast suffered when one head received a death stroke?

14. When was the death stroke administered, and how did a military officer describe its effect on Satan's wild beast?

15. How did the seventh head of the wild beast receive its death stroke?

16. During the first world war, how did the United States show that it was part of a dual world power?

torian Esmé Wingfield-Stratford wrote, "it was all a question of whether, at this hour of supreme crisis, Britain and the United States would sink their differences in the realization of [their] overmastering unity and common trusteeship." As events turned out, they did. In 1917 the United States contributed her resources and manpower to bolster the war effort of the staggering Allies. Thus, the seventh head, combining Britain and the United States, came out on the winning side.

[17] The world after the war was vastly different. Satan's earthly system, although devastated by the death stroke, revived and became more powerful than ever and so won the admiration of humans because of its recuperative power.

[18] Historian Charles L. Mee, Jr., writes: "The collapse of the old order [caused by the first world war] was a necessary prelude to the spread of self-rule, the liberation of new nations and classes, the release of new freedom and independence." Leading in the development of this postwar era was the seventh head of the wild beast, now healed, and with the United States of America moving into the dominant role. The dual world power took the lead in advocating both the League of Nations and the United Nations. By the 1980's, U.S. political power had led the more privileged nations in creating a higher standard of living, in fighting disease, and in advancing technology. It had even placed 12 men on the moon. It is no wonder, therefore, that mankind in general has "followed the wild beast with admiration."

[19] Mankind has even gone beyond admir-ing the wild beast, as John next states: **"And they worshiped the dragon because it gave the authority to the wild beast, and they worshiped the wild beast with the words: 'Who is like the wild beast, and who can do battle with it?'"** (**Revelation 13:4**) While Jesus was here on earth, Satan claimed to have authority over all the kingdoms of the earth. Jesus did not dispute this; in fact, he himself referred to Satan as the ruler of the world and refused to participate in the politics of that day. John later wrote of true Christians: "We know we originate with God, but the whole world is lying in the power of the wicked one." (1 John 5:19; Luke 4:5-8; John 6:15; 14:30) Satan delegates authority to the wild beast, and he does this on a nationalistic basis. Thus, instead of being united in bonds of godly love, mankind has become divided by pride of tribe, race, and nation. The great majority of people worship, in effect, that part of the wild beast having authority in the land where they happen to live. Thus the whole beast gains admiration and worship.

[20] Worship in what sense? In the sense of putting love of country ahead of love of God. Most people love the land of their birth. As good citizens, true Christians also respect the rulers and the emblems of the country where they reside, obey the laws, and make a positive contribution to the welfare of their community and their neighbors. (Romans 13: 1-7; 1 Peter 2:13-17) They cannot, however, give blind devotion to one country as against all others. "Our country, right or wrong" is not a Christian teaching. So Christians who worship Jehovah God cannot share in giving prideful patriotic worship to any part of the wild beast, for this would amount to worshiping the dragon—the source of authority of the beast. They cannot ask admiringly: "Who is like the wild beast?" Rather, they follow the example of Michael—his name

17. What happened to Satan's earthly system after the war?
18. How can it be said that mankind in general has "followed the wild beast with admiration"?
19. (a) How has mankind even gone beyond admir-ing the wild beast? (b) Who has undisputed author-ity over all the kingdoms of the earth, and how do we know? (c) How does Satan delegate authority to the wild beast, and with what effect on the majority of people?

20. (a) In what sense do people worship the wild beast? (b) Why do Christians who worship Jehovah God not take part in such worship of the wild beast, and whose example do they follow?

meaning "Who Is Like God?"—as they uphold Jehovah's universal sovereignty. At God's appointed time, this Michael, Christ Jesus, will do battle with the wild beast and conquer it, even as he triumphed in expelling Satan from heaven.—Revelation 12:7-9; 19:11, 19-21.

Waging War Against the Holy Ones

21 The wily Satan had plans for manipulating the wild beast to his own ends. John explains this: *"And a mouth speaking great things and blasphemies was given it* [the seven-headed beast]*, and authority to act forty-two months was given it. And it opened its mouth in blasphemies against God, to blaspheme his name and his residence, even those residing in heaven. And there was granted it to wage war with the holy ones and conquer them, and authority was given it over every tribe and people and tongue and nation. And all those who dwell on the earth will worship it; the name of not one of them stands written in the scroll of life of the Lamb who was slaughtered, from the founding of the world."—Revelation 13:5-8.*

22 The 42 months mentioned here appear to be the same as the three and a half years during which the holy ones are harassed by a horn arising from one of the beasts in Daniel's prophecy. (Daniel 7:23-25; see also Revelation 11:1-4.) Thus, from the latter part of 1914 on into 1918, while the warring nations were literally tearing at one another like wild beasts, citizens of those nations were pressured to worship the wild beast, to indulge in the religion of nationalism, even to be ready to die for their country. Such pressure led to intense suffering on the part of many of the anointed ones, who felt that their higher obedience belonged to Jehovah God and his Son, Christ Jesus. (Acts 5:29)

Their trials came to a climax in May 1918, when they were 'conquered.' In the United States, prominent officers and other representatives of the Watch Tower Society were wrongly imprisoned, and the organized preaching by their Christian brothers was greatly hindered. Having authority "over every tribe and people and tongue and nation," the wild beast clamped down on God's work worldwide.

23 This seemed like a victory for Satan and his organization. But it could bring them no long-term benefits, since no one in Satan's visible organization had his name written in "the scroll of life of the Lamb." Figuratively, this scroll contains the names of those who will rule with Jesus in his heavenly Kingdom. The first names were written in it at Pentecost 33 C.E. And in the years since then, more and more names have been added. Since 1918, the sealing of the remaining ones of the 144,000 Kingdom heirs has been proceeding to completion. Soon, the names of all of them will be written indelibly in the Lamb's scroll of life. As for the opposers who worship the wild beast, not one of these will have his name written in that scroll. So any apparent victory these may have over "the holy ones" is an empty one, merely temporary.

24 John now calls upon those with discernment to listen very carefully: *"If anyone has an ear, let him hear."* Then he goes on to say: *"If anyone is meant for captivity, he goes away into captivity. If anyone will kill with the sword, he must be killed with the sword. Here is where it means the endurance and faith of the holy ones."* (Revelation 13:9, 10) Jeremiah wrote words quite similar to these in the

---

21. How does John describe Satan's manipulation of the wild beast?
22. (a) To what time period do the 42 months refer? (b) During the 42 months, how were the anointed Christians 'conquered'?

---

23. (a) What is "the scroll of life of the Lamb," and what has been proceeding to completion since 1918? (b) Why was any apparent victory for Satan's visible organization over "the holy ones" merely an empty one?
24. What does John call upon those with discernment to hear, and what do the words heard mean for God's people?

(handwritten annotations on image: "INDICATES PARTNERSHIP", "HORNS... OF... POLITICAL", "POWERS", "SPEAKING OF ... GOD")

The Two-Horned Wild Beast START 3/8/92

²⁵ But now another wild beast comes onto the world scene. John reports: *"And I saw another wild beast ascending out of the earth, and it had two horns like a lamb, but it began speaking as a dragon. And it exercises all the authority of the first wild beast in its sight. And it makes the earth and those who dwell in it worship the first wild beast, whose death-stroke got healed. And it performs great signs, so that it should even make fire come down out of heaven to the earth in the sight of mankind."* (*Revelation 13:11-13*) This wild beast has two horns, indicating a partnership of two political powers. And it is described as coming out of the earth, not out of the sea. Thus, it comes out of Satan's already established earthly system of things. It must be a world power, already existing, that takes on a significant role during the Lord's day.

years preceding 607 B.C.E., to show that there was no turning back of Jehovah's judgments for the unfaithful city of Jerusalem. (Jeremiah 15:2; see also Jeremiah 43:11; Zechariah 11:9.) In his time of great trial, Jesus made it plain that his followers must not compromise when he said: "All those who take the sword will perish by the sword." (Matthew 26:52) Similarly, now in the Lord's day God's people must hold fast to Bible principles. There will be no final escape for unrepentant ones who worship the wild beast. All of us will need endurance, along with unshakable faith, in order to survive the persecutions and trials that lie ahead.—Hebrews 10:36-39; 11:6.

———

25. (a) How does John describe another symbolic wild beast that comes onto the world scene? (b) What is indicated by the two horns of the new wild beast and by its coming out of the earth?

CONTENDING WITH TWO FEROCIOUS BEASTS

26 What can it be? The Anglo-American World Power—the same as the seventh head of the first wild beast but in a special role! Isolating it in the vision as a separate wild beast helps us to see more clearly how it acts independently on the world stage. This figurative two-horned wild beast is made up of two coexisting, independent, but cooperating political powers. Its two horns "like a lamb" suggest that it makes itself out to be mild and inoffensive, with an enlightened form of government to which all the world should turn. But it speaks "as a dragon" in that it uses pressure and threats and even outright violence wherever its version of rulership is not accepted. It has not encouraged submission to God's Kingdom under the rule of the Lamb of God but, rather, to the interests of Satan, the great dragon. It has promoted nationalistic divisions and hatreds that add up to worshiping the first wild beast.*

27 This two-horned wild beast performs great signs, even making fire come down from heaven. (Compare Matthew 7:21-23.) This latter sign reminds us of Elijah, the ancient prophet of God who engaged in a

---

* Commentators have noted that nationalism, in effect, is a religion. Hence, people who are nationalistic are really worshiping that portion of the wild beast represented by the country in which they live. Regarding nationalism in the United States, we read: "Nationalism, viewed as a religion, has much in common with other great religious systems of the past . . . On his own national god the modern religious nationalist is conscious of dependence. Of His powerful help he feels the need. In Him he recognises the source of his own perfection and happiness. To Him, in a strictly religious sense, he subjects himself. . . . The nation is conceived of as eternal, and the deaths of her loyal sons do but add to her undying fame and glory." —Carlton J. F. Hayes, as quoted on page 359 of the book *What Americans Believe and How They Worship*, by J. Paul Williams.

26. (a) What is the two-horned wild beast, and how does it relate to the original wild beast? (b) In what sense are the horns of the two-horned beast lamblike, and how is it "as a dragon" when speaking? (c) What are nationalistic people really worshiping, and to what has nationalism been likened? (See footnote.)

27. (a) What attitude of the two-horned wild beast is indicated by the fact that it makes fire come down out of heaven? (b) How do many people view the modern counterpart of the two-horned wild beast?

contest with the prophets of Baal. When he successfully called down fire from heaven in the name of Jehovah, it proved beyond doubt that he was a true prophet and that the Baal prophets were false. (1 Kings 18: 21-40) Like those Baal prophets, the two-horned wild beast feels that it has adequate credentials as a prophet. (Compare Revelation 13:14, 15; 19:20.) Why, it claims to have vanquished the forces of evil in two world wars, and now it stands firm against so-called godless communism! Many, indeed, view the modern counterpart of the two-horned wild beast as a guardian of liberty and a font of material good things.

The Image of the Wild Beast

28 Is this two-horned wild beast as innocent as its lamblike horns would indicate? John goes on to say: **"And it misleads those who dwell on the earth, because of the signs that were granted it to perform in the sight of the wild beast, while it tells those who dwell on the earth to make an image to the wild beast that had the sword-stroke and yet revived. And there was granted it to give breath to the image of the wild beast, so that the image of the wild beast should both speak and cause to be killed all those who would not in any way worship the image of the wild beast."**—Revelation 13: 14, 15.

29 What is this "image of the wild beast," and what is its purpose? The purpose is to promote the worship of the seven-headed wild beast of which it is an image and thus, in effect, to perpetuate the existence of the wild beast. This image is constructed after the seven-headed wild beast revives from its sword stroke, that is, after the end of the first world war. It is no lifeless statue, such as

---

28. How does John show that the two-horned wild beast is not as innocent as its lamblike horns would indicate?

29. (a) What is the purpose of the image of the wild beast, and when was this image constructed? (b) Why is the image of the wild beast no lifeless statue?

REVELATION CLIMAX

There was granted it to give breath to the image of the wild beast

Nebuchadnezzar erected on the plains of Dura. (Daniel 3:1) The two-horned wild beast breathes life into this image so that the image can live and play a role in world history.

30 The outworking of history identifies this image as the organization proposed, promoted, and supported by Britain and the United States and known initially as the League of Nations. Later, in Revelation chapter 17, it will appear under a different symbol, that of a living, breathing scarlet-colored wild beast having an independent existence. This international body 'speaks,' in that it makes boastful claims to be the only one able to bring peace and security to mankind. But in reality it has become a forum for member nations to exchange verbal tirades and insults. It has threatened with ostracism, or a living death, any nation or people that does not bow to its authority. It has actually ex-

pelled nations that fail to abide by its ideologies. At the onset of the great tribulation, militaristic "horns" of this image of the wild beast will fulfill a devastating role.—Revelation 7:14; 17:8, 16.

31 Since World War II, the image of the wild beast—now manifested as the United Nations organization—has already killed in a literal way. For example, in 1950 a UN force took the field in the war between North Korea and South Korea. The UN force, along with the South Koreans, killed an estimated 1,420,000 North Koreans and Chinese. Similarly, from 1960 to 1964, United Nations armies were active in the Congo (now Zaire). Moreover, world leaders, including popes Paul VI and John Paul II, have continued to affirm that this image is man's last and best hope for peace. If mankind fails to serve it, they insist, the human race will destroy itself. They thus figuratively cause to be killed all humans who refuse to go along with the image and worship it.—Compare Deuteronomy 5:8, 9.

30, 31. (a) What do the facts of history identify this image to be? (b) Have any been killed for refusing to worship this image? Explain.

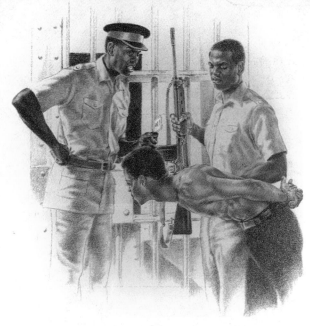

The Mark of the Wild Beast

³² John now sees how Satan maneuvers the political parts of his visible organization to cause the maximum suffering for the remaining ones of the seed of God's woman. (Genesis 3:15) He returns to describing "the wild beast" itself: *"And it puts under compulsion all persons, the small and the great, and the rich and the poor, and the free and the slaves, that they should give these a mark in their right hand or upon their forehead, and that nobody might be able to buy or sell except a person having the mark, the name of the wild beast or the number of its name. Here is where wisdom comes in: Let the one that has intelligence calculate the number of the wild beast, for it is a man's number; and its number is six hundred and sixty-six."—Revelation 13:16-18.*

³³ The wild beast has a name, and this name is a number: 666. Six, as a number, is associated with Jehovah's enemies. A Philistine man of the Rephaim was of "extraordi-

nary size," and his "fingers and toes were in sixes." (1 Chronicles 20:6) King Nebuchadnezzar erected a golden image 6 cubits in breadth and 60 cubits high, to unify his political officials in one worship. When God's servants refused to worship the image of gold, the king had them thrown into a fiery furnace. (Daniel 3:1-23) The number six falls short of seven, which stands for completeness from God's standpoint. Therefore, a triple six represents gross imperfection.

³⁴ A name identifies a person. So how does this number identify the beast? John says that it "is a man's number," not that of a spirit person, so the name helps to confirm that the wild beast is earthly, symbolizing human government. Just as six fails to measure up to seven, so 666—six to the third degree—is a fitting name for the world's gigantic political system that fails so miserably to measure up to God's standard of perfection. The world's political wild beast rules supreme under the name-number 666, while big politics, big religion, and big busi-

---

32. How does John describe Satan's maneuvering of the political parts of his visible organization to cause suffering for the remaining ones of the seed of God's woman?

33. (a) What is the name of the wild beast? (b) With what is the number six associated? Explain.

34. (a) What is indicated by the fact that the number of the wild beast "is a man's number"? (b) Why is 666 a fitting name for Satan's world political system?

way the wild beast does, as, for example, in celebrating holidays. They are expected to worship the wild beast, letting it rule their lives, so as to receive its mark.

36 Those who refuse to accept the mark of the wild beast have had constant problems. Starting in the 1930's, for example, they had to fight many court battles and endure violent mobbings and other persecutions. In the totalitarian countries, they were thrown into concentration camps, where many died. Since the second world war, countless young men have suffered lengthy imprisonments; some even being tortured and killed, because of their refusal to compromise their Christian neutrality. In other lands Christians are literally unable to buy or sell; some are unable to own property; others are raped, murdered, or chased from their native land. Why? Because in good conscience they refuse to buy a political party card.*—John 17:16.

* See, for example, the *Watchtower* issues of September 1, 1971, page 520; June 15, 1974, page 373; June 1, 1975, page 341; February 1, 1979, page 23; June 1, 1979, page 20; May 15, 1980, page 10.

36. Those who refuse to accept the mark of the wild beast have had what problems?

ness keep that wild beast functioning as an oppressor of mankind and a persecutor of God's people.

35 What does it mean to be marked on the forehead or in the right hand with the name of the wild beast? When Jehovah gave Israel the Law, he told them: "You must apply these words of mine to your heart and your soul and bind them as a sign upon your hand, and they must serve as a frontlet band between your eyes." (Deuteronomy 11:18) This meant that the Israelites had to keep that Law constantly before them, so that it influenced all their actions and thoughts. The 144,000 anointed ones are said to have the Father's name and that of Jesus written on their foreheads. This identifies them as belonging to Jehovah God and Jesus Christ. (Revelation 14:1) In imitation, Satan uses the demonic mark of the wild beast. Anybody engaged in everyday activities such as buying and selling is pressured to do things the

35. What does it mean to be marked on the forehead or in the right hand with the name of the wild beast?

³⁷ In some areas of the earth, religion is so ingrained in community life that anyone who stands for Bible truth is ostracized by family and former friends. It takes great faith to endure. (Matthew 10:36-38; 17:22) In a world where the majority worship material wealth and where dishonesty is rampant, the true Christian often has to trust implicitly in Jehovah that He will uphold him in pursuing an upright course. (Psalm 11:7; Hebrews 13:18) In a world awash with immorality, it takes great determination to remain clean and pure. Christians who fall sick are often pressured by doctors and nurses to break God's law on the sanctity of blood; they even have to resist court orders that conflict with their faith. (Acts 15:28, 29; 1 Peter 4:3, 4) And in these days of rising unemployment, it is becoming increasingly difficult for a true Christian to avoid work that would mean compromising his integrity before God.—Micah 4:3, 5.

³⁸ Yes, the world is a difficult place for those who do not have the mark of the wild beast. It is an outstanding demonstration of Jehovah's power and blessing that the remaining ones of the seed of the woman, as well as more than three million of the great crowd, are keeping integrity despite all the pressures to break God's laws. (Revelation 7:9) Unitedly, throughout the earth, may all of us continue to magnify Jehovah and his righteous ways, as we refuse to receive the mark of the wild beast.—Psalm 34:1-3.

37, 38. (a) Why is the world a difficult place for those who refuse to have the mark of the wild beast? (b) Who are keeping integrity, and what are they determined to do?

Singing the Triumphal New Song

Start 3/8/92 17

HOW refreshing it is to turn to John's next vision! In contrast with the dragon's grotesque beastlike organizations, we now see Jehovah's loyal servants and their activities during the Lord's day. (Revelation 1:10) Already, Revelation 7:1, 3 has disclosed to us that the four winds of destruction are being held back until all 144,000 of these anointed slaves are sealed. Revelation 12:17 has made known that these "remaining ones of [the woman's] seed" become the special target of Satan, the dragon, during that time. And Revelation chapter 13 has vividly depicted the political organizations raised up on earth by Satan to bring intense pressure and cruel persecution on Jehovah's faithful servants. But that archenemy cannot thwart God's purpose! We will now learn that despite Satan's malevolent activity, all the 144,000 are triumphantly gathered.

² John, and with him the John class today, is given a preview of that happy outcome: **"And I saw, and, look! the Lamb standing upon**

---

1. What have we already learned regarding Revelation chapters 7, 12, and 13, and what will we now learn?

2. What preview of a happy finale does John give us at Revelation 14:1, and who is the Lamb?

the Mount Zion, and with him a hundred and forty-four thousand having his name and the name of his Father written on their foreheads." (*Revelation 14:1*) As we have seen, this Lamb is the same as the Michael who cleansed the heavens by casting out the Devil and his demons. He is the Michael whom Daniel describes as "standing in behalf of the sons of [God's] people" as he prepares to "stand up" in executing Jehovah's righteous judgments. (Daniel 12:1; Revelation 12:7, 9) Since 1914 this self-sacrificing Lamb of God has been standing on Mount Zion as the Messianic King.

³ It is just as Jehovah foretold: "I, even I, have installed my king upon Zion, my holy mountain." (Psalm 2:6; 110:2) This no longer refers to the earthly Mount Zion, the geographical location of earthly Jerusalem, in which city human kings in the line of David used to reign. (1 Chronicles 11:4-7; 2 Chronicles 5:2) No, for Jesus, after his death and resurrection in 33 C.E., was installed as a foundation cornerstone on the heavenly Mount Zion, the celestial location where Jehovah determined to place the "city of the living God, heavenly Jerusalem." Hence, "the Mount Zion" here represents the exalted position of Jesus and his joint heirs, who make up heavenly Jerusalem, which is the Kingdom. (Hebrews 12:22, 28; Ephesians 3:6) It is the glorious royal situation to which Jehovah

---

3. What is "the Mount Zion" upon which the Lamb and the 144,000 are "standing"?

Vision   9

Revelation 14:1-20

Subject: The 144,000 are with the Lamb on Mount Zion; angelic pronouncements sound through the earth; harvests are reaped

Time of fulfillment: 1914 to the great tribulation

elevates them during the Lord's day. Over the centuries, anointed Christians, as "living stones," have earnestly looked forward to standing on that heavenly Mount Zion, united with the glorified Lord Jesus Christ in his majestic Kingdom.—1 Peter 2:4-6; Luke 22:28-30; John 14:2, 3.

⁴ John sees not only Jesus but the complete body of the 144,000 fellow heirs of the heavenly Kingdom standing upon the Mount Zion. At the time represented by the vision, many, but not all, of the 144,000 are already in heaven. Later in the same vision, John learns that some of the holy ones still have to endure and die faithful. (Revelation 14:12, 13) Evidently, then, some of the 144,000 are still on earth. So how is it that John sees all of them standing with Jesus on Mount Zion?* In that, as members of the congregation of anointed Christians, these have now "approached a Mount Zion and a city of the living God, heavenly Jerusalem." (Hebrews 12:22) Like Paul when he was still on earth, they have already—in a spiritual sense—been raised up to be in union with Christ Jesus in heavenly places. (Ephesians 2:5, 6) Additionally, in 1919 they responded to the invitation, "Come on up here," and in a figurative way "went up into heaven in the cloud." (Revelation 11:12) In view of these scriptures, we can see that all the 144,000—spiritually speaking—are located on Mount Zion with Jesus Christ.

⁵ The 144,000 have no part with the worshipers of the wild beast, who are marked with the symbolic number 666. (Revelation 13:15-18) In contrast, these loyal ones have the name of God and of the Lamb written on

---

* As 1 Corinthians 4:8 shows, anointed Christians do not rule as kings while here on earth. Nevertheless, according to the context at Revelation 14:3, 6, 12, 13, they share in singing the new song by preaching the good news as they endure to the end of their earthly course.

---

4. How is it that all the 144,000 are standing on Mount Zion?
5. Whose names are written on the foreheads of the 144,000, and what is the significance of each name?

their foreheads. No doubt John, a Jew, saw God's name in Hebrew lettering, יהוה.* In having the name of Jesus' Father symbolically written on their foreheads, these sealed ones make known to all that they are *Jehovah's* witnesses, *His* slaves. (Revelation 3:12) Their having Jesus' name also displayed on their foreheads indicates that they acknowledge being owned by him. He is their betrothed "husband," and they are his prospective "bride," "a new creation" serving God with heavenly life in view. (Ephesians 5:22-24; Revelation 21:2, 9; 2 Corinthians 5:17) Their intimate relationship with Jehovah and Jesus Christ affects all their thoughts and actions.

Singing as if a New Song

⁶ In harmony with this, John reports: *"And I heard a sound out of heaven as the sound of many waters and as the sound of loud thunder; and the sound that I heard was as of singers who accompany themselves on the harp playing on their harps. And they are singing as if a new song before the throne and before the four living creatures and the elders; and no one was able to master that song but the hundred and forty-four thousand, who have been bought from the earth."* (*Revelation 14:2, 3*) It is no wonder that John, upon hearing 144,000 voices joined in one melodious chorus, is reminded of roaring waterfalls and pealing thunderclaps. How pleasant that clear harplike accompaniment! (Psalm 81:2) What choir on earth could ever attain to the grandeur of that magnificent chorus?

⁷ And what is this "new song"? As we noted in discussing Revelation 5:9, 10, the song has to do with Jehovah's Kingdom purposes and his wonderful provision, through Jesus Christ, for making spiritual Israel "a kingdom and priests to our God." It is a song of praise to Jehovah publicizing the new things he is accomplishing by means of the Israel of God and in behalf of it. (Galatians 6:16) Members of this spiritual Israel respond to the psalmist's invitation: "Praise Jah, you people! Sing to Jehovah a new song, his praise in the congregation of loyal ones. Let Israel rejoice in its grand Maker, the sons of Zion—let them be joyful in their King." (Psalm 149:1, 2) True, those words were written centuries ago, but in our day, they have been sung with new understanding. In 1914 the Messianic Kingdom was born. (Revelation 12:10) In 1919 Jehovah's people on earth began to announce "the word of the kingdom" with renewed zeal. (Matthew 13:19) Stimulated by the Society's yeartext for 1919 (Isaiah 54:17) and encouraged by their restoration to a spiritual paradise, they began in that year to 'sing to Jehovah with music in their hearts.'—Ephesians 5:19.

⁸ Why is it, though, that only the 144,000 are able to learn the song mentioned at Revelation 14:3? Because it has to do with their experiences as chosen heirs of God's Kingdom. They alone are adopted as sons of God and anointed with holy spirit. They alone are bought from the earth to become part of that heavenly Kingdom, and they alone "will be priests . . . and will rule as kings" with Jesus Christ for a thousand years to bring mankind to perfection. They alone are seen to be "singing as if a new song" in the very presence of Jehovah.* These unique experiences

---

* This is supported by the use of Hebrew names in other visions; Jesus is given the Hebrew name "Abaddon" (meaning "Destruction") and executes judgment at the place "called in Hebrew Har–Magedon."—Revelation 9:11; 16:16.

6. What singing does John hear, and how does he describe it?
7. (a) What is the new song of Revelation 14:3? (b) How is it that the song of Psalm 149:1 is new in our day?

---

* The scripture says *"as if* a new song," for the song itself was recorded in the prophetic word in ancient times. But there was no one qualified to sing it. Now, with the establishing of the Kingdom and the resurrecting of the holy ones, the realities had burst forth in fulfillment of the prophecies, and it was time to vocalize the song in all its grandeur.

---

8. Why is it that only the 144,000 are able to learn the new song of Revelation 14:3?

and prospects give them a singular appreciation of the Kingdom and enable them to sing about it in a way that no one else can. —Revelation 20:6; Colossians 1:13; 1 Thessalonians 2:11, 12.

9 Nevertheless, others listen and respond to their singing. Since 1935 a growing great crowd of other sheep has heard their triumphant song and been moved to join with them in publicizing God's Kingdom. (John 10:16; Revelation 7:9) True, these newcomers cannot learn to sing exactly the same new song that the future rulers of God's Kingdom sing. But they too sound a melodious chorus of praise to Jehovah that is an anthem lauding Jehovah for the new things he is accomplishing. They thus fulfill the psalmist's exhortation: "Sing to Jehovah a new song. Sing to Jehovah, all you people of the earth. Sing to Jehovah, bless his name. From day to day tell the good news of salvation by him. Declare among the nations his glory, among all the peoples his wonderful works. Ascribe to Jehovah, O you families of the peoples, ascribe to Jehovah glory and strength. Say among the nations: 'Jehovah himself has become king.'"—Psalm 96:1-3, 7, 10; 98:1-9.

10 How can the 144,000 sing "before" the elders, since the 24 elders are the 144,000 in their glorious heavenly position? Early in the Lord's day, those "dead in union with Christ" were resurrected as spirit creatures. Thus, faithful anointed Christians who have conquered are now in heaven, symbolically fulfilling functions comparable to those of 24 divisions of priestly elders. They are included in the vision of Jehovah's heavenly organization. (1 Thessalonians 4:15, 16; 1 Chronicles 24:1-18; Revelation 4:4; 6:11) The remnant of the 144,000 still on earth are therefore singing the new song before, or in the sight of, their resurrected brothers in heaven.

11 At this point we might also ask: Why is it that these anointed overcomers are referred to as the symbolic 24 elders as well as the 144,000? It is because Revelation views this one group from two different standpoints. The 24 elders are always shown in their ultimate position around Jehovah's throne, installed as kings and priests in the heavens. They symbolize the entire group of 144,000 in their heavenly position, although at present a small remnant of these is still on earth. (Revelation 4:4, 10; 5:5-14; 7:11-13; 11: 16-18) Revelation chapter 7, however, focuses on the 144,000 as brought forth from humankind, and it stresses Jehovah's grand purpose to seal the complete number of individual spiritual Israelites and to grant salvation to an unnumbered great crowd. Revelation chapter 14 provides a picture confirming that the complete Kingdom class of 144,000 individual overcomers will be assembled with the Lamb on Mount Zion. The qualifications to be met in order to be numbered with the 144,000 are also made known, as we shall now see.*

Followers of the Lamb

12 Continuing his description of the 144,-000 who are "bought from the earth," John tells us: *"These are the ones that did not defile themselves with women; in fact, they are virgins. These are the ones that keep following the Lamb no matter where he goes. These were*

* The situation may be compared to that of the faithful and discreet slave that gives food to the domestics at the proper time. (Matthew 24:45) The slave as a body is responsible for supplying the food, but the domestics, the *individual* members of that body, are sustained by partaking of that spiritual provision. They are the same group but described in different terms—collectively and individually.

9. How have the great crowd responded to the singing of the anointed ones, and what exhortation have they thus fulfilled?
10. How is it possible for the 144,000 to sing "before" the symbolic 24 elders?

11. Why are the anointed overcomers referred to as the 24 elders as well as the 144,000?
12. (a) How does John continue his description of the 144,000? (b) In what sense are the 144,000 referred to as virgins?

144,000

bought from among mankind as firstfruits to God and to the Lamb, and no falsehood was found in their mouths; they are without blemish." (Revelation 14:4, 5) The fact that the 144,000 "are virgins" does not mean that members of this class are necessarily unmarried in the flesh. The apostle Paul wrote to Christians who had a heavenly calling that, whereas there are advantages to Christian singleness, marriage is preferable under certain circumstances. (1 Corinthians 7:1, 2, 36, 37) What characterizes this class is a *spiritual* virginity. They have avoided spiritual adultery with worldly politics and with false religion. (James 4:4; Revelation 17:5) As the betrothed bride of Christ, they have kept themselves pure, "without a blemish in among a crooked and twisted generation." —Philippians 2:15.

13 Additionally, "no falsehood was found in their mouths." In this, they are like their King, Jesus Christ. As a perfect human, "he committed no sin, nor was deception found in his mouth." (1 Peter 2:21, 22) In being simultaneously without blemish and truth-

ful, the 144,000 are prepared as a chaste bride for Jehovah's great High Priest. When Jesus was on earth, he invited righthearted ones to follow him. (Mark 8:34; 10:21; John 1:43) Those who responded imitated his way of life and obeyed his teachings. Thus, during their earthly course, they "keep following the Lamb no matter where he goes" as he guides them through Satan's world.

14 The 144,000 are "bought from the earth," "bought from among mankind." They are adopted as spirit sons of God, and after their resurrection, they will no longer be mere flesh-and-blood humans. As mentioned in verse 4, they become the "firstfruits to God and to the Lamb." True, back in the first century, Jesus was "the firstfruits of those who have fallen asleep in death." (1 Corinthians 15:20, 23) But the 144,000 are the "certain firstfruits" of imperfect mankind, purchased by means of Jesus' sacrifice. (James 1:18) Nevertheless, the ingathering of fruitage from mankind does not end with them. The book of Revelation has already pointed to the harvesting of an unnumbered

---

13. Why are the 144,000 a fitting bride for Jesus Christ, and how do they "keep following the Lamb no matter where he goes"?

14. (a) How is it that the 144,000 are "firstfruits to God and to the Lamb"? (b) In what sense are the great crowd also firstfruits?

24 elders

great crowd that cries with a loud voice: "Salvation we owe to our God, who is seated on the throne, and to the Lamb." This great crowd will survive the great tribulation, and as they continue to be refreshed by "fountains of waters of life," they will be raised to human perfection on earth. Sometime after the great tribulation, Hades will be emptied, and countless millions of other humans will be resurrected and have the opportunity to drink from those same waters of life. With this in mind, it would be correct to call the great crowd a firstfruits of the other sheep —they are the first to 'wash their robes and make them white in the blood of the Lamb' with the hope of living forever on earth. —Revelation 7:9, 10, 14, 17; 20:12, 13.

¹⁵ These three firstfruits (Jesus Christ, the 144,000, and the great crowd) have interesting correspondencies in the festivals celebrated according to the ancient Mosaic Law. On Nisan 16, during the Festival of Unfermented Cakes, a sheaf of the firstfruits of the barley harvest was offered to Jehovah. (Leviticus 23:6-14) Nisan 16 was the day Jesus was

Coheirs of the Lamb, Christ Jesus, as viewed from two different standpoints

resurrected from the dead. On the 50th day from Nisan 16, in the third month, the Israelites celebrated the festival of the harvest of the first ripe fruits of the wheat harvest. (Exodus 23:16; Leviticus 23:15, 16) This festival came to be called Pentecost (from a Greek word meaning "fiftieth"), and it was at Pentecost 33 C.E. that the first members of the 144,000 were anointed with holy spirit. Finally, in the seventh month when the whole harvest was gathered in, there was the Festival of Booths, a time of joyful thanksgiving when the Israelites dwelt for a week in booths made of, among other things, palm branches. (Leviticus 23:33-43) Correspondingly, the great crowd, who are part of the great ingathering, give thanks before the throne with "palm branches in their hands." —Revelation 7:9.

---

15. What correspondencies are there between the three different firstfruits and the festivals celebrated under the Mosaic Law?

Declaring Everlasting Good News

16 John next writes: **"And I saw another angel flying in midheaven, and he had everlasting good news to declare as glad tidings to those who dwell on the earth, and to every nation and tribe and tongue and people, saying in a loud voice: 'Fear God and give him glory, because the hour of the judgment by him has arrived, and so worship the One who made the heaven and the earth and sea and fountains of waters.'"** (*Revelation 14:6, 7*) The angel is

16, 17. (a) John sees an angel flying where, and what proclamation is the angel making? (b) Who are involved in the Kingdom-preaching work, and what experiences indicate this?

flying "in midheaven," where the birds fly. (Compare Revelation 19:17.) Hence, his voice can be heard around the globe. Of how much greater range than any television news flash is this angel's worldwide proclamation!

[17] Everyone is urged to fear, not the wild beast and its image, but Jehovah, who is incomparably more powerful than any symbolic beast controlled by Satan. Why, Jehovah created heaven and earth, and now the time has come for him to judge the earth! (Compare Genesis 1:1; Revelation 11:18.) When on earth, Jesus prophesied concerning our day: "And this good news of the kingdom will be preached in all the inhabited earth for a witness to all the nations; and then the end will come." (Matthew 24:14)

The congregation of anointed Christians is fulfilling this commission. (1 Corinthians 9:16; Ephesians 6:15) Revelation here reveals that invisible angels are also involved in this preaching work. How often angelic guidance has been apparent in bringing one of Jehovah's Witnesses to a home where some distressed soul was yearning, even praying, for spiritual help!

[18] As the angel flying in midheaven has declared, the hour for judgment has arrived. What judgment will God now render? Ears will tingle at the announcements now to be made by a second, a third, a fourth, and a fifth angel.—Jeremiah 19:3.

---

18. According to the angel flying in midheaven, the hour for what has arrived, and who will be making further announcements?

Chapter 30

4/6/92
Start

"Babylon the Great Has Fallen!"

IT IS the hour of God's judgment! Listen, then, to the divine message: *"And another, a second angel, followed, saying: 'She has fallen! Babylon the Great has fallen, she who made all the nations drink of the wine of the anger of her fornication!'"* (*Revelation 14:8*) For the first time, but not the last, Revelation focuses attention on Babylon the Great. Later, chapter 17 will describe her as a voluptuous harlot. Who is she? As we shall see, she is a global empire, she is religious, and she is Satan's counterfeit system that he uses in fighting against the seed of God's woman. (Revelation 12:17) Babylon the Great is the entire world empire of false religion. She includes all religions that preserve the religious teachings and practices of ancient Babylon and that manifest her spirit.

[2] It was at Babylon, more than 4,000 years ago, that Jehovah confused the tongues of the would-be builders of the Tower of Babel. The different language groups were scattered to the ends of the earth, taking with them the apostate beliefs and practices that are the basis of most religions to this day. (Genesis 11:1-9) Babylon the Great is the religious part of Satan's organization. (Compare John 8:

---

1. What does the second angel announce, and who is Babylon the Great?

2. (a) How was it that Babylonish religion was scattered to all parts of the earth? (b) What is the most prominent segment of Babylon the Great, and when did it emerge as a powerful organization?

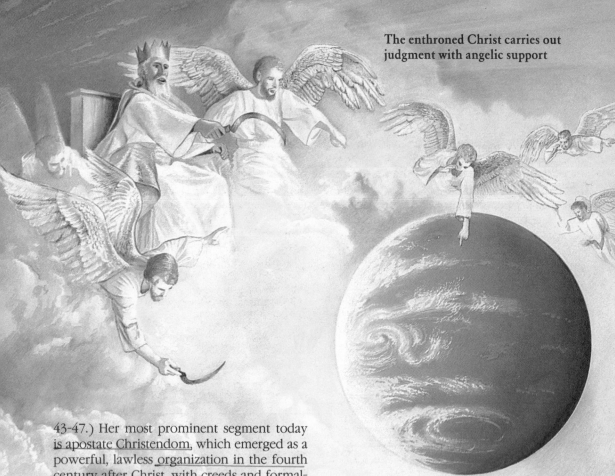

The enthroned Christ carries out judgment with angelic support

43-47.) Her most prominent segment today is apostate Christendom, which emerged as a powerful, lawless organization in the fourth century after Christ, with creeds and formalisms derived, not from the Bible, but largely from Babylonish religion.—2 Thessalonians 2:3-12.

³ You may ask, 'Since religion still exercises great influence in the earth, why does the angel announce that Babylon the Great has fallen?' Well, what resulted in 539 B.C.E. when ancient Babylon fell? Why, Israel was freed to return to its homeland and restore true worship there! So the restoration of spiritual Israel in 1919 to a radiant spiritual prosperity, which continues and expands to this day, stands as evidence that Babylon the Great fell in that year. No longer does she have power of restraint over God's people.

Moreover, she has come into deep trouble within her own ranks. Since 1919 her corruption, dishonesty, and immorality have been widely exposed. In most of Europe, few people go to church anymore, and in many socialistic countries, religion is regarded as "the opium of the people." Disgraced in the eyes of all lovers of God's Word of truth, Babylon the Great now waits on death row, as it were, for the execution of Jehovah's righteous judgment on her.

Babylon's Disgraceful Fall

⁴ Let us examine in more detail the circumstances surrounding the disgraceful fall

---

3. How can it be said that Babylon the Great has fallen?

4-6. How is it that "Babylon the Great . . . made all the nations drink of the wine of the anger of her fornication"?

of Babylon the Great. The angel here tells us that "Babylon the Great . . . made all the nations drink of the wine of the anger of her fornication." What does this mean? It relates to conquest. For example, Jehovah told Jeremiah: "Take this cup of the wine of rage out of my hand, and you must make all the nations to whom I am sending you drink it. And they must drink and shake back and forth and act like crazed men because of the sword that I am sending among them." (Jeremiah 25:15, 16) In the sixth and seventh centuries B.C.E., Jehovah used ancient Babylon to pour out a symbolic cup of tribulation for many nations to drink, including apostate Judah, so that even his own people were taken into exile. Then, in her turn, Babylon fell because her king exalted himself against Jehovah, "the Lord of the heavens."—Daniel 5:23.

5 Babylon the Great has also made conquests, but for the most part, these have been more subtle. She has "made all the nations drink" by using the wiles of a prostitute, committing religious fornication with them. She has enticed political rulers into alliances and friendships with her. Through religious allurements, she has schemed political, commercial, and economic oppression. She has fomented religious persecution and religious wars and crusades, as well as national wars, for purely political and commercial reasons. And she has sanctified these wars by saying they are God's will.

6 Religion's involvement in the wars and politics of this 20th century is common knowledge—as in Shinto Japan, Hindu India, Buddhist Vietnam, "Christian" Northern Ireland and Latin America, as well as others—not to overlook the army chaplains' part on both sides of the two world wars in urging young men to slaughter one another. A classic example of the philandering of Babylon the Great is the share she had in the Spanish Civil War of 1936-39, in which at least 600,000 people were killed. This bloodspilling was provoked by supporters of the Catholic clergy and their allies, in part because the wealth and position

After Babylon fell in 539 B.C.E., her prisoners were released

'The Wine of Her Fornication'

A prominent part of Babylon the Great is the Roman Catholic Church. The church is governed by the pope in Rome and claims that each pope is a successor of the apostle Peter. Following are some published facts about these so-called successors:

Formosus (891-96): "Nine months after his death, Formosus' body was disinterred from the papal crypt and arraigned for trial before a 'cadaveric' council, at which Stephen [the new pope] presided. The deceased pope was accused of inordinate ambition for the papal office and all his acts were declared invalid. . . . The corpse was stripped of pontifical robes; the fingers of the right hand were amputated."—*New Catholic Encyclopedia*.

Stephen VI (896-97): "Within a few months [of the trial of Formosus' corpse] a violent reaction ended the pontificate of Pope Stephen; he was deprived of the pontifical insignia, imprisoned, and strangled."—*New Catholic Encyclopedia*.

Sergius III (904-11): "His two immediate predecessors . . . were strangled in prison. . . . In Rome he was supported by the Theophylactus family, by one of whose daughters, Marozia, he is supposed to have had a son (later Pope John XI)."—*New Catholic Encyclopedia*.

Stephen VII (928-31): "In the last years of his pontificate, Pope John X . . . had incurred the wrath of Marozia, the *Donna Senatrix* of Rome, and had been imprisoned and assassinated. Marozia then conferred the papacy on Pope Leo VI, who died after 6 1/2 months in office. Stephen VII succeeded him, probably through the influence of Marozia. . . . During his 2 years as Pope, he was powerless under the domination of Marozia."—*New Catholic Encyclopedia*.

John XI (931-35): "Upon the death of Stephen VII . . . , Marozia, of the House of Theophylactus, obtained the papacy for her son John, a youth in his early 20s. . . . As pope, John was dominated by his mother."—*New Catholic Encyclopedia*.

John XII (955-64): "He was hardly eighteen, and contemporary reports agree about his disinterest in spiritual things, addiction to boorish pleasures, and uninhibitedly debauched life."—*The Oxford Dictionary of Popes*.

Benedict IX (1032-44; 1045; 1047-48): "He was notorious for selling the papacy to his godfather and then subsequently reclaiming the office twice."—*The New Encyclopædia Britannica*.

Thus, rather than following the example of faithful Peter, these and other popes were an evil influence. They allowed bloodguilt and spiritual and physical fornication, as well as a Jezebel influence, to corrupt the church they ruled. (James 4:4) In 1917 the Watch Tower Society's book *The Finished Mystery* set out many of these facts in stark detail. This was one way that the Bible Students in those days 'struck the earth with every sort of plague.'—Revelation 11:6; 14:8; 17:1, 2, 5.

of the church was threatened by Spain's legal government.

⁷ Since Babylon the Great is the religious part of Satan's seed, she has always made Jehovah's "woman," "Jerusalem above," her main target. In the first century, the congregation of anointed Christians was clearly identified as the woman's seed. (Genesis 3:15; Galatians 3:29; 4:26) Babylon the Great tried hard to conquer that chaste congregation by seducing it into committing religious fornication. The apostles Paul and Peter warned that many would succumb and a great apostasy would result. (Acts 20:29, 30; 2 Peter 2:1-3) Jesus' messages to the seven congregations indicated that toward the end of John's life, Babylon the Great was making some progress in her efforts to corrupt. (Revelation 2:6, 14, 15, 20-23) But Jesus had already shown how far she would be permitted to go.

The Wheat and the Weeds

⁸ In his parable of the wheat and the weeds, Jesus spoke of a man who sowed fine seed in a field. But "while men were sleeping," an enemy came and oversowed weeds. Hence, the wheat came to be obscured by the weeds. Jesus explained his parable in these words: "The sower of the fine seed is the Son of man; the field is the world; as for the fine seed, these are the sons of the kingdom; but the weeds are the sons of the wicked one, and the enemy that sowed them is the Devil." He then showed that the wheat and the weeds would be allowed to grow together until "the conclusion of the system of things," when the angels would "collect out" the symbolic weeds.—Matthew 13:24-30, 36-43.

⁹ What Jesus and the apostles Paul and

---

7. Who has been the main target of Babylon the Great, and what methods has she used against this target?

8, 9. (a) What did Jesus' parable of the wheat and the weeds indicate? (b) What happened "while men were sleeping"?

Peter warned about happened. "While men were sleeping," either after the apostles fell asleep in death or when Christian overseers became drowsy in guarding the flock of God, Babylonish apostasy sprouted right inside the congregation. (Acts 20:31) Soon the weeds greatly outnumbered the wheat and hid it from view. For a number of centuries, it might have appeared that the seed of the woman had been completely engulfed by the voluminous skirts of Babylon the Great.

¹⁰ In the 1870's anointed Christians began to make determined efforts to disassociate themselves from the whorish ways of Babylon the Great. They abandoned false doctrines that Christendom had brought in from paganism and boldly used the Bible in preaching that the times of the Gentiles would end in 1914. The chief instrument of Babylon the Great, the clergy of Christendom, opposed these stirrings of restoration of true worship. During the first world war, they took advantage of wartime hysteria to try to stamp out that small group of faithful Christians. In 1918, when their activities were almost completely suppressed, it appeared that Babylon the Great had succeeded. She seemed to have triumphed over them.

¹¹ As we previously noted, the proud city of Babylon experienced a disastrous fall from power in 539 B.C.E. Then the cry was heard: "She has fallen! Babylon has fallen!" The great seat of the world empire had fallen to the armies of Medo-Persia under Cyrus the Great. Although the city itself survived the conquest, her fall from power was real, and it resulted in the release of her Jewish captives. They returned to Jerusalem to reestablish pure worship there.—Isaiah 21:9; 2 Chronicles 36:22, 23; Jeremiah 51:7, 8.

¹² In our century the cry that Babylon the Great has fallen has also been heard! Babylonish Christendom's temporary success in 1918 was sharply reversed in 1919 when the remnant of anointed ones, the John class, was restored by a spiritual resurrection. Babylon the Great had fallen as far as having any captive hold on God's people was concerned. Like locusts, Christ's anointed brothers swarmed out of the abyss, ready for action. (Revelation 9:1-3; 11:11, 12) They were the modern "faithful and discreet slave," and the Master appointed them over all his belongings on earth. (Matthew 24:45-47) Their being used in this way proved that Jehovah had utterly rejected Christendom despite her claim to be his representative on earth. Pure worship was reestablished, and the way was open to complete the work of sealing the remnant of the 144,000—the remaining ones of the seed of the woman, the age-old enemy of Babylon the Great. All of this signaled a crushing defeat for that satanic religious organization.

Endurance for the Holy Ones

¹³ Now the third angel speaks. Listen! *"And another angel, a third, followed them, saying in a loud voice: 'If anyone worships the wild beast and its image, and receives a mark on his forehead or upon his hand, he will also drink of the wine of the anger of God that is poured out undiluted into the cup of his wrath.'"* (Revelation 14:9, 10a) At Revelation 13:16, 17, it was revealed that during the Lord's day those who do not worship the image of the wild beast would suffer—even be killed. Now we learn that Jehovah has determined to bring to judgment those "having the mark, the name of the wild beast or the number of its

---

10. What took place in the 1870's, and how did Babylon the Great react to this?
11. What resulted from the fall of ancient Babylon?

12. (a) In our century, how can it be said that Babylon the Great has fallen? (b) What proves that Jehovah has utterly rejected Christendom?
13. (a) What does the third angel announce? (b) What judgment does Jehovah make of those who receive the mark of the wild beast?

name." They will be forced to drink a bitter 'cup of wrath' of Jehovah's anger. What will this mean for them? In 607 B.C.E., when Jehovah forced Jerusalem to drink "his cup of rage," the city experienced "despoiling and breakdown, and hunger and sword" at the hands of the Babylonians. (Isaiah 51:17, 19) Similarly, when idolizers of earth's political powers and their image, the United Nations, get to drink the cup of Jehovah's wrath, the result will be a calamity for them. (Jeremiah 25:17, 32, 33) They will be utterly destroyed.

14 Even before that happens, however, those with the mark of the beast have to undergo the tormenting effects of Jehovah's disapproval. Speaking of the worshiper of the wild beast and its image, the angel informs John: *"And he shall be tormented with fire and sulphur in the sight of the holy angels and in the sight of the Lamb. And the smoke of their torment ascends forever and ever, and day and night they have no rest, those who worship the wild beast and its image, and whoever receives the mark of its name."—Revelation 14: 10b, 11.*

NOT HELL FIRE

15 Some have viewed the mention here of fire and sulfur ("fire and brimstone," *King James Version*) as a proof of the existence of a hellfire. But a brief look at a similar prophecy shows the real import of these words in this context. Back in the days of Isaiah, Jehovah warned the nation of Edom that they would be punished because of their enmity toward Israel. He said: "Her torrents must be changed into pitch, and her dust into sulphur, and her land must become as burning pitch. By night or by day it will not be extinguished; to time indefinite its smoke will keep ascending. From generation to generation she will be parched; forever and ever

no one will be passing across her."—Isaiah 34:9, 10.

16 Was Edom hurled into some mythical hellfire to burn forever? Of course not. Rather, the nation completely disappeared from the world scene as if she had been totally consumed with fire and sulfur. The final result of the punishment was not everlasting torment but "emptiness . . . wasteness . . . nothing." (Isaiah 34:11, 12) The (smoke) 'ascending to time indefinite' vividly illustrates this. When a house burns down, smoke keeps coming from the ashes for some time after the flames have died down, providing onlookers with evidence that there has been a destructive conflagration. Even today God's people remember the lesson to be learned from the destruction of Edom. In this way 'the smoke of her burning' is still ascending in a symbolic way.

17 Those who have the mark of the wild beast will also be destroyed completely, as if by fire. As the prophecy later reveals, their dead bodies will be left unburied for animals and birds to eat. (Revelation 19:17, 18) So, clearly, they are not being literally tortured forever! How are they "tormented with fire and sulphur"? In that the proclamation of truth exposes them and warns them of God's coming judgment. Therefore they vilify God's people and, where possible, slyly persuade the political wild beast to persecute and even kill Jehovah's Witnesses. As a climax, these opposers will be destroyed as with fire and brimstone. Then "the smoke of their torment ascends forever and ever" in that God's judgment of them will serve as a touchstone if ever again Jehovah's rightful sovereignty is challenged. That issue will have been settled for all eternity.

18 Who deliver the tormenting message

---

14. Even before the destruction of those who worship the wild beast and its image, what must such ones undergo, and how does John describe this?
15, 16. What is the import of the words "fire and sulphur" at Revelation 14:10?

17, 18. (a) What is the outcome for those who receive the mark of the wild beast? (b) In what way is it that worshipers of the wild beast are tormented? (c) How is it that "the smoke of their torment ascends forever and ever"?

today? Remember, the symbolic locusts have authority to torment the men who do not have the seal of God on their foreheads. (Revelation 9:5) Evidently, these ones under angelic direction are the tormentors. Such is the persistence of the symbolic locusts that "day and night they have no rest, those who worship the wild beast and its image, and whoever receives the mark of its name." And finally, after their destruction, the monumental evidence of that vindication of Jehovah's sovereignty, "the smoke of their torment," will ascend forever and ever. May the John class endure until that vindication is complete! As the angel concludes: *"Here is where it means endurance for the holy ones, those who observe the commandments of God and the faith of Jesus."—Revelation 14:12.*

19 Yes, "endurance for the holy ones" means their worshiping Jehovah in exclusive devotion through Jesus Christ. Their message is not popular. It leads to opposition, persecution, even martyrdom. But they are strengthened by what John next reports: *"And I heard a voice out of heaven say: 'Write: Happy are the dead who die in union with the Lord from this time onward. Yes, says the spirit, let them rest from their labors, for the things they did go right with them.'"—Revelation 14:13.*

20 This promise harmonizes well with Paul's prophecy concerning Jesus' presence: "Those who are dead in union with Christ will rise first. Afterward we the living who are surviving [those of the anointed ones who survive into the Lord's day] will, together with them, be caught away in clouds to meet the Lord in the air." (1 Thessalonians 4:15-17) After Satan's ouster from heaven, those who were dead in union with Christ rose first. (Compare Revelation 6:9-11.) Afterward, those of the anointed ones who die during the Lord's day are promised a special privilege. Their resurrection to spirit life in heaven is instantaneous, "in the twinkling of an eye." (1 Corinthians 15:52) How marvelous this is! And their works of righteousness continue right on in the heavenly realm.

Harvest of the Earth *4/4/92*

21 Others are also to benefit in this day of judgment, as John goes on to tell us: *"And I saw, and, look! a white cloud, and upon the cloud someone seated like a son of man, with a golden crown on his head and a sharp sickle in his hand. And another angel [the fourth] emerged from the temple sanctuary, crying with a loud voice to the one seated on the cloud: 'Put your sickle in and reap, because the hour has come to reap, for the harvest of the earth is thoroughly ripe.' And the one seated on the cloud thrust in his sickle on the earth, and the earth was reaped."—Revelation 14:14-16.*

22 The identity of the one seated on the white cloud is not in doubt. Seated on a white cloud, resembling a son of man and with a golden crown, he is clearly Jesus, the Messianic King that Daniel also saw in vision. (Daniel 7:13, 14; Mark 14:61, 62) But what is the harvest here prophesied? While on earth, Jesus likened the discipling work to the harvesting of the world field of humanity. (Matthew 9:37, 38; John 4:35, 36) The climax of this harvesting comes in the Lord's day, when Jesus is crowned as King and executes judgment on behalf of his Father. Thus, his time of ruling, since 1914, is also the joyful time for bringing in the harvest.—Compare Deuteronomy 16:13-15.

---

19. Why is endurance required on the part of the holy ones, and what does John report that strengthens them?

20. (a) How does the promise reported by John harmonize with Paul's prophecy about Jesus' presence? (b) Those of the anointed who die after Satan's ouster from heaven are promised what special privilege?

---

21. What does John tell us about "the harvest of the earth"?

22. (a) Who is the one wearing a golden crown and seated upon the white cloud? (b) When does the climax of the harvesting take place, and how?

²³ Although he is a King and a Judge, Jesus waits for word from Jehovah his God before beginning to reap. That word comes from "the temple sanctuary" by means of an angel. Immediately, Jesus obeys. First, from 1919 on, he has his angels complete the harvesting of the 144,000. (Matthew 13:39, 43) Next, the harvest ingathering of the great crowd of other sheep takes place. (Matthew 25:31-33; John 10:16; Revelation 7:9) History shows that between 1931 and 1935 a goodly number of these other sheep began to appear. In 1935 Jehovah opened to the understanding of the John class the real identity of the great crowd of Revelation 7:9-17. Thenceforth, much emphasis was placed on the ingathering of this crowd. By the year 1988, its number has far exceeded the three million mark, and it is still increasing. Surely, the one like a son of man has reaped a bountiful, joyous harvest during this time of the end. —Compare Exodus 23:16; 34:22.

Treading the Vine of the Earth

²⁴ With the harvest of salvation completed, it is time for another harvest. John reports: *"And still another angel [the fifth] emerged from the temple sanctuary that is in heaven, he, too, having a sharp sickle. And still another angel [the sixth] emerged from the altar and he had authority over the fire. And he called out with a loud voice to the one that had the sharp sickle, saying: 'Put your sharp sickle in and gather the clusters of the vine of the earth, because its grapes have become ripe.'"* (*Revelation 14:17, 18*) The angelic hosts are entrusted with much harvesting during the Lord's day, separating the good from the bad!

²⁵ The fifth angel comes from Jehovah's presence in the temple sanctuary; hence, the final harvest also takes place according to Jehovah's will. The angel is commanded to begin his work by a message relayed through another angel that "emerged from the altar." This fact is most significant, since faithful souls underneath the altar had asked: "Until when, Sovereign Lord holy and true, are you refraining from judging and avenging our blood upon those who dwell on the earth?" (Revelation 6:9, 10) With the harvesting of the vine of the earth, this cry for vengeance will be satisfied.

²⁶ But what is "the vine of the earth"? In the Hebrew Scriptures, the Jewish nation was spoken of as Jehovah's vine. (Isaiah 5:7; Jeremiah 2:21) Similarly, Jesus Christ and those who will serve with him in God's Kingdom are spoken of as a vine. (John 15:1-8) In this setting, the significant characteristic of a vine is that it produces fruit, and the true Christian vine has produced abundant fruit to Jehovah's praise. (Matthew 21:43) "The vine of the earth," therefore, must be, not this genuine vine, but Satan's imitation of it, his corrupt visible system of government over mankind, with its various "clusters" of demonic fruitage produced over the centuries. Babylon the Great, in which apostate Christianity is so prominent, has exercised great influence over this poisonous vine.—Compare Deuteronomy 32:32-35.

²⁷ Judgment must be executed! *"And the angel thrust his sickle into the earth and gathered the vine of the earth, and he hurled it into the great winepress of the anger of God. And the winepress was trodden outside the city, and blood came out of the winepress as high up as the bridles of the horses, for a distance of a thousand six hundred furlongs."* (*Revelation 14:19, 20*) Jehovah's indignation against this

---

23. (a) From whom does the word to begin reaping come? (b) What harvesting has taken place from 1919 down till now?

24. What is in the hands of the fifth angel, and what does the sixth angel call out?

25. (a) What is indicated by the fact that the fifth angel came from the temple sanctuary? (b) Why is it fitting that the command to begin reaping comes from an angel who "emerged from the altar"?

---

26. What is "the vine of the earth"?

27. (a) What takes place when the angel with the sickle gathers the vine of the earth? (b) What prophecies in the Hebrew Scriptures indicate the extent of the harvest?

vine has long since been announced. (Zephaniah 3:8) A prophecy in the book of Isaiah leaves no doubt that whole nations will be destroyed when the winepress is trampled. (Isaiah 63:3-6) Joel too prophesied that huge "crowds," whole nations, would be trampled to destruction in "the winepress," in "the low plain of the decision." (Joel 3:12-14) Truly, a stupendous harvest the like of which will never again occur! According to John's ❯

vision, not only are the grapes harvested but the whole symbolic vine is cut down and thrown into the winepress to be trampled. So the vine of the earth will be stamped out and will never be able to grow again.

28 The visionary treading is done by horses, for the blood trodden out from the vine reaches "the bridles of the horses." Since the term "horses" usually refers to war operations, this must be a time of war. The armies of the heavens that follow Jesus into the final war against Satan's system of things are said to tread "the winepress of the anger of the wrath of God the Almighty." (Revelation 19:11-16) These are clearly the ones that do the treading of the vine of the earth. The winepress is "trodden outside the city," that is, outside heavenly Zion. Indeed, it is fitting that the vine of the earth should be trodden on earth. But it will also be "trodden outside the city" in that no harm will come to the

remaining ones of the woman's seed, who represent the heavenly Zion on earth. These together with the great crowd will be safely hidden within Jehovah's earthly organizational arrangement.—Isaiah 26: 20, 21.

29 This vivid vision has a parallel in the crushing of the kingdoms of the earth by the Kingdom stone described at Daniel 2:34, 44. There will be an extermination. The river of blood from the winepress is very deep, up to the bridles of the horses, and it extends for a distance of 1,600 furlongs.* This huge figure, produced by multiplying the square of four by the square of ten (4 x 4 x 10 x 10), emphatically conveys the message that evidence of the destruction will involve all the earth. (Isaiah 66:15, 16) The destruction will be complete and irreversible. Never, no never again, will Satan's vine of the earth take root! —Psalm 83:17, 18.

---

* 1,600 furlongs is about 300 kilometers, or 180 English miles.—Revelation 14:20, *New World Translation Reference Bible,* footnote.

---

28. Who do the treading of the vine of the earth, and what does it mean that the winepress is "trodden outside the city"?

29. How deep is the blood from the winepress, how far does it extend, and what does all of this indicate?

REVELATION CLIMAX

30 Living as we do deep in the time of the end, the vision of these two harvests is very meaningful. We have only to look around us to see the fruits of Satan's vine. Abortions and other forms of murder; homosexuality, adultery, and other forms of immorality; dishonesty and lack of natural affection—all such things make this world vile in Jehovah's eyes. Satan's vine bears "the fruit of a poisonous plant and worm-

---

30. What are the fruits of Satan's vine, and what should be our determination?

wood." Its ruinous, idolatrous course dishonors mankind's Grand Creator. (Deuteronomy 29:18; 32:5; Isaiah 42:5, 8) What a privilege it is to be actively associated with the John class in the harvest of wholesome fruitage that Jesus is bringing forth to Jehovah's praise! (Luke 10:2) May all of us be determined that we will never be tainted by the vine of this world, and may we thus avoid being trampled with the vine of the earth when Jehovah's adverse judgment is executed.

Jehovah's Works
—Great and Wonderful

A WOMAN giving birth to a male child! A great dragon seeking to devour that child! Those two heavenly signs, so vividly portrayed in Revelation chapter 12, brought home to us that the agelong controversy involving the Seed of God's woman and Satan and his demonic seed is reaching its climax. In highlighting these symbols, John says: "And a great sign was seen in heaven . . . And another sign was

---

1, 2. (a) What third sign does John report? (b) What angelic role has long been known by Jehovah's servants?

seen." (Revelation 12:1, 3, 7-12) Now John reports a third sign: *"And I saw in heaven another sign, great and wonderful, seven angels with seven plagues. These are the last ones, because by means of them the anger of God is brought to a finish." (Revelation 15:1)* This third sign also has vital meaning for Jehovah's servants.

² Notice the important roles that angels again have in accomplishing God's will. This fact has long been known by Jehovah's servants. Why, under inspiration the ancient psalmist even spoke to such angels, urging them: "Bless Jehovah, O you angels of his, mighty in power, carrying out his word, by listening to the voice of his word"! (Psalm 103:20) Now, in this new scene, angels are assigned to pour out the seven last plagues.

³ What are these plagues? Like the seven trumpet blasts, they are scathing judgment

---

3. What are the seven plagues, and what does the pouring out of them denote?

> ## Vision _____ *10*
>
> ### Revelation 15:1–16:21
>
> **Subject:** Jehovah in his sanctuary; the seven bowls of his wrath poured into the earth
>
> **Time of fulfillment:** 1919 to Armageddon

pronouncements <u>publicizing Jehovah's view</u> <u>of various features of this world and warning</u> <u>of the final outcome of his judicial decisions.</u> (Revelation 8:1–9:21) The pouring out of them points to the execution of those judgments, when the objects of Jehovah's wrath are de-stroyed in the day of his burning anger. (Isaiah 13:9-13; Revelation 6:16, 17) Thus, by means of them "the anger of God is brought to a fin-ish." <u>But before describing the pouring out</u> of the plagues, John tells us about some humans who will not be adversely affected by them. Having refused the mark of the wild beast, these loyal ones sing praises to Jehovah as they proclaim his day of vengeance.—Revelation 13:15-17.

START ①

The Song of Moses and of the Lamb

⁴ A remarkable panorama now comes into <u>John's view</u>: "*And <u>I saw what seemed to be</u> a glassy sea <u>mingled with fire,</u> and <u>those who come</u> off <u>victorious from the wild beast</u> and from its <u>image</u> and from <u>the number of its name</u> standing by the glassy sea,* <u>having harps of God</u>."—Reve-lation 15:2.

⁵ The "<u>glassy sea</u>" is the same one that John saw earlier, positioned before the throne of God. (<u>Revelation 4:6</u>) It is similar to "the mol-ten sea" (water container) of Solomon's tem-ple, where <u>the priests obtained water</u> to <u>cleanse themselves.</u> (1 Kings 7:23) It is thus a fine representation <u>of "the bath of water,"</u> that <u>is, God's Word,</u> by which <u>Jesus cleanses the</u> <u>priestly congregation of anointed Christians.</u> (Ephesians 5:25, 26; Hebrews 10:22) This glassy sea is "mingled with fire," <u>indicating that these</u> <u>anointed ones are tested</u> and <u>purged</u> as they

---

4. What now comes into John's view?
5. What is pictured by the "glassy sea mingled with fire"?

obey the high standard set for them. Further, it reminds us that God's Word also contains expressions of fiery judgments against his enemies. (Deuteronomy 9:3; Zephaniah 3:8) Some of these fiery judgments are manifested in the seven last plagues that are about to be poured out.

⁶ The fact that the molten sea in Solomon's temple was for the use of the priests indicates that the singers standing before the heavenly glassy sea are a priestly class. They have "harps of God," and we therefore associate them with the 24 elders and the 144,000, since these groups also sing to a harp accompaniment. (Revelation 5:8; 14:2) The singers that John sees "come off victorious from the wild beast and from its image and from the number of its name." So they must be those from among the 144,000 who live on earth during the last days. As a group, they do indeed come off victorious. For some 70 years since 1919, they have refused to accept the mark of the wild beast or look to its image as man's only hope for peace. Many of them have already endured faithful to the death, and these, now in heaven, doubtless follow with special delight the singing of their brothers who are still on earth. —Revelation 14:11-13.

⁷ These loyal overcomers have harps of God. In this, they are like the temple Levites of old, who worshiped Jehovah with song to the accompaniment of harps. Some also prophesied to a harp accompaniment. (1 Chronicles 15:16; 25:1-3) The beautiful strains of the harp embellished Israel's songs of joy and prayers of praise and thanksgiving to Jehovah. (1 Chronicles 13:8; Psalm 33:2; 43:4; 57:7, 8) In times of depression or captivity, the harp was not heard. (Psalm 137:2) The presence of harps of God in this vision should whet our antici-

pation for an exultant, triumphant song of praise and thanksgiving to our God.*

⁸ That is what John reports: **"And they are singing the song of Moses the slave of God and the song of the Lamb, saying: 'Great and wonderful are your works, Jehovah God, the Almighty. Righteous and true are your ways, King of eternity. Who will not really fear you, Jehovah, and glorify your name, because you alone are loyal? For all the nations will come and worship before you, because your righteous decrees have been made manifest.'"—Revelation 15:3, 4.**

⁹ These victors sing "the song of Moses," that is, a song similar to one that Moses sang in like circumstances. After the Israelites had witnessed the ten plagues in Egypt and the destruction of the Egyptian armies in the Red Sea, Moses led them in such a song of triumphant praise to Jehovah, proclaiming: "Jehovah will rule as king to time indefinite, even forever." (Exodus 15:1-19) How fitting that the singers in John's vision, coming off victorious from the wild beast and being involved in proclaiming the seven last plagues, should also sing "to the King of eternity"!—1 Timothy 1:17.

¹⁰ In another song, composed as Israel prepared for the conquest of Canaan, the aged Moses told that nation: "I shall declare the name of Jehovah. Do you attribute greatness to our God!" The last verse of this song also gave encouragement to non-Israelites, and Moses' inspired words reach right down to the great crowd of today: "Be glad, you nations, with his people." And why should they be glad? Because now Jehovah "will avenge the blood of his servants, and he will pay back vengeance to his adversaries." This execution

* Interestingly, in 1921 the John class released the Bible study aid *The Harp of God,* which had a circulation of more than five million copies in over 20 languages. It helped bring in more anointed singers.

6. (a) Who are the singers standing before the heavenly glassy sea, and how do we know? (b) In what way have they "come off victorious"?
7. How was the harp used in ancient Israel, and how should the presence of harps of God in John's vision affect us?

8. What song is being sung, and what are its words?
9. Why is the song called, in part, "the song of Moses"?
10. What other song was composed by Moses, and how does the last verse of it relate to the great crowd of today?

JEHOVAH'S WORKS—GREAT AND WONDERFUL

217

of righteous judgment will bring jubilation to all who hope in Jehovah.—Deuteronomy 32: 3, 43; Romans 15:10-13; Revelation 7:9.

[11] How Moses himself would have rejoiced to be in the Lord's day now, singing along with the heavenly chorus: "All the nations will come and worship before you"! That transcendent song continues to have marvelous fulfillment today as we see, not just in vision but as a living reality, the millions from "the nations" who are now flocking joyfully to Jehovah's earthly organization.

[12] Nevertheless, this is the song not only of Moses but also "of the Lamb." How so? Moses was Jehovah's prophet to Israel, but Moses himself prophesied that Jehovah would raise up a prophet like him. This One proved to be the Lamb, Jesus Christ. Whereas Moses was "the slave of God," Jesus was God's Son, in effect, the Greater Moses. (Deuteronomy 18: 15-19; Acts 3:22, 23; Hebrews 3:5, 6) Hence, the singers also sing "the song of the Lamb."

[13] Like Moses, Jesus publicly sang God's praises and prophesied about His victory over all enemies. (Matthew 24:21, 22; 26:30; Luke 19: 41-44) Jesus too looked forward to the time when the nations would come in to praise Jehovah, and as the self-sacrificing "Lamb of God," he laid down his human life to make this possible. (John 1:29; Revelation 7:9; compare Isaiah 2:2-4; Zechariah 8:23.) And just as Moses came to appreciate God's name, Jehovah, and extol that name, so Jesus made God's name manifest. (Exodus 6:2, 3; Psalm 90:1, 17; John 17:6) Since Jehovah is loyal, his glorious promises are certain of fulfillment. Surely, then, we are at one with these loyal singers, with the Lamb, and with Moses, in subscribing to the words of the song: "Who will not really fear you, Jehovah, and glorify your name?"

---

11. How does the song that John heard continue to have a fulfillment?
12. Why is the song of the victorious ones also called "the song of the Lamb"?
13. (a) How is it that Jesus, although greater than Moses, is like him? (b) How may we unite with the singers?

The Angels With the Bowls

[14] It is fitting that we hear the song of these anointed conquerors. Why? Because they have publicized on earth the judgments contained in the bowls that were full of the anger of God. But the pouring out of these bowls involves more than mere humans, as John goes on to show: *"And after these things I saw, and the sanctuary of the tent of the witness was opened in heaven, and the seven angels with the seven plagues emerged from the sanctuary, clothed with clean, bright linen and girded about their breasts with golden girdles. And one of the four living creatures gave the seven angels seven golden bowls that were full of the anger of God, who lives forever and ever."—Revelation 15:5-7.*

[15] As respects the Israelite temple, which contained representations of heavenly things, only the high priest could enter the Most Holy, here called "the sanctuary." (Hebrews 9:3, 7) It represents the place of Jehovah's presence in heaven. In heaven itself, however, not only does the High Priest Jesus Christ have the privilege of entering in before Jehovah but the angels do also. (Matthew 18:10; Hebrews 9: 24-26) It is not surprising, then, that seven angels should be seen coming out from the sanctuary in heaven. They have a commission from Jehovah God himself: Pour out the bowls full of the anger of God.—Revelation 16:1.

[16] These angels are well qualified for this work. They are clothed with clean, bright linen, showing that they are spiritually clean and holy, righteous in Jehovah's sight. Also, they wear golden girdles. Girdles are usually used when a person girds himself for a task to be accomplished. (Leviticus 8:7, 13; 1 Samuel

---

14. Whom does John see emerging from the sanctuary, and what is given to them?
15. Why is it not surprising that the seven angels emerge from the sanctuary?
16. (a) What shows that the seven angels are well qualified for their work? (b) What indicates that others are involved in the great task of pouring out the symbolic bowls?

2:18; Luke 12:37; John 13:4, 5) So the angels are girded for carrying out an assignment. Moreover, their girdles are golden. In the ancient tabernacle, gold was used to represent divine, heavenly things) (Hebrews 9:4, 11, 12) That means that these angels have a precious, divine commission of service to perform. Others too are involved in this great task. One of the four living creatures hands the actual bowls to them. Doubtless, this was the first living creature, which resembled a lion, symbolizing the boldness and indomitable courage needed to proclaim Jehovah's judgments.—Revelation 4:7.

start **Jehovah in His Sanctuary** ✓

1/20/92 ¹⁷ Finally, completing this part of the vision, John tells us: *"And the sanctuary became filled with smoke because of the glory of God and*

17. What does John tell us about the sanctuary, and how does that remind us of the sanctuary in ancient Israel?

because of his power, and no one was able to enter into the sanctuary until the seven plagues of the seven angels were finished." (*Revelation 15:8*) There were occasions in Israel's history when a cloud covered the literal sanctuary, and this manifestation of Jehovah's glory prevented the priests from entering there. (1 Kings 8: 10, 11; 2 Chronicles 5:13, 14; compare Isaiah 6: 4, 5.) These were times when Jehovah was actively involved with developments on earth.

18 Jehovah is also deeply interested in things happening on earth now. He wants the seven angels to complete their assignment. It is a climactic time of judgment, as described at Psalm 11:4-6: "Jehovah is in his holy temple. Jehovah—in the heavens is his throne. His own eyes behold, his own beaming eyes examine the sons of men. Jehovah himself examines the righteous one as well as the wicked one, and anyone loving violence His soul certainly hates. He will rain down upon the wicked ones traps, fire and sulphur and a scorching wind, as the portion of their cup." Until these seven plagues are poured out upon the wicked ones, the seven angels will not return to Jehovah's lofty presence.

19 The awesome command thunders forth: *"And I heard a loud voice out of the sanctuary say to the seven angels: 'Go and pour out the seven bowls of the anger of God into the earth.'"* (*Revelation 16:1*) Who issues this command? It must be Jehovah himself, since the radiance of his glory and power prevented anyone else from entering the sanctuary. Jehovah came to his spiritual temple for judgment in 1918. (Malachi 3:1-5) It must, then, have been shortly after that date that he gave the command to pour out the bowls of the anger of God. In fact, the judgments contained in the symbolic bowls started to be proclaimed with intensity in 1922. And their proclamation is increasing to a crescendo today.

The Bowls and the Trumpet Blasts

20 The bowls of Jehovah's anger reveal fea-

tures of the world scene as Jehovah views them and warn of judgments that Jehovah will execute. The angels pour out the bowls through the agency of the congregation of anointed Christians on earth, the ones singing the song of Moses and the song of the Lamb. While proclaiming the Kingdom as good news, the John class have boldly revealed the contents of these bowls of anger. (Matthew 24:14; Revelation 14:6, 7) Thus, their twofold message has been peaceful in proclaiming liberty to mankind but warlike in warning of "the day of vengeance on the part of our God." —Isaiah 61:1, 2.

21 The targets of the first four bowls of God's anger correspond to those of the first four trumpet blasts, that is, the earth, the sea, the rivers and fountains of water, and the heavenly sources of light. (Revelation 8:1-12) But the trumpet blasts announced plagues on "a third," whereas an entirety is afflicted by the pouring out of the bowls of God's anger. Thus, while Christendom, as "a third," has received first attention during the Lord's day, not one part of Satan's system has been exempted from being plagued by Jehovah's vexatious judgment messages and the sorrows they bring.

22 The final three trumpet blasts were different, for they were called woes. (Revelation 8:13; 9:12) The first two of these consisted particularly of the locusts and the armies of cavalry, while the third introduced the birth of Jehovah's Kingdom. (Revelation 9:1-21; 11: 15-19) As we shall see, the final three bowls of his wrath also cover some of these aspects, but they are somewhat different from the three woes. Let us now pay close attention to the dramatic disclosures that result from the pouring out of the bowls of Jehovah's anger.

---

18. When will the seven angels return to make a report to Jehovah?
19. (a) What command is issued, and by whom? (b) When must the pouring out of the symbolic bowls have begun?
20. What do the bowls of Jehovah's anger reveal and warn of, and how are they poured out?

21. How do the targets of the first four bowls of God's anger correspond to those of the first four trumpet blasts, and wherein do they differ?
22. How were the final three trumpet blasts different, and how do they relate to the final three bowls of Jehovah's anger?

REVELATION CLIMAX

Chapter 32

God's Anger Brought to a Finish

JOHN has already introduced the angels commissioned to pour out the seven bowls. He tells us that "these are the last ones, because

1. What will have taken place when the seven bowls have been poured out to a finality, and what questions now arise regarding the bowls?

"Into the Earth"

The John class has publicized Jehovah's wrath against "the earth" with statements such as the following:

"After centuries of effort, political parties have proved their inadequacy to meet the present conditions and to solve the distressing problems. Economists and statesmen, studying the question diligently, find that they are able to do nothing."—*Millions Now Living Will Never Die*, 1920, page 61.

"There is not a government on earth today that satisfies any reasonable proportion of the world. Many of the nations are ruled by dictators. The whole world is practically bankrupt."—*A Desirable Government*, 1924, page 5.

"Bringing an end to this system of things . . . is the only way to rid the world of evil and make room for peace and righteousness to flourish."—*"This Good News of the Kingdom,"* 1954, page 25.

"The present world arrangement has distinguished itself by increasing sin, unrighteousness and rebellion against God and his will. . . . It is unreformable. Therefore, it must go!"—*The Watchtower*, November 15, 1981, page 6.

---

by means of them the anger of God is brought to a finish." (Revelation 15:1; 16:1) These plagues, revealing Jehovah's sanctions for wickedness in the earth, must be poured out to a finality. When they are over, God's judgments will have been executed. Satan's world will be no more! What do these plagues portend for mankind and the rulers of the present wicked system? How can Christians avoid being plagued along with this doomed world? Vital questions, these, and now they are to be answered. All who long for the triumph of righteousness will have keen interest in what John next sees.

Jehovah's Wrath Against "the Earth"

2 The first angel goes into action! *"And the first one went off and poured out his bowl into the earth. And a hurtful and malignant ulcer came to be upon the men that had the mark of the wild beast and that were worshiping its image."* (*Revelation 16:2*) As in the case of the first trumpet blast, "the earth" here symbolizes the stable-looking political system that Satan began to build here on earth back in Nimrod's time, over 4,000 years ago.—Revelation 8:7.

3 In these last days, many governments have

---

2. What results from the first angel's pouring out his bowl into the earth, and what is symbolized by "the earth"?

3. (a) How have many governments demanded what amounts to worship from their subjects? (b) What have the nations produced as a substitute for God's Kingdom, and what is the effect on those who worship it?

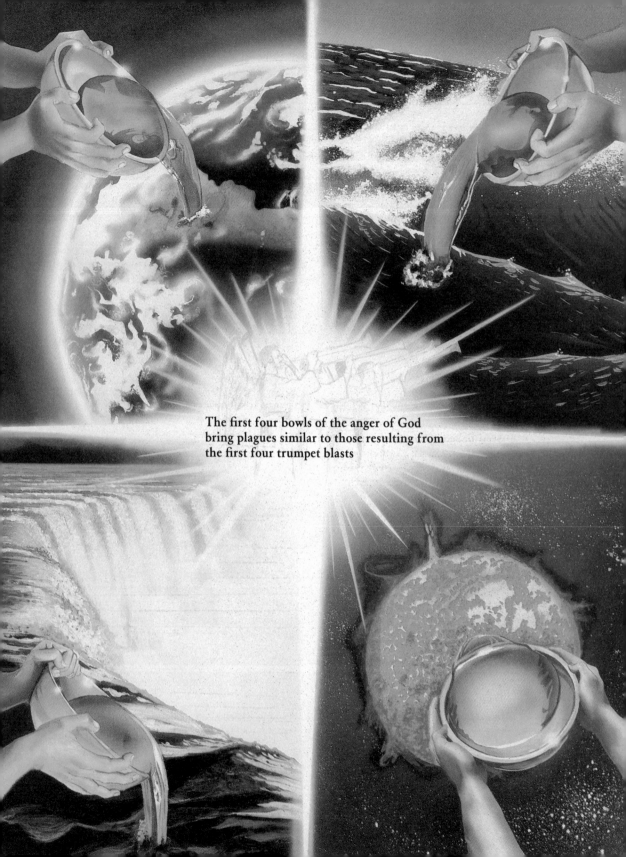

The first four bowls of the anger of God bring plagues similar to those resulting from the first four trumpet blasts

demanded what amounts to worship from their subjects, insisting that the State must be exalted above God or any other loyalty. (2 Timothy 3:1; compare Luke 20:25; John 19:15.) Since 1914 it has become common for nations to conscript their youth in order for them to fight, or be ready to fight, the kind of total warfare that has so bloodied the pages of modern history. During the Lord's day, the nations have also produced, as a substitute for God's Kingdom, the image of the beast—the League of Nations and its successor, the United Nations. What blasphemy to proclaim, as recent popes have done, that this man-made body is the nations' sole hope for peace! It staunchly opposes God's Kingdom. Those who worship it become spiritually unclean, ulcerated, just as the Egyptians who opposed Jehovah in Moses' day were plagued by literal sores and ulcers.—Exodus 9:10, 11.

⁴ The contents of this bowl strongly emphasize the choice that lies before humans. They must suffer either the world's disapproval or Jehovah's indignation. Mankind has been put under compulsion to accept the mark of the wild beast, with the intent that "nobody might be able to buy or sell except a person having the mark, the name of the wild beast or the number of its name." (Revelation 13:16, 17) But there is a price to pay for this! Jehovah regards those who accept the mark as being stricken with "a hurtful and malignant ulcer." Since 1922 they have been marked in public as having rejected the living God. Their political schemes have no success, and they suffer anguish. Spiritually, they are unclean. Unless they repent, this "hurtful" illness will be terminal, for it is now Jehovah's day of judgment. There is no neutral ground between being a part of the world's system of things and serving Jehovah on the side of his Christ.—Luke 11:23; compare James 4:4.

---

4. (a) What do the contents of the first bowl of the anger of God strongly emphasize? (b) How does Jehovah regard those who accept the mark of the wild beast?

The Sea Becomes Blood

⁵ The second bowl of God's anger must now be poured out. What will it mean for mankind? John tells us: *"And the second one poured out his bowl into the sea. And it became blood as of a dead man, and every living soul died, yes, the things in the sea."* (*Revelation 16:3*) Like the second trumpet blast, this bowl is directed against "the sea"—the seething, rebellious mass of humanity alienated from Jehovah. (Isaiah 57:20, 21; Revelation 8:8, 9) In Jehovah's eyes, this "sea" is like blood, unfit for creatures to live in. That is why Christians must be no part of the world. (John 17:14) The pouring out of the second bowl of God's anger reveals that all of mankind who inhabit this sea are dead in Jehovah's eyes. By reason of community responsibility, mankind is guilty of gross shedding of innocent blood. When Jehovah's day of anger arrives, they will

---

5. (a) What takes place when the second bowl is poured out? (b) How does Jehovah view those who inhabit the symbolic sea?

"Into the Sea"

The following are just a few of the statements published over the years by the John class proclaiming God's wrath against the restless, rebellious "sea" of ungodly mankind alienated from Jehovah:

"The history of every nation shows that it has been a struggle between the classes. It has been a few against the many. . . . These struggles have resulted in many revolutions, great suffering, and much bloodshed." —*Government*, 1928, page 244.

In the new world, "the symbolic 'sea' of the restless, rebellious, ungodly peoples out of whom the symbolic wild beast ascended long ago for the Devil's use will be gone."—*The Watchtower*, September 15, 1967, page 567.

"The present human society is spiritually sick and diseased. None of us can save it, for God's Word shows its sickness is leading to its death."—*True Peace and Security—From What Source?*, 1973, page 131.

literally die at the hands of his executional forces.—Revelation 19:17, 18; compare Ephesians 2:1; Colossians 2:13.

Giving Them Blood to Drink

4/27/92
START. a

⁶ The third bowl of God's anger, like the third trumpet blast, has an effect on fresh-

6. What takes place when the third bowl is poured out, and what words are heard from an angel and from the altar?

"Into the Rivers and the Fountains"

The third plague has exposed "the rivers and the fountains of the waters" by statements such as the following:

"The clergy, who claim to be teachers of [Christ's] doctrines, have sanctified war and made it a holy thing. They have delighted to have their portraits and statues exhibited side by side with those of bloody warriors."—The Watch Tower, September 15, 1924, page 275.

"Spiritualism [spiritism] is founded on a great untruth, the lie of survival after death and of the immortality of the human soul."—What Do the Scriptures Say About "Survival After Death?," 1955, page 51.

"Human philosophies, political theorists, social organizers, economic advisers and advocates of religious traditions have resulted in no real life-giving refreshment . . . Such waters have even led the drinkers to violate the Creator's law concerning the sacredness of blood and to engage in religious persecutions."—Resolution adopted at the "Everlasting Good News" International Convention, 1963.

"Not the scientific salvation, but the destruction of the human race is the thing to be expected from man himself. . . . We cannot look to all the psychologists and psychiatrists of the world to change mankind's way of thinking . . . We cannot depend upon any international police force to be formed . . . and make this earth a safe place in which to live."—Saving the Human Race—In the Kingdom Way, 1970, page 5.

---

water sources. "And the third one poured out his bowl into the rivers and the fountains of the waters. And they became blood. And I heard the angel over the waters say: 'You, the One who is and who was, the loyal One, are righteous, because you have rendered these decisions, because they poured out the blood of holy ones and of prophets, and you have given them blood to drink. They deserve it.' And I heard the altar say: 'Yes, Jehovah God, the Almighty, true and righteous are your judicial decisions.'"—Revelation 16:4-7.

⁷ These "rivers and the fountains of the waters" picture the so-called fresh sources of guidance and wisdom accepted by this world, such as the political, economic, scientific, educational, social, and religious philosophies that guide human actions and decisions. Rather than look to Jehovah, the Fountain of life, for life-giving truth, men have 'hewn out for themselves broken cisterns' and drunk deeply of "the wisdom of this world [that] is foolishness with God."—Jeremiah 2:13; 1 Corinthians 1:19; 2:6; 3:19; Psalm 36:9.

⁸ Such tainted "waters" have led men to become bloodguilty, for example, in encouraging them to shed blood on a monumental scale in the wars of this century, which have now taken more than a hundred million lives. Particularly in Christendom, where the two world wars erupted, have men been "in a hurry to shed innocent blood," and this has included the blood of God's own witnesses. (Isaiah 59:7; Jeremiah 2:34) Mankind has also incurred bloodguilt by its misuse of huge quantities of blood for transfusions, in violation of Jehovah's righteous laws. (Genesis 9:3-5; Leviticus 17:14; Acts 15:28, 29) On this account, they have already reaped sorrow by the proliferation, through blood transfusions, of AIDS, hepatitis, and other diseases. Full retribution for all bloodguilt will come shortly when transgressors pay the supreme penalty,

---

7. What is pictured by "the rivers and the fountains of the waters"?
8. In what ways has mankind incurred bloodguilt?

being trampled in "the great winepress of the anger of God."—Revelation 14:19, 20.

⁹ In Moses' day, when the Nile River was turned into blood, the Egyptians were able to keep alive by seeking other sources of water. (Exodus 7:24) Today, though, during the spiritual plague, there is nowhere in Satan's world that people can find life-giving waters. The pouring out of this third bowl involves proclaiming that the world's "rivers and the fountains of the waters" are as blood, bringing spiritual death to all who imbibe them. Unless people turn to Jehovah, they reap his adverse judgment.—Compare Ezekiel 33:11.

¹⁰ "The angel over the waters," that is, the angel who pours this bowl into the waters, magnifies Jehovah as the Universal Judge, whose righteous decisions are absolute. Therefore, he says of this judgment: "They deserve it." Doubtless, the angel personally witnessed much of the bloodshed and cruelty fomented over thousands of years by the false teachings and philosophies of this wicked world. Hence, he knows that Jehovah's judicial decision is right. Even God's "altar" speaks out. At Revelation 6:9, 10, the souls of those who were martyred are said to be at the base of that altar. So "the altar" adds powerful testimony as to the justice and righteousness of Jehovah's decisions.* Certainly, it is fitting that those who have shed and misused so much blood should themselves be force-fed with blood, in symbol of Jehovah's sentencing them to death.

Scorching Men With Fire

¹¹ The fourth bowl of the anger of God has the sun as its target. John tells us: *"And the fourth one poured out his bowl upon the sun; and to the sun it was granted to scorch the men with fire. And the men were scorched with great heat, but they blasphemed the name of God, who has the authority over these plagues, and they did not repent so as to give glory to him."*—Revelation 16:8, 9.

¹² Today, at the conclusion of the system of things, Jesus' spiritual brothers "shine as brightly as the sun in the kingdom of their

---

12. What is this world's "sun," and what is granted to this symbolic sun?

"Upon the Sun"

As the "sun" of human rulership has "scorched" mankind during the Lord's day, the John class, with statements such as the following, has drawn attention to what is happening:

"Today Hitler and Mussolini, the arbitrary dictators, threaten the peace of the whole world, and they are fully supported in their destruction of freedom by the Roman Catholic Hierarchy."—*Fascism or Freedom,* 1939, page 12.

"Throughout history the policy followed by human dictators has been, Rule or ruin! But the regulation now to be applied to all the earth by God's installed King, Jesus Christ, is, Be ruled or be ruined."—*When All Nations Unite Under God's Kingdom,* 1961, page 23.

"Since 1945 more than *25 million persons* have been killed in some 150 wars fought around the globe."—*The Watchtower,* January 15, 1980, page 6.

"The nations around the world . . . care little about international responsibility or rules of conduct. To reach their ends, some nations feel fully justified in using any means that they consider necessary—massacres, assassinations, hijackings, bombings, and so on . . . How long will the nations put up with one another in such senseless and irresponsible conduct?"—*The Watchtower,* February 15, 1985, page 4.

---

* For examples of inanimate things serving as a witness or giving testimony, compare Genesis 4:10; 31:44-53; Hebrews 12:24.

9. What does the pouring out of the third bowl involve?
10. What does "the angel over the waters" make known, and what testimony does "the altar" add?
11. What is the target of the fourth bowl of the anger of God, and what takes place when it is poured out?

The fifth bowl exposes the throne of the wild beast as being the authority Satan has given to the wild beast

Father." (Matthew 13:40, 43) Jesus himself is "the sun of righteousness." (Malachi 4:2) Mankind, though, has its own "sun," its own rulers who try to shine in opposition to God's Kingdom. The fourth trumpet blast proclaimed that the 'sun, moon, and stars' in Christendom's heavens are really sources of darkness, not light. (Revelation 8:12) The fourth bowl of God's anger now shows that the world's "sun" would get unbearably hot. Those looked to as sunlike leaders would "scorch" mankind. This would be granted to the symbolic sun. In other words, Jehovah would allow this as part of his fiery judgment on mankind. In what way has this scorching taken place?

[13] After the first world war, the rulers of this world formed the League of Nations in an effort to solve the problem of world security, but this failed. So other experimental types of rulership were tried, such as Fascism and Nazism. Communism continued to expand. Rather than improve mankind's lot, the sunlike rulers in these systems began to 'scorch mankind with great heat.' Local wars in Spain, Ethiopia, and Manchuria led up to the second world war. Modern history records that Mussolini, Hitler, and Stalin as dictators became responsible directly and indirectly for the deaths of tens of millions, including many of their own nationals. More recently, interna-

13. In what way have sunlike rulers of this world "scorched" mankind?

tional or civil conflicts have "scorched" the people of countries such as Vietnam, Kampuchea, Iran, Lebanon, and Ireland, as well as countries in Latin America and Africa. Add to this the ongoing struggle between the superpowers, whose horrendous nuclear weapons are capable of incinerating all mankind. In these last days, humanity has surely been exposed to a scorching "sun," its unrighteous rulers. The pouring out of the fourth bowl of God's anger has pinpointed these historic facts, and God's people have proclaimed them throughout the earth.

14 Jehovah's Witnesses have consistently taught that the only solution to mankind's baffling problems is God's Kingdom, through which Jehovah purposes to sanctify his name. (Psalm 83:4, 17, 18; Matthew 6:9, 10) Mankind, however, has as a whole turned a deaf ear to this solution. Many who reject the Kingdom also blaspheme the name of God, even as Pharaoh did when he refused to acknowledge Jehovah's sovereignty. (Exodus 1:8-10; 5:2) Having no interest in the Messianic Kingdom, these opposers choose to suffer under their own torrid "sun" of oppressive human rulership.

The Throne of the Wild Beast

15 Upon what does the next angel pour out his bowl? *And the fifth one poured out his bowl upon the throne of the wild beast.*" (*Revelation 16:10a*) "The wild beast" is Satan's governmental system. It does not have a literal throne, any more than the wild beast itself is literal. Mention of a throne, however, shows that the wild beast has exercised royal authority over mankind; this is in harmony with the fact that each of the beast's heads bears a royal diadem. In fact, "the throne of the wild beast"

is the foundation, or source, of that authority.* The Bible reveals the true situation of the royal authority of the wild beast when it says that "the dragon gave to the beast its power and its throne and great authority." (Revelation 13:1, 2; 1 John 5:19) Thus, the pouring out of the bowl upon the throne of the wild beast involves a proclamation revealing the true role that Satan has played and still plays in supporting and promoting the wild beast.

16 How is this relationship between Satan and the nations maintained? When Satan

---

* A similar use of "throne" appears in the words addressed prophetically to Jesus: "God is your throne to time indefinite, even forever." (Psalm 45:6) Jehovah is the source, or foundation, of Jesus' royal authority.

---

16. (a) Whom do the nations serve, whether they are aware of it or not? Explain. (b) How does the world reflect Satan's personality? (c) When will the throne of the wild beast be overthrown?

"Upon the Throne of the Wild Beast"

Jehovah's Witnesses have exposed the throne of the wild beast and publicized Jehovah's condemnation of it with statements such as these:

"**The rulers** and political guides of the nations are influenced by malicious superhuman forces that are irresistibly driving them on in a suicidal march to the decisive conflict of Armageddon."—*After Armageddon—God's New World*, 1953, page 8.

"**The 'wild beast'** of untheocratic human government got its power, authority and throne from the Dragon. So it must hew to the party line, the Dragon line."—*After Armageddon—God's New World*, 1953, page 15.

"**The Gentile nations** can locate their own selves only on . . . the side of God's Chief Adversary, Satan the Devil."—Resolution adopted at the "Divine Victory" International Convention, 1973.

---

14. What have Jehovah's Witnesses consistently taught to be the only solution to mankind's problems, with what response by mankind as a whole?
15. (a) Upon what is the fifth bowl poured out? (b) What is "the throne of the wild beast," and what is involved in the pouring out of the bowl upon it?

tempted Jesus, he showed him all the kingdoms of the world in a vision and offered "all this authority and the glory of them." But there was a condition—Jesus first had to perform an act of worship before Satan. (Luke 4: 5-7) Can we imagine that the governments of the world receive their authority at a lesser price? Not at all. According to the Bible, Satan is the god of this system of things, so that, whether the nations are aware of it or not, they serve him. (2 Corinthians 4:3, 4)* This situation is revealed in the makeup of the present world system, which is built on narrow nationalism, hatred, and self-interest. It is organized the way Satan wants it—to keep mankind under his control. The corruption in government, the lust for power, the lying diplomacy, the armaments race—these reflect Satan's debased personality. The world subscribes to Satan's unrighteous standards, thus making him its god. The throne of the wild beast will be overthrown when that beast suffers extinction and the Seed of God's woman finally abysses Satan himself.—Genesis 3:15; Revelation 19:20, 21; 20:1-3.

Darkness and Gnawing Pain

17 The kingdom of this wild beast has been in spiritual darkness ever since its beginning. (Compare Matthew 8:12; Ephesians 6:11, 12.) The fifth bowl brings intensified public announcement of this darkness. It even dramatizes it, in that this bowl of God's anger is poured out upon the very throne of the symbolic wild beast. *"And its kingdom became darkened, and they began to gnaw their tongues for their pain, but they blasphemed the God of heaven for their pains and for their ulcers, and they did not repent of their works."—Revelation 16: 10b, 11.*

---

* See also Job 1:6, 12; 2:1, 2; Matthew 4:8-10; 13:19; Luke 8:12; John 8:44; 12:31; 14:30; Hebrews 2:14; 1 Peter 5:8.

---

17. (a) How does the pouring out of the fifth bowl relate to the spiritual darkness that has always enveloped the kingdom of the wild beast? (b) How do people react to the pouring out of the fifth bowl of God's anger?

18 The fifth trumpet blast is not exactly the same as the fifth bowl of God's anger, since the trumpet blast heralded a plague of locusts. But notice that at the release of that plague of locusts, there was a darkening of the sun and the air. (Revelation 9:2-5) And at Exodus 10: 14, 15, we read concerning the locusts with which Jehovah plagued Egypt: "They were very burdensome. Before them there had never turned up in this way locusts like them, and there will never turn up any in this way after them. And they went covering the visible surface of the entire land, and the land grew dark." Yes, darkness! Today, the world's spiritual darkness has become all too evident as a result of the sounding of the fifth trumpet and the pouring out of the fifth bowl of God's anger. The stinging message proclaimed by the modern-day locust swarm brings torment and pain to those wicked ones who "have loved the darkness rather than the light."—John 3:19.

19 As world ruler, Satan has caused much unhappiness and suffering. Famine, wars, violence, crime, drug abuse, immorality, sexually transmitted diseases, dishonesty, religious hypocrisy—these and more are the hallmarks of Satan's system of things. (Compare Galatians 5:19-21.) Even so, the public exposure of Satan as the god of this system of things caused pain and embarrassment to those who live by his standards. "They began to gnaw their tongues for their pain," especially in Christendom. Many resent that the truth exposes their lifestyle. Some find it threatening, and they persecute those who publish it. They reject God's Kingdom and revile Jehovah's holy name. Their religiously diseased, ulcerous condition is laid bare, so that they blaspheme the God of heaven. No, they do "not repent of their works." So we cannot expect a mass conversion before the end of this system of things. —Isaiah 32:6.

---

18. What correspondency is there between the fifth trumpet blast and the fifth bowl of God's anger?
19. In harmony with Revelation 16:10, 11, what does the public exposure of Satan as the god of this system of things cause?

5/4/92 start

The River Euphrates Dried Up

20 The sixth trumpet blast heralded the releasing of "the four angels that are bound at the great river Euphrates." (Revelation 9:14) Historically, Babylon was the great city that sat on the river Euphrates. And in 1919 the release of the symbolic four angels accompanied a significant fall of Babylon the Great. (Revelation 14:8) It is noteworthy, then, that the sixth bowl of God's anger also involves the river Euphrates: *"And the sixth one poured out his bowl upon the great river Euphrates, and its water was dried up, that the way might be prepared for the kings from the rising of the sun."* (*Revelation 16:12*) This too is bad news for Babylon the Great!

21 In ancient Babylon's heyday, the abundant waters of the Euphrates were a major part of her defense system. In 539 B.C.E. those waters dried up when they were diverted from their course by the Persian leader Cyrus. Thus, the way was open for Cyrus the Persian and Darius the Mede, the kings from "the rising of the sun" (that is, the east), to enter Babylon and conquer it. In the hour of crisis, the river Euphrates failed in the defense of that great city. (Isaiah 44:27–45:7; Jeremiah 51:36) Something similar is due to happen to modern Babylon, the worldwide system of false religion.

22 Babylon the Great "sits on many waters." According to Revelation 17:1, 15, these symbolize "peoples and crowds and nations and tongues"—hordes of adherents that she has regarded as a protection.

---

20. How do both the sixth trumpet blast and the pouring out of the sixth bowl involve the river Euphrates?
21, 22. (a) How did the protective waters of the river Euphrates dry up for Babylon in 539 B.C.E.? (b) What are the "waters" that Babylon the Great sits on, and how are these symbolic waters even now drying up?

"Its Water Was Dried Up"

Even now, support for Babylonish religion is drying up in many places, indicating what will happen when "the kings from the rising of the sun" make their attack.

"A nationwide survey found that 75 per cent of those who live in municipal areas [of Thailand] do not go to Buddhist temples to listen to sermons at all, while the number in the countryside who visit the temples is steadily declining to about fifty per cent." —*Bangkok Post*, September 7, 1987, page 4.

"The magic has gone out of Taoism in the land [China] where it was founded some two millennia ago. . . . Deprived of the magical devices by which they and their predecessors used to gain large followings, members of the priesthood find themselves without successors, facing the virtual extinction of Taoism as an organized faith on the mainland."—*The Atlanta Journal and Constitution*, September 12, 1982, page 36-A.

"Japan . . . has one of the world's largest concentrations of foreign missionaries, nearly 5,200, yet . . . less than 1% of the population is Christian. . . . A Franciscan priest working here since the 1950s . . . believes that 'the day of the foreign missionary in Japan is finished.' "—*The Wall Street Journal*, July 9, 1986, page 1.

In England during the past three decades, "nearly 2,000 of the 16,000 Anglican churches have been closed because of disuse. Attendance has fallen to among the lowest of avowedly Christian countries. . . . 'It is not now the case that England is a Christian country,' [the Bishop of Durham] said." —*The New York Times*, May 11, 1987, page A4.

"After hours of heated debate, [Greece's] Parliament approved legislation today, enabling the Socialist Government to take over huge estates held by the Greek Orthodox Church . . . Moreover, the law gives nonclerics control of church councils and committees responsible for the administration of prized church investments including hotels, marble quarries and office blocks." —*The New York Times*, April 4, 1987, page 3.

But the "waters" are drying up! In Western Europe, where formerly she had great influence, hundreds of millions have openly ignored religion. In some Eastern European lands, there is a declared policy to try to destroy the influence of religion. The masses in those lands have not risen up on her behalf. Similarly, when the time comes for Babylon the Great to be destroyed, the dwindling number of her adherents will prove to be no protection at all. (Revelation 17:16) Though she claims a membership of thousands of millions, Babylon the Great will find herself defenseless against "the kings from the rising of the sun."

23 Who are these kings? In 539 B.C.E. they were Darius the Mede and Cyrus the Persian, who were used by Jehovah to conquer the ancient city of Babylon. In this the Lord's day, the false religious system of Babylon the Great will also be destroyed by human rulers. But again, this will be a divine judgment. Jehovah God and Jesus Christ, "the kings from the rising of the sun," will have put into the hearts of human rulers the "thought" to turn on Babylon the Great and destroy her utterly. (Revelation 17:16, 17) The pouring out of the sixth bowl proclaims publicly that this judgment is about to be executed!

24 These first six bowls of Jehovah's anger carry a sobering message. God's earthly servants, supported by the angels, have been busy publicizing their contents on an earth-wide scale. In this way, due warning has been served on all sectors of Satan's world system, and Jehovah has provided individuals an opportunity to turn to righteousness and keep living. (Ezekiel 33: 14-16) Still, one more bowl of God's anger remains. But before telling us about it, Revelation reveals how Satan and his earthly agents are trying to counteract the publicizing of Jehovah's judgments.

The Gathering to Armageddon

25 John tells us: *"And I saw three unclean inspired expressions that looked like frogs come out of the mouth of the dragon and out of the mouth of the wild beast and out of the mouth of the false prophet. They are, in fact, expressions inspired by demons and perform signs, and they go forth to the kings of the entire inhabited earth, to gather them together to the war of the great day of God the Almighty."* (*Revelation 16:13, 14*) In Moses' day, Jehovah brought a loathsome plague of frogs on Pharaoh's Egypt, so that "the land began to stink." (Exodus 8:5-15) During the Lord's day, there has also been a disgusting froglike visitation, though from a different source. It consists of Satan's "unclean inspired expressions," clearly symbolizing propaganda designed to maneuver all human rulers, "kings," into opposition to Jehovah God. Satan thus makes sure that they are not swayed by the pouring out of the bowls of God's anger but are firmly on Satan's side when "the war of the great day of God the Almighty" begins.

26 The propaganda comes from "the dragon" (Satan) and "the wild beast" (Satan's earthly political setup), creatures that we have already met up with in Revelation. What, though, is "the false prophet"? This is a newcomer in name only. Previously, we were shown a wild beast with two horns like a lamb that performed great signs before the seven-headed wild beast. This deceptive

---

23. (a) Who were the kings from "the rising of the sun" in 539 B.C.E.? (b) Who are "the kings from the rising of the sun" during the Lord's day, and how will they destroy Babylon the Great?
24. (a) How have the contents of the first six bowls of Jehovah's anger been publicized, and with what result? (b) Before telling us of the remaining bowl of God's anger, what does Revelation reveal?

25. (a) What does John tell us about unclean, froglike "inspired expressions"? (b) How has there been a disgusting froglike visitation of "unclean inspired expressions" in the Lord's day, and with what result?
26. (a) From what three sources does satanic propaganda come? (b) What is "the false prophet," and how do we know?

creature acted like a prophet for that wild beast. It promoted worship of the wild beast, even causing an image to be built to it. (Revelation 13:11-14) This wild beast with two horns like a lamb must be the same as "the false prophet" mentioned here. Confirming this, we read later that the false prophet, like the symbolic wild beast with two horns, "performed in front of [the seven-headed wild beast] the signs with which he misled those who received the mark of the wild beast and those who render worship to its image."—Revelation 19:20.

²⁷ With so much satanic propaganda around, the next words that John records are indeed timely: *"Look! I am coming as a thief. Happy is the one that stays awake and keeps his outer garments, that he may not walk naked and people look upon his shamefulness." (Revela-*

---

27. (a) What timely warning does Jesus Christ himself give? (b) What warning did Jesus give when he was on the earth? (c) How did the apostle Paul echo Jesus' warning?

tion 16:15) Who is coming "as a thief"? Jesus himself, coming at an unannounced time as Jehovah's Executioner. (Revelation 3:3; 2 Peter 3:10) While still on earth, Jesus also likened his coming to that of a thief, saying: "Keep on the watch, therefore, because you do not know on what day your Lord is coming. On this account you too prove yourselves ready, because at an hour that you do not think to be it, the Son of man is coming." (Matthew 24:42, 44; Luke 12:37, 40) Echoing this warning, the apostle Paul said: "Jehovah's day is coming exactly as a thief in the night. Whenever it is that they are saying: 'Peace and security!' then sudden destruction is to be instantly upon them." Satan is even now

Demonic propaganda is gathering earth's rulers to the focal situation, Har–Magedon, where Jehovah's judgments will be poured out upon them

maneuvering the nations toward making that false proclamation of "Peace and security!"—1 Thessalonians 5:2, 3.

28 Jesus also warned of the kind of pressures that this world, saturated with propaganda, would put on Christians. He said: "Pay attention to yourselves that your hearts never become weighed down with overeating and heavy drinking and anxieties of life, and suddenly that day be instantly upon you as a snare. . . . Keep awake, then, all the time making supplication that you may succeed in escaping all these things that are destined to occur, and in standing before the Son of man." (Luke 21:34-36) "That day" is "the great day of God the Almighty." (Revelation 16:14) As "that day" of the vindication of Jehovah's sovereignty approaches, it becomes ever more difficult to cope with the anxieties of life. Christians need to be alert and watchful, staying awake until that day arrives.

29 What, though, is implied by the warning that those found sleeping would be shamed by losing their "outer garments"? In ancient Israel, any priest or Levite on guard duty at the temple had a heavy responsibility. Jewish commentators tell us that if anyone was caught sleeping on such duty, his garments could be stripped from him and burned, so that he was publicly shamed.

30 Jesus here warns that something similar can happen today. The priests and Levites foreshadowed Jesus' anointed brothers. (1 Peter 2:9) But Jesus' warning applies by extension to the great crowd too. The outer garments here referred to identify the wearer as a Christian witness of Jehovah.

(Compare Revelation 3:18; 7:14.) If any allow the pressures of Satan's world to lull them to sleep or into inactivity, they are likely to lose these outer garments—in other words, lose their clean identification as Christians. Such a situation would be shameful. It would put one in danger of losing out completely.

31 The need for Christians to stay awake becomes even more pressing as the next verse of Revelation comes closer to fulfillment: *"And they* [the expressions inspired by demons] *gathered them* [the earthly kings, or rulers] *together to the place that is called in Hebrew Har–Magedon."* (*Revelation 16:16*) This name, more commonly rendered Armageddon, occurs only once in the Bible. But it has fired mankind's imagination. World leaders have warned of a possible nuclear Armageddon. Armageddon has been linked also with the ancient city of Megiddo, the site of many decisive battles in Bible times, and some religious leaders have therefore speculated that the final war on earth will take place in that limited area. In this, they are far wide of the truth.

32 The name Har–Magedon means "Mountain of Megiddo." But rather than being a literal place, it represents the world situation into which all nations are gathered in opposition to Jehovah God and where he will finally destroy them. This is global in extent. (Jeremiah 25:31-33; Daniel 2:44) It is similar to "the great winepress of the anger of God" and "the low plain of the decision," or "the low plain of Jehoshaphat," where the nations are gathered for execution by Jehovah. (Revelation 14:19; Joel 3:12, 14) It is also related

28. What warning did Jesus give about resisting worldly pressures, and what is "that day" that Christians do not want to be upon them "as a snare"?
29, 30. (a) What is implied by Jesus' warning that those found sleeping would be shamed by losing their "outer garments"? (b) What do outer garments identify the wearer as being? (c) How might a person lose his symbolic outer garments, and with what result?

31. (a) How does Revelation 16:16 stress the need for Christians to stay awake? (b) What speculation have some religious leaders made regarding Armageddon?
32, 33. (a) Rather than being a literal place, what does the name Har–Magedon, or Armageddon, represent? (b) What other Bible terms are similar to "Armageddon" or related to it? (c) When will it be time for the seventh angel to pour out the final bowl of the anger of God?

to "the soil of Israel" where the satanic armies of Gog of Magog are destroyed and that location "between the grand sea and the holy mountain of Decoration" where the king of the north comes "all the way to his end" at the hands of Michael the great prince.—Ezekiel 38:16-18, 22, 23; Daniel 11:45–12:1.

33 When the nations have been maneuvered into this situation by the croaking propaganda originating with Satan and his earthly agents, it will be time for the seventh angel to pour out the final bowl of the anger of God.

"It Has Come to Pass!"

5/11/92

34 *"And the seventh one poured out his bowl*

34. Upon what does the seventh angel pour out his bowl, and what proclamation issues "out of the sanctuary from the throne"?

upon the air. At this a loud voice issued out of the sanctuary from the throne, saying: 'It has come to pass!' "—Revelation 16:17.

35 "The air" is the final life-sustaining medium to be plagued. But this is not the literal air. There is nothing about the literal air that makes it deserving of Jehovah's adverse judgments, any more than the literal earth, sea, freshwater sources, or sun deserve to suffer judgments at Jehovah's hand. Rather,

———
35. (a) What is "the air" of Revelation 16:17? (b) In pouring out his bowl upon the air, what does the seventh angel express?

Those motivated by Satan's polluted "air" must suffer the execution of Jehovah's righteous judgments

this is "the air" Paul was discussing when he called Satan "the ruler of the authority of the air." (Ephesians 2:2) It is the satanic "air" breathed by the world today, the spirit, or general mental inclination, that characterizes his whole wicked system of things, the satanic thinking that permeates every aspect of life outside Jehovah's organization. So in pouring out his bowl upon the air, the seventh angel expresses God's wrath against Satan, his organization, and everything that motivates mankind to support Satan in defying Jehovah's sovereignty.

36 This and the previous six plagues give the sum total of Jehovah's judgments against Satan and his system. They are a declaration of doom for Satan and his seed. When this final bowl is poured out, Jehovah himself proclaims: "It has come to pass!" There is nothing else to say. When the contents of the bowls of God's anger have been publicized to Jehovah's satisfaction, there will be no delay in his executing the judgments proclaimed by these messages.

37 John continues: **"And lightnings and voices and thunders occurred, and a great earthquake occurred such as had not occurred since men came to be on the earth, so extensive an earthquake, so great. And the great city split into three parts, and the cities of the nations fell; and Babylon the Great was remembered in the sight of God, to give her the cup of the wine of the anger of his wrath. Also, every island fled, and mountains were not found. And a great hail with every stone about the weight of a talent descended out of heaven upon the men, and the men blasphemed God due to the plague of hail, because the plague of it was unusually great."—Revelation 16:18-21.**

---

36. (a) What do the seven plagues constitute? (b) What is indicated by Jehovah's proclamation: "It has come to pass!"?
37. How does John describe what takes place after the pouring out of the seventh bowl of the anger of God?

38 Once again, Jehovah acts unmistakably toward mankind, this being signaled by "lightnings and voices and thunders." (Compare Revelation 4:5; 8:5.) Mankind will be shaken in a way that has never happened before, as if by a devastating earthquake. (Compare Isaiah 13:13; Joel 3:16.) This blockbuster shaking will shatter "the great city," Babylon the Great, so that it splits into "three parts"—symbolic of its collapse into unredeemable ruin. Also, "the cities of the nations" will fall. "Every island" and "mountains"—institutions and organizations that seem so permanent in this system—will go. "A great hail," much greater than that which afflicted Egypt during the seventh plague, with each hailstone weighing about a talent, will pummel mankind painfully.* (Exodus 9:22-26) This punishing downpour of congealed waters likely pictures unusually heavy verbal expressions of Jehovah's judgments, signaling that the end of this system of things has arrived at last! Jehovah could well use literal hail too in his destructive work. —Job 38:22, 23.

39 Thus, Satan's world will meet up with Jehovah's righteous judgment. To the end, most of humankind will continue to defy and blaspheme God. As with Pharaoh of old, their hearts will not be softened by the repeated plagues or by the final death-dealing culmination of those plagues. (Exodus 11:9, 10) There will be no last-minute, large-scale change of heart. With their dying breath, they will rail against the God who declares: "They will have to know that I am Jehovah." (Ezekiel 38:23) Nevertheless, the sovereignty of Jehovah God the Almighty will have been vindicated.

---

* If John had in mind the Greek talent, each hailstone would weigh about 45 pounds. It would be a devastating hailstorm.

---

38. What is symbolized by (a) the "great earthquake"? (b) the fact that "the great city," Babylon the Great, is split into "three parts"? (c) the fact that "every island fled, and mountains were not found"? (d) "the plague of hail"?
39. Despite the pouring out of the seven plagues, what course of action will most of humankind take?

Judging the Infamous Harlot

JEHOVAH'S righteous anger must be poured out to completion, seven bowls of it! When the sixth angel emptied his bowl at the location of ancient Babylon, it fittingly symbolized the plaguing of Babylon the Great as events move swiftly toward the final war of Armageddon. (Revelation 16:1, 12, 16) Likely, it is this same angel that now reveals why and how Jehovah executes his righteous judgments. John is struck with wonderment at what he next hears and sees: *"And one of the seven angels that had the seven bowls came and spoke with me, saying: 'Come, I will show you the judgment upon the great harlot who sits on many waters, with whom the kings of the earth committed fornication, whereas those who inhabit the earth were made drunk with the wine of her fornication.'"*—Revelation 17:1, 2.

2 "The great harlot"! Why so shocking a designation? Who is she? Some have identified this symbolic harlot with ancient Rome. But

---

1. What does one of the seven angels reveal to John?
2. What evidence is there that "the great harlot" (a) is not ancient Rome? (b) is not big business? (c) is a religious entity?

Rome was a political power. This harlot commits fornication with the kings of the earth, and this evidently includes the kings of Rome. Besides, after her destruction, "the kings of the earth" are said to mourn her passing. Therefore, she cannot be a political power. (Revelation 18:9, 10) Additionally, since she is mourned also by the world's merchants, she could not picture big business. (Revelation 18:15, 16) We read, however, that 'by her spiritistic practice all the nations were misled.' (Revelation 18:23) This makes it clear that the great harlot must be a worldwide religious entity.

3 Which religious entity? Is she the Roman Catholic Church, as some have maintained? Or is she all of Christendom? No, she must be even larger than these if she is to mislead all the nations. She is, in fact, the entire world empire of false religion. Her origin in the mysteries of Babylon is shown in that many Babylonish doctrines and practices are common to religions around the earth. For example, belief in the inherent immortality of the human soul, in a hell of torment, and in a trinity of gods is to be found in most Oriental religions as well as in the sects of Christendom. False religion, spawned more than 4,000 years ago in the ancient city of Babylon, has developed into the modern monstrosity

---

3. (a) Why must the great harlot symbolize more than the Roman Catholic Church or even all of Christendom? (b) What Babylonish doctrines are to be found in most Oriental religions as well as in the sects of Christendom? (c) What did Roman Catholic cardinal John Henry Newman admit regarding the origin of many of Christendom's doctrines, ceremonies, and practices? (See footnote.)

Vision _____ *11*

Revelation 17:1-18

Subject: Babylon the Great rides a scarlet-colored wild beast that finally turns on her and devastates her

Time of fulfillment: From 1919 to the great tribulation

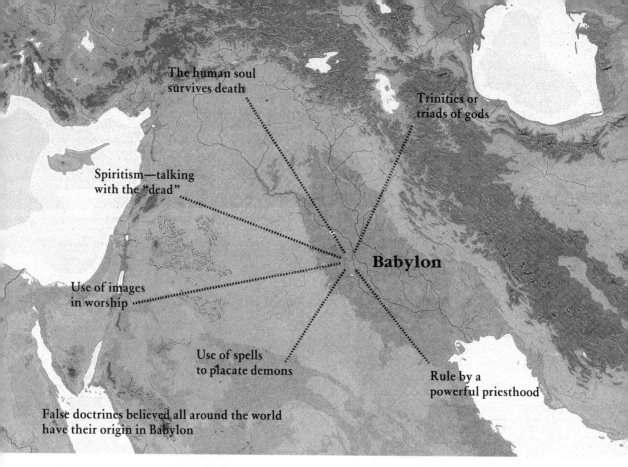

The human soul
survives death

Trinities or
triads of gods

Spiritism—talking
with the "dead"

Babylon

Use of images
in worship

Use of spells
to placate demons

Rule by a
powerful priesthood

False doctrines believed all around the world
have their origin in Babylon

that is called, appropriately, Babylon the Great.* Why, though, is she described by the repugnant term "the great harlot"?

⁴ Babylon (or Babel, meaning "Confu-sion") came to its peak of greatness in Nebuchadnezzar's time. It was a religio-political state with more than a thousand temples and chapels. Its priesthood exercised great power. Though Babylon has long since ceased to exist as a world power, religious Babylon the Great lives on, and after the ancient pattern, she still seeks to influence and mold political affairs. But does God approve of religion in politics? In the Hebrew Scriptures, Israel was said to prostitute herself when she got involved with false worship and when, instead of trusting in Jehovah, she made alliances with the nations. (Jeremiah 3:6, 8, 9; Ezekiel 16:28-30) Babylon the Great also commits fornication. Outstandingly, she has done whatever she deems expedient in order to gain influence and power over the ruling kings of the earth.—1 Timothy 4:1.

---

* Indicating the non-Christian origin of many of apostate Christendom's doctrines, ceremonies, and practices, 19th-century Roman Catholic cardinal John Henry Newman wrote in his *Essay on the Development of Christian Doctrine:* "The use of temples, and these dedicated to particular saints, and ornamented on occasions with branches of trees; incense, lamps, and candles; votive offerings on recovery from illness; holy water; asylums; holydays and seasons, use of calendars, processions, blessings on the fields; sacerdotal vestments, the tonsure, the ring in marriage, turning to the East, images at a later date, perhaps the ecclesiastical chant, and the Kyrie Eleison [the song "Lord, Have Mercy"], are all of pagan origin, and sanctified by their adoption into the Church."

Rather than sanctify such idolatry, "Jehovah the Almighty" admonishes Christians: "Get out from among them, and separate yourselves, . . . and quit touching the unclean thing."—2 Corinthians 6:14-18.

---

4. (a) In what ways did ancient Israel commit fornication? (b) In what outstanding way has Babylon the Great committed fornication?

5 Today, religious leaders frequently campaign for high government office, and in some lands, they share in government, even holding cabinet posts. In 1988 two well-known Protestant clergymen ran for the office of president of the United States. Leaders in Babylon the Great love the limelight; their photos are often to be seen in the public press as they consort with prominent politicians. In contrast, Jesus shunned political involvement and said of his disciples: "They are no part of the world, just as I am no part of the world."—John 6:15; 17:16; Matthew 4:8-10; see also James 4:4.

Modern-Day 'Harlotry'

6 Through her meddling in politics, the great harlot has brought untold sorrow to mankind. Consider, for example, the facts behind Hitler's rise to power in Germany —ugly facts that some would like to expunge from the history books. In May 1924 the Nazi Party held 32 seats in the German Reichstag. By May 1928 these had dwindled to 12 seats. However, the Great Depression engulfed the world in 1930; riding in its wake, the Nazis made a remarkable recovery, gaining 230 out of 608 seats in the German elections of July 1932. Soon after, former chancellor Franz von Papen, a Papal Knight, came to the Nazis' aid. According to historians, von Papen envisioned a new Holy Roman Empire. His own short tenure as chancellor had been a failure, so now he hoped to gain power through the Nazis. By January 1933, he had mustered support for Hitler from the industrial barons, and through wily intrigues he ensured that Hitler became Germany's chancellor on January 30, 1933. He himself was made vice-chancellor and was used by Hitler to win the support of Catholic sections of Germany. Within two months of gaining power, Hitler dissolved parliament, dispatched thousands of opposition leaders to concentration camps, and began an open campaign of oppressing the Jews.

7 On July 20, 1933, the Vatican's interest in the rising power of Nazism was displayed when Cardinal Pacelli (who later became Pope Pius XII) signed a concordat in Rome between the Vatican and Nazi Germany. Von Papen signed the document as Hitler's representative, and Pacelli there conferred on von Papen the high papal decoration of the Grand Cross of the Order of Pius.* In his book *Satan in Top Hat,* Tibor Koeves writes of this, stating: "The Concordat was a great victory for

---

* William L. Shirer's historical work *The Rise and Fall of the Third Reich* states that von Papen was "more responsible than any other individual in Germany for Hitler's coming to power." In January 1933 former German chancellor von Schleicher had said of von Papen: "He proved to be the kind of traitor beside whom Judas Iscariot is a saint."

Churchill Exposes 'Harlotry'

In his book *The Gathering Storm* (1948), Winston Churchill reports that Hitler appointed Franz von Papen as German minister to Vienna for "the undermining or winning over of leading personalities in Austrian politics." Churchill quotes the U.S. minister in Vienna as saying of von Papen: "In the boldest and most cynical manner . . . Papen proceeded to tell me that . . . he intended to use his reputation as a good Catholic to gain influence with Austrians like Cardinal Innitzer."

After Austria had capitulated and Hitler's storm troopers had goose-stepped into Vienna, Catholic cardinal Innitzer ordered that all Austrian churches fly the swastika flag, ring their bells, and pray for Adolf Hitler in honor of his birthday.

---

5. (a) What limelight do religious clergymen enjoy? (b) Why is a desire for worldly prominence a direct contradiction of the words of Jesus Christ?
6, 7. (a) How did Hitler's Nazi Party come to power in Germany? (b) How did the concordat that the Vatican made with Nazi Germany help Hitler in his push for world domination?

Hitler. It gave him the first moral support he had received from the outer world, and this from the most exalted source." The concordat required the Vatican to withdraw its support from Germany's Catholic Center Party, thus sanctioning Hitler's one-party "total state."* Further, its article 14 stated: "The appointments for archbishops, bishops, and the like will be issued only after the governor, installed by the Reich, has duly ascertained that no doubts exist with respect to general political considerations." By the end of 1933 (proclaimed a "Holy Year" by Pope Pius XI), Vatican support had become a major factor in Hitler's push for world domination.

8 Though a handful of priests and nuns

---

* In addressing the College of Mondragone on May 14, 1929, Pope Pius XI said that he would negotiate with the Devil himself if the good of souls required it.

8, 9. (a) How did the Vatican as well as the Catholic Church and its clergy react to the Nazi tyranny? (b) What statement did the German Catholic bishops issue at the start of World War II? (c) In what have religio-political relationships resulted?

This item appeared in the first edition only of _The New York Times,_ December 7, 1941, the same day Nazi Germany's ally Japan attacked Pearl Harbor

'WAR PRAYER' FOR REICH

Catholic Bishops at Fulda Ask Blessing and Victory

By Telephone to THE NEW YORK TIMES.

FULDA, Germany, Dec. 6—The Conference of German Catholic Bishops assembled in Fulda has recommended the introduction of a special "war prayer" which is to be read at the beginning and end of all divine services.

The prayer implores Providence to bless German arms with victory and grant protection to the lives and health of all soldiers. The Bishops further instructed Catholic clergy to keep and remember in a special Sunday sermon at least once a month German soldiers "on land, on sea and in the air."

---

protested Hitler's atrocities—and suffered for it—the Vatican as well as the Catholic Church and its army of clergy gave either active or tacit support to the Nazi tyranny, which they regarded as a bulwark against the advance of world communism. Sitting pretty in the Vatican, Pope Pius XII let the Holocaust on the Jews and the cruel persecutions of Jehovah's Witnesses and others proceed uncriticized. It is ironical that Pope John Paul II, on visiting Germany in May 1987, should glorify the anti-Nazi stand of one sincere priest. What were the other thousands of the German clergy doing during Hitler's reign of terror? A pastoral letter issued by the German Catholic bishops in September 1939 at the outbreak of World War II provides enlightenment on this point. It reads in part: "In this decisive hour we admonish our Catholic soldiers to do their duty in obedience to the Fuehrer and to be ready to sacrifice their whole individuality. We appeal to the Faithful to join in ardent prayers that Divine Providence may lead this war to blessed success."

9 Such Catholic diplomacy illustrates the kind of harlotry that religion has engaged in over the past 4,000 years in wooing the political State in order to gain power and advantage. Such religio-political relationships have fostered warfare, persecutions, and human misery on a vast scale. How happy mankind can be that Jehovah's judgment upon the great harlot is at hand. May it soon be executed!

Sitting on Many Waters

10 Ancient Babylon sat on many waters —the Euphrates River and numerous canals. These were a protection to her as well as a source of commerce producing wealth, until they dried up in one night. (Jeremiah 50:38; 51:9, 12, 13) Babylon the Great also looks to

10. What are the "many waters" that Babylon the Great looks to for protection, and what is happening to them?

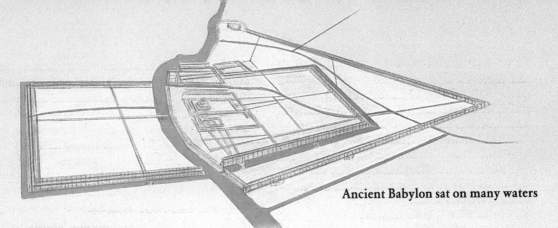

Ancient Babylon sat on many waters

"many waters" to protect and enrich her. These symbolic waters are "peoples and crowds and nations and tongues," that is, all the thousands of millions of humans over whom she has dominated and from whom she has drawn material support. But these waters are also drying up, or withdrawing support.—Revelation 17:15; compare Psalm 18:4; Isaiah 8:7.

[11] Further, Babylon of old was described as "a golden cup in the hand of Jehovah, she making all the earth drunk." (Jeremiah 51:7) Ancient Babylon forced neighboring nations to swallow expressions of Jehovah's anger *a* when she conquered them militarily, making

11. (a) How did ancient Babylon 'make all the earth drunk'? (b) How has Babylon the Great 'made all the earth drunk'?

The great harlot today also sits on "many waters"

them as weak as drunken men. In that respect, she was Jehovah's instrument. Babylon the Great, too, has made conquests to the point of becoming a worldwide empire. But she is certainly not God's instrument. Rather, she has served "the kings of the earth" with whom she commits religious fornication. She has gratified these kings by using her lying doctrines and enslaving practices to keep the masses of the people, "those who inhabit the earth," weak as drunken men, passively subservient to their rulers.

[12] Shinto Japan provides a notable example of this. The indoctrinated Japanese soldier regarded it as the highest honor to give his life for the emperor—the supreme Shinto god. During World War II, some 1,500,000 Japanese soldiers died in battle; almost to a man, they looked at surrender as dishonorable. But as a consequence of Japan's defeat, Emperor Hirohito was compelled to renounce his claim to divinity. This resulted in a notable withdrawing of the "waters" supporting the Shinto segment of Babylon the Great—alas, after Shintoism had sanctioned the shedding of buckets of blood in the Pacific war theater! This weakening of Shinto influence also opened the way in recent years for more than 120,000 Japanese, the great majority of whom were formerly Shintoists and Buddhists, to become dedicated, baptized ministers of the Sovereign Lord Jehovah.

The Harlot Rides a Beast

[13] What more does the prophecy disclose as to the great harlot and her fate? As John now relates, a further vivid scene comes to view: *"And he* [the angel] *carried me away in the power of the spirit into a wilderness. And I caught sight of a woman sitting upon a scarlet-colored wild beast that was full of blasphemous names and that had seven heads and ten horns."* —Revelation 17:3.

[14] Why is John carried into a wilderness? An earlier pronouncement of doom against ancient Babylon was described as being "against the wilderness of the sea." (Isaiah 21:1, 9) This gave due warning that, despite all its watery defenses, ancient Babylon would become a lifeless desolation. It is fitting, then, that John should be carried in his vision to a wilderness to see the fate of Babylon the Great. She too must become desolate and waste. (Revelation 18: 19, 22, 23) John is amazed, though, by what he sees out there. The great harlot is not alone! She is sitting on a monstrous wild beast!

[15] This wild beast has seven heads and ten horns. Is it, then, the same as the wild beast that John saw earlier, which also has seven heads and ten horns? (Revelation 13:1) No, there are differences. This wild beast is scarlet-colored and, unlike the previous wild beast, is not said to have diadems. Rather than having blasphemous names on its seven heads only, it is "full of blasphemous names." Nevertheless, there must be a relationship between this new wild beast and the previous one; the similarities between them are too pronounced to be coincidental.

[16] What, then, is this new scarlet-colored wild beast? It must be the image to the wild beast that was brought forth under the urging of the Anglo-American wild beast that has two horns like a lamb. After the image was made, that two-horned wild beast was allowed to give breath to the image of the

---

12. (a) How was a segment of Babylon the Great in Japan responsible for much bloodshed during World War II? (b) How were "waters" in support of Babylon the Great withdrawn in Japan, and with what result?

13. What amazing sight does John see when the angel carries him in the power of the spirit into a wilderness?

---

14. Why is it fitting that John was carried into a wilderness?

15. What differences are there between the wild beast of Revelation 13:1 and that of Revelation 17:3?

16. What is the identity of the scarlet-colored wild beast, and what has been stated as to its purpose?

NO-DIADEMS
Like Pg. 189
which has them

**Babylon the Great
sitting upon a dangerous
wild beast**

wild beast. (Revelation 13:14, 15) John now sees the living, breathing image. It pictures the League of Nations organization that the two-horned wild beast brought to life in 1920. U.S. President Wilson had envisioned that the League "would be a forum for the dispensation of justice for all men and wipe out the threat of war forever." When it was resurrected after the second world war as the United Nations, its chartered purpose was "to maintain international peace and security."

17 In what way is this symbolic wild beast full of blasphemous names? In that men have set up this multinational idol as a substitute for God's Kingdom—to accomplish what God says his Kingdom alone can accomplish. (Daniel 2:44; Matthew 12:18, 21) What is remarkable about John's vision,

17. (a) In what way is the symbolic scarlet-colored wild beast full of blasphemous names? (b) Who is riding the scarlet-colored wild beast? (c) How did Babylonish religion link itself with the League of Nations and its successor right from the beginning?

The religious harlot has committed fornication with the kings of the earth

though, is that Babylon the Great is riding the scarlet-colored wild beast. True to the prophecy, Babylonish religion, particularly in Christendom, has linked itself with the League of Nations and its successor. As early as December 18, 1918, the body now known as the National Council of the Churches of Christ in America adopted a declaration that declared in part: "Such a League is not a mere political expedient; it is rather the political expression of the Kingdom of God on earth. . . . The Church can give a spirit of good-will, without which no League of Nations can endure. . . . The League of Nations is rooted in the Gospel. Like the Gospel, its objective is 'peace on earth, good-will toward men.'"

[18] On January 2, 1919, the *San Francisco Chronicle* carried the front-page headline: "Pope Pleads for Adoption of Wilson's League of Nations." On October 16, 1919, a petition signed by 14,450 clergymen of leading denominations was presented to the U.S. Senate, urging that body "to ratify the Paris peace treaty embodying the league of nations covenant." Though the U.S. Senate failed to ratify the treaty, Christendom's clergy continued to campaign for the League. And how was the League inaugurated? A news dispatch from Switzerland, dated November 15, 1920, read: "Opening of the first assembly of the League of Nations

18. How did Christendom's clergy show their support for the League of Nations?

was announced at eleven o'clock this morning by the ringing of all the church bells in Geneva."

19 Did the John class, the one group on earth that eagerly accepted the incoming Messianic Kingdom, share with Christendom in paying homage to the scarlet-colored wild beast? Far from it! On Sunday, September 7, 1919, the convention of Jehovah's people in Cedar Point, Ohio, featured the public talk "The Hope for Distressed Humanity." On the following day, the Sandusky *Star-Journal* reported that J. F. Rutherford, president of the Watch Tower Society, in addressing nearly 7,000 persons, had "asserted that the Lord's displeasure is certain to be visited upon the League . . . because the clergy—Catholic and Protestant—claiming to be God's representatives, have abandoned his plan and endorsed the League of Nations, hailing it as a political expression of Christ's kingdom on earth."

20 The dismal failure of the League of Nations should have signaled to the clergy that such man-made organs are no part of a Kingdom of God on earth. What blasphemy to make such a claim! It makes it seem as though God was a party to the colossal botch that the League turned out to be. As for God, "perfect is his activity." Jehovah's heavenly Kingdom under Christ—and not a combine of squabbling politicians, many of them atheists—is the means by which he will bring in peace and have his will done on earth as in heaven.—Deuteronomy 32:4; Matthew 6:10.

21 What of the League's successor, the United Nations? From its inception, this body has also had the great harlot riding on its back, visibly associated with it and trying to guide its destiny. For example, on its 20th anniversary, in June 1965, representatives of the Roman Catholic Church and the Eastern Orthodox Church, together with Protestants, Jews, Hindus, Buddhists, and Muslims—said to represent two thousand million of earth's population—assembled in San Francisco to celebrate their support and admiration of the UN. On visiting the UN in October 1965, Pope Paul VI described it as "that greatest of all international organizations" and added: "The peoples of the earth turn to the United Nations as the last hope of concord and peace." Another papal visitor, Pope John Paul II, addressing the UN in October 1979, said: "I hope the United Nations will ever remain the supreme forum of peace and justice." Significantly, the pope made no mention of Jesus Christ or of God's Kingdom in his speech. During his visit to the United States in September 1987, as reported by *The New York Times*, "John Paul spoke at length about the positive role of the United Nations in promoting . . . 'new worldwide solidarity.'"

A Name, a Mystery

22 The apostle John is soon to learn that the great harlot has chosen a dangerous beast to ride. First, though, his attention turns to Babylon the Great herself. She is richly adorned, but, oh, how repulsive she is! ***"And the woman was arrayed in purple and scarlet, and was adorned with gold and precious stone and pearls and had in her hand a golden cup that was full of disgusting things and the unclean things of her fornication. And upon her forehead was written a name, a mystery: 'Babylon the Great, the mother of the harlots and of the disgusting things of the earth.' And I saw that the woman was drunk with the blood of the holy ones and with the blood of the witnesses of Jesus."***—Revelation 17:4-6a.

23 As was the custom in ancient Rome, this

---

19. When the scarlet-colored wild beast made its appearance, what course of action did the John class take?
20. Why was it blasphemous for the clergy to hail the League of Nations as "the political expression of the Kingdom of God on earth"?
21. What shows that the great harlot supports and admires the League's successor, the United Nations?

22. (a) What kind of beast has the great harlot chosen to ride? (b) How does John describe the symbolic harlot Babylon the Great?
23. What is the full name of Babylon the Great, and what is its significance?

"Blasphemous Names"

When the wild beast with two horns promoted the League of Nations after World War I, its many religious paramours immediately sought to give a religious sanction to this move. As a result, the new peace organization became "full of blasphemous names."

"Christianity can furnish the good-will, the dynamic behind the league [of nations], and so change the treaty from a scrap of paper into an instrument of the kingdom of God."—*The Christian Century,* U.S.A., June 19, 1919, page 15.

"The League of Nations idea is the extension to international relationships of the idea of the Kingdom of God as a world order of good will. . . . It is the thing all Christians pray for when they say, 'Thy Kingdom come.'"—*The Christian Century,* U.S.A., September 25, 1919, page 7.

"The Cement of the League of Nations is the Blood of Christ."—Dr. Frank Crane, Protestant minister, U.S.A.

"The [National] Council [of Congregational Churches] supports the Covenant [of the League of Nations] as the only political instrument now available by which the Spirit of Jesus Christ may find wider scope in practical application to the affairs of nations."—*The Congregationalist and Advance,* U.S.A., November 6, 1919, page 642.

"The conference calls upon all Methodists to uphold and promote highly the ideals [of the League of Nations] as expressed by the idea of God the Father and God's earthly children."—The Wesleyan Methodist Church, Britain.

"When we consider the aspirations, the possibilities and the resolutions of this agreement, we see that it contains the heart of the teachings of Jesus Christ: The Kingdom of God and his righteousness . . . It is nothing less than that."—Sermon by the Archbishop of Canterbury at the opening of the League of Nations Assembly in Geneva, December 3, 1922.

"The League of Nations Association in this country has the same holy right as any humanitarian missionary society, because she is at present the most effective agency of the rule of Christ as the Prince of peace among the nations."—Dr. Garvie, Congregationalist minister, Britain.

prostitute is identified by the name on her forehead.* It is a long name: "Babylon the Great, the mother of the harlots and of the disgusting things of the earth." That name is "a mystery," something with hidden meaning. But in God's due time, the mystery is to be explained. In fact, the angel gives John enough information to allow Jehovah's servants today to discern the full significance of this descriptive name. We recognize Babylon the Great as being all of false religion. She is "the mother of the harlots" because all the individual false religions in the world, including the many sects in Christendom, are like her daughters, imitating her in committing spiritual harlotry. She is also the "mother of disgusting things" in that she has given birth to such revolting offspring as idolatry, spiritism, fortune-telling, astrology, palmistry, human sacrifice, temple prostitution, drunkenness in honor of false gods, and other obscene practices.

[24] Babylon the Great is dressed in "purple and scarlet," the colors of royalty, and is "adorned with gold and precious stone and pearls." How appropriate! Just reflect on all the magnificent buildings, rare statues and paintings, priceless icons, and other religious paraphernalia, as well as astronomical amounts of property and cash, that this world's religions have accumulated. Whether at the Vatican, in the TV empire of evangelism centered in the United States, or in the exotic wats and temples of the Orient, Babylon the Great has amassed—and at times lost—fabulous wealth.

[25] Look now at what the harlot has in her

---

* Compare the words of Roman author Seneca to an errant priestess (as quoted by Swete): "You stood, girl, in the house of ill repute . . . your name hung from your forehead; you accepted money for your dishonor."—*Controv.* i, 2.

---

24. Why is it appropriate that Babylon the Great is seen to be dressed in "purple and scarlet" and is "adorned with gold and precious stone and pearls"?
25. (a) What is symbolized by the contents of the "golden cup that was full of disgusting things?" (b) In what sense is the symbolic harlot drunk?

hand. John must have gasped at the sight of it —a golden cup "full of disgusting things and the unclean things of her fornication"! This is the cup containing "the wine of the anger of her fornication" with which she has made all the nations drunk. (Revelation 14:8; 17:2) It looks rich on the outside, but its contents are disgusting, unclean. (Compare Matthew 23:25, 26.) It contains all the filthy practices and lies that the great harlot has used to seduce the nations and bring them under her influence. Even more revolting, John sees that the harlot herself is inebriated, drunk with the blood of God's servants! In fact, we later read that "in her was found the blood of prophets and of holy ones and of all those who have been slaughtered on the earth." (Revelation 18:24) What massive bloodguilt!

26 Over the centuries, the world empire of false religion has shed oceans of blood. For example, in medieval Japan, temples in Kyoto were transformed into fortresses, and warrior-monks, invoking "the holy name of Buddha," battled one another until the streets ran red with blood. In this 20th century, the clergy of Christendom have marched with the armies of their respective countries, and these have slaughtered one another, with the loss of at least a hundred million lives. In October 1987 former U.S. president Nixon said: "The 20th century has been the bloodiest in history. More people have been killed in the wars of this century than in all the wars fought before the century began." The religions of the world are judged adversely by God for their share in all of this; Jehovah detests "hands that are shedding innocent blood." (Proverbs 6:16, 17) Earlier, John heard a cry from the altar: "Until when, Sovereign Lord holy and true, are you refraining from judging and avenging our blood upon those who dwell on the earth?" (Revelation 6:10) Babylon the Great, the mother of the harlots and of the disgusting things of the earth will be deeply involved when the time comes to answer that question.

26. What evidence is there of bloodguilt on the part of Babylon the Great?

The woman is "drunk with the blood of the holy ones"

An Awesome Mystery Solved

WHAT is John's reaction at seeing the great harlot and her fearsome mount? He himself answers: *"Well, on catching sight of her I wondered with great wonderment."* (*Revelation 17:6b*) Mere human imagination could never conjure up such a sight. Yet, there it is—away out in a wilderness—a debauched prostitute perched on a gruesome, scarlet-colored wild beast! (Revelation 17:3) The John class today also wonders with great wonderment as events unfold in fulfillment of the prophetic vision. If people of the world could see it, they would exclaim, 'Incredible!' and the world's rulers would echo, 'Unthinkable!' But the vision becomes a startling 20th-century reality. God's people have already had a remarkable share in the vision's fulfillment, and this assures them that the prophecy will move right on to its astounding climax.

² The angel notices John's amazement. *"And so,"* John continues, *"the angel said to me: 'Why is it you wondered? I will tell you the mystery of the woman and of the wild beast that is carrying her and that has the seven heads and the ten horns.'"* (*Revelation 17:7*) Ah, the angel will now unravel the mystery! He explains to the wide-eyed John the various facets of the vision and the dramatic events that are about to unfold. Likewise, as it serves

under angelic direction today, the watchful John class has had revealed to it the understanding of the prophecy. "Do not interpretations belong to God?" Like faithful Joseph, we believe that they do. (Genesis 40:8; compare Daniel 2:29, 30.) God's people are placed, as it were, center stage as Jehovah interprets to them the meaning of the vision and its impact on their lives. (Psalm 25:14) Right on time, he has opened up to their understanding the mystery of the woman and of the wild beast.—Psalm 32:8. √

³ From September 18 to 20, 1942, at the height of World War II, Jehovah's Witnesses in the United States held their New World Theocratic Assembly. The key city, Cleveland, Ohio, was tied in by telephone with more than 50 other convention cities, for a peak attendance of 129,699. Where wartime conditions permitted, other conventions repeated the program around the world. At the time, many of Jehovah's people expected that the war would escalate into God's war of Armageddon; hence the title of the public talk, "Peace—Can It Last?," aroused much curiosity. How could the new president of the Watch Tower Society, N. H. Knorr, presume to talk about peace when the very opposite seemed to be in store for the nations?* The reason was that the John class was paying "more than the usual attention"

---

* J. F. Rutherford died on January 8, 1942, and N. H. Knorr succeeded him as president.

---

1. (a) How does John react at seeing the great harlot and her fearsome mount, and why? (b) How does the John class today react as events unfold in fulfillment of the prophetic vision?

2. (a) In response to John's amazement, what does the angel tell him? (b) What has the John class had revealed to it, and how has this been done?

3, 4. (a) What public talk was given by the Society's president in 1942, and how did it identify the scarlet-colored wild beast? (b) What words spoken by the angel to John were discussed by President Knorr?

Building GENEVA wbH *NYC*

Japan, Germany, and Italy withdrew, and the Soviet Union was dropped from the League. In September 1939 the Nazi dictator of Germany launched World War II.* Having failed to keep peace in the world, the League of Nations virtually plunged into an abyss of inactivity. By 1942 it had become a has-been. Neither before this nor at some later date —but right at that critical time—did Jehovah interpret to his people the full depth of

* On November 20, 1940, Germany, Italy, Japan, and Hungary signed up for a "new League of Nations," followed four days later by the Vatican's broadcasting a Mass and a prayer for a religious peace and for a new order of things. That "new League" never materialized.

to God's prophetic Word.—Hebrews 2:1; 2 Peter 1:19.

⁴ What light did the talk "Peace—Can It Last?" throw on the prophecy? Clearly identifying the scarlet-colored wild beast of Revelation 17:3 as the League of Nations, President Knorr went on to discuss its stormy career on the basis of the angel's following words to John: **"The wild beast that you saw was, but is not, and yet is about to ascend out of the abyss, and it is to go off into destruction."**—Revelation 17:8a.

⁵ "The wild beast . . . *was.*" Yes, it had existed as the League of Nations from January 10, 1920, onward, with 63 nations participating at one time or another. But, in turn,

5. (a) How was it that "the wild beast . . . was" and then "is not"? (b) How did President Knorr answer the question, "Will the League remain in the pit?"

AN AWESOME MYSTERY SOLVED

As prophesied about the scarlet-colored wild beast, the League of Nations was abyssed during World War II but was revived as the United Nations

meaning of the vision! At the New World Theocratic Assembly, President Knorr could declare, in line with the prophecy, that "the wild beast . . . *is not.*" He then asked the question, "Will the League remain in the pit?" Quoting Revelation 17:8, he answered: "The association of worldly nations will rise again." That is just how it proved to be—in vindication of Jehovah's prophetic Word!

Ascending out of the Abyss

6 The scarlet-colored wild beast did indeed climb out of the abyss. On June 26, 1945, with noisy fanfare in San Francisco, U.S.A., 50 nations voted to accept the Charter of the United Nations organization. This body was "to maintain international peace and security." There were many similarities between the League and the UN. *The World Book Encyclopedia* notes: "In some ways, the UN resembles the League of Nations, which was organized after World War I. . . . Many of the nations that founded the UN had also founded the League. Like the League, the UN was established to help keep peace between nations. The main organs of the UN are much like those of the League." The UN, then, is actually a revival of the scarlet-colored wild beast. Its membership of over 150 nations far exceeds that of the League's 63; it has also taken on broader responsibilities than its predecessor.

7 At first, great hopes were expressed for the UN. This was in fulfillment of the angel's words: ***"And when they see how the wild beast was, but is not, and yet will be present, those who dwell on the earth will wonder admiringly, but their names have not been written upon the***

scroll of life from the founding of the world." *(Revelation 17:8b)* Earth's dwellers have admired this new colossus, operating from its imposing headquarters on New York's East River. But true peace and security have eluded the UN. In this diabolical nuclear age, world peace has been maintained only by the threat of "mutual assured destruction" —MAD, as it is abbreviated—and the arms race has continued to escalate astronomically. After almost 40 years of effort by the United Nations, its secretary-general, Javier Pérez de Cuéllar, lamented in 1985: "We are living in another age of fanatics, and we don't know what to do about it."

8 The UN does not have the answers. And why? Because the Giver of life to all mankind is not the UN's life-giver. Its life span will be short, for according to God's decree, "it is to go off into destruction." The UN's founders and admirers do not have their names recorded in God's scroll of life. How could sinful, mortal men, many of whom mock God's name, achieve through the UN what Jehovah God has declared he is about to accomplish, not by human means, but through the Kingdom of his Christ?—Daniel 7:27; Revelation 11:15.

9 The UN is actually a blasphemous counterfeit of God's Messianic Kingdom by his Prince of Peace, Jesus Christ—to whose princely rule there will be no end. (Isaiah 9: 6, 7) Even if the UN were to patch up some temporary peace, wars would soon erupt again. This is in the nature of sinful men. "Their names have not been written upon the scroll of life from the founding of the world." Jehovah's Kingdom by Christ will not only establish eternal peace on earth but, on the

---

6. (a) When did the scarlet-colored wild beast climb out of the abyss, and with what new name? (b) Why is the United Nations actually a revival of the scarlet-colored wild beast?
7. (a) In what way have earth's dwellers wondered admiringly at the revived scarlet-colored wild beast? (b) What goal has eluded the UN, and what did its secretary-general say in this regard?

8, 9. (a) Why does the UN not have the answers to the world's problems, and what will shortly happen to it according to God's decree? (b) Why do the UN's founders and admirers not have their names recorded in God's "scroll of life"? (c) What will Jehovah's Kingdom successfully accomplish?

In support of the UN's "Year of Peace," representatives of the world's religions offered up a babel of prayers at Assisi, Italy, but not one of them prayed to the living God, Jehovah

basis of Jesus' ransom sacrifice, raise the dead, the righteous and the unrighteous who are in God's memory. (John 5:28, 29; Acts 24:15) This includes everyone who has remained steadfast despite the attacks of Satan and his seed, and others who have yet to show themselves obedient. Obviously, God's scroll of life will never contain the names of die-hard adherents of Babylon the Great or of any who continued to worship the wild beast. —Exodus 32:33; Psalm 86:8-10; John 17:3; Revelation 16:2; 17:5. *Luke 10:20*

Peace and Security—A Vain Hope

START 6/1/92

¹⁰ In an effort to bolster the hopes of mankind, the United Nations proclaimed 1986 to be an "International Year of Peace," with the theme "To Safeguard Peace and the Future of Humanity." Warring nations were called

upon to lay down their weapons, at least for one year. What was their response? According to a report by the International Peace Research Institute, more than five million soldiers were killed in combat during 1986 alone! Though some special coins and commemorative stamps were issued, most of the nations did little about pursuing the ideal of peace in that year. Nevertheless, the world's religions—always anxious for a fine rapport with the UN—set about publicizing the year in various ways. On January 1, 1986, Pope John Paul II praised the work of the UN and dedicated the new year to peace. And on October 27, he assembled the leaders of many of the world's religions at Assisi, Italy, to pray for peace.

¹¹ Does God answer such prayers for peace? Well, to which God were those religious leaders praying? If you asked them, each group would give a different answer. Is there a pantheon of millions of gods that can

10, 11. (a) What did the UN proclaim in 1986, and what was the response? (b) How many "religious families" assembled at Assisi, Italy, to pray for peace, and does God answer such prayers? Explain.

hear and grant petitions made in many different ways? Many of the participants worshiped Christendom's Trinity.* Buddhists, Hindus, and others chanted prayers to gods without number. In all, 12 "religious families" assembled, being represented by such notables as the Anglican Archbishop of Canterbury, Buddhism's Dalai Lama, a Russian

---

* The Trinity concept stems from ancient Babylon, where the sun-god Shamash, the moon god Sin, and the star god Ishtar were worshiped as a triad. Egypt followed the same pattern, worshiping Osiris, Isis, and Horus. Assyria's chief god, Asshur, is portrayed as having three heads. Following the same pattern, images are to be found in Catholic churches depicting God as having three heads.

The "Peace" Paradox

Though 1986 was proclaimed by the UN to be the International Year of Peace, the suicidal armaments race escalated. *World Military and Social Expenditures 1986* supplies these sobering details:

In 1986 global military expenditures reached $900 thousand million.

One hour's global military expenditure would suffice to immunize the 3.5 million that die annually from preventable infectious disease.

Worldwide, one person in five lives in gnawing poverty. All these starving people could be fed for one year at the cost of what the world spends for armaments in two days.

The explosive energy in the world's stockpile of nuclear weapons is 160,000,000 times greater than that of the Chernobyl explosion.

Today a nuclear bomb can be delivered having an explosive power more than 500 times as powerful as the bomb dropped on Hiroshima in 1945.

Today's nuclear arsenals contain the equivalent of more than one million Hiroshimas. They represent 2,700 times the explosive energy released in World War II, when 38 million people died.

Wars have become more frequent and more deadly. War deaths totaled 4.4 million in the 18th century, 8.3 million in the 19th century, 98.8 million in 86 years of the 20th century. Since the 18th century, war deaths have increased more than six times faster than the world's population. There have been ten times as many deaths per war in the 20th century as in the 19th.

Orthodox metropolitan, the president of Tokyo's Shinto Shrine Association, African animists, and two American Indians decked out in plumed headdresses. It was a colorful group, to say the least, making for spectacular TV coverage. One group prayed unceasingly for 12 hours at one time. (Compare Luke 20: 45-47.) But did any of those prayers reach beyond the rain clouds that hovered over the gathering? No, for the following reasons:

¹² In contrast with those who "walk in the name of Jehovah," not one of those religionists was praying to Jehovah, the living God, whose name appears some 7,000 times in the original text of the Bible. (Micah 4:5; Isaiah 42: 8, 12)* As a group, they did not approach God in the name of Jesus, the majority of them not even believing in Jesus Christ. (John 14:13; 15:16) None of them are doing God's will for our day, which is to proclaim worldwide God's incoming Kingdom—not the UN—as the real hope for mankind. (Matthew 7:21-23; 24:14; Mark 13:10) For the most part, their religious organizations have been involved in the bloody wars of history, including the two world wars of this century. To such, God says: "Even though you make many prayers, I am not listening; with bloodshed your very hands have become filled." —Isaiah 1:15; 59:1-3.

¹³ Further, it is deeply significant that the world's religious leaders should join hands with the United Nations in calling for peace at this time. They would like to influence the UN to their own advantage, especially in this modern age when so many of their people are abandoning religion. Like the unfaithful

---

* *Webster's Third New International Dictionary* of 1981 defines Jehovah God as "a supreme deity recognized and the only deity worshiped by Jehovah's Witnesses."

12. For what reasons did God not answer the prayers for peace of the world's religious leaders?
13. (a) Why is it significant that the world's religious leaders should join hands with the UN in calling for peace? (b) The cries for peace will culminate in what divinely foretold climax?

leaders in ancient Israel, they call out, "'There is peace! There is peace!' when there is no peace." (Jeremiah 6:14) No doubt their cries for peace will continue, rising in support of the climax concerning which the apostle Paul prophesied: "Jehovah's day is coming exactly as a thief in the night. Whenever it is that they are saying: 'Peace and security!' then sudden destruction is to be instantly upon them just as the pang of distress upon a pregnant woman; and they will by no means escape."—1 Thessalonians 5:2, 3.

¹⁴ What form will this significant cry of "Peace and security!" take? It is here men-

tioned as being outstanding just before the sudden destruction of those making the cry. Hence, it will have to be something more pronounced than any previous declarations, by world leaders. No doubt it will be on an earth-wide scale. Yet, it will be no more than a facade. Underneath, nothing will really have changed. Selfishness, hatred, crime, family breakdown, immorality, sickness, sorrow, and death will still be here. That is why the coming cry will mislead those who are not awake to Bible prophecy. But it need not mislead *you*, if you have been awake to the meaning of world events and have heeded the prophetic warnings in God's Word. —Mark 13:32-37; Luke 21:34-36.

---

14. What form will the cry of "Peace and security!" take, and how can one avoid being misled by it?

Chapter 35

Executing Babylon the Great

IN FURTHER describing the scarlet-colored wild beast of Revelation 17:3, the angel tells John: *"Here is where the intelligence that has wisdom comes in: The seven heads mean seven mountains, where the woman sits on top. And there are seven kings: five have fallen, one is, the other has not yet arrived, but when he does arrive he must remain a short while."* (Revelation 17:9, 10) The angel is here conveying wisdom from above, the only wisdom that can give understanding of the symbols in Revelation. (James 3:17) This wisdom enlightens the John class and its companions as to the seriousness of the times in which we live. It builds in devoted hearts appreciation of Jehovah's judgments, now about to

be carried out, and inculcates a healthy fear of Jehovah. As Proverbs 9:10 states: "The fear of Jehovah is the start of wisdom, and the knowledge of the Most Holy One is what understanding is." What does divine wisdom reveal to us about the wild beast?

² The seven heads of that ferocious beast stand for seven "mountains," or seven "kings." Both terms are used Scripturally to refer to governmental powers. (Jeremiah 51: 24, 25; Daniel 2:34, 35, 44, 45) In the Bible, six world powers are mentioned as having an impact on the affairs of God's people: Egypt, Assyria, Babylon, Medo-Persia, Greece, and Rome. Of these, five had already come and gone by the time John received

---

1. How does the angel describe the scarlet-colored wild beast, and what kind of wisdom is needed to understand the symbols of Revelation?

2. What is the meaning of the seven heads of the scarlet-colored wild beast, and how is it that "five have fallen, one is"?

Revelation, whereas Rome was still very much a world power. This corresponds well with the words, "five have fallen, one is." But what of "the other" that was due to come?

³ The Roman Empire endured and even expanded for hundreds of years after John's day. In 330 C.E., Emperor Constantine moved his capital from Rome to Byzantium, which he renamed Constantinople. In 395 C.E., the Roman Empire was split into Eastern and Western parts. In 410 C.E., Rome itself fell to Alaric, king of the Visigoths (a Germanic tribe that had converted to the Arian brand of "Christianity"). Germanic tribes (also "Christian") conquered Spain and much of the territory of Rome in North Africa. There were centuries of upheaval, unrest, and readjustment in Europe. Notable emperors arose in the West, such as Charlemagne, who formed an alliance with Pope Leo III in the 9th century, and Frederick II, who reigned in the 13th century. But their domain, though named the Holy Roman Empire, was much smaller than that of the earlier Roman Empire at its zenith. It was more of a restoration or a continuation of this ancient power than a new empire.

⁴ Rome's Eastern Empire, centered at Constantinople, endured in a somewhat uneasy relationship with the Western Empire. In the sixth century, Eastern emperor Justinian I was able to reconquer much of North Africa, and he also intervened in Spain and Italy. In the seventh century, Justinian II recovered for the Empire areas of Macedonia that had been conquered by Slavic tribesmen. By the eighth century, however, much of the former territory of ancient Rome in North Africa, Spain, and Syria had come under the

3. (a) How did the Roman Empire come to be divided? (b) What developments took place in the West? (c) How is the Holy Roman Empire to be viewed?
4. What successes did the Eastern Empire have, but what happened to much of the former territory of ancient Rome in North Africa, Spain, and Syria?

**The Succession of
Seven World Powers**

EGYPT

ASSYRIA

BABYLON

MEDO-
PERSIA

GREECE

ROME

ANGLO-
AMERICA

new empire of Islam and thus passed from the control of both Constantinople and Rome.

5 The city of Constantinople itself endured somewhat longer. It survived frequent attacks from Persians, Arabs, Bulgars, and Russians until in 1203 it finally fell—not to Muslims but to Crusaders from the West. In 1453, though, it came under the power of the Muslim Ottoman ruler Mehmed II and soon became capital of the Ottoman, or Turkish, Empire. Thus, although the city of Rome fell in 410 C.E., it took many more centuries for all traces of the political Roman Empire to pass from the world scene. And even then, its influence was still discernible in religious empires based on the papacy of Rome and the Eastern Orthodox churches.

6 By the 15th century, however, some countries were building brand-new empires. While some of these new imperial powers were found in the territory of former colonies of Rome, their empires were not mere continuations of the Roman Empire. Portugal, Spain, France, and Holland all became seats of far-flung domains. But the most successful was Britain, which came to preside over a huge empire on which 'the sun never set.' This empire spread at different times over much of North America, Africa, India, and Southeast Asia, as well as the expanse of the South Pacific.

7 By the 19th century, some of the colonies in North America had already broken away from Britain to form the independent United States of America. Politically, some conflict between the new nation and the former motherland continued. Nevertheless, the first world war forced both countries to recognize their common interests and cemented a special relationship between them. Thus, a kind of dual world power came to exist, made up of the United States of America, now the world's wealthiest nation, and Great Britain, seat of the world's largest empire. Here, then, is the seventh 'head,' or world power, that continues into the time of the end and in the territories of which the modern-day witnesses of Jehovah first got established. Compared with the long reign of the sixth head, the seventh remains only "a short while," until God's Kingdom destroys all national entities.

Why Called an Eighth King?

8 The angel further explains to John: *"And the wild beast that was but is not, it is also itself an eighth king, but springs from the seven, and it goes off into destruction."* (*Revelation 17: 11*) The symbolic scarlet-colored wild beast "springs from" the seven heads; that is, it is born from, or owes its existence to, those heads of the original "wild beast . . . out of the sea," of which the scarlet-colored wild beast is an image. In what way? Well, in 1919 the Anglo-American power was the ascendant head. The previous six heads had fallen, and the position of dominant world power had passed to this dual head and was now centered in it. This seventh head, as the current representative of the line of world powers, was the moving force in establishing the League of Nations and is still the major promoter and financial support of the United Nations. Thus, in symbol, the scarlet-colored wild beast—the eighth king— "springs from" the original seven heads. Viewed in this way, the statement that it sprang from the seven harmonizes well with

---

5. Though the city of Rome fell in 410 C.E., how is it that it took many more centuries for all traces of the political Roman Empire to pass from the world scene?

6. What brand-new empires developed, and which one became the most successful?

7. How did a kind of dual world power come to exist, and how long did John say that the seventh 'head,' or world power, would continue?

8, 9. What does the angel call the symbolic scarlet-colored wild beast, and in what way does it spring from the seven?

the earlier revelation that the wild beast with two horns like a lamb (the Anglo-American World Power, the seventh head of that original wild beast) urged the making of the image and gave it life.—Revelation 13:1, 11, 14, 15.

⁹ Additionally, original members of the League of Nations included, along with Great Britain, governments that ruled in the seats of some of the previous heads, namely Greece, Iran (Persia), and Italy (Rome). Eventually, governments ruling the territory controlled by the previous six world powers came to be supportive members of the image of the wild beast. In this sense, too, it could be said that this scarlet-colored wild beast sprang from the seven world powers.

¹⁰ Notice that the scarlet-colored wild beast "is also itself an eighth king." Thus, the United Nations today is designed to look like a world government. At times it has even acted like one, sending armies into the field to resolve international disputes, as in Korea, the Sinai Peninsula, some African countries, and Lebanon. But it is only the *image* of a king. Like a religious image, it has no real

10. (a) How can it be said that the scarlet-colored wild beast "is also itself an eighth king"? (b) How did a Soviet leader express support for the United Nations?

"It is also itself an eighth king"

influence or power apart from what is invested in it by those who brought it into existence and worship it. On occasion, this symbolic wild beast looks weak; but it has never experienced the kind of wholesale abandonment by dictator-oriented members that sent the League of Nations reeling into the abyss. (Revelation 17:8) Though holding radically different opinions in other areas, a prominent Soviet leader in 1987 joined the popes of Rome in expressing support for the UN. He even called for "a comprehensive system of international security" based on the UN. As John soon learns, the time will come when the UN will act with considerable authority. Then it, in its turn, "goes off into destruction."

Ten Kings for One Hour

¹¹ In the previous chapter of Revelation, the sixth and seventh angels poured out bowls of the anger of God. Thus we were advised that earth's kings are being gathered to God's war at Armageddon and that 'Babylon the Great is to be remembered in the sight of God.' (Revelation 16:1, 14, 19) Now we will learn in greater detail how God's judgments on these are to be executed. Listen again to Jehovah's angel as he speaks to John. **"And the ten horns that you saw mean ten kings, who have not yet received a kingdom, but they do receive authority as kings one hour with the wild beast. These have one thought, and so they give their power and authority to the wild beast. These will battle with the Lamb, but, because he is Lord of lords and King of kings, the Lamb will conquer them. Also, those called and chosen and faithful with him will do so."—Revelation 17:12-14.**

¹² The ten horns depict all the political

11. What does Jehovah's angel tell about the ten horns on the symbolic scarlet-colored wild beast?
12. (a) What do the ten horns depict? (b) How is it that the symbolic ten horns 'had not yet received a kingdom'? (c) How do the symbolic ten horns have "a kingdom" now, and for how long?

powers that presently hold sway on the world scene and that support the image of the wild beast. Very few of the countries that now exist were known in John's day. And those that were, such as Egypt and Persia (Iran), today have an entirely different political setup. Hence, in the first century, the 'ten horns had not yet received a kingdom.' But now in the Lord's day, they have "a kingdom," or political authority. With the collapse of the great colonial empires, particularly since the second world war, many new nations have been born. These, as well as the longer-established powers, must rule with the wild beast for a short period—just "one hour"—before Jehovah brings an end to all worldly political authority at Armageddon.

¹³ Today, nationalism is one of the strongest forces motivating these ten horns. They have "one thought" in that they want to preserve their national sovereignty rather than accept God's Kingdom. This was their purpose in subscribing to the League of Nations and the United Nations organization in the first place—to preserve world peace and thus safeguard their own existence. Such an attitude ensures that the horns will oppose the Lamb, the "Lord of lords and King of kings," because Jehovah has purposed that his Kingdom under Jesus Christ will shortly replace all these kingdoms.—Daniel 7:13, 14; Matthew 24:30; 25:31-33, 46.

¹⁴ Of course, there is nothing that the rulers of this world can do against Jesus himself. He is in heaven, far out of their reach. But Jesus' brothers, the remaining ones of the woman's seed, are still on earth and apparently vulnerable. (Revelation 12:17) Many of the horns have already demonstrat-

Turning their backs on the Lamb, "they give their power and authority to the wild beast"

ed bitter hostility toward them, and in this way they have battled with the Lamb. (Matthew 25:40, 45) Soon, though, the time will come for God's Kingdom to "crush and put an end to all these kingdoms." (Daniel 2:44) Then, the kings of the earth will be in a fight to the finish with the Lamb, as we shall soon see. (Revelation 19:11-21) But here we learn enough to realize that the nations will not succeed. Though they and the UN scarlet-colored wild beast have their "one thought," they cannot defeat the great "Lord of lords and King of kings," nor can they defeat "those called and chosen and faithful with him," which includes his anointed followers

13. In what way do the ten horns have "one thought," and what attitude toward the Lamb does this ensure?
14. How is it possible for the rulers of the world to battle with the Lamb, and what will be the outcome?

watery defenses, Babylon the Great today relies on her huge membership of "peoples and crowds and nations and tongues." The angel appropriately draws our attention to these before telling of a shocking development: Political governments of this earth will turn violently upon Babylon the Great. What will all those "peoples and crowds and nations and tongues" do then? God's people are already warning Babylon the Great that the water of the river Euphrates will dry up. (Revelation 16:12) Those waters will finally drain away completely. They will not be able to give the disgusting old harlot any effectual support in her hour of greatest need.—Isaiah 44:27; Jeremiah 50:38; 51: 36, 37.

17 Certainly, the immense material wealth of Babylon the Great will not save her. It may even hasten her destruction, for the vision shows that when the wild beast and the ten horns vent their hatred on her they will strip off her royal robes and all her jewelry. They will plunder her wealth. They "make her . . . naked," shamefully exposing her real character. What devastation! Her end is also far from dignified. They destroy her, "eat up her fleshy parts," reducing her to a lifeless skeleton. Finally, they "completely burn her with fire." She is burned up like a carrier of the plague, without even a decent burial! It is not the nations alone, as represented by the ten horns, that destroy the great harlot, but "the wild beast," meaning the UN itself, joins them in this rampage. It will give its sanction to the destruction of false religion. A majority of the 150-and-more nations within the UN have already displayed, by their voting pattern, a hostility

still on earth. These too will have conquered by keeping integrity in answer to Satan's vile accusations.—Romans 8:37-39; Revelation 12:10, 11.

Devastating the Harlot

15 God's people are not the only objects of the enmity of the ten horns. The angel now draws John's attention back to the harlot: *"And he says to me: 'The waters that you saw, where the harlot is sitting, mean peoples and crowds and nations and tongues. And the ten horns that you saw, and the wild beast, these will hate the harlot and will make her devastated and naked, and will eat up her fleshy parts and will completely burn her with fire.'"—Revelation 17:15, 16.*

16 Just as ancient Babylon relied on her

---

15. What does the angel say about the harlot and the attitude and action of the ten horns and the wild beast toward her?
16. Why will Babylon the Great not be able to rely on her waters for protective support when political governments turn against her?

17. (a) Why will the wealth of Babylon the Great not save her? (b) How will the end of Babylon the Great be far from dignified? (c) Besides the ten horns, or individual nations, what else joins in the rampage against Babylon the Great?

Albania, Russia

toward religion, especially that of Christendom.

¹⁸ Why would the nations treat their former paramour so outrageously? We have seen in recent history the *potential* for such a turning against Babylonish religion. Official government opposition has tremendously reduced the influence of religion in lands such as the Soviet Union and China. In Protestant sectors of Europe, widespread apathy and doubt have emptied the churches, so that religion is practically dead. The vast Catholic empire is torn by rebellion and disagreement, which the itinerant pope has been unable to calm. We should not, though, lose sight of the fact that this final, all-out attack on Babylon the Great comes as an expression of God's unalterable judgment on the great harlot.

Carrying Out God's Thought

¹⁹ How does Jehovah execute this judgment? This may be illustrated by Jehovah's action against his apostate people in ancient times, concerning whom he said: "In the prophets of Jerusalem I have seen horrible things, committing adultery and walking in falsehood; and they have strengthened the hands of evildoers in order that they should not return, each one from his own badness.

---

18. (a) What *potential* for the nations to turn against Babylonish religion has already been seen? (b) What will be the basic reason for the all-out attack on the great harlot?

19. (a) How can the execution of Jehovah's judgment against the great harlot be illustrated by his judgment on apostate Jerusalem in 607 B.C.E.? (b) What did the desolated, uninhabited condition of Jerusalem after 607 B.C.E. prefigure for our day?

To me all of them have become like Sodom, and the inhabitants of her like Gomorrah." . (Jeremiah 23:14) In 607 B.C.E., Jehovah used Nebuchadnezzar to 'strip off the garments, take away the beautiful articles, and leave naked and nude' that spiritually adulterous city. (Ezekiel 23:4, 26, 29) Jerusalem of that time was a pattern of Christendom today, and as John saw in earlier visions, Jehovah will administer to Christendom and the rest of false religion a similar punishment. The desolated, uninhabited condition of Jerusalem after 607 B.C.E. shows what religious Christendom will look like after being stripped of her wealth and shamefully exposed. And the rest of Babylon the Great will fare no better.

²⁰ Again Jehovah uses human rulers in executing judgment. *"For God put it into their hearts to carry out his thought, even to carry out their one thought by giving their kingdom to the wild beast, until the words of God will have been accomplished."* (*Revelation 17:17*) What is God's "thought"? To arrange for the executioners of Babylon the Great to band together, in order to destroy her completely. Of course, the rulers' motive in attacking her will be to carry out their own "one thought." They will feel that it is in their nationalistic interests to turn upon the great harlot. They may come to view the continued existence of organized religion within their boundaries as a threat to their sovereignty. But Jehovah

---

20. (a) How does John show that Jehovah once again will use human rulers in executing judgment? (b) What is God's "thought"? (c) In what way will the nations carry out their "one thought," but whose thought will really be carried out?

Christendom as the principal part of Babylon the Great will resemble ancient Jerusalem in utter ruin

will actually be maneuvering matters; they will carry out *his* thought by destroying his age-old, adulterous enemy at one stroke! —Compare Jeremiah 7:8-11, 34.

²¹ Yes, the nations will use the scarlet-colored wild beast, the United Nations, in destroying Babylon the Great. They do not act on their own initiative, for Jehovah puts it into their hearts "even to carry out their one thought by giving their kingdom to the wild beast." When the time comes, the nations will evidently see the need to strengthen the United Nations. They will give it teeth, as it were, lending it whatever authority and power they possess so that it can turn upon false religion and fight successfully against her "until the words of God will have been accomplished." Thus, the ancient harlot will come to her complete end. And good riddance to her!

---

21. Since the scarlet-colored wild beast will be used in destroying Babylon the Great, what will the nations evidently do with regard to the United Nations?

²² As if to emphasize the certainty of Jehovah's execution of judgment on the world empire of false religion, the angel concludes his testimony by saying: *"And the woman whom you saw means the great city that has a kingdom over the kings of the earth."* (*Revelation 17:18*) Like Babylon of Belshazzar's time, Babylon the Great has "been weighed in the balance and found wanting." (Daniel 5:27, *The New English Bible*) Her execution will be swift and final. And how do Jehovah's Witnesses respond to the unraveling of the mystery of the great harlot and of the scarlet-colored wild beast? They show zeal in proclaiming Jehovah's day of judgment, while answering "with graciousness" sincere searchers for truth. (Colossians 4:5, 6; Revelation 17:3, 7) As our next chapter will show, all who are desirous of surviving when the great harlot is executed must act, and act quickly!

---

22. (a) At Revelation 17:18, what is signified by the way the angel concludes his testimony? (b) How do Jehovah's Witnesses respond to the unraveling of the mystery?

Chapter 36

The Great City Devastated

START
6/15/92
To 2614 #12

SUDDEN, shocking, devastating—such will be the demise of Babylon the Great! It will be one of the most catastrophic events in all history, marking the start of the "great tribulation such as has not occurred since the world's beginning until now, no, nor will occur again."—Matthew 24:21.

² False religion has been around for a long time. It has existed without a break since the

days of bloodthirsty Nimrod, who opposed Jehovah and set men to building the Tower of Babel. When Jehovah confused the tongues of those rebels and scattered them over the earth, Babylon's false religion traveled with them. (Genesis 10:8-10; 11:4-9) Since then, political empires have risen and fallen, but Babylonish religion has endured. It has taken many shapes and forms, becoming a world empire of false religion, the prophesied Babylon the Great. Its most prominent part is Christendom, which grew

---

1. What will mark the start of the great tribulation?
2. Though political empires have risen and fallen, what kind of empire has endured?

Revelation 18:1–19:10

Subject: The fall and destruction of Babylon the Great; the marriage of the Lamb announced

Time of fulfillment: From 1919 until after the great tribulation

out of a fusion of early Babylonish teachings with apostate "Christian" doctrine. Because of the long, long history of Babylon the Great, many people find it hard to believe that it will ever be destroyed.

[3] It is therefore appropriate that Revelation should confirm the doom of false religion by giving us two detailed descriptions of her fall and subsequent events leading to her total desolation. We have already seen her as "the great harlot" that is finally devastated by her erstwhile lovers of the political realm. (Revelation 17:1, 15, 16) Now, in still another vision, we are to view her as a city, the religious antitype of ancient Babylon.

Babylon the Great Takes a Tumble

[4] John continues the account, telling us: *"After these things I saw another angel descending from heaven, with great authority; and the earth was lighted up from his glory. And he cried out with a strong voice, saying: 'She has fallen!*

3. How does Revelation confirm the doom of false religion?
4. (a) What vision does John next see? (b) How may we identify the angel, and why is it fitting for him to announce the fall of Babylon the Great?

As humans spread into all the earth, they took Babylonish religion with them

Babylon the Great has fallen.'" (*Revelation 18: 1, 2a*) It is the second time that John hears that angelic announcement. (See Revelation 14:8.) This time, however, its significance is emphasized by the magnificence of the heavenly angel, for his glory lights up the whole earth! Who can he be? Centuries earlier the prophet Ezekiel, reporting on a heavenly vision, stated that "the earth itself shone because of his [Jehovah's] glory." (Ezekiel 43:2) The only angel to shine with glory comparable to Jehovah's would be the Lord Jesus, who is "the reflection of [God's] glory and the exact representation of his very being." (Hebrews 1:3) In 1914 'the Son of man arrived in his glory,' and since that time Jesus, installed "on his glorious throne" in the heavens, has been exercising authority over the earth as Jehovah's associate King and Judge. It is fitting, then, that he should announce the fall of Babylon the Great.—Matthew 25:31, 32.

[5] Whom does this angel with great authority use in heralding such amazing news before mankind? Why, it is the very people that are released as a result of that fall, the remaining anointed ones on earth, the John class. From 1914 to 1918, these suffered

5. (a) Whom does the angel use in heralding the fall of Babylon the Great? (b) When judgment began on those professing to be "the house of God," how did Christendom fare?

greatly at the hands of Babylon the Great, but in 1918 the Lord Jehovah and his "messenger of the [Abrahamic] covenant," Jesus Christ, began judgment with "the house of God," those professing to be Christians. Thus apostate Christendom was brought to trial. (Malachi 3:1; 1 Peter 4:17) Her tremendous bloodguilt incurred during the first world war, her complicity in persecuting Jehovah's faithful witnesses, and her Babylonish creeds did not help her in the time of judgment; nor did any other part of Babylon the Great merit God's approval.—Compare Isaiah 13:1-9.

6 So by 1919 Babylon the Great had fallen, opening the way for God's people to be released and restored, in one day as it were, to their land of spiritual prosperity. (Isaiah 66:8) By that year, Jehovah God and Jesus Christ, the Greater Darius and the Greater Cyrus, had maneuvered matters so that false religion could no longer keep a hold on Jehovah's people. No more could it prevent them from serving Jehovah and making known to all who might hear that harlotlike Babylon the Great is doomed and the vindication of Jehovah's sovereignty is at hand!—Isaiah 45:1-4; Daniel 5:30, 31.

7 True, Babylon the Great was not destroyed in 1919—any more than the ancient city Babylon was destroyed in 539 B.C.E. when it fell to the armies of Cyrus the Persian. But from Jehovah's viewpoint, that organization had fallen. She was judicially condemned, awaiting execution; therefore, false religion could no longer hold Jehovah's people in captivity. (Compare Luke 9:59, 60.) These were released to serve as the Master's faithful and discreet slave in providing spiritual food at the proper time. They had re-

ceived a judgment of "Well done" and were commissioned to get busy again in Jehovah's work.—Matthew 24:45-47; 25:21, 23; Acts 1:8.

8 Millenniums ago Jehovah used other prophets to foretell this epoch-marking event. Isaiah spoke of a watchman who "proceeded to call out like a lion: 'Upon the watchtower, O Jehovah, I am standing constantly by day, and at my guardpost I am stationed all the nights.'" And what event does that watchman discern and proclaim with lionlike boldness? This: "She has fallen! Babylon has fallen, and all the graven images of her gods he [Jehovah] has broken to the earth!" (Isaiah 21:8, 9) This watchman well foreshadows the wide-awake John class today, as it uses the *Watchtower* magazine and other theocratic publications to sound abroad the news that Babylon has fallen.

Decline of Babylon the Great

9 Ancient Babylon's fall in 539 B.C.E. was the start of a long decline that ended in her desolation. Similarly, since the first world war, the influence of Babylonish religion has declined remarkably on a global scale. In Russia, the Bolshevik Revolution has continued to stifle the influence of the Russian Orthodox Church. In Japan, Shinto emperor worship was proscribed following the second world war. In China, the communist government controls all religious appointments and activity. In Protestant northern Europe, most people have become indifferent to religion. And the Roman Catholic Church has recently been weakened by schisms and internal dissent in its global domain.—Compare Mark 3:24-26.

10 All these trends are doubtless part of the 'drying up of the river Euphrates' in prepara-

---

6. Why can it be said that Babylon the Great had fallen by 1919?
7. (a) Though Babylon the Great was not destroyed in 1919, how did Jehovah view her? (b) When Babylon the Great fell in 1919, what resulted to Jehovah's people?

8. What event does the watchman of Isaiah 21:8, 9 proclaim, and who today is foreshadowed by that watchman?
9, 10. (a) The influence of Babylonish religion has suffered what decline since World War I? (b) How does the mighty angel describe the fallen condition of Babylon the Great?

REVELATION CLIMAX

tion for the coming militaristic attack on Babylon the Great. This 'drying up' is reflected, too, in the pope's announcement of October 1986 that the church must "again become mendicant"—because of huge deficits. (Revelation 16:12) Particularly since 1919 has Babylon the Great been exposed to public gaze as a spiritual wasteland, just as the mighty angel here announces: *"And she has become a dwelling place of demons and a lurking place of every unclean exhalation and a lurking place of every unclean and hated bird!"* (*Revelation 18: 2b*) Soon she will be literally such a wasteland, as desolate as Babylon's ruins in 20th-century Iraq.—See also Jeremiah 50:25-28.

[11] The word "demons" here is likely a reflection of the word "goat-shaped demons" (*se'i·rim'*) found in Isaiah's description of fallen Babylon: "And there the haunters of waterless regions will certainly lie down, and their houses must be filled with eagle owls. And there the ostriches must reside, and goat-shaped demons themselves will go skipping about there." (Isaiah 13:21) It may not refer to literal demons but rather to shaggy-haired, desert-dwelling animals whose appearance made onlookers think of demons. In the ruins of Babylon the Great, the figurative existence of such animals, along with stagnant, poisonous air ("unclean exhalation") and unclean birds, signifies her spiritually dead condition. She holds forth no life prospect whatever for mankind.—Compare Ephesians 2:1, 2.

[12] Her situation also matches Jeremiah's prophecy: "'There is a sword against the Chaldeans,' is the utterance of Jehovah, 'and against the inhabitants of Babylon and against her princes and against her wise ones. . . . There is a devastation upon her waters, and they must be dried up. For it is a

The John class, like a watchman, proclaims that Babylon has fallen

land of graven images, and because of their frightful visions they keep acting crazy. Therefore the haunters of waterless regions will dwell with the howling animals, and in her the ostriches must dwell; and she will nevermore be dwelt in, nor will she reside for generation after generation.'" Idolatry and chanting of repetitious prayers cannot save Babylon the Great from a retribution resembling God's overthrow of Sodom and Gomorrah.—Jeremiah 50:35-40.

Passion-Arousing Wine

[13] The mighty angel next calls attention to the broad extent of the harlotry of Babylon the Great, proclaiming: *"For because of the passion-arousing wine of her fornication* all the nations have fallen victim, and the kings of the earth committed fornication with her, and*

---

* *New World Translation Reference Bible,* footnote.

---

11. In what sense has Babylon the Great become "a dwelling place of demons" and 'a lurking place of unclean exhalations and of unclean birds'?
12. How does the situation of Babylon the Great match Jeremiah's prophecy in chapter 50?

13. (a) How does the mighty angel call attention to the broad extent of the harlotry of Babylon the Great? (b) What immorality that was rife in ancient Babylon is also found in Babylon the Great?

THE GREAT CITY DEVASTATED

the traveling merchants of the earth became rich due to the power of her shameless luxury." (*Revelation 18:3*) She has indoctrinated all nations of mankind in her unclean religious ways. In ancient Babylon, according to Greek historian Herodotus, each maiden was required to prostitute her virginity in temple worship. Revolting sexual corruption is portrayed to this day in the war-damaged Buddhist sculptures at Angkor Wat in Kampuchea and in the temples at Khajuraho, India, which show the Hindu god Vishnu surrounded by disgusting erotic scenes. In the United States, the disclosures of immorality that shook the world of TV evangelists in 1987, and again in 1988, as well as the revelation of the widespread practice of homosexuality by ministers of religion, illustrate that even Christendom tolerates shocking excesses of literal fornication. Yet, all the nations have fallen victim to an even more serious kind of fornication in this 20th century.

[14] We have already reviewed the illicit religio-political relationship that catapulted Hitler into power in Nazi Germany. Other nations also suffered because of religion's meddling in secular affairs. For example: In Fascist Italy, on February 11, 1929, the Lateran Treaty was signed by Mussolini and Cardinal Gasparri, making Vatican City a sovereign state. Pope Pius XI claimed that he had "given Italy back to God, and God back to Italy." Was that the truth? Consider what happened six years later. On October 3, 1935, Italy invaded Abyssinia, claiming that it was "a barbarous land which still practises slavery." Who, really, was being barbarous? Did the Catholic Church condemn Mussolini's barbarity? While the pope issued ambiguous statements, his bishops were quite vocal in blessing the armed forces of their Italian

"fatherland." In the book *The Vatican in the Age of the Dictators,* Anthony Rhodes reports:

[15] "In his Pastoral Letter of the 19th October [1935], the Bishop of Udine [Italy] wrote, 'It is neither timely nor fitting for us to pronounce on the rights and wrongs of the case. Our duty as Italians, and still more as Christians is to contribute to the success of our arms.' The Bishop of Padua wrote on the 21st October, 'In the difficult hours through which we are passing, we ask you to have faith in our statesmen and armed forces.' On the 24th October, the Bishop of Cremona consecrated a number of regimental flags and said: 'The blessing of God be upon these soldiers who, on African soil, will conquer new and fertile lands for the Italian genius, thereby bringing to them Roman and Christian culture. May Italy stand once again as the Christian mentor to the whole world.'"

[16] Abyssinia was raped, with the blessing of the Roman Catholic clergy. Could any of these claim, in any sense, that they were like the apostle Paul in being "clean from the blood of all men"?—Acts 20:26.

[17] Add to Germany, Italy, and Abyssinia another nation that has fallen victim to the fornication of Babylon the Great—Spain. The Civil War of 1936-39 in that land was sparked, in part, by the democratic government's taking steps to reduce the huge power of the Roman Catholic Church. As the war got under way, the Catholic Fascist leader of the revolutionary forces, Franco, described himself as "the Christian Generalissimo of the Holy Crusade," a title that he later dropped. Several hundred thousand Spaniards died in the fighting. Apart from this, according to a conservative estimate, Franco's Nationalists had murdered 40,000 Popular Front members, while the latter had murdered 8,000 clerics—monks, priests, nuns, and novices. Such is the horror and tragedy

---

14-16. (a) What spiritually illicit religio-political relationship developed in Fascist Italy? (b) When Italy invaded Abyssinia, what statements did bishops of the Roman Catholic Church make?

---

17. How did Spain suffer because its clergy failed to "beat their swords into plowshares"?

"The Kings . . . Committed Fornication With Her"

In the early 1800's European merchants were smuggling large quantities of opium into China. In March 1839 Chinese officials tried to stop the illegal trade by seizing 20,000 chests of the drug from British merchants. This led to tension between Britain and China. As relations between the two countries deteriorated, some Protestant missionaries urged Britain to go to war, with statements such as the following:

"How these difficulties do rejoice my heart because I think the English government may be enraged, and God, in His power may break down the barriers which prevent the gospel of Christ from entering China."—Henrietta Shuck, Southern Baptist missionary.

Finally, war broke out—the war that is today known as the Opium War. Missionaries wholeheartedly encouraged Britain with comments such as these:

"I am constrained to look back upon the present state of things not so much as an opium or an English affair, as the great design of Providence to make the wickedness of man subserve His purposes of mercy toward China in breaking through her wall of exclusion." —Peter Parker, Congregationalist missionary.

Another Congregationalist missionary, Samuel W. Williams, added: "The hand of God is apparent in all that has transpired in a remarkable manner, and we doubt not that He who said He came to bring a sword upon the earth has come here and that for the speedy destruction of His enemies and the establishment of His own kingdom. He will overturn and overturn until He has established the Prince of Peace."

Regarding the horrendous slaughter of Chinese nationals, missionary J. Lewis Shuck wrote: "I regard such scenes . . . as the direct instruments of the Lord in clearing away the rubbish which impedes the advancement of Divine Truth."

Congregationalist missionary Elijah C. Bridgman added: "God has often made use of the strong arm of civil power to prepare the way for His kingdom . . . The agency in these great moments is human; the directing power divine. The high governor of all the nations has employed England to chastize and humble China."—Quotations taken from "Ends and Means," 1974, an essay by Stuart Creighton Miller published in *The Missionary Enterprise in China and America* (a Harvard Study edited by John K. Fairbank).

of civil war, illustrating the wisdom of heeding Jesus' words: "Return your sword to its place, for all those who take the sword will perish by the sword." (Matthew 26:52) How disgusting that Christendom gets involved in such massive bloodshed! Her clergy have indeed failed utterly to "beat their swords into plowshares"!—Isaiah 2:4.

The Traveling Merchants

18 Who are "the traveling merchants of the earth"? No doubt we would today call them traders, commercial giants, wheeler-dealers of big business. This is not to say that it is wrong to engage in legitimate business. The Bible provides wise counsel for business people, warning against dishonesty, greed, and the like. (Proverbs 11:1; Zechariah 7:9, 10; James 5:1-5) The greater gain is "godly devotion along with self-sufficiency." (1 Timothy 6:6, 17-19) However, Satan's world does not follow righteous principles. Corruption abounds. It is to be found in religion, in politics—and in big business. From time to time the news media expose scandals, such as embezzlement by high government officials and illegal trafficking in arms.

19 International trading in arms is soaring beyond $1,000,000,000,000 each year, while hundreds of millions of humans are deprived of life's necessities. That is bad enough. But armaments appear to be a basic support of the world's economy. On April 11, 1987, an article in London's *Spectator* reported: "Counting only directly related industries, some 400,000 jobs are involved in the U.S. and 750,000 in Europe. But curiously enough, as the social and economic role of building weapons has grown, the actual question of whether the producers are well defended has slipped into the background." Huge profits are made as bombs and other

---

18. Who are "the traveling merchants of the earth"?
19. What fact about the world's economy helps explain why the merchants of the earth come up for unfavorable mention in Revelation?

weaponry are traded all over the earth, even to potential enemies. Some day those bombs may come back in a fiery holocaust to destroy those selling them. What a paradox! Add to this the graft that surrounds the arms industry. In the United States alone, according to the *Spectator,* "every year the Pentagon inexplicably loses $900-million worth of arms and equipment." It is no wonder that the merchants of the earth come up for unfavorable mention in Revelation!

[20] As foretold by the glorious angel, religion has been deeply involved in such corrupt business practices. For example, there is the Vatican's involvement in the collapse of Italy's Banco Ambrosiano in 1982. The case has dragged on through the 1980's, the unanswered question being: Where did the money go? In February 1987 Milan magistrates issued arrest warrants for three Vatican clerics, including an American archbishop, on charges that they were accessories to fraudulent bankruptcy, but the Vatican rejected an extradition request. In July 1987, amid an uproar of protest, the warrants were nullified by Italy's highest Court of Appeals on the basis of an old treaty between the Vatican and the Italian government.

[21] Did Jesus have a tie-in with questionable business practices of his day? No. He was not even a property owner, for he had "nowhere to lay down his head." A rich young ruler was advised by Jesus: "Sell all the things you have and distribute to poor people, and you will have treasure in the heavens; and come be my follower." That was fine admonition, for it could have resulted in his getting rid of all anxieties over business matters. (Luke 9:58; 18:22) In contrast, Babylonish religion often has unsavory links with big business. For example, in 1987 the *Albany Times Union* reported that the financial administrator of the Catholic archdiocese of Miami, Florida, U.S.A., admitted to the church's owning stocks in companies that make nuclear weapons, R-rated movies, and cigarettes.

"The Traveling Merchants . . . Became Rich"

"Between 1929 and the outbreak of World War II, [Bernadino] Nogara [the Vatican financial administrator] assigned Vatican capital and Vatican agents to work in diversified areas of Italy's economy —particularly in electric power, telephone communications, credit and banking, small railroads, and the production of agricultural implements, cement, and artificial textile fibers. Many of these ventures paid off.

"Nogara gobbled up a number of companies including La Società Italiana della Viscosa, La Supertessile, La Società Meridionale Industrie Tessili, and La Cisaraion. Fusing these into one company, which he named CISA-Viscosa and placed under the command of Baron Francesco Maria Oddasso, one of the most highly trusted Vatican laymen, Nogara then maneuvered the absorption of the new company by Italy's largest textile manufacturer, SNIA-Viscosa. Eventually the Vatican interest in SNIA-Viscosa grew larger and larger, and in time the Vatican took control—as witness the fact that Baron Oddasso subsequently became vice president.

"Thus did Nogara penetrate the textile industry. He penetrated other industries in other ways, for Nogara had many tricks up his sleeve. This selfless man . . . probably did more to infuse life into the Italian economy than did any other single businessman in Italy's history . . . Benito Mussolini had never quite been able to achieve the empire of which he dreamed, but he enabled the Vatican and Bernadino Nogara to create a dominion of another kind." —*The Vatican Empire,* by Nino Lo Bello, pages 71-3.

This is just one example of the close cooperation between the merchants of the earth and Babylon the Great. No wonder these merchants will mourn when their business partner is no more!

---

20. What example shows religion's involvement in corrupt business practices?
21. How do we know that Jesus had no tie-in with questionable business practices of his day, but what do we see today with Babylonish religion?

"Get Out of Her, My People"

22 John's next words point to a further fulfillment of the prophetic pattern: *"And I heard another voice out of heaven say: 'Get out of her, my people, if you do not want to share with her in her sins, and if you do not want to receive part of her plagues.'"* (*Revelation 18:4*) Prophecies of ancient Babylon's fall in the Hebrew Scriptures also include Jehovah's command to his people: "Take your flight out of the midst of Babylon." (Jeremiah 50:8, 13) Similarly, in view of the coming desolation of Babylon the Great, God's people are now urged to escape. In 537 B.C.E. the opportunity to escape from Babylon caused much rejoicing on the part of faithful Israelites. In the same way, the release of God's people from Babylonish captivity in 1919 led to rejoicing on their part. (Revelation 11:11, 12) And since that time millions of others have obeyed the order to flee.—Compare Matthew 24:15, 16.

23 Is it really so urgent to flee out of Babylon the Great, withdrawing from membership in the world's religions and making a complete separation? It is, for we need to take God's view of this age-old religious monstrosity, Babylon the Great. He did not mince words in calling her the great harlot. So now the voice out of heaven informs John further concerning this whore: *"For her sins have massed together clear up to heaven, and God has called her acts of injustice to mind. Render to her even as she herself rendered, and do to her twice as much, yes, twice the number of the things she did; in the cup in which she put a mixture put twice as much of the mixture for her. To the extent that she glorified herself and lived in shameless luxury, to that extent give her torment and mourning. For in her heart she keeps saying, 'I sit a queen, and I am no widow, and I shall never see mourning.' That is why in one day her plagues will come, death and* mourning and famine, and she will be completely burned with fire, because Jehovah God, who judged her, is strong."*—Revelation 18:5-8.

24 Strong words, those! So action is required. Jeremiah urged the Israelites in his day to act, saying: "Flee out of the midst of Babylon, . . . for it is the time of vengeance belonging to Jehovah. There is treatment that he is paying back to her. Get out of the midst of her, O my people, and provide each one his soul with escape from the burning anger of Jehovah." (Jeremiah 51:6, 45) In a similar way, the voice out of heaven warns God's people today to flee from Babylon the Great in order not to receive part of her plagues. Jehovah's plaguelike judgments on this world, including Babylon the Great, are now being proclaimed. (Revelation 8:1–9:21; 16:1-21) God's people need to separate themselves from false religion if they themselves do not want to suffer these plagues and ultimately die with her. Besides, remaining within that organization would make them share in her sins. They would be as guilty as she is of spiritual adultery and of shedding the blood "of all those who have been slaughtered on the earth."—Revelation 18:24; compare Ephesians 5:11; 1 Timothy 5:22.

25 How, though, do God's people get out of Babylon the Great? In the case of ancient Babylon, the Jews had to make the physical journey from the city of Babylon all the way back to the Promised Land. But more was involved than that. Isaiah prophetically told the Israelites: "Turn away, turn away, get out of there, touch nothing unclean; get out from the midst of her, keep yourselves clean, you who are carrying the utensils of Jehovah." (Isaiah 52:11) Yes, they had to abandon all unclean practices of Babylonish religion that might tarnish their worship of Jehovah.

---

22. (a) What does a voice out of heaven say? (b) What led to rejoicing on the part of God's people in 537 B.C.E. and in 1919 C.E.?
23. How does the voice out of heaven emphasize the urgency of fleeing out of Babylon the Great?

24. (a) God's people must flee out of Babylon the Great to avoid what? (b) Those who fail to flee out of Babylon the Great share with her in what sins?
25. In what ways did God's people get out of ancient Babylon?

26 The apostle Paul quoted Isaiah's words in his letter to the Corinthians, saying: "Do not become unevenly yoked with unbelievers. For what fellowship do righteousness and lawlessness have? Or what sharing does light have with darkness? . . . 'Therefore get out from among them, and separate yourselves,' says Jehovah, 'and quit touching the unclean thing.'" The Corinthian Christians did not have to leave Corinth in order to obey that command. They did, however, physically have to avoid the unclean temples of false religion, as well as spiritually separate themselves from the unclean acts of those idol worshipers. In 1919 God's people began to flee from Babylon the Great in this way, cleansing themselves of any residual unclean teachings and practices. Thus, they were able to serve him as his purified people.—2 Corinthians 6:14-17; 1 John 3:3.

27 Ancient Babylon's fall and eventual desolation was a punishment for her sins. "For clear to the heavens her judgment has reached." (Jeremiah 51:9) Similarly, the sins of Babylon the Great have "massed together clear up to heaven," so as to come to the attention of Jehovah himself. She is guilty of injustice, idolatry, immorality, oppression, robbery, and murder. Ancient Babylon's fall was, in part, vengeance for what she had done to Jehovah's temple and his true worshipers. (Jeremiah 50:8, 14; 51:11, 35, 36) The fall of Babylon the Great and her eventual destruction are likewise expressions of vengeance for what she has done to true worshipers over the centuries. Indeed, her final destruction is the beginning of "the day of vengeance on the part of our God."—Isaiah 34:8-10; 61:2; Jeremiah 50:28.

28 Under the Mosaic Law, if an Israelite stole from his fellow countrymen, he had to pay back at least double in compensation. (Exodus 22:1, 4, 7, 9) In the coming destruction of Babylon the Great, Jehovah will apply a comparable standard of justice. She is to receive twice as much as she gave out. There will be no mercy to temper this justice because Babylon the Great has shown no mercy to her victims. She fed parasitically on the peoples of the earth to keep herself in "shameless luxury." Now she will experience suffering and mourning. Ancient Babylon felt that she was in an absolutely secure position, boasting: "I shall not sit as a widow, and I shall not know the loss of children." (Isaiah 47:8, 9, 11) Babylon the Great also feels secure. But her destruction, decreed by Jehovah who "is strong," will happen quickly, as if "in one day"!

26. How did the Corinthian Christians obey the words, 'Get out from among them and quit touching the unclean thing'?
27. What parallels are there between the judgments on ancient Babylon and those on Babylon the Great?
28. What standard of justice does Jehovah apply to Babylon the Great, and why?

Ancient Babylon's ruins portend the coming ruination of Babylon the Great

Chapter 37

Mourning and Rejoicing at Babylon's End

BABYLON'S end is good news for Jehovah's people, but how do the nations view it? John tells us: *"And the kings of the earth who committed fornication with her and lived in shameless luxury will weep and beat themselves in grief over her, when they look at the smoke from the burning of her, while they stand at a distance because of their fear of her torment and say, 'Too bad, too bad, you great city, Babylon you strong city, because in one hour your judgment has arrived!'"—Revelation 18:9, 10.*

2 The nations' reaction may seem surprising in view of the fact that Babylon was destroyed by the symbolic ten horns of the scarlet-colored wild beast. (Revelation 17:16) But when Babylon is gone, "the kings of the earth" will evidently realize how useful she was to them in keeping the people pacified and in subjection. The clergy have declared wars to be sacred, acted as recruiting agents, and preached the youth into the battle lines. Religion has provided a screen of holiness behind which corrupt rulers have operated in oppressing the common people. (Compare Jeremiah 5:30, 31; Matthew 23:27, 28.) Notice, however, that these grief-stricken kings now stand at a distance from the doomed city. They do not get close enough to come to her

aid. They are sad to see her go but not sad enough to take risks in her behalf.

Merchants Weep and Mourn

3 The kings of the earth are not the only ones to regret the passing of Babylon the Great. *"Also, the traveling merchants of the earth are weeping and mourning over her, because there is no one to buy their full stock anymore, a full stock of gold and silver and precious stone and pearls and fine linen and purple and silk and scarlet; and everything in scented wood and every sort of ivory object and every sort of object out of most precious wood and of copper and of iron and of marble; also cinnamon and Indian spice and incense and perfumed oil and frankincense and wine and olive oil and fine flour and wheat and cattle and sheep, and horses and coaches and slaves and human souls. Yes, the fine fruit that your soul desired has departed from you [Babylon the Great], and all the dainty things and the gorgeous things have perished from you, and never again will people find them."—Revelation 18:11-14.*

4 Yes, Babylon the Great was a close friend and a good customer of wealthy merchants. For example, the monasteries, nunneries, and churches in Christendom have over the centuries acquired huge amounts of gold, silver, precious stones, valuable woods, and other forms of material wealth. Further, religion's blessing has been bestowed on the lavish

---

1. How will "the kings of the earth" react to the sudden destruction of Babylon the Great?
2. (a) Since the symbolic ten horns of the scarlet-colored wild beast destroy Babylon the Great, why do "the kings of the earth" grieve over her end? (b) Why do the grief-stricken kings stand at a distance from the doomed city?

---

3. Who else regret the passing of Babylon the Great, and what reasons for this does John give?
4. Why do "the traveling merchants" weep and mourn over the end of Babylon the Great?

"Too bad, too bad," say the rulers

"Too bad, too bad," say the merchants

buying sprees and drunken orgies that accompany the celebration of the Christ-dishonoring Christmas and other so-called holy days. Christendom's missionaries have penetrated distant lands, opening up new markets for "the traveling merchants" of this world. In 17th-century Japan, Catholicism, which had come with the traders, even became involved in feudal warfare. Reporting on a decisive battle under the walls of Osaka castle, *The Encyclopædia Britannica* states: "The Tokugawa troops found themselves fighting against a foe whose banners were emblazoned with the cross and with images of the Saviour and St James, the patron saint of Spain." The victorious faction persecuted and practically wiped out Catholicism in that land. The church's participation in worldly affairs today will likewise bring her no blessing.

⁵ The voice out of heaven says further: *"The traveling merchants of these things, who became rich from her, will stand at a distance because of their fear of her torment and will weep and mourn, saying, 'Too bad, too bad—the great city, clothed with fine linen and purple and scarlet, and richly adorned with gold ornament*

and precious stone and pearl, because in one hour such great riches have been devastated!'" (Revelation 18:15-17a) With the destruction of Babylon the Great, the "merchants" mourn at the loss of that commercial partner. Truly, it is "too bad, too bad" for them. Notice, though, that their reasons for mourning are entirely selfish and that they—like the kings—"stand at a distance." They do not get close enough to be of any help to Babylon the Great.

⁶ The account goes on: *"And every ship captain and every man that voyages anywhere, and sailors and all those who make a living by the sea, stood at a distance and cried out as they looked at the smoke from the burning of her and said, 'What city is like the great city?' And they threw dust upon their heads and cried out, weeping and mourning, and said, 'Too bad, too bad—the great city, in which all those having boats at sea became rich by reason of her costliness, because in one hour she has been devastated!'"* (Revelation 18:17b-19) Ancient Babylon was a commercial city and had a great fleet of ships. Similarly, Babylon the Great does much business by the "many waters" of her people. This provides employment for many of her religious subjects. What an economic blow the destruction of Babylon the Great will be for these! There will never be another source of livelihood like her.

Rejoicing Over Her Annihilation

⁷ When ancient Babylon was overthrown

---

5. (a) How does the voice out of heaven further describe the mourning of "the traveling merchants"? (b) Why do the merchants also "stand at a distance"?

6. How does the voice out of heaven describe the mourning of ship captains and sailors, and why do they weep?

7, 8. How does the voice out of heaven climax its message regarding Babylon the Great, and who will respond to those words?

by the Medes and the Persians, Jeremiah prophetically said: "And over Babylon the heavens and the earth and all that is in them will certainly cry out joyfully." (Jeremiah 51:48) When Babylon the Great is destroyed, the voice out of heaven climaxes its message, saying of Babylon the Great: *"Be glad over her, O heaven, also you holy ones and you apostles and you prophets, because God has judicially exacted punishment for you from her!"* (*Revelation 18:20*) Jehovah and the angels will be delighted to see the annihilation of God's ancient enemy, as will the apostles and early Christian prophets, who by now are resurrected and have taken their position in the 24-elders arrangement.—Compare Psalm 97:8-12.

8 Indeed, all the "holy ones"—whether resurrected to heaven or still surviving on earth—will cry out for joy, as will the associated great crowd of other sheep. In time, all the faithful men of old will be resurrected into the new system of things, and they too will join in the rejoicing. God's people have not tried to avenge themselves on their false religious persecutors. They have remembered Jehovah's words: "Vengeance is mine; I will repay, says Jehovah." (Romans 12:19; Deuteronomy 32:35, 41-43) Well, Jehovah has now repaid. All the blood spilled by Babylon the Great will have been avenged.

Hurling a Great Millstone

9 What John next sees confirms that Jehovah's judgment of Babylon the Great is final: *"And a strong angel lifted up a stone like a great millstone and hurled it into the sea, saying: 'Thus with a swift pitch will Babylon the great city be hurled down, and she will never be found again.'"* (*Revelation 18:21*) In Jeremiah's time, a similar act with powerful prophetic meaning was performed. Jeremiah was inspired to write in a book "all the calamity that would come upon Babylon." He gave the book to Seraiah and told him to travel to Babylon. There, following Jeremiah's instructions, Seraiah read a declaration against the city: "O Jehovah, you yourself have spoken against this place, in order to cut it off so that there may come to be in it no inhabitant, either man or even domestic animal, but that she may become mere desolate wastes to time indefinite." Seraiah then tied a stone to the book and threw it into the river Euphrates, saying: "This is how Babylon will sink down and never rise up because of the calamity that I am bringing in upon her."—Jeremiah 51:59-64.

10 The throwing of the book with the attached stone into the river was a guarantee that Babylon would plunge into oblivion, never to recover. The apostle John's seeing a strong angel perform a similar act is likewise a powerful guarantee that Jehovah's purpose toward Babylon the Great will be fulfilled. The completely ruined condition of ancient Babylon today testifies powerfully to what will befall false religion in the near future.

11 The strong angel now addresses Babylon the Great, saying: *"And the sound of singers who accompany themselves on the harp and of musicians and of flutists and of trumpeters will never be heard in you again, and no craftsman of any trade will ever be found in you again, and*

9, 10. (a) What does a strong angel now do and say? (b) What act similar to that performed by the strong angel of Revelation 18:21 took place in Jeremiah's time, and what did it guarantee? (c) What does the action taken by the strong angel seen by John guarantee?

11, 12. (a) How does the strong angel now address Babylon the Great? (b) How did Jeremiah prophesy concerning apostate Jerusalem, and what did it signify for our day?

no sound of a millstone will ever be heard in you again, and no light of a lamp will ever shine in you again, and no voice of a bridegroom and of a bride will ever be heard in you again; because your traveling merchants were the top-ranking men of the earth, for by your spiritistic practice all the nations were misled."—Revelation 18: 22, 23.

[12] In comparable terms, Jeremiah prophesied concerning apostate Jerusalem: "I will destroy out of them the sound of exultation and the sound of rejoicing, the voice of the bridegroom and the voice of the bride, the sound of the hand mill and the light of the lamp. And all this land must become a devastated place, an object of astonishment." (Jeremiah 25:10, 11) As the principal part of Babylon the Great, Christendom will become a lifeless ruin, as so vividly depicted by Jerusalem's desolate condition after 607 B.C.E. The

Christendom that once rejoiced lightheartedly and bustled with everyday noise will find herself conquered and abandoned.

[13] Indeed, as the angel here tells John, *all* of Babylon the Great will change from a powerful, international empire to an arid, desertlike wasteland. Her "traveling merchants," including top-ranking millionaires, have used her religion for personal advantage or as a cover-up, and the clergy have found it profitable to share the limelight with them. But those merchants will no longer have Babylon the Great as their accomplice. No more will she be hoodwinking the nations of earth with her mystic religious practices.

An Appalling Bloodguilt

[14] In conclusion, the strong angel tells why Jehovah judges Babylon the Great so severely. *"Yes,"* says the angel, *"in her was found the blood of prophets and of holy ones and of all those who have been slaughtered on the earth."* (*Revelation 18:24*) When on earth, Jesus told the religious leaders in Jerusalem that they were accountable for "all the righteous blood spilled on earth, from the blood of righteous Abel" onward. Accordingly, that crooked generation was destroyed in 70 C.E. (Matthew 23: 35-38) Today, another generation of religionists bears bloodguilt for its persecution of God's servants.

[15] In his book *The Catholic Church and Nazi Germany*, Guenter Lewy writes: "When Jehovah's Witnesses were suppressed in Bavaria on April 13 [1933] the Church even accepted the assignment given it by the Ministry of Education and Religion of reporting on any member of the sect still practicing the forbidden religion." The Catholic Church thus

---

The Price of Compromise

Guenter Lewy writes in his book *The Catholic Church and Nazi Germany:* "Had German Catholicism from the start adhered to a policy of resolute opposition to the Nazi regime, world history might well have taken a different course. Even if this struggle had ultimately failed to defeat Hitler and prevent all of his many crimes, it would in this view have raised the moral prestige of the Church immeasurably. The human cost of such resistance would undeniably have been great, but these sacrifices would have been made for the greatest of all causes. With the home front unreliable, Hitler might not have dared going to war and literally millions of lives would have been saved. . . . When thousands of German anti-Nazis were tortured to death in Hitler's concentration camps, when the Polish intelligentsia was slaughtered, when hundreds of thousands of Russians died as a result of being treated as Slavic *Untermenschen* [subhumans], and when 6,000,000 human beings were murdered for being 'non-Aryan,' Catholic Church officials in Germany bolstered the regime perpetrating these crimes. The Pope in Rome, the spiritual head and supreme moral teacher of the Roman Catholic Church, remained silent."—Pages 320, 341.

---

13. What sudden change overtakes Babylon the Great, and what is the effect on her "traveling merchants"?
14. What reason does the strong angel give for the severity of Jehovah's judgment, and what did Jesus similarly say when he was on the earth?
15. How was the Catholic Church in Nazi Germany bloodguilty on two counts?

REVELATION CLIMAX

shares responsibility for consigning thousands of Witnesses to concentration camps; its hands are stained by the lifeblood of hundreds of Witnesses who were executed. When young Witnesses, such as Wilhelm Kusserow, showed that they could die courageously by a firing squad, Hitler decided that the firing squad was too good for conscientious objectors; so Wilhelm's brother Wolfgang, at 20 years of age, died by the guillotine. At the same time, the Catholic Church was encouraging young German Catholics to die in the army of the fatherland. The bloodguilt of the church is plain to see!

16 However, the prophecy says that the blood of *"all* those who have been slaughtered on the earth" must be charged to Babylon the Great. That has certainly been true in modern times. For example, since Catholic intrigue helped to bring Hitler to power in Germany, the Vatican shares in a terrible bloodguilt with regard to the six million Jews that died in Nazi pogroms. Further, in this 20th century alone, well over a hundred million people have been killed in hundreds of wars. Is false religion to blame in this connection? Yes, in two ways.

17 One way is that many wars are related to religious differences. For example, the violence in India between Muslims and Hindus in 1946-48 was religiously motivated. Hundreds of thousands of lives were lost. The conflict between Iraq and Iran in the 1980's is related to sectarian differences, with hundreds of thousands being killed. Violence between Catholics and Protestants in Northern Ireland has taken thousands of lives. The continuing violence in Lebanon is religiously based. Surveying this field, columnist C. L. Sulzberger said in 1976: "It is a dismal

truth that probably half or more of the wars now being fought around the world are either openly religious conflicts or involved with religious disputes." Indeed, it has been so throughout the turbulent history of Babylon the Great.

18 What is the second way? From Jehovah's viewpoint, the world's religions are bloodguilty because they have not convincingly taught their followers the truth of Jehovah's requirements for his servants. They have not convincingly taught people that God's true worshipers must imitate Jesus Christ and show love toward others regardless of their national origin. (Micah 4:3, 5; John 13:34, 35; Acts 10:34, 35; 1 John 3:10-12) Because the religions making up Babylon the Great have not taught these things, their adherents have been drawn into the vortex of international warfare. How evident this was in the two world wars of the first half of this century, both of which started in Christendom and resulted in fellow religionists' slaughtering one another! If all who claimed to be Christians had adhered to Bible principles, those wars could never have taken place.

19 Jehovah lays the blame for all this bloodshed at the feet of Babylon the Great. Had the religious leaders, and particularly those in Christendom, taught their people Bible truth, such massive bloodshed would not have occurred. Truly, then, directly or indirectly, Babylon the Great—the great harlot and world empire of false religion—must answer to Jehovah not only for "the blood of prophets and of holy ones" whom she has persecuted and killed but for the blood "of *all* those who have been slaughtered on the earth." Babylon the Great does indeed carry an appalling bloodguilt. Good riddance when her final destruction takes place!

16, 17. (a) What bloodguilt must be charged to Babylon the Great, and how did the Vatican become bloodguilty regarding the Jews who died in Nazi pogroms? (b) What is one way in which false religion is to blame for the killing of millions of people in hundreds of wars in this century alone?

---

18. What is the second way in which the world's religions are bloodguilty?
19. What appalling bloodguilt does Babylon the Great carry?

7/13/92 Start
2272 70
2 different bread Crowd

Praise Jah for His Judgments!

BABYLON THE GREAT is no more! This is truly joyous news. No wonder John hears happy exclamations of praise in heaven! *"After these things I heard what was as a loud voice of a great crowd in heaven. They said: 'Hallelujah!'* The salvation and the glory and the power belong to our God, because his judgments are true and righteous. For he has executed judgment upon the great harlot who corrupted the earth with her fornication, and he has avenged the blood of his slaves at her hand.' And right away for the second time they said: 'Hallelujah!'* And the smoke from her goes on ascending forever and ever."—Revelation 19:1-3.*

² Hallelujah indeed! The word means "Praise Jah, you people," "Jah" being the shortened form of the divine name, Jehovah. We are here reminded of the exhortation of the psalmist: "Every breathing thing—let it praise Jah. Praise Jah, you people!" (Psalm 150:6) John's hearing the exultant heavenly chorus sing "Hallelujah!" twice at this point in Revelation demonstrates the continuity of the divine revelation of truth. The God of the Christian Greek Scriptures is the same as the God of the earlier Hebrew Scriptures, and Jehovah is his name. The God that caused the fall of ancient Babylon has now judged and destroyed Babylon the Great. Ascribe to him all glory for that feat! The power that

maneuvered her downfall belongs to him rather than to the nations that he used as instruments in desolating her. To Jehovah alone we must attribute salvation.—Isaiah 12:2; Revelation 4:11; 7:10, 12.

³ Why has the great harlot been so deserving of this judgment? According to the law that Jehovah gave to Noah—and through him to all mankind—the wanton shedding of blood calls for the death sentence. This was stated again in God's Law to Israel. (Genesis 9:6; Numbers 35:20, 21) Moreover, under that Mosaic Law both physical and spiritual adultery merited death. (Leviticus 20:10; Deuteronomy 13:1-5) For thousands of years, Babylon the Great has been bloodguilty, and she is a gross fornicatrix. For example, the policy of the Roman Catholic Church of forbidding her priests to marry has resulted in gross immorality on the part of many of them, not a few of these today contracting AIDS. (1 Corinthians 6:9, 10; 1 Timothy 4:1-3) But her major sins, 'massing together clear up to heaven,' are her shocking acts of spiritual fornication—this latter in teaching falsehoods and allying herself with corrupt politicians. (Revelation 18:5) Since her punishment has finally overtaken her, the heavenly multitude now echoes a second Hallelujah.

⁴ Babylon the Great has been set afire like a conquered city, and the smoke from her

---

* *New World Translation Reference Bible,* footnote.

1. What words does John hear "as a loud voice of a great crowd in heaven"?
2. (a) What does the word "Hallelujah" mean, and what does John's hearing it twice at this point demonstrate? (b) Who receives the glory for destroying Babylon the Great? Explain.

3. Why has the great harlot been so deserving of her judgment?
4. What is symbolized by the fact that the smoke from Babylon the Great "goes on ascending forever and ever"?

"goes on ascending forever and ever." When a literal city is burned by conquering armies, the smoke keeps ascending as long as the ashes are hot. Anyone who tries to rebuild it while it is still smoking will simply get burned by the smoldering ruins. Since the smoke from Babylon the Great will rise "forever and ever" in token of the finality of her judgment, no one will ever be able to restore that iniquitous city. False religion is gone forever. Hallelujah, indeed!—Compare Isaiah 34:5, 9, 10.

[5] In an earlier vision, John saw around the throne four living creatures, together with the 24 elders that picture the Kingdom heirs in their glorious heavenly position. (Revelation 4:8-11) Now he sees them again as they thunder forth a third Hallelujah over the destruction of Babylon the Great: *"And the twenty-four elders and the four living creatures*

---

5. (a) What do the 24 elders and the four living creatures do and say? (b) Why is the Hallelujah refrain far more melodious than Hallelujah choruses sung in Christendom's churches?

"Epistle to Sodom and Gomorrah"

Under this feature heading, London's *Daily Telegraph* of November 12, 1987, reported on a motion before the General Synod of the Church of England. This called for ousting homosexual "Christians" from the church. Columnist Godfrey Barker stated: "The Archbishop of Canterbury gloomily opined yesterday: 'If St Paul were to write an epistle to the Church of England, we might well ask what sort of letter it might be.'" Mr. Barker himself commented: "An epistle to Sodom and Gomorrah is the answer," and added: "Dr Runcie [the archbishop] fancied it would read like Romans, Ch 1."

The writer quoted Paul's words at Romans 1:26-32: "God gave them up in the lusts of their hearts to impurities. . . . Men committing shameless acts with men . . . though they know God's decree that those who do such things deserve to die, they not only do them but approve those who practise them." He concluded: "St Paul was merely worried about the chaps in the pews. Dr Runcie's problem is the chaps in the pulpits."

Why does the archbishop have such a problem? Large headlines in the London *Daily Mail* of October 22, 1987, had declared: "'One vicar in three gay' . . . Campaign to drive out homosexuals 'would shut Church of England.'" The reports quoted the "reverend" general secretary of the Lesbian and Gay Christian Movement as saying: "If this motion were accepted it would wreck the Church, and the Archbishop of Canterbury knows it. As a general figure, we believe between 30 and 40 per cent of Church of England clergymen are gay. And they are the most active people contributing to the ministry of the Church." The dwindling numbers of churchgoers is no doubt in part a reflection of disgust at that burgeoning homosexual ministry.

What did the church synod decide? An overwhelming majority of 388 members (95 percent of the clergy) voted in favor of a watered-down motion. Concerning this, *The Economist* of November 14, 1987, reported: "The Church of England is against homosexual practices, but not very much. The general synod, the Church's parliament, with homosexual clergy in mind, this week decided that homosexual acts, unlike fornication and adultery, are not a sin: they merely 'fall short of the ideal' that 'sexual intercourse is an act of total commitment which belongs properly within a permanent married relationship.'" Contrasting the stance of the Archbishop of Canterbury with the apostle Paul's forthright statement at Romans 1:26, 27, *The Economist* displayed a quotation of Paul's words above the caption "St Paul knew what he thought."

Jesus Christ also knew what he thought and stated it in explicit terms. He said that it would be "more endurable for the land of Sodom on Judgment Day" than for the religionists who spurned his message. (Matthew 11:23, 24) Jesus was here using hyperbole to show that those religious leaders who rejected the Son of God and his teaching were even more reprehensible than the Sodomites. Jude 7 states that those Sodomites underwent "the judicial punishment of everlasting fire," meaning eternal destruction. (Matthew 25:41, 46) How severe, then, will be the judgment of so-called Christian leaders who blindly lead their blinded flocks away from the high moral standards of God's Kingdom into the permissive, debauched ways of this world! (Matthew 15:14) Concerning false religion, Babylon the Great, the voice from heaven calls with urgency: "Get out of her, my people, if you do not want to share with her in her sins, and if you do not want to receive part of her plagues."—Revelation 18:2, 4.

fell down and worshiped God seated upon the throne, and said: 'Amen! Hallelujah!'"* (*Revelation 19:4*) This grand Hallelujah chorus is in addition, then, to the "new song" of praise to the Lamb. (Revelation 5:8, 9) They sing now the magnificent victory refrain, ascribing all glory to the Sovereign Lord Jehovah because of his decisive victory over the great harlot, Babylon the Great. These Hallelujahs peal forth far more melodiously than any Hallelujah choruses sung in Christendom's churches, where Jehovah, or Jah, has been dishonored and despised. Such hypocritical singing that reproaches Jehovah's name is now silenced forever!

⁶ It was in 1918 that Jehovah began rewarding 'those fearing his name, the small and the great'—the first of these being the anointed Christians who had died faithful, whom he resurrected and stationed in the heavenly ranks of the 24 elders. (Revelation 11:18) Others join with these in singing the Hallelujahs, for John reports: *"Also, a voice issued forth from the throne and said: 'Be praising our God, all you his slaves, who fear him, the small ones and the great.'"* (*Revelation 19:5*) This is the "voice" of Jehovah's Mouthpiece, his own Son, Jesus Christ, who stands "in the midst of the throne." (Revelation 5:6) Not only in heaven but also here on earth, "all you his slaves" share in the singing, with the anointed John class taking the lead on earth. How exultantly these share in obeying the command: "Be praising our God"!

⁷ Yes, those of the great crowd are also numbered among these slaves. Since 1935 these have been coming out of Babylon the Great and have experienced the fulfillment of God's promise: "He will bless those fearing Jehovah, the small ones as well as the great ones." (Psalm 115:13) When harlotlike Bab-

ylon is destroyed, millions of them will join in "praising our God"—along with the John class and all the heavenly host. Later, those resurrected on earth, whether previously prominent or not, will no doubt sing further Hallelujahs on learning that Babylon the Great is gone forever. (Revelation 20: 12, 15) All praise to Jehovah for his resounding victory over the age-old harlot!

⁸ What an incentive all of this gives us to share fully in God's work for today! May all of Jah's servants devote themselves heart and soul to declaring God's judgments, together with the grand Kingdom hope, *now,* before Babylon the Great is unseated and destroyed. —Isaiah 61:1-3; 1 Corinthians 15:58.

'Hallelujah—Jehovah Is King!'

⁹ There are further reasons for rejoicing, as John goes on to tell us: *"And I heard what was as a voice of a great crowd and as a sound of many waters and as a sound of heavy thunders. They said: 'Hallelujah,* because Jehovah our God, the Almighty, has begun to rule as king.'"* (*Revelation 19:6*) This last Hallelujah is the one that makes the proclamation foursquare, or symmetrical. It is a mighty celestial sound, more magnificent than any human choir, more majestic than any earthly waterfall, and more fear-inspiring than any terrestrial thunderstorm. The myriads of heavenly voices celebrate the fact that "Jehovah our God, the Almighty, has begun to rule as king."

¹⁰ How is it, though, that Jehovah *begins* to rule? Millenniums have passed since the psalmist declared: "God is my King from long ago." (Psalm 74:12) Jehovah's kingship was ancient even then, so how can the universal chorus sing that "Jehovah . . . has *begun* to

---

* *New World Translation Reference Bible,* footnote.

8. What incentive should the heavenly choruses of praise witnessed by John give us now, before Babylon the Great is destroyed?
9. Why is the last Hallelujah such a full, rich sound?
10. In what sense can it be said that Jehovah *begins* to rule as king after Babylon the Great's devastation?

---

* *New World Translation Reference Bible,* footnote.

6. Whose "voice" is heard, what does it urge, and who share in the response?
7. After Babylon the Great is destroyed, who will be praising Jehovah?

Heaven resounds with four Hallelujahs, praising Jah for his final victory over Babylon the Great

god remains to contest the sovereignty of the true God, Jehovah!

The Lamb's Marriage Is at Hand!

¹¹ "You woman enemy of mine"! That is how Jerusalem, the location of Jehovah's temple of worship, addressed idolatrous Babylon. (Micah 7:8) Likewise, "the holy city, New Jerusalem," made up of the bride of 144,000 members, has had every reason to address Babylon the Great as her enemy. (Revelation 21:2) But at last the great harlot

---

11, 12. (a) How did ancient Jerusalem address ancient Babylon, setting what pattern with regard to New Jerusalem and Babylon the Great? (b) With the victory over Babylon the Great, what do the heavenly throngs sing and announce?

rule as king"? In that when Babylon the Great is destroyed, Jehovah will no longer have that presumptuous rival to detract from obedience to him as the Universal Sovereign. No longer will false religion incite earth's rulers to oppose him. When ancient Babylon fell from world dominance, Zion heard the victorious proclamation: "Your God has become king!" (Isaiah 52:7) After the Kingdom's birth in 1914, the 24 elders proclaimed: "We thank you, Jehovah God . . . because you have taken your great power and begun ruling as king." (Revelation 11:17) Now, after the devastation of Babylon the Great, the cry is again uttered: "Jehovah . . . has begun to rule as king." No man-made

has suffered adversity, calamity, and ruin. Her spiritistic practices and astrologers have been unable to save her. (Compare Isaiah 47: 1, 11-13.) A major victory, indeed, for true worship!

¹² With the disgusting harlot, Babylon the Great, gone forever, attention can now be focused on the virgin-pure bride of the Lamb! Hence, the heavenly throngs sing exultantly in praise of Jehovah: *"Let us rejoice and be overjoyed, and let us give him the glory, because the marriage of the Lamb has arrived and his wife has prepared herself. Yes, it has been granted to her to be arrayed in bright, clean, fine linen, for the fine linen stands for the righteous acts of the holy ones."—Revelation 19:7, 8.*

¹³ Down through the centuries, Jesus has made loving preparation for this celestial marriage. (Matthew 28:20; 2 Corinthians 11:2) He has been cleansing the 144,000 of spiritual Israel so that "he might present the congregation to himself in its splendor, not having a spot or a wrinkle or any of such things, but that it should be holy and without blemish." (Ephesians 5:25-27) With a view to attaining to "the prize of the upward call of God," each anointed Christian has had to strip off the old personality with its practices, put on the new Christian personality, and perform righteous acts "whole-souled as to Jehovah."—Philippians 3:8, 13, 14; Colossians 3:9, 10, 23.

¹⁴ From Pentecost 33 C.E. on, Satan used Babylon the Great as his tool in trying to contaminate the prospective members of the Lamb's wife. By the end of the first century, he had sown seeds of Babylonish religion in the congregation. (1 Corinthians 15:12; 2 Timothy 2:18; Revelation 2:6, 14, 20) The apostle Paul describes those who were subverting the faith in these words: "For such

men are false apostles, deceitful workers, transforming themselves into apostles of Christ. And no wonder, for Satan himself keeps transforming himself into an angel of light." (2 Corinthians 11:13, 14) In succeeding centuries, apostate Christendom, like the rest of Babylon the Great, dressed herself in the clothing of wealth and privilege, "purple and scarlet, . . . gold and precious stone and pearls." (Revelation 17:4) Her clergy and popes consorted with bloodthirsty emperors, such as Constantine and Charlemagne. She was never arrayed in "the righteous acts of the holy ones." As a counterfeit bride, she was truly a masterpiece of satanic deception. At last, she is gone forever!

The Lamb's Wife Has Prepared Herself

¹⁵ So now, after almost 2,000 years, all 144,- 000 of the bride class have made themselves ready. But at what point of time may it be said that 'the Lamb's wife has prepared herself'? Progressively, from Pentecost 33 C.E on, believing anointed ones "were sealed with the promised holy spirit," this in view of a coming "day of releasing by ransom." As the apostle Paul expressed it, God "has also put his seal upon us and has given us the token of what is to come, that is, the spirit, in our hearts." (Ephesians 1:13; 4:30; 2 Corinthians 1:22) Each anointed Christian is "called and chosen," and he has proved himself "faithful."—Revelation 17:14.

¹⁶ After decades of testing, Paul himself could declare: "I have fought the fine fight, I have run the course to the finish, I have observed the faith. From this time on there is reserved for me the crown of righteousness, which the Lord, the righteous judge, will give me as a reward in that day, yet not

---

13. What preparation for the marriage of the Lamb has taken place down through the centuries?
14. How has Satan tried to contaminate the prospective members of the Lamb's wife?

15. How does the sealing take place, and what is required of an anointed Christian?
16. (a) When was the apostle Paul's sealing complete, and how do we know? (b) When will the Lamb's wife have "prepared herself" fully?

only to me, but also to all those who have loved his manifestation." (2 Timothy 4:7, 8) The apostle's sealing appears to have been complete, even though he was still in the flesh and would yet face martyrdom. Similarly, the time must come when all remaining ones on earth of the 144,000 will have been sealed individually as belonging to Jehovah. (2 Timothy 2:19) This will be when the Lamb's wife will have fully prepared herself —the great majority of the 144,000 having already received their heavenly reward and those still on earth having been finally approved and sealed as faithful ones.

17 At this point in Jehovah's timetable, when the sealing of the 144,000 has reached completion, the angels release the four winds of the great tribulation. (Revelation 7:1-3) First, judgment is executed on harlotlike Babylon the Great. The victorious Christ next moves on quickly to Armageddon to destroy the rest of Satan's organization on earth and, finally, to abyss Satan and his demons. (Revelation 19:11–20:3) No doubt, anointed ones who survive on earth will soon enter into their heavenly reward to join their fellow

members of the bride class. Then, amid a setting of universal peace, the marriage of the Lamb can take place!

18 The prophetic description of events in Psalm 45 confirms that order. First the enthroned King rides forth to the conquest of his enemies. (Verses 1-7) Then the marriage is performed, the heavenly bride being attended on earth by her virgin companions, the great crowd. (Verses 8-15) Next the marriage becomes fruitful, with resurrected mankind being raised to perfection under oversight of "princes in all the earth." (Verses 16, 17) What glorious blessings accompany the marriage of the Lamb!

Happy Are Those Invited

19 John now records the fourth of the seven happinesses in Revelation: **"And he** [the angel who has been revealing these things to John] **tells me: 'Write: Happy are those invited to the evening meal of the Lamb's marriage.' Also, he tells me: 'These are the true sayings of God.'"**

---

17. When can the marriage of the Lamb take place?

18. How does Psalm 45 confirm the sequence of events with regard to the marriage of the Lamb?
19. What is the fourth of the seven happinesses in Revelation, and who share in this particular happiness?

(*Revelation 19:9*)* The ones invited to "the evening meal of the Lamb's marriage" are the members of the bride class. (Compare Matthew 22:1-14.) All the anointed bridal company share the happiness of having received this invitation. Most of the invitees have already gone to heaven, the place of the marital evening meal. Those who are still on earth are happy, too, that they have the invitation. Their place at the marital evening meal is secure. (John 14:1-3; 1 Peter 1:3-9) When they are resurrected to heaven, then the entire, united bride will proceed to share with the Lamb in that supremely happy marriage.

20 The angel adds that "these are the true sayings of God." This word "true" translates the Greek *a·le·thi·nos′* and means "genuine" or "dependable." Since these sayings are really from Jehovah, they are faithful and reliable. (Compare 1 John 4:1-3; Revelation 21:5; 22:6.) As one invited to that marriage feast, John must have been filled with joy at hearing this and at contemplating the blessings ahead for the bride class. He was so deeply moved, in fact, that the angel had to give him counsel, as John relates: *"At that I fell down before his feet to worship him. But he tells me: 'Be careful! Do not do that! All I am is a fellow slave of you and of your brothers who have the work of witnessing to Jesus. Worship God.'"*—Revelation 19:10a.

21 Throughout Revelation a remarkable witness is given to the faithfulness and diligence of the angels. They are involved in the channel of revealed truth. (Revelation 1:1) They work along with humans in preaching

---

* See also Revelation 1:3; 14:13; 16:15.

---

20. (a) What is the import of the words: "These are the true sayings of God"? (b) How was John affected by the words of the angel, and what was the angel's response?
21. (a) What does Revelation disclose as to the angels? (b) What attitude should Christians have toward the angels?

the good news and pouring out the symbolic plagues. (Revelation 14:6, 7; 16:1) They fought alongside Jesus to cast Satan and his angels from heaven, and they will fight alongside him again at Armageddon. (Revelation 12:7; 19:11-14) Indeed, they have access to the very person of Jehovah. (Matthew 18:10; Revelation 15:6) Nevertheless, they are no more than humble slaves of God. There is no room in pure worship for worship of the angels or even for relative worship, directing worship to God via some "saint" or angel. (Colossians 2:18) Christians worship only Jehovah, making their petitions to him in Jesus' name.—John 14:12, 13.

Jesus' Role in Prophecy

22 The angel then says: *"For the bearing witness to Jesus is what inspires prophesying."* (*Revelation 19:10b*) How so? This means that all inspired prophecy is evoked because of Jesus and the role he plays in Jehovah's purposes. The first prophecy in the Bible promised the coming of a seed. (Genesis 3:15) Jesus became that Seed. Subsequent revelations built a huge edifice of prophetic truth on this basic promise. The apostle Peter told the believing Gentile Cornelius: "To him [Jesus] all the prophets bear witness." (Acts 10:43) Some 20 years later, the apostle Paul said: "No matter how many the promises of God are, they have become Yes by means of him [Jesus]." (2 Corinthians 1:20) After another 43 years, John himself reminds us: "The truth came to be through Jesus Christ."—John 1:17.

23 Does this detract in any way from the worship we give to Jehovah? No. Remember the angel's cautionary advice: "Worship God." Jesus never tries to rival Jehovah. (Philippians 2:6) True, all the angels are told to "do obeisance to [Jesus]," and all creation

---

22. What does the angel say to John, and what do the words mean?
23. Why does the high position and authority of Jesus not detract from the worship we give to Jehovah?

must recognize his high position so that "in the name of Jesus every knee should bend." But notice, this is "to the glory of God the Father" and by his order. (Hebrews 1:6; Philippians 2:9-11) Jehovah gave Jesus his high authority, and by acknowledging that authority, we give glory to God. If we refuse to submit to Jesus' rule, it is equivalent to rejecting Jehovah God himself.—Psalm 2:11, 12.

STOP

²⁴ So, then, let us unitedly voice the opening words of Psalms 146 to 150: "Praise Jah, you people!" May the Hallelujah chorus thunder forth in anticipation of Jehovah's triumph over the Babylonish world empire of false religion! And may joy abound as the marriage of the Lamb approaches!

24. What two astounding events do we contemplate, and what words should we therefore voice?

Chapter 39

The Warrior-King Triumphs at Armageddon

ARMAGEDDON—a fearsome word to many! But to lovers of righteousness, it betokens the long-awaited day when Jehovah will execute final judgment on the nations. It is not man's war but "the war of the great day of God the Almighty"—his day of vengeance against earth's rulers. (Revelation 16: 14, 16; Ezekiel 25:17) With the desolating of Babylon the Great, the great tribulation will already have started. Then, urged on by Satan, the scarlet-colored wild beast and its ten horns will concentrate their attack on Jehovah's people. The Devil, more wrathful than ever at God's womanlike organization, is determined to use his dupes in waging war to a finish with the remaining ones of her seed. (Revelation 12:17) This is Satan's last opportunity!

² The Devil's vicious assault is vividly described in Ezekiel chapter 38. There, the Devil-based Satan is called "Gog of the land of Magog." Jehovah puts figurative hooks in Gog's jaws, drawing him and his numerous military force to the attack. How does he do this? By causing Gog to see His witnesses as a defenseless people "gathered together out of the nations, one that is accumulating wealth and property, those who are dwelling in the center of the earth." These hold the center stage on earth as the one people to have refused to worship the wild beast and its image. Their spiritual strength and prosperity enrage Gog. So Gog and his numerous military force, including the wild beast out of the sea with its ten horns,

1. What is Armageddon, and what leads up to it?

2. Who is Gog of Magog, and how does Jehovah maneuver him to attack His own people?

Vision 13

Revelation 19:11–21

Subject: Jesus leads the armies of heaven to destroy Satan's system of things

Time of fulfillment: After the destruction of Babylon the Great

279

swarm in for the kill. Unlike Babylon the Great, however, God's clean people enjoy divine protection!—Ezekiel 38:1, 4, 11, 12, 15; Revelation 13:1.

3 How does Jehovah dispose of Gog and all his crowd? Listen! "'I will call forth against him throughout all my mountainous region a sword,' is the utterance of the Sovereign Lord Jehovah. 'Against his own brother the sword of each one will come to be.'" But neither nuclear nor conventional arms will avail in that strife, for Jehovah declares: "I will bring myself into judgment with him, with pestilence and with blood; and a flooding downpour and hailstones, fire and sulphur I shall rain down upon him and upon his bands and upon the many peoples that will be with him. And I shall certainly magnify myself and sanctify myself and make myself known before the eyes of many nations; and they will have to know that I am Jehovah."—Ezekiel 38:21-23; 39:11; compare Joshua 10:8-14; Judges 7:19-22; 2 Chronicles 20:15, 22-24; Job 38: 22, 23.

The One Called "Faithful and True"

4 Jehovah calls forth a sword. Who is it that wields this sword? Returning to Revelation, we find the answer in still another thrilling vision. Before John's eyes the heavens open to reveal something truly awe inspiring—Jesus Christ himself in battle array! John tells us: *"And I saw the heaven opened, and, look! a white horse. And the one seated upon it is called Faithful and True, and he judges and carries on war in righteousness. His eyes are a fiery flame, and upon his head are many diadems."—Revelation 19:11, 12a.*

5 As in the earlier vision of the four horse-

men, this "white horse" is a fitting symbol of righteous warfare. (Revelation 6:2) And who of God's sons could be more righteous than this mighty Warrior? Being "called Faithful and True," he must be "the faithful and true witness," Jesus Christ. (Revelation 3:14) He makes war in order to execute Jehovah's righteous judgments. Thus, he is acting in his capacity as Jehovah's appointed Judge, the "Mighty God." (Isaiah 9:6) His eyes are fear inspiring, like "a fiery flame," looking to the coming fiery destruction of his foes.

6 Diadems crown the head of this Warrior-King. The wild beast that John saw coming out of the sea had ten diadems, picturing its temporary rulership of the earthly scene. (Revelation 13:1) Jesus, though, has "many diadems." His glorious rulership is unmatched, since he is "King of those who rule as kings and Lord of those who rule as lords."—1 Timothy 6:15.

7 John's description continues: *"He has a name written that no one knows but he himself." (Revelation 19:12b)* The Bible already speaks of God's Son by names such as Jesus, Immanuel, and Michael. But this unstated "name" appears to stand for the position and privileges that Jesus enjoys during the Lord's day. (Compare Revelation 2:17.) Isaiah, describing Jesus since 1914, says: "His name will be called Wonderful Counselor, Mighty God, Eternal Father, Prince of Peace." (Isaiah 9:6) The apostle Paul associated Jesus' name with His very high privileges of service when he wrote: "God exalted [Jesus] to a superior position and kindly gave him the name that is above every other name, so that in the name of Jesus every knee should bend."—Philippians 2:9, 10.

8 Jesus' privileges are unique. Apart from Jehovah himself, only Jesus can comprehend what it means to hold such a high

---

3. How does Jehovah dispose of Gog's militarized forces?

4. How does John describe Jesus Christ in battle array?

5, 6. What is signified by (a) the "white horse"? (b) the name "Faithful and True"? (c) eyes like "a fiery flame"? (d) "many diadems"?

---

7. What is the written name that Jesus has?

8. Why is it that only Jesus can know the name written, and with whom does he share some of his lofty privileges?

position. (Compare Matthew 11:27.) Therefore, of all God's creatures, only Jesus can fully appreciate this name. Nevertheless, Jesus does include his bride in some of these privileges. So he makes this promise: "The one that conquers . . . I will write upon him . . . that new name of mine."—Revelation 3:12.

9 John adds: *"And he is arrayed with an outer garment sprinkled with blood, and the name he is called is The Word of God." (Revelation 19:13)* Whose "blood" is this? It could be Jesus' lifeblood, shed for the sake of mankind. (Revelation 1:5) But, in this context, it more likely refers to the blood of his enemies that is spilled when Jehovah's judgments are executed upon them. We are reminded of the earlier vision in which the vine of the earth is reaped and trodden in the great winepress of the anger of God until the blood reaches "as high up as the bridles of the horses"—signifying a great victory over God's enemies. (Revelation 14:18-20) Likewise, the blood sprinkled on Jesus' outer garment confirms that his victory is decisive and complete. (Compare Isaiah 63:1-6.) Now John again speaks of Jesus' being called by a name. This time it is a widely known name—"The Word of God"—identifying this Warrior-King as Jehovah's Chief Spokesman and Champion of truth.—John 1:1; Revelation 1:1.

Jesus' Fellow Warriors

10 Jesus is not alone in fighting this battle. John tells us: *"Also, the armies that were in heaven were following him on white horses, and they were clothed in white, clean, fine linen." (Revelation 19:14)* The fact that the

horses are "white" denotes righteous warfare. "Fine linen" is appropriate for the King's horsemen, and its glistening, clean whiteness indicates a pure, righteous standing before Jehovah. Who, then, make up these "armies"? Doubtless, they include the holy angels. It was early in the Lord's day that Michael and his angels hurled Satan and his demons out of heaven. (Revelation 12:7-9) Further, "all the angels" now attend upon Jesus as he sits on his glorious throne and proceeds to judge the nations and people of earth. (Matthew 25:31, 32) Surely, in the decisive war, when God's judgments are executed to a finality, Jesus will again be accompanied by his angels.

11 Others too will be involved. When sending his message to the congregation in Thyatira, Jesus promised: "To him that conquers and observes my deeds down to the end I will give authority over the nations, and he shall shepherd the people with an iron rod so that they will be broken to pieces like clay vessels, the same as I have received from my Father." (Revelation 2:26, 27) Without a doubt, when the time comes, those of Christ's brothers already in heaven will have a part in shepherding people and nations with that iron rod.

12 What, though, of God's servants here on earth? The John class will have no active part in the fighting at Armageddon; neither will its loyal companions, those peoples out of all nations who have been streaming to Jehovah's spiritual house of worship. These peaceable humans have already beaten swords into plowshares. (Isaiah 2:2-4) Yet, they are very much involved! As we have already noted, it is Jehovah's seemingly defenseless people that are viciously attacked by Gog and all his crowd. That is the signal for Jehovah's Warrior-King, supported by the armies in heaven, to start fighting a

---

9. What is indicated by (a) Jesus' being "arrayed with an outer garment sprinkled with blood"? (b) Jesus' being called "The Word of God"?
10, 11. (a) How does John show that Jesus is not alone in the battle? (b) What is denoted by the fact that the horses are white and that the horsemen are clothed in "white, clean, fine linen"? (c) Who make up the heavenly "armies"?

---

12. (a) Will God's servants on earth take part in the fighting at Armageddon? (b) How are Jehovah's people on earth involved in Armageddon?

war of extermination against those nations. (Ezekiel 39:6, 7, 11; compare Daniel 11:44–12:1.) As spectators, God's people on earth will be most interested. Armageddon will mean their salvation, and they will live for eternity as having been eyewitnesses of Jehovah's great war of vindication.

STOP

13 Does this mean that Jehovah's Witnesses are against all government? Far from it! They obey the apostle Paul's counsel: "Let every soul be in subjection to the superior authorities." They realize that as long as the present system lasts, those "superior authorities" exist by God's permission for maintaining a measure of order in human society. Thus, Jehovah's Witnesses pay their taxes, obey the laws, respect traffic ordinances, comply with registrations, and so forth. (Romans 13:1, 6, 7) Further, they follow Bible principles in being truthful and honest; showing love of neighbor; building a strong, moral family unit; and training their children to be exemplary citizens. In this way they pay back not only "Caesar's things to Caesar, but God's things to God." (Luke 20:25; 1 Peter 2:13-17) Since God's Word shows that the governmental powers of this world are temporary, Jehovah's Witnesses prepare now for the fuller life, the real life, soon to be enjoyed under Christ's Kingdom rule. (1 Timothy 6:17-19) Though they will have no part in overturning the powers of this world, the Witnesses experience reverential awe at what God's inspired Word, the Holy Bible, says regarding the judgment Jehovah is about to execute at Armageddon. —Isaiah 26:20, 21; Hebrews 12:28, 29.

To the Final Battle!

START
Aug
1992
14

14 By what authority does Jesus complete his conquest? John informs us: *"And out of his mouth there protrudes a sharp long sword,*

that he may strike the nations with it, and he will shepherd them with a rod of iron." (Revelation 19:15a) That "sharp long sword" represents Jesus' God-given authority to issue orders for the execution of all who refuse to support God's Kingdom. (Revelation 1:16; 2:16) This vivid symbolism parallels Isaiah's words: "He [Jehovah] proceeded to make my mouth like a sharp sword. In the shadow of his hand he has hidden me. And he gradually made me a polished arrow." (Isaiah 49:2) Here Isaiah foreshadowed Jesus, who proclaims God's judgments and executes them, as with an unerring arrow.

15 At this point in time, Jesus will already have acted in fulfillment of Paul's words: "Then, indeed, the lawless one will be revealed, whom the Lord Jesus will do away with by the spirit of his mouth and bring to nothing by the manifestation of his presence." Yes, Jesus' presence (Greek, *pa·rou·si′a*) has been demonstrated from 1914 onward by the exposing and judging of the man of lawlessness, the clergy of Christendom. That presence will be strikingly manifested when the ten horns of the scarlet-colored wild beast execute that judgment and ravage Christendom, along with the rest of Babylon the Great. (2 Thessalonians 2:1-3, 8) That will be the start of the great tribulation! After that, Jesus turns his attention to what remains of Satan's organization, in line with the prophecy: "He must strike the earth with the rod of his mouth; and with the spirit of his lips he will put the wicked one to death."—Isaiah 11:4.

16 The Warrior-King, as Jehovah's appointee, will make a distinction between those who will survive and those who will die. Jehovah, speaking prophetically to this Son of God, says: "You will break them [earth's

---

13. How do we know that Jehovah's Witnesses are not against all government?
14. What is symbolized by the "sharp long sword" protruding from Jesus' mouth?

15. At this point in time, who will already have been exposed and judged so as to mark the start of what?
16. How do the Psalms and Jeremiah describe the role of Jehovah's appointed Warrior-King?

REVELATION CLIMAX

rulers] with an iron scepter, as though a potter's vessel you will dash them to pieces." And Jeremiah addresses such corrupt governmental leaders and their lackeys, saying: "Howl, you shepherds, and cry out! And wallow about, you majestic ones of the flock, because your days for slaughtering and for your scatterings have been fulfilled, and you must fall like a desirable vessel!" However desirable those rulers may have appeared to a wicked world, one blow from the King's iron scepter will shatter them, as if smashing an attractive vessel. It will be just as David prophesied concerning the Lord Jesus: "The rod of your strength Jehovah will send out of Zion, saying: 'Go subduing in the midst of your enemies.' Jehovah himself at your right hand will certainly break kings to pieces on the day of his anger. He will execute judgment among the nations; he will cause a fullness of dead bodies."—Psalm 2:9, 12; 83:17, 18; 110:1, 2, 5, 6; Jeremiah 25:34.

[17] This mighty Warrior-King appears again in the next scene of the vision: *"He treads too the winepress of the anger of the wrath of God the Almighty." (Revelation 19:15b)* In a previous vision, John had already seen the treading of the "winepress of the anger of God." (Revelation 14:18-20) Isaiah also describes an executional winepress, and other prophets tell how calamitous the day of God's anger will be for all the nations.—Isaiah 24:1-6; 63:1-4; Jeremiah 25:30-33; Daniel 2:44; Zephaniah 3:8; Zechariah 14:3, 12, 13; Revelation 6:15-17.

[18] The prophet Joel associates a winepress with Jehovah's coming to "judge all the nations round about." And it is Jehovah who issues the command, no doubt to His

17. (a) How does John describe the executional action of the Warrior-King? (b) Relate some prophecies that show how calamitous the day of God's anger will be for the nations.
18. What does the prophet Joel disclose as to Jehovah's judging of all the nations?

¹⁹ That will be a day of doom, indeed, for disobedient nations and humans but a day of relief for all who have made Jehovah and his Warrior-King their refuge! (2 Thessalonians 1:6-9) The judgment that started with the house of God in 1918 will have run through to its climax, answering the question at 1 Peter 4:17: "What will the end be of those who are not obedient to the good news of God?" The glorious Victor will have trodden the winepress to a finish, demonstrating that he is the exalted One of whom John says: *"And upon his outer garment, even upon his thigh, he has a name written, King of kings and Lord of lords." (Revelation 19:16)* He has proved to be far, far mightier than any earthly ruler, any human king or lord. His dignity and splendor are transcendent. He has ridden "in the cause of truth and humility and righteousness" and has triumphed for all time! (Psalm 45:4) Upon his blood-sprinkled garments is written the name bestowed on him by the Sovereign Lord Jehovah, whose Vindicator he is!

The Great Evening Meal of God

²⁰ In Ezekiel's vision, after the destruction of Gog's crowd, the birds and the wild animals are invited to a feast! They rid the landscape of carcasses by eating the dead bodies of Jehovah's enemies. (Ezekiel 39:11, 17-20) John's next words bring that earlier prophecy vividly to mind: *"I saw also an angel standing in the sun, and he cried out with a loud voice and said to all the birds that fly in midheaven: 'Come here, be gathered together to the great evening meal of God, that you may eat the fleshy parts of kings and the fleshy parts of military commanders and the fleshy parts of strong men and the fleshy parts of horses and*

associate Judge, Jesus, and his heavenly armies: "Thrust in a sickle, for harvest has grown ripe. Come, descend, for the winepress has become full. The press vats actually overflow; for their badness has become abundant. Crowds, crowds are in the low plain of the decision, for the day of Jehovah is near in the low plain of the decision. Sun and moon themselves will certainly become dark, and the very stars will actually withdraw their brightness. And out of Zion Jehovah himself will roar, and out of Jerusalem he will give forth his voice. And heaven and earth certainly will rock; but Jehovah will be a refuge for his people, and a fortress for the sons of Israel. And you people will have to know that I am Jehovah your God."—Joel 3: 12-17.

---

19. (a) How will the question asked at 1 Peter 4:17 be answered? (b) What name is written on Jesus' outer garment, and why will it prove to be appropriate?

20. How does John describe "the great evening meal of God," bringing to mind what earlier, but similar, prophecy?

of those seated upon them, and the fleshy parts of all, of freemen as well as of slaves and of small ones and great.'"—Revelation 19:17, 18.

21 The angel is "standing in the sun," a commanding position for attracting the attention of the birds. He invites them to be ready to gorge themselves on the flesh of those about to be slain by the Warrior-King and his heavenly armies. The fact that the dead are to be left on the surface of the ground indicates that they will die in public shame. Like Jezebel of old, they will not have an honorable burial. (2 Kings 9:36, 37) The list of those whose corpses would be left lying there shows the range of the destruction: kings, military commanders, strong men, freemen, and slaves. No exceptions. Every last trace of the rebellious world in opposition to Jehovah will be eliminated. After this, there will no more be a restless sea of confused humans. (Revelation 21:1) This is "the great evening meal of God," since it is Jehovah who invites the birds to share therein.

22 John summarizes the course of the final war: *"And I saw the wild beast and the kings of the earth and their armies gathered together*

to wage the war with the one seated on the horse and with his army. And the wild beast was caught, and along with it the false prophet that performed in front of it the signs with which he misled those who received the mark of the wild beast and those who render worship to its image. While still alive, they both were hurled into the fiery lake that burns with sulphur. But the rest were killed off with the long sword of the one seated on the horse, which sword proceeded out of his mouth. And all the birds were filled from the fleshy parts of them."—Revelation 19:19-21.

23 After the pouring out of the sixth bowl of Jehovah's wrath, John reported that "the kings of the earth and of the whole world" were gathered by demonic propaganda to "the battle of that great day of God Almighty." This is fought at Armageddon—not a literal location, but the global situation that calls for the execution of Jehovah's judgment. (Revelation 16:12, 14, 16, *King James Version*) Now John sees the battle lines. There, ranged against God, are all "the kings of the earth and their armies." They have stubbornly refused to submit themselves to Jehovah's King. He gave them fair warning in the inspired message: "Kiss the son, that [Jehovah] may not become incensed and you may not perish from the way." Not

---

21. What is indicated by (a) the angel's "standing in the sun"? (b) the fact that the dead are left lying on the surface of the ground? (c) the list of those whose corpses would be left lying on the ground? (d) the expression "the great evening meal of God"?
22. How does John summarize the course of the final war?

---

23. (a) In what sense is "the battle of that great day of God Almighty" fought at "Armageddon"? (b) What warning have "the kings of the earth" failed to heed, and with what consequence?

having submitted to Christ's rule, they must die.—Psalm 2:12.

24 The seven-headed, ten-horned wild beast out of the sea, representing Satan's political organization, is tumbled into oblivion, and along with it goes the false prophet, the seventh world power. (Revelation 13:1, 11-13; 16:13) While still "alive" or still functioning in their united opposition to God's people on earth, they are cast into "the lake of fire." Is this a literal lake of fire? No, not any more than the wild beast and the false prophet are literal animals. Rather, it is a symbol of complete, final destruction, a place of no return. Here is where, later, death and Hades, as well as the Devil himself, will be hurled. (Revelation 20:10, 14) It is certainly not an inferno of eternal torture for the wicked, since the very idea of such a place is detestable to Jehovah.—Jeremiah 19:5; 32:35; 1 John 4:8, 16.

25 All others who were not directly part of government but who were nevertheless an irreformable part of this corrupt world of mankind are likewise "killed off with the long sword of the one seated on the horse." Jesus will pronounce them deserving of death. Since in their case the lake of fire is not mentioned, are we to expect that they will have a resurrection? Nowhere are we told that those executed by Jehovah's Judge at that time are to be resurrected. As Jesus himself stated, all those who are not "sheep" go off "into the everlasting fire prepared for the Devil and his angels," that is, "into everlasting cutting-off." (Matthew 25:33, 41, 46) This climaxes "the day of judgment and of destruction of the ungodly men."—2 Peter 3:7; Nahum 1:2, 7-9; Malachi 4:1.

26 In this way, all of Satan's earthly organization comes to an end. The "former heaven" of political rulership has passed away. The "earth," the seemingly permanent system that Satan has built up over the centuries, is now utterly destroyed. The "sea," the mass of wicked humanity opposed to Jehovah, is no more. (Revelation 21:1; 2 Peter 3:10) What, though, does Jehovah have in store for Satan himself? John goes on to tell us.

---

24. (a) What judgment is executed on the wild beast and the false prophet, and in what sense are they "still alive"? (b) Why must "the lake of fire" be figurative?
25. (a) Who are those "killed off with the long sword of the one seated on the horse"? (b) Are we to expect that any of those "killed off" will have a resurrection?

---

26. State in brief the outcome of Armageddon.

Crushing the Serpent's Head

DO YOU recall the first Bible prophecy? It was uttered by Jehovah God when he said to the serpent: "I shall put enmity between you and the woman and between your seed and

---

1. How has the fulfillment of the first Bible prophecy proceeded?

her seed. He will bruise you in the head and you will bruise him in the heel." (Genesis 3:15) Now the fulfillment of that prophecy comes to its climax! We have traced the history of Satan's warring against Jehovah's heavenly womanlike organization. (Revelation 12:1, 9) The Serpent's earthly seed, with its religion, politics, and big business, has heaped cruel persecution on the woman's seed, Jesus Christ and his 144,000 anointed followers, here on earth. (John 8:37, 44; Galatians 3:16, 29) Satan inflicted an agonizing death on Jesus. But this proved to be like a heel wound, for God resurrected his faithful Son on the third day.—Acts 10:38-40.

² What about the Serpent and his seed? About 56 C.E. the apostle Paul wrote a long letter to the Christians in Rome. In concluding it, he encouraged them by saying: "For his part, the God who gives peace will crush Satan under your feet shortly." (Romans 16: 20) This is more than a superficial bruising. Satan is to be crushed! Paul here used a Greek word, *syn·tri'bo,* that means to bruise into a jellylike state, to trample down, to destroy utterly by crushing. As for the human seed of the Serpent, this is due for a real plaguing in the Lord's day, climaxing at the great tribulation in the complete crushing of Babylon the Great and the political systems of the world, together with their financial and military henchmen. (Revelation, chapters 18 and 19) Thus Jehovah brings to a climax the enmity between the two seeds. The Seed of God's woman triumphs over the earthly seed of the Serpent, and that seed is no more!

---

2. How is the Serpent bruised, and what happens to the Serpent's earthly seed?

Vision _____ 14

Revelation 20:1-10

Subject: The abyssing of Satan, the Millennial Reign, mankind's final test, and Satan's destruction

Time of fulfillment: From the end of the great tribulation to the destruction of Satan

---

Satan Abyssed

³ What, then, is in store for Satan himself and his demons? John tells us: *"And I saw an angel coming down out of heaven with the key of the abyss and a great chain in his hand. And he seized the dragon, the original serpent, who is the Devil and Satan, and bound him for a thousand years. And he hurled him into the abyss and shut it and sealed it over him, that he might not mislead the nations anymore until the thousand years were ended. After these things he must be let loose for a little while."*—Revelation 20:1-3.

⁴ Who is this angel? He must have tremendous power to be able to dispose of Jehovah's archenemy. He has "the key of the abyss and a great chain." Does this not remind us of an earlier vision? Why, yes, the king over the locusts is called "the angel of the abyss"! (Revelation 9:11) So here we again observe Jehovah's Chief Vindicator, the glorified Jesus Christ, in action. This archangel that cast Satan out of heaven, that judged Babylon the Great, and that disposed of "the kings of the earth and their armies" at Armageddon would surely not step aside to let a lesser angel deliver the masterstroke in abyssing Satan! —Revelation 12:7-9; 18:1, 2; 19:11-21.

⁵ When the great fiery-colored dragon was hurled down from heaven, he was spoken of as "the original serpent, the one called Devil and Satan, who is misleading the entire inhabited earth." (Revelation 12:3, 9) Now, at the point of being seized and abyssed, he is described again in full as "the dragon, the original serpent, who is the Devil and Satan." This infamous devourer, deceiver, slanderer, and opposer is chained and hurled "into the abyss," which is closed and sealed off tightly, "that he might not mislead the nations

---

3. What does John tell us is going to happen to Satan?
4. Who is the angel with the key of the abyss, and how do we know?
5. How does the angel of the abyss deal with Satan the Devil, and why?

anymore." This abyssing of Satan is for a thousand years, during which time his influence on mankind will be no more than that of a prisoner in a deep dungeon. The angel of the abyss removes Satan completely from any contact with the Kingdom of righteousness. What a relief for mankind!

6 What happens to the demons? They too have been "reserved for judgment." (2 Peter 2:4) Satan is called "Beelzebub the ruler of the demons." (Luke 11:15, 18; Matthew 10:25) In view of their longtime collaboration with Satan, should not the same judgment be meted out to them? The abyss has long been an object of fear to those demons; on one occasion when Jesus confronted them, they "kept entreating him not to order them to go away into the abyss." (Luke 8:31) But when Satan is abyssed, his angels will surely be hurled into the abyss with him. (Compare Isaiah 24: 21, 22.) After the abyssing of Satan and his demons, the Thousand Year Reign of Jesus Christ can begin.

7 Will Satan and his demons be active while in the abyss? Well, remember the scarlet-colored, seven-headed wild beast that "was, but is not, and yet is about to ascend out of the abyss." (Revelation 17:8) While in the

abyss, it "was not." It was nonfunctioning, immobilized, to all intents and purposes dead. Likewise, speaking of Jesus, the apostle Paul said: "'Who will descend into the abyss?' that is, to bring Christ up from the dead." (Romans 10:7) While in that abyss, Jesus was dead.* It is reasonable to conclude, then, that Satan and his demons will be in a state of deathlike inactivity for the thousand years of their abyssing. What good tidings for lovers of righteousness!

Judges for a Thousand Years

8 After the thousand years, Satan is released from the abyss for a short while. Why? Before giving the answer, John brings our attention back to the beginning of that time period. We read: ***"And I saw thrones, and there were those who sat down on them, and power of judging was given them."*** (*Revelation 20:4a*) Who are these ones sitting on thrones and ruling in the heavens with the glorified Jesus?

9 They are "the holy ones" that Daniel described as ruling in the Kingdom with the One "like a son of man." (Daniel 7:13, 14, 18) They are the same as the 24 elders who sit on heavenly thrones in the very presence of Jehovah. (Revelation 4:4) They include the 12 apostles, to whom Jesus gave the promise: "In the re-creation, when the Son of man sits down upon his glorious throne, you who have followed me will also yourselves sit

---

* Other scriptures say that Jesus was in Hades while he was dead. (Acts 2:31) We should not conclude, however, that Hades and the abyss are always the same. While the wild beast and Satan go into the abyss, only humans are said to go to Hades, where they are asleep in death until their resurrection.—Job 14:13; Revelation 20:13.

8, 9. What does John now tell us about those sitting on thrones, and who are such ones?

---

6. (a) What evidence is there that the demons also go into the abyss? (b) What can now begin, and why?

7. (a) In what state will Satan and his demons be while in the abyss, and how do we know? (b) Are Hades and the abyss the same? (See footnote.)

upon twelve thrones, judging the twelve tribes of Israel." (Matthew 19:28) They also include Paul, as well as the Corinthian Christians who remained faithful. (1 Corinthians 4:8; 6:2, 3) They would include, too, members of the congregation of Laodicea who conquered.—Revelation 3:21.

10 Thrones—144,000 of them—are prepared for these anointed conquerors who are "bought from among mankind as firstfruits to God and to the Lamb." (Revelation 14:1, 4) *"Yes,"* continues John, *"I saw the souls of those executed with the ax for the witness they bore to Jesus and for speaking about God, and those who had worshiped neither the wild beast nor its image and who had not received the mark upon their forehead and upon their hand."* (*Revelation 20:4b*) Among those kings, then, are the anointed Christian martyrs who earlier, at the opening of the fifth seal, asked Jehovah how much longer he would wait to avenge their blood. At that time they were given a white robe and told to wait a little longer. But now they have been avenged through the devastating of Babylon the Great, the destruction of the nations by the King of kings and Lord of lords, and the abyssing of Satan.—Revelation 6:9-11; 17:16; 19:15, 16.

11 Were all these 144,000 royal judges physically "executed with the ax"? Likely, relatively few of them were in a literal sense. This expression, though, doubtless is intended to embrace all those anointed Christians who endure martyrdom in one way or another.* (Matthew 10:22, 28) Certainly, Satan would like to have executed *all* of them with the ax,

but, in fact, not all of Jesus' anointed brothers die as martyrs. Many of them die of disease or old age. Such ones, however, also belong to the group that John now sees. The death of all of them is, in a sense, sacrificial. (Romans 6:3-5) Additionally, none of them were part of the world. Hence, all of them have been hated by the world and, in effect, become dead in its eyes. (John 15:19; 1 Corinthians 4:13) None of them worshiped the wild beast or its image, and when they died, none of them carried the mark of the beast. All of them died as conquerors.—1 John 5:4; Revelation 2:7; 3:12; 12:11.

12 Now these conquerors live again! John reports: *"And they came to life and ruled as kings with the Christ for a thousand years."* (*Revelation 20:4c*) Does this mean that these judges are not resurrected until after the destruction of the nations and the abyssing of Satan and his demons? No. Most of them are already very much alive, since they rode with Jesus against the nations at Armageddon. (Revelation 2:26, 27; 19:14) Indeed, Paul indicated that their resurrection commences soon after the beginning of Jesus' presence in 1914 and that some are resurrected before others. (1 Corinthians 15:51-54; 1 Thessalonians 4: 15-17) Therefore, their coming to life occurs over a period of time as they individually receive the gift of immortal life in the heavens.—2 Thessalonians 1:7; 2 Peter 3:11-14.

13 Their reigning and judging will be for a thousand years. Is this a literal thousand years, or should we view it symbolically as being an undefined, long period of time? "Thousands" may mean a large, indefinite number, as at 1 Samuel 21:11. But here the "thousand" is literal, since it appears three times in Revelation 20:5-7 as *"the* thousand years." Paul called

---

* The ax (Greek, *pe′le·kus*) was seemingly the traditional instrument of execution in Rome, although by John's day the sword was more generally used. (Acts 12:2) Therefore, the Greek word here used, *pe·pe·le·kis·me′non* ("executed with the ax"), simply means "executed."

10. (a) How does John now describe the 144,000 kings? (b) From what John earlier told us, whom do the 144,000 kings include?

11. (a) How are we to understand the expression "executed with the ax"? (b) Why may it be said that all the 144,000 died a sacrificial death?

12. What does John report about the 144,000 kings, and when does their coming to life occur?

13. (a) How should we view the thousand years during which the 144,000 rule, and why? (b) How did Papias of Hierapolis view the thousand years? (See footnote.)

CRUSHING THE SERPENT'S HEAD

this time of judgment "a day" when he stated: "He [God] has set a day in which he purposes to judge the inhabited earth in righteousness." (Acts 17:31) Since Peter tells us that one day with Jehovah is as a thousand years, it is appropriate that this Day of Judgment be a literal thousand years.*—2 Peter 3:8.

The Rest of the Dead

14 Whom, though, will these kings judge if, as the apostle John here inserts, *"(the rest of the dead did not come to life until the thousand years were ended)"*? (*Revelation 20:5a*) Again, the expression "come to life" has to be understood according to context. This expression can have varying meanings in varying circumstances. For example, Paul said of his anointed fellow Christians: "It is you God made alive though you were dead in your trespasses and sins." (Ephesians 2:1) Yes, spirit-anointed Christians were "made alive," even in the first century, being declared righteous on the basis of their faith in Jesus' sacrifice.—Romans 3:23, 24.

15 Similarly, pre-Christian witnesses of Jehovah were declared righteous as to friendship with God; and Abraham, Isaac, and Jacob were spoken of as "living" even though they were physically dead. (Matthew 22:31, 32; James 2:21, 23) However, they and all others who are resurrected, as well as the great crowd of faithful other sheep who survive Armageddon and any children that may be born to these in the new world, must yet be raised to human perfection. This will be accomplished by Christ and his associate kings and priests during the thousand-year Judgment Day, on the basis of Jesus' ransom sacrifice. By the end of that Day, "the rest of the dead" will have "come to life" in the sense that they will be perfect humans. As we shall see, they must then pass a final test, but they will face that test as perfected humans. When they pass the test, God will declare them worthy of living forever, righteous in the fullest sense. They will experience the complete fulfillment of the promise: "The righteous themselves will possess the earth, and they will reside forever upon it." (Psalm 37: 29) What a delightful future is in store for obedient mankind!

The First Resurrection

16 Returning now to those who "came to life and ruled as kings with the Christ," John writes: *"This is the first resurrection."* (*Revelation 20:5b*) How is it first? It is "the first resurrection" as to time, for the ones who experience it are a "firstfruits to God and to the Lamb." (Revelation 14:4) It is also first in importance, since those who share in it become corulers with Jesus in his heavenly Kingdom and judge the rest of mankind. Finally, it is first in quality. Apart from Jesus Christ himself, those raised in the first resurrection are the only creatures spoken of in the Bible as receiving immortality.—1 Corinthians 15:53; 1 Timothy 6:16.

17 What a blessed prospect for these anointed ones! As John declares: *"Happy and holy is anyone having part in the first resurrection; over these the second death has no authority."* (*Revelation 20:6a*) As Jesus promised the Christians in Smyrna, these conquerors that share

---

* Interestingly, Papias of Hierapolis, who is understood to have received some of his Bible knowledge from pupils of John, the writer of Revelation, is reported by fourth-century historian Eusebius to have believed in a literal Thousand Year Reign of Christ (although Eusebius strongly disagreed with him).—*The History of the Church*, Eusebius, III, 39.

---

14. (a) What statement does John insert about "the rest of the dead"? (b) How do expressions made by the apostle Paul throw light on the term "come to life"?
15. (a) The pre-Christian witnesses of Jehovah enjoyed what standing with God? (b) How do the other sheep "come to life," and when will they possess the earth in the fullest sense?

---

16. How does John describe the resurrection experienced by those who rule as kings with Christ, and why?
17. (a) How does John describe the blessed prospect for the anointed Christians? (b) What is "the second death," and why does it have "no authority" over the 144,000 conquerors?

in "the first resurrection" will be in no danger of harm by "the second death," which means annihilation, destruction without hope of a resurrection. (Revelation 2:11; 20:14) The second death has "no authority" over such conquerors, for they will have put on incorruption and immortality.—1 Corinthians 15:53.

18 How different from earth's kings during Satan's tenure of authority! These have ruled at most for a mere 50 or 60 years, and the great majority for just a few years. Many of them have oppressed mankind. In any case, how could the nations benefit permanently under ever-changing rulers with ever-changing policies? In contrast, John says of earth's new rulers: *"But they will be priests of God and of the Christ, and will rule as kings with him for the thousand years."* (Revelation 20:6b) With Jesus, they will form the sole government for a thousand years. Their priestly service, in applying the merit of Jesus' perfect human sacrifice, will lift obedient humans to spiritual, moral, and physical perfection. Their kingly service will result in building a global human society that reflects Jehovah's righteousness and holiness. As judges for a thousand years, they, with Jesus, will lovingly guide responsive humans toward the goal of everlasting life.—John 3:16.

The Final Test

19 By the end of the Thousand Year Reign,

all earth will have come to resemble the original Eden. It will be a veritable paradise. Perfect mankind will no longer need a high priest to intercede for it before God, since all traces of Adamic sin will have been removed and the last enemy, death, brought to nothing. Christ's Kingdom will have achieved God's purpose to create one world with one government. At this point, Jesus "hands over the kingdom to his God and Father."—1 Corinthians 15:22-26; Romans 15:12.

20 It is now time for a final test. Will that perfected world of mankind, in contrast with the first humans in Eden, stand firm in its integrity? John tells us what happens: *"Now as soon as the thousand years have been ended, Satan will be let loose out of his prison, and he will go out to mislead those nations in the four corners of the earth, Gog and Magog, to gather them together for the war. The number of these is as the sand of the sea. And they advanced over the breadth of the earth and encircled the camp of the holy ones and the beloved city."—Revelation 20:7-9a.*

21 How will Satan's last effort fare? He deceives "those nations in the four corners of the earth, Gog and Magog," and leads them to

---

18. What does John now say of earth's new rulers, and what will they accomplish?
19. What will be earth's state and mankind's state by the end of the Thousand Year Reign, and what does Jesus now do?

20. What does John tell us will happen when it is time for the final test?
21. For his last effort, how does Satan proceed, and why should we not be surprised that some will follow Satan even after the Thousand Year Reign?

"the war." Who could possibly side with Satan after a thousand years of joyful, upbuilding theocratic rule? Well, do not forget that Satan was able to mislead the perfect Adam and Eve while they were enjoying life in the Paradise of Eden. And he was able to lead astray heavenly angels who had seen the bad results of the original rebellion. (2 Peter 2:4; Jude 6) So we should not be surprised that some perfect humans will be enticed to follow Satan even after a delightful thousand years of rule by God's Kingdom.

²² The Bible calls these rebels "nations in the four corners of the earth." This does not mean that mankind will have been divided once again into mutually exclusive national entities. It merely indicates that these will separate themselves from Jehovah's righteous, loyal ones and manifest the same bad spirit that the nations show today. They will "think up an injurious scheme," as did the Gog of Magog in Ezekiel's prophecy, with a goal of destroying theocratic government on earth. (Ezekiel 38:3, 10-12) Hence, they are called "Gog and Magog."

²³ The number of those who join Satan in his revolt will be "as the sand of the sea." How many is that? There is no foreordained number. (Compare Joshua 11:4; Judges 7:12.) The final total number of rebels will depend on how each individual reacts to Satan's deceptive wiles. Doubtless, though, there will be a considerable number, since they will feel strong enough to overcome "the camp of the holy ones and the beloved city."

²⁴ "The beloved city" must be the city that is spoken of by the glorified Jesus Christ to his followers at Revelation 3:12 and that he calls "the city of my God, the new Jerusalem which descends out of heaven from my God." Since this is a heavenly organization, how could those earthly forces 'encircle' it? In that they encircle "the camp of the holy ones." A camp is outside a city; therefore, "the camp of the holy ones" must represent those on earth outside the heavenly location of New Jerusalem who loyally support Jehovah's governmental arrangement. When the rebels under Satan attack those faithful ones, the Lord Jesus regards it as an assault on him. (Matthew 25: 40, 45) "Those nations" will try to wipe out all that the heavenly New Jerusalem has accomplished in making earth a paradise. So in attacking "the camp of the holy ones," they are also attacking "the beloved city."

The Lake of Fire and Sulfur

²⁵ Will this final effort by Satan succeed? Certainly not—no more than the attack that

---

22. (a) What is indicated by the expression "those nations in the four corners of the earth"? (b) Why are the rebels called "Gog and Magog"?
23. What is indicated by the fact that the number of the rebels is "as the sand of the sea"?

24. (a) What is "the beloved city," and how can it be encircled? (b) What is represented by "the camp of the holy ones"?
25. How does John describe the outcome of the rebels' attack on "the camp of the holy ones," and what will this mean for Satan?

Gog of Magog is due to make on spiritual Israel in our day will succeed! (Ezekiel 38: 18-23) John vividly describes the outcome: *"But fire came down out of heaven and devoured them. And the Devil who was misleading them was hurled into the lake of fire and sulphur, where both the wild beast and the false prophet already were."* (*Revelation 20:9b-10a*) Rather than being merely abyssed, this time Satan, the original Serpent, will actually be crushed out of existence, pulverized, completely annihilated as if by fire.

[26] We have already noted that "the lake of fire and sulphur" could not be a literal place of torment. (Revelation 19:20) If Satan were to suffer excruciating torture there for all eternity, Jehovah would have to preserve him alive. Yet, life is a gift, not a punishment. Death is the punishment for sin, and according to the Bible, dead creatures feel no pain. (Romans 6:23; Ecclesiastes 9:5, 10) Moreover, we read later that death itself, along with Hades, is cast into this same lake of fire and sulfur. Surely, death and Hades cannot suffer pain!—Revelation 20:14.

[27] All of this reinforces the view that the lake of fire and sulfur is symbolic. Further, the mention of fire and sulfur calls to mind the fate of ancient Sodom and Gomorrah, destroyed by God because of their gross wickedness. When their time came, "Jehovah made it rain sulphur and fire from Jehovah, from the heavens, upon Sodom and upon Gomorrah." (Genesis 19:24) What befell the two cities is called "the judicial punishment of everlasting fire." (Jude 7) Yet, those two cities did not suffer everlasting torment. Rather, they were blotted out, obliterated for all time, along with their depraved inhabitants. Those

The Dead Sea. Possible location of Sodom and Gomorrah

cities do not exist today, and no one can say for sure where they were located.

[28] In harmony with this, the Bible itself explains the meaning of the lake of fire and sulfur: "This means the second death, the lake of fire." (Revelation 20:14) It is clearly the same as the Gehenna that Jesus spoke of, a place where the wicked remain destroyed, not tortured forever. (Matthew 10:28) It is complete, utter destruction without hope of a resurrection. Thus, while there are keys for death, Hades, and the abyss, there is no mention of a key for opening the lake of fire and sulfur. (Revelation 1:18; 20:1) It will never release its captives.—Compare Mark 9:43-47.

Tormented Day and Night Forever

[29] Referring to the Devil as well as the wild beast and the false prophet, John now tells us: *"And they will be tormented day and night forever and ever."* (*Revelation 20:10b*) What

---

26. Why cannot "the lake of fire and sulphur" be a literal place of torment?
27. How does what happened to Sodom and Gomorrah help us understand the term the lake of fire and sulfur?

28. What is the lake of fire and sulfur, and how is it unlike death, Hades, and the abyss?
29, 30. What does John say about the Devil as well as the wild beast and the false prophet, and how is this to be understood?

could this mean? As mentioned already, it is not logical to say that symbols, such as the wild beast and the false prophet, as well as death and Hades, could suffer torture in a literal way. Hence, we have no reason to believe that Satan will be suffering for all eternity. He is to be annihilated.

30 The Greek word used here for "torment," *ba·sa·ni′zo,* means primarily "to test (metals) by the touchstone." "To question by applying torture" is a second meaning. (*The New Thayer's Greek-English Lexicon of the New Testament*) In the context, the use of this Greek word indicates that what happens to Satan will serve, for all eternity, as a touchstone on the issue of the rightness and righteousness of Jehovah's rule. That issue of sovereign rulership will have been settled once and for all time. Never again will a challenge to Jehovah's sovereignty need to be tested over an extended period of time in order to be proved wrong.—Compare Psalm 92:1, 15.

31 Additionally, the related word *ba·sa·ni·stes′,* "tormentor," is used in the Bible to mean "jailer." (Matthew 18:34, *Kingdom Interlinear*) In harmony with this, Satan will be imprisoned in the lake of fire forever; he will never be released. Finally, in the Greek *Septuagint,* which was well known to John, the related word *ba′sa·nos* is used to refer to humiliation that leads to death. (Ezekiel 32:24, 30) This helps us to see that the punishment that Satan undergoes is a humiliating, everlasting death in the lake of fire and sulfur. His works die with him.—1 John 3:8.

32 Again, the demons are not mentioned in this verse. Will they be released with Satan at the end of the thousand years and then undergo the punishment of everlasting death along with him? The evidence answers yes. In the parable of the sheep and the goats, Jesus

---

31. How do two Greek words related to the one meaning "torment" help us to understand the punishment that Satan the Devil undergoes?
32. What punishment will the demons undergo, and how do we know?

"I shall put enmity between you and the woman and between your seed and her seed. He will bruise you in the head and you will bruise him in the heel"

said that the goats would go off "into the everlasting fire prepared for the Devil and his angels." (Matthew 25:41) The expression "everlasting fire" must refer to the lake of fire and sulfur where Satan is to be hurled. The Devil's angels were cast out of heaven with him. Evidently, they went into the abyss with him at the beginning of the Thousand Year Reign. Consistently, then, they will also be destroyed with him in the lake of fire and sulfur.—Matthew 8:29.

33 In this way, the final detail of the proph-

---

33. What final detail of Genesis 3:15 will then be fulfilled, and to what matter does Jehovah's spirit now draw John's attention?

ecy recorded at Genesis 3:15 is fulfilled. When Satan is hurled into the lake of fire, he will become as dead as a snake the head of which has been ground under an iron heel. He and his demons will be gone forever. There is no further mention of them in the book of Revelation. Now, having prophetically disposed of these, Jehovah's spirit draws attention to a matter of pressing interest to those who cherish an earthly hope: What will result to humankind from the heavenly reign of the "King of kings" and "those called and chosen and faithful with him"? (Revelation 17:14) To answer, John brings us back once again to the beginning of the Thousand Year Reign.

God's Day of Judgment —Its Joyful Outcome!

As HUMANS, we were created to live forever. If Adam and Eve had obeyed God's commands, they would never have died. (Genesis 1:28; 2:8, 16, 17; Ecclesiastes 3:10, 11) But when they sinned, they lost perfection and life both for themselves and for their offspring, and death came to reign over mankind as a relentless enemy. (Romans 5:12, 14; 1 Corinthians 15:26) Nevertheless, God's purpose to have perfect humans live forever on a paradise earth did not change. Out of his great love for mankind, he sent to earth his only-begotten Son, Jesus, who gave his perfect human life as a ransom for "many" of Adam's offspring. (Matthew 20:28; John 3:16) Jesus can now use this legal merit of his sacrifice to restore be-

---

1. (a) What did mankind lose when Adam and Eve sinned? (b) What purpose of God has not changed, and how do we know?

lieving humans to life in perfection on a paradise earth. (1 Peter 3:18; 1 John 2:2) What grand reason for mankind to "be joyful and rejoice"!—Isaiah 25:8, 9.

2 With Satan confined in the abyss, Jesus' glorious Thousand Year Reign begins. It is

---

2. What does John report at Revelation 20:11, and what is the "great white throne"?

Vision _____ 15

Revelation 20:11–21:8

Subject: The general resurrection, Judgment Day, and blessings of new heavens and a new earth

Time of fulfillment: The Thousand Year Reign

---

now the "day" in which God "purposes to judge the inhabited earth in righteousness by a man whom he has appointed." (Acts 17:31; 2 Peter 3:8) John declares: *"And I saw a great white throne and the one seated on it. From before him the earth and the heaven fled away, and no place was found for them."* (*Revelation 20:11*) What is this "great white throne"? It can be none other than the judgment seat of "God the Judge of all." (Hebrews 12:23) Now he will judge mankind as to who will benefit from Jesus' ransom sacrifice.—Mark 10:45.

3 God's throne is "great," emphasizing Jehovah's grandeur as Sovereign Lord, and it is "white," calling attention to his flawless righteousness. He is the ultimate Judge of mankind. (Psalm 19:7-11; Isaiah 33:22; 51:5, 8) He has, however, delegated the work of judging to Jesus Christ: "The Father judges no one at all, but he has committed all the judging to the Son." (John 5:22) With Jesus are his 144,000 associates, to whom the "power of judging was given . . . for a thousand years." (Revelation 20:4) Even so, it is Jehovah's standards that decide what will happen to each individual during Judgment Day.

4 How is it that "the earth and the heaven fled away"? This is the same heaven that departed as a scroll at the opening of the sixth seal—the human ruling powers that are "stored up for fire and are being reserved to the day of judgment and of destruction of the ungodly men." (Revelation 6:14; 2 Peter 3:7) The earth is the organized system of things that exists under this rulership. (Revelation 8:7) The destruction of the wild beast and the kings of the earth and their armies, along with those who received the mark of the wild beast and those who render worship to its image, marks the fleeing away of this heaven and earth. (Revelation 19:19-21) Judg-

ment having been executed on Satan's earth and heaven, the Great Judge decrees another Day of Judgment.

The Thousand-Year Judgment Day

5 Who are left to be judged after the old earth and the old heaven flee away? Not the anointed remnant of the 144,000, for these have already been judged and sealed. Those still alive on earth after Armageddon must shortly thereafter die and receive their heavenly reward by resurrection. (1 Peter 4:17; Revelation 7:2-4) However, the millions of the great crowd who have now come out of the great tribulation stand conspicuously "before the throne." These have already been counted righteous for survival because of their faith in Jesus' shed blood, but their judging must continue through the thousand years as Jesus keeps on guiding them to "fountains of waters of life." Then, having been restored to human perfection and thereafter tested, they will be declared righteous in the fullest sense. (Revelation 7:9, 10, 14, 17) Children who survive the great tribulation and any children born to the great crowd during the Millennium will similarly need to be judged during the thousand years.—Compare Genesis 1:28; 9:7; 1 Corinthians 7:14.

6 John, however, observes a throng far more numerous than the surviving great crowd. It will number into the thousands of millions! *"And I saw the dead, the great and the small, standing before the throne, and scrolls were opened."* (*Revelation 20:12a*) "The great and the small" embraces the prominent as well as the less prominent ones of humans that have lived and died on this earth during the past 6,000 years. In the Gospel that the apostle John wrote shortly after Revelation, Jesus said of the Father: "He has given him [Jesus] authority

---

3. (a) What is indicated by the fact that God's throne is said to be "great" and "white"? (b) Who will do the judging on Judgment Day, and on what basis?
4. What does it mean that "the earth and the heaven fled away"?

5. After the old earth and the old heaven flee away, who are the ones left to be judged?
6. (a) What throng does John see, and what is indicated by the words "the great and the small"? (b) How will the countless millions in God's memory no doubt be brought forth?

to do judging, because Son of man he is. Do not marvel at this, because the hour is coming in which all those in the memorial tombs will hear his voice and come out." (John 5:27-29) What a stupendous project—the undoing of the deaths and burials throughout all history! No doubt those countless millions in God's memory will be brought forth gradually so that the great crowd—so few by comparison—will be able to handle problems that may arise because resurrected ones may tend at first to follow their old life-style, with its fleshly weaknesses and attitudes.

Who Are Raised and Judged?

7 John adds: *"But another scroll was opened; it is the scroll of life. And the dead were judged out of those things written in the scrolls according to their deeds. And the sea gave up those dead in it, and death and Hades gave up those dead in them, and they were judged individually according to their deeds."* (*Revelation 20:12b, 13*) A breathtaking spectacle indeed! 'The sea, death, and Hades' each plays a part, but note that these terms are not mutually exclusive.* Jonah, when in the belly of a fish and therefore in the midst of the sea, spoke of himself as being in Sheol, or Hades. (Jonah 2:2) If a person is held in the grip of Adamic death, then likely he is also in Hades. These prophetic words give strong assurance that no one will be overlooked.

8 There are, of course, an unknown number who will not be resurrected. Among these would be the unrepentant scribes and Pharisees who rejected Jesus and the apostles, the religious "man of lawlessness," and anointed Christians "who have fallen away." (2 Thessalonians 2:3; Hebrews 6:4-6; Matthew 23:29-33) Jesus also spoke of goatlike people at the

---

* Those resurrected from the sea would not include earth's corrupted inhabitants that perished in the Deluge of Noah's day; that destruction was final, as will be the execution of Jehovah's judgment in the great tribulation. —Matthew 25:41, 46; 2 Peter 3:5-7.

7, 8. (a) What scroll is opened, and what takes place thereafter? (b) For whom will there be no resurrection?

world's end who go into "the everlasting fire prepared for the Devil and his angels," namely, "everlasting cutting-off." (Matthew 25:41, 46) No resurrection for these!

9 On the other hand, some will be specially favored in the resurrection. The apostle Paul indicated this when he said: "I have hope toward God . . . that there is going to be a resurrection of both the righteous and the unrighteous." (Acts 24:15) With regard to the earthly resurrection, "the righteous" will include faithful men and women of old—Abraham, Rahab, and many others—who were declared righteous as to friendship with God. (James 2:21, 23, 25) In this same group will be those righteous other sheep who died faithful to Jehovah in modern times. Likely, all such integrity keepers will be resurrected early in Jesus' Millennial Reign. (Job 14:13-15; 27:5; Daniel 12:13; Hebrews 11:35, 39, 40) No doubt many of these resurrected righteous ones will be assigned special privileges in overseeing the tremendous work of restoration in Paradise.—Psalm 45:16; compare Isaiah 32:1, 16-18; 61:5; 65:21-23.

10 Who, though, are "the unrighteous" mentioned at Acts 24:15? These would include the great masses of mankind who have died throughout history, particularly those who lived in 'times of ignorance.' (Acts 17:30) These, because of where they were born or when they lived, had no opportunity to learn obedience to Jehovah's will. Additionally, there may be some who did hear the message of salvation but who did not respond fully at that time or who died before they had progressed to dedication and baptism. In the resurrection such ones will have to make further adjustments in their thinking and life course if they are going to benefit from this opportunity for gaining everlasting life.

---

9. How does the apostle Paul indicate that some will be specially favored in the resurrection, and whom do these include?
10. Of those to be resurrected, who are "the unrighteous"?

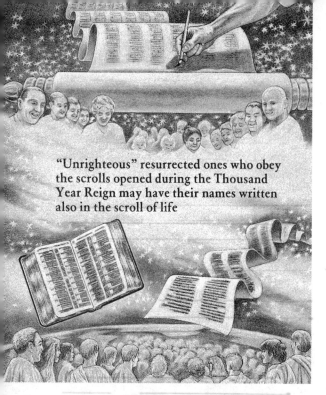

"Unrighteous" resurrected ones who obey the scrolls opened during the Thousand Year Reign may have their names written also in the scroll of life

The Scroll of Life

¹¹ John speaks of "the scroll of life." This is a record of those in line to receive everlasting life from Jehovah. The names of the anointed brothers of Jesus, of the great crowd, and of faithful men of old, such as Moses, have been recorded in this scroll. (Exodus 32:32, 33; Daniel 12:1; Revelation 3:5) As yet, none of the "unrighteous" resurrected ones have their names in the scroll of life. So the scroll of life will be opened during the Thousand Year Reign to permit the writing of names of others that come to qualify. Those whose names do not get written in the scroll, or book, of life are "hurled into the lake of fire."—Revelation 20: 15; compare Hebrews 3:19.

¹² What, then, will determine whether a person gets his name written in the opened scroll

of life at that time? The key factor will be the same as it was in the days of Adam and Eve: obedience to Jehovah. As the apostle John wrote to beloved fellow Christians: "The world is passing away and so is its desire, but *he that does the will of God remains forever."* (1 John 2: 4-7, 17) In the matter of obedience, Jehovah's appointed Judge set the example: "Although [Jesus] was a Son, he learned obedience from the things he suffered; and after he had been made perfect he became responsible for everlasting salvation to all those obeying him." —Hebrews 5:8, 9.

Opening Other Scrolls

¹³ How must these resurrected ones demonstrate their obedience? Jesus himself pointed to the two great commandments, saying: "The first is, 'Hear, O Israel, Jehovah our God is one Jehovah, and you must love Jehovah your God with your whole heart and with your whole soul and with your whole mind and with your whole strength.' The second is this, 'You must love your neighbor as yourself.'" (Mark 12:29-31) There are also Jehovah's well-established principles that they must follow, such as to repudiate stealing, lying, murdering, and immorality.—1 Timothy 1:8-11; Revelation 21:8.

¹⁴ However, John has just mentioned other scrolls that will be opened during the Millennial Reign. (Revelation 20:12) What will these be? At times, Jehovah has given specific instructions for particular situations. For example, in Moses' day he provided a detailed series of laws that meant life for the Israelites if they obeyed. (Deuteronomy 4:40; 32:45-47) During the first century, new instructions were given to help faithful ones to follow Jehovah's principles under the Christian system of things. (Matthew 28:19, 20; John 13:34; 15:9, 10) Now

---

11. (a) What is "the scroll of life," and whose names are recorded in this scroll? (b) Why will the scroll of life be opened during the Thousand Year Reign?
12. What will determine whether a person gets his name written in the opened scroll of life, and how did Jehovah's appointed Judge set the example?

---

13. How must resurrected ones demonstrate their obedience, and what principles must they follow?
14. What other scrolls are opened, and what do they contain?

John reports that the dead are to be "judged out of those things written in the scrolls according to their deeds." Evidently, then, the opening of these scrolls will publish Jehovah's detailed requirements for mankind during the thousand years. By applying in their lives the regulations and commandments of those scrolls, obedient humans will be able to lengthen their days, attaining finally to everlasting life.

¹⁵ What an extensive campaign of theocratic education will be needed! In 1987 Jehovah's Witnesses worldwide were conducting, on the

---

15. What kind of educational campaign will be needed during the resurrection, and how will the resurrection likely proceed?

average, 3,005,048 Bible studies in various locations. But during the resurrection, countless millions of studies, based on the Bible and the new scrolls, will no doubt be conducted! All of God's people will need to become teachers and to exert themselves. Resurrected ones, as they progress, will no doubt share in this vast teaching program. Likely, the resurrection will proceed in such a way that those who are alive may have the joy of welcoming and instructing former family members and acquaintances, who, in their turn, may welcome and instruct others. (Compare 1 Corinthians 15: 19-28, 58.) The more than three million witnesses of Jehovah who are active in spreading the truth today are laying a good foundation for the privileges they hope to have during the resurrection.—Isaiah 50:4; 54:13.

[16] With regard to the earthly resurrection, Jesus said that 'those who did good things come out to a resurrection of life, those who practiced vile things to a resurrection of judgment.' Here "life" and "judgment" contrast with each other, showing that those resurrected ones who "practiced vile things" after being instructed in the inspired Scriptures and scrolls are judged to be unworthy of life. Their names will not be written in the scroll, or book, of life. (John 5:29) This would also be true of any who previously followed a faithful course but who, for some reason, turn aside during the Thousand Year Reign. Names can be erased. (Exodus 32:32, 33) On the other hand, those who obediently follow the things written in the scrolls will keep their names on the written record, the scroll of life, and continue living. For them, the resurrection will have proved to be one "of life."

The End of Death and Hades

[17] Next, John describes something truly wonderful! *"And death and Hades were hurled into the lake of fire. This means the second death, the lake of fire. Furthermore, whoever was not found written in the book of life was hurled into the lake of fire."* (*Revelation 20:14, 15*) By the end of the millennial Judgment Day, "death and Hades" are completely removed. Why does this involve a thousand years? Hades, the common grave of all mankind, is emptied when the last one in God's memory is resurrected. But as long as any humans are tainted by inherited sin, Adamic death is still with them. All those resurrected on earth, as well as the great crowd that survives Armageddon, will need to obey what is written in the scrolls until Jesus' ransom merit has been applied in fully removing sickness, old age, and other inherited disabilities. Then Adamic death, along with Hades, is "hurled into the lake of fire." They will be gone forever!

[18] Thus, the program that the apostle Paul describes in his letter to the Corinthians will come to completion: "For [Jesus] must rule as king until God has put all enemies under his feet. As the last enemy, [Adamic] death is to be brought to nothing." What happens next? "When all things will have been subjected to him, then the Son himself will also subject himself to the One who subjected all things to him." In other words, Jesus "hands over the kingdom to his God and Father." (1 Corinthians 15:24-28) Yes, Jesus, having conquered Adamic death through the merit of his ransom sacrifice, will hand over a perfected human family to his Father, Jehovah. It is evidently at this point, at the end of the thousand years, that Satan is released and the final test takes place to determine whose names will remain *permanently* recorded in the scroll of life. "Exert yourselves vigorously" so that your name may be among them!—Luke 13:24; Revelation 20:5.

---

16. (a) Whose names will not be written in the scroll, or book, of life? (b) Who are those whose resurrection will prove to be one "of life"?
17. (a) What wonderful action does John describe? (b) When is Hades emptied? (c) When will Adamic death be "hurled into the lake of fire"?

---

18. (a) How does the apostle Paul describe the success of Jesus' rule as King? (b) What does Jesus do with the perfected human family? (c) What other things take place at the end of the thousand years?

Chapter 42

A New Heaven and a New Earth

THIS glorious vision continues to unfold as the angel takes John back to the beginning of the Thousand Year Reign. What does he describe? *"And I saw a new heaven and a new earth; for the former heaven and the former earth had passed away, and the sea is no more."* (*Revelation 21:1*) A captivating panorama comes to view!

2 Hundreds of years before John's day, Jehovah had said to Isaiah: "For here I am creating new heavens and a new earth; and the former things will not be called to mind, neither will they come up into the heart." (Isaiah 65:17; 66:22) This prophecy was initially fulfilled when faithful Jews returned to Jerusalem in 537 B.C.E. after their 70-year exile in Babylon. In that restoration, they formed a cleansed society, "a new earth," under a new governmental system, "new

1. What does John describe when the angel takes him back to the beginning of the Thousand Year Reign?

2. (a) How was Isaiah's prophecy about new heavens and a new earth fulfilled upon the restored Jews in 537 B.C.E.? (b) How do we know that there will be a further application of Isaiah's prophecy, and how is this promise fulfilled?

heavens." The apostle Peter, however, pointed to a further application of the prophecy, saying: "But there are new heavens and a new earth that we are awaiting according to his promise, and in these righteousness is to dwell." (2 Peter 3:13) John now shows that this promise is fulfilled during the Lord's day. "The former heaven and the former earth," Satan's organized system of things with its governmental structure influenced by Satan and his demons, will pass away. The turbulent "sea" of wicked, rebellious mankind will cease to exist. In its place will be "a new heaven and a new earth"—a new earthly society under a new government, God's Kingdom.—Compare Revelation 20:11.

3 John continues: *"I saw also the holy city, New Jerusalem, coming down out of heaven from God and prepared as a bride adorned for her husband."* (*Revelation 21:2*) New Jerusalem is the bride of Christ, made up of the anointed Christians who remain faithful to death and who are raised to become kings and priests with the glorified Jesus. (Revelation 3:12; 20:6) Just as earthly Jerusalem became the seat of government in ancient Israel, the magnificent New Jerusalem and her Bridegroom make up the government of the new system of things. This is the new heaven. The 'bride comes down out of heaven,' not literally, but in the sense of directing attention to the earth. The Lamb's bride is to be his loyal helpmeet in operating a righteous government over all mankind. A blessing indeed for the new earth!

3. (a) What does John describe, and what is New Jerusalem? (b) How does New Jerusalem 'come down out of heaven'?

In the new earth society,
there will be joyful work
and fellowship for all

4 John tells us further: *"With that I heard a loud voice from the throne say: 'Look! The tent of God is with mankind, and he will reside with them, and they will be his peoples. And God himself will be with them.'"* (*Revelation 21:3*) When Jehovah made the Law covenant with the then new nation of Israel, he promised: "I shall certainly put my tabernacle in the midst of you, and my soul will not abhor you. And I shall indeed walk in the midst of you and prove myself your God, and you, on your part, will prove yourselves my people." (Leviticus 26:11, 12) Now Jehovah is making a similar promise to faithful humans. During the thousand-year Judgment Day, they will become a very special people to him.

5 During the Millennial Reign, Jehovah will "reside" among mankind in a temporary arrangement, he being represented by his royal Son, Jesus Christ. At the end of the Thousand Year Reign, however, when Jesus hands the Kingdom over to his Father, no royal representative or intercessor will be needed. Jehovah will reside spiritually with "his peoples" in a permanent and direct way. (Compare John 4:23, 24.) What a lofty privilege for restored humanity! *SPIRIT & Truth*

6 John goes on to say: *"And he will wipe out every tear from their eyes, and death will be no more, neither will mourning nor outcry nor pain be anymore. The former things have passed away."* (*Revelation 21:4*) Once again, we are reminded of earlier inspired promises. Isaiah also looked forward to the time when death and mourning would be no more and grief would be replaced by exultation. (Isaiah 25:8;

35:10; 51:11; 65:19) John now confirms that these promises have a wonderful fulfillment during the thousand-year Judgment Day. First the great crowd will enjoy the blessings. "The Lamb, who is in the midst of the throne," continuing to shepherd them, "will guide them to fountains of waters of life. And God will wipe out every tear from their eyes." (Revelation 7:9, 17) But eventually all those who are resurrected and exercise faith in Jehovah's provisions will be there with them, enjoying a paradise that is both spiritual and physical.

7 "At that time," says Isaiah, "the eyes of the blind ones will be opened, and the very ears of the deaf ones will be unstopped." Yes, "at that time the lame one will climb up just as a stag does, and the tongue of the speechless one will cry out in gladness." (Isaiah 35:5, 6) At that time, too, "they will certainly build houses and have occupancy; and they will certainly plant vineyards and eat their fruitage. They will not build and someone else have occupancy; they will not plant and someone else do the eating. For like the days of a tree will the days of my people be; and the work of their own hands my chosen ones will use to the full." (Isaiah 65:21, 22) So they will not be uprooted from the earth.

8 What magnificent foregleams fill our minds as we meditate on these promises! Wondrous provisions are in store for faithful mankind under heaven's loving government. Are such promises too good to be true? Are they just the dreams of an old man exiled on the island of Patmos? Jehovah himself answers: *"And the One seated on the throne said: 'Look! I am making all things new.' Also, he says: 'Write, because these words are faithful and true.' And he said to me: 'They have come to pass! I am the Alpha and the Omega, the beginning and the end.'"*—Revelation 21:5, 6a.

---

4. What promise does God make that is similar to the one he made to the newly formed nation of Israel?

5. (a) How will God reside with mankind during the Millennial Reign? (b) How will God reside among mankind after the Thousand Year Reign?

6, 7. (a) What grand promises does John disclose, and who will enjoy the blessings? (b) How does Isaiah describe a paradise that is both spiritual and physical?

---

8. What does Jehovah himself say with regard to the reliability of these grand promises?

⁹ It is as though Jehovah himself were signing for faithful mankind a guarantee, or title deed, to these future blessings. Who would dare question such a Guarantor? Why, so certain are these promises of Jehovah that he speaks as though they were already fulfilled: "They have come to pass!" Is not Jehovah "the Alpha and the Omega . . . , the One who is and who was and who is coming, the Almighty"? (Revelation 1:8) Indeed he is! He himself declares: "I am the first and I am the last, and besides me there is no God." (Isaiah 44:6) As such, he can inspire prophecies and fulfill them in every detail. How faith strengthening! So he promises: "Look! I am making all things new"! Rather than questioning whether these marvels will really happen, surely we should be wondering: 'What do I personally have to do to inherit such blessings?'

"Water" for the Thirsty Ones

¹⁰ It is Jehovah himself who declares: *"To anyone thirsting I will give from the fountain of the water of life free."* (*Revelation 21:6b*) To quench that thirst, a person has to be conscious of his spiritual need and be willing to accept "the water" that Jehovah provides. (Isaiah 55:1; Matthew 5:3) What "water"? Jesus himself answered that question when witnessing to a woman beside a well in Samaria. He told her: "Whoever drinks from the water that I will give him will never get thirsty at all, but the water that I will give him will become in him a fountain of water bubbling up to impart everlasting life." That "fountain of the water of life" flows from God through Christ as his provision for restoring mankind to perfection of life. Like the Samaritan woman, how eager we should be to drink deep from that fountain! And like that woman, how ready we should be to

drop mundane interests in favor of telling others the good news!—John 4:14, 15, 28, 29.

The Ones Conquering

¹¹ Those who drink of that refreshing "water" must also conquer, as Jehovah goes on to say: *"Anyone conquering will inherit these things, and I shall be his God and he will be my son."* (*Revelation 21:7*) This promise is similar to the promises found in the messages to the seven congregations; hence, these words must apply in the first place to anointed disciples. (Revelation 2:7, 11, 17, 26-28; 3:5, 12, 21) Christ's spiritual brothers throughout the ages have eagerly anticipated the privilege of being part of New Jerusalem. If they conquer, as Jesus conquered, their hopes will be realized.—John 16:33.

¹² The great crowd out of all nations also look to this promise. They too must conquer, loyally serving God until they come out of the great tribulation. Then they will enter into their earthly inheritance, 'the kingdom prepared for them from the founding of the world.' (Matthew 25:34) These and others of the Lord's earthly sheep who pass the test at the end of the thousand years are called "holy ones." (Revelation 20:9) They will enjoy a sacred and filial relationship with their Creator, Jehovah God, as members of his universal organization.—Isaiah 66:22; John 20:31; Romans 8:21.

¹³ With this grand prospect in view, how important it is that Jehovah's Witnesses now remain clean from the defiling things of Satan's world! We need to be strong, resolute, and determined that the Devil will never drag us down into the company that Jehovah himself here describes: *"But as for the cowards and those without faith and those who are disgusting in their filth and murderers and*

9. Why can these future blessings be viewed as absolutely certain of realization?
10. What "water" does Jehovah offer, and what does it stand for?

11. What promise does Jehovah make, and to whom do the words first apply?
12. How will Jehovah's promise at Revelation 21:7 be fulfilled toward the great crowd?
13, 14. To inherit God's grand promises, what practices must we resolutely avoid, and why?

fornicators and those practicing spiritism and idolaters and all the liars, their portion will be in the lake that burns with fire and sulphur. This means the second death." (*Revelation 21:8*) Yes, the would-be inheritor has to avoid the practices that have befouled this old system of things. He has to conquer by remaining faithful in the face of all pressures and temptations.—Romans 8:35-39.

¹⁴ Christendom, though she claims to be the bride of Christ, is characterized by the disgusting practices that John here describes. So she goes down to eternal destruction with the rest of Babylon the Great. (Revelation 18: 8, 21) Likewise, any of the anointed or of the great crowd who take up the practice of such

evildoing, or start encouraging it, face everlasting destruction. If they persist in these actions, they will not inherit the promises. And in the new earth, any who try to introduce such practices will be destroyed speedily, going into the second death without hope of a resurrection.—Isaiah 65:20.

¹⁵ Outstanding as conquerors are the Lamb, Jesus Christ, and his bride of 144,000, New Jerusalem. How fitting, then, that Revelation should be brought to a sublime climax by a final, transcendent view of New Jerusalem! John now describes one last vision.

---

15. Who are outstanding as conquerors, and with what vision is Revelation brought to a sublime climax?

The Resplendent City

AN ANGEL had taken John into a wilderness to show him Babylon the Great. Now one of the same angelic group conducts John to a lofty mountain. What a contrast he sees! Here is no unclean, immoral city like the Babylonish harlot, but New Jerusalem—pure,

---

1, 2. (a) Where does an angel take John to see New Jerusalem, and what contrast do we here note? (b) Why is this the grand Revelation climax?

Vision	16

Revelation 21:9–22:5

Subject: A description of New Jerusalem

Time of fulfillment: After the great tribulation and the abyssing of Satan

spiritual, holy—and it is descending from heaven itself.—Revelation 17:1, 5.

² Even earthly Jerusalem never had a glory such as this. John tells us: *"And there came one of the seven angels who had the seven bowls which were full of the seven last plagues, and he spoke with me and said: 'Come here, I will show you the bride, the Lamb's wife.' So he carried me away in the power of the spirit to a great and lofty mountain, and he showed me the holy city Jerusalem coming down out of heaven from God and having the glory of God."* (*Revelation 21: 9-11a*) From the vantage point of that towering mountain, John surveys the beauteous city in all its lovely detail. Men of faith have been in eager expectation of its coming ever since mankind's fall into sin and death. At last it is here! (Romans 8:19; 1 Corinthians 15: 22, 23; Hebrews 11:39, 40) It is the magnificent spiritual city, composed of 144,000 loyal

305

integrity keepers, resplendent in its holiness and reflecting the very glory of Jehovah. Here is the grand Revelation climax!

3 New Jerusalem is breathtaking in its beauty: *"Its radiance was like a most precious stone, as a jasper stone shining crystal-clear. It had a great and lofty wall and had twelve gates, and at the gates twelve angels, and names were inscribed which are those of the twelve tribes of the sons of Israel. On the east were three gates, and on the north three gates, and on the south three gates, and on the west three gates. The wall of the city also had twelve foundation stones, and on them the twelve names of the twelve apostles of the Lamb."* (*Revelation 21:11b-14*) How fitting that the first impression John records is of glowing brightness! Radiant as a new bride, New Jerusalem makes a fitting consort for Christ. It positively glows, as is proper for a creation of "the Father of the celestial lights."—James 1:17.

4 On its 12 gates, there are inscribed the names of the 12 tribes of Israel. Therefore, this symbolic city is made up of the 144,000, who were sealed "out of every tribe of the sons of Israel." (Revelation 7:4-8) In harmony with this, the foundation stones have on them the names of the 12 apostles of the Lamb. Yes, New Jerusalem is not the fleshly nation of Israel founded on the 12 sons of Jacob. It is the spiritual Israel, founded on "the apostles and prophets."—Ephesians 2:20.

5 The symbolic city has a huge wall. In ancient times, city walls were built for security to keep out enemies. New Jerusalem's "great and lofty wall" shows that she is spiritually secure. No enemy of righteousness, no one unclean or dishonest, will ever be able to gain entrance. (Revelation 21:27) But for those allowed in, entering this beauteous city is like entering Paradise. (Revelation 2:7) After Adam's expulsion, cherubs were posted in front of the original Paradise to keep out unclean humans. (Genesis 3:24) Similarly, angels are posted at each entrance of the holy city Jerusalem to ensure the spiritual security of the city. Indeed, throughout the last days, angels have been guarding the congregation of anointed Christians, which becomes New Jerusalem, from Babylonish contamination. —Matthew 13:41.

Measuring the City

6 John continues his account: *"Now the one who was speaking with me was holding as a measure a golden reed, that he might measure the city and its gates and its wall. And the city lies foursquare, and its length is as great as its breadth. And he measured the city with the reed, twelve thousand furlongs; its length and breadth and height are equal. Also, he measured its wall, one hundred and forty-four cubits, according to a man's measure, at the same time an angel's."* (*Revelation 21:15-17*) When the temple sanctuary was measured, this guaranteed the fulfillment of Jehovah's purposes with regard to it. (Revelation 11:1) Now, the angel's measuring New Jerusalem shows how unchangeable Jehovah's purposes are with regard to this glorious city.*

7 What a remarkable city this is! A perfect cube 12,000 furlongs (about 1,380 miles) in perimeter, surrounded by a wall 144 cubits,

---

* The fact that the measure used was "according to a man's measure, at the same time an angel's" may have to do with the fact that the city is made up of the 144,000, who originally were human but who become spirit creatures among the angels.

---

3. How does John describe the beauty of New Jerusalem?
4. What indicates that New Jerusalem is not the fleshly nation of Israel?
5. What is denoted by New Jerusalem's "great and lofty wall" and by the fact that angels are posted at each entrance?

6. (a) How does John describe the measuring of the city, and what does this measuring indicate? (b) What may explain that the measure used was "according to a man's measure, at the same time an angel's"? (See footnote.)
7. What is remarkable about the city's measurements?

or 210 feet, in height. No literal city could ever have such measurements. It would cover a territory about 14 times as large as modern Israel, and it would tower almost 350 miles into outer space! Revelation was given in signs. So, what do these measurements tell us about heavenly New Jerusalem?

8 The 144-cubit-high walls remind us that the city is made up of 144,000 spiritually adopted sons of God. The figure 12 that appears in the 12,000-furlong measurement of the city—with the length, breadth, and height being equal—is used figuratively in organizational settings in Bible prophecy. Hence, New Jerusalem is a superbly designed organizational arrangement for accomplishing God's eternal purpose. New Jerusalem, together with the King Jesus Christ, is Jehovah's Kingdom organization. Then there is the shape of the city: a perfect cube. In Solomon's temple, the Most Holy, containing a symbolic representation of Jehovah's pres-

ence, was a perfect cube. (1 Kings 6:19, 20) How fitting, then, that New Jerusalem, illuminated by the glory of Jehovah himself, is seen as a perfect, large-scale cube! All its measurements are perfectly balanced. It is a city without irregularities or defects.—Revelation 21:22.

Precious Building Materials

9 John continues his description: *"Now the structure of its wall was jasper, and the city was pure gold like clear glass. The foundations of the city's wall were adorned with every sort of precious stone: the first foundation was jasper, the second sapphire, the third chalcedony, the fourth emerald, the fifth sardonyx, the sixth sardius, the seventh chrysolite, the eighth beryl, the ninth topaz, the tenth chrysoprase, the eleventh hyacinth, the twelfth amethyst. Also, the twelve gates were twelve pearls; each one of the gates was made of one pearl. And the broad way of the city was pure gold, as transparent glass."* —Revelation 21:18-21.

10 The city's construction is truly resplendent. Instead of mundane, earthly building

---

8. What is denoted by (a) the city's 144-cubit-high walls? (b) the city's 12,000-furlong measurement? (c) the city's being a perfect cube in shape?

9. How does John describe the building materials of the city?

10. What is denoted by the fact that the city is constructed of jasper, gold, and "every sort of precious stone"?

materials like clay or stone, we read of jasper, refined gold, and "every sort of precious stone." How fittingly these portray celestial building materials! Nothing could be more magnificent. The ancient ark of the covenant was overlaid with pure gold, and in the Bible this element often represents things that are good and valuable. (Exodus 25:11; Proverbs 25:11; Isaiah 60:6, 17) But the entire New Jerusalem, and even its broad way, are constructed of "pure gold like clear glass," portraying a beauty and intrinsic value that stagger the imagination.

[11] No human smelter could produce gold of such purity. But Jehovah is the Master Refiner. He sits "as a refiner and cleanser of silver," and he refines the individual, faithful members of spiritual Israel "like gold and like silver," removing from them all impurities. Only individuals who have truly been refined and cleansed will finally make up New Jerusalem, and in this way Jehovah builds the city with living building materials that are aglow with the highest excellence of spiritual purity.—Malachi 3:3, 4.

[12] Even the city's foundations are beautiful,

being adorned with 12 precious gems. This calls to mind the ancient Jewish high priest, who on ceremonial days wore an ephod studded with 12 different precious stones somewhat similar to the ones described here. (Exodus 28:15-21) Surely this is no coincidence! Rather, it emphasizes the priestly function of New Jerusalem, of which Jesus, the great High Priest, is the "lamp." (Revelation 20:6; 21:23; Hebrews 8:1) Also, it is through New Jerusalem that the benefits of Jesus' high-priestly ministry are channeled to mankind. (Revelation 22:1, 2) The city's 12 gates, each being a pearl of great beauty, call to mind Jesus' illustration that likened the Kingdom to a pearl of high value. All who enter through those gates will have shown true appreciation for spiritual values.—Matthew 13:45, 46; compare Job 28:12, 17, 18.

---

11. What ensures that those who make up New Jerusalem will be aglow with the highest excellence of spiritual purity?

12. What is signified by the fact that (a) the city's foundations are adorned with 12 precious gems? (b) the city's gates are pearls?

A City of Light

9/21/92 Start

13 In Solomon's time, Jerusalem was dominated by a temple built at the city's highest elevation on Mount Moriah to the north. But what of New Jerusalem? John says: *"And I did not see a temple in it, for Jehovah God the Almighty is its temple, also the Lamb is. And the city has no need of the sun nor of the moon to shine upon it, for the glory of God lighted it up, and its lamp was the Lamb."* (*Revelation 21: 22, 23*) In truth, there is no need to construct a literal temple here. The ancient Jewish temple was just a pattern, and the reality of that pattern, the great spiritual temple, has existed since Jehovah anointed Jesus as High Priest in 29 C.E. (Matthew 3:16, 17; Hebrews 9:11, 12, 23, 24) A temple also presupposes a priestly class offering sacrifices to Jehovah on behalf of the people. But all those who are part of New Jerusalem are priests. (Revelation 20:6) And the great sacrifice, Jesus' perfect human life, has been offered once for all time. (Hebrews 9:27, 28) Moreover, Jehovah is personally accessible to everyone living in the city.

14 When Jehovah's glory passed by Moses on Mount Sinai, it caused Moses' face to shine so brightly that he had to cover it from his fellow Israelites. (Exodus 34:4-7, 29, 30, 33) Can you imagine, then, the brightness of a city that is permanently lighted up with Jehovah's glory? Such a city could have no nighttime. It would have no need of a literal sun or moon. It would be eternally shedding light. (Compare 1 Timothy 6:16.) New Jerusalem is bathed in that kind of radiant brilliance. Indeed, this bride and its Bridegroom King become the capital of Jehovah's universal organization—his "woman," "the Jerusalem above"—concerning which Isaiah prophesied: "For you the sun will no more prove to be a light by day, and for brightness the moon itself will no more give you light. And Jehovah must become to you an indefinitely lasting light, and your God your beauty. No more will your sun set, nor will your moon go on the wane; for Jehovah himself will become for you an indefinitely

---

13. What does John next say regarding New Jerusalem, and why does the city not need any literal temple?

14. (a) Why does New Jerusalem not need the sun and the moon to shine on it? (b) What did Isaiah's prophecy foretell concerning Jehovah's universal organization, and how is New Jerusalem involved in this?

lasting light, and the days of your mourning will have come to completion."—Isaiah 60:1, 19, 20; Galatians 4:26.

A Light for the Nations

15 This same prophecy also foretold: "And nations will certainly go to your light, and kings to the brightness of your shining forth." (Isaiah 60:3) Revelation shows that these words would include New Jerusalem: *"And the nations will walk by means of its light, and the kings of the earth will bring their glory into it. And its gates will not be closed at all by day, for night will not exist there. And they will bring the glory and the honor of the nations into it."* —*Revelation 21:24-26.*

16 Who are these "nations" walking by means of the light of New Jerusalem? They are people, once a part of the nations of this wicked world, who respond to the light shed through this glorious heavenly city. Foremost among them are the great crowd, who have already come out of "all nations and tribes and peoples and tongues" and who worship God day and night in company with the John class. (Revelation 7:9, 15) After New Jerusalem comes down from heaven and Jesus uses the keys of death and of Hades to resurrect the dead, they will be joined by millions more, originally from "the nations," who come to love Jehovah and his Son, the Lamb-like Husband of New Jerusalem.—Revelation 1:18.

17 Who, then, are "the kings of the earth" who "bring their glory into it"? They are not the literal kings of the earth as a group, for they go down to destruction fighting against God's Kingdom at Armageddon. (Revelation 16:14, 16; 19:17, 18) Could the kings be some high-ranking ones of the nations who become a part of the great crowd, or are they

resurrected kings who submit to God's Kingdom in the new world? (Matthew 12:42) Hardly, because for the most part, the glory of such kings was worldly and has long since faded. "The kings of the earth," then, who bring their glory into New Jerusalem must be the 144,000, who are "bought . . . out of every tribe and tongue and people and nation" to rule as kings with the Lamb, Jesus Christ. (Revelation 5:9, 10; 22:5) They bring their God-given glory into the city to add to its radiance.

18 John continues: *"But anything not sacred and anyone that carries on a disgusting thing and a lie will in no way enter into it; only those written in the Lamb's scroll of life will."* (*Revelation 21:27*) Nothing tainted by Satan's system of things can be a part of New Jerusalem. Even though its gates are permanently open, no one who "carries on a disgusting thing and a lie" will be allowed to enter. There will be no apostates in that city nor any members of Babylon the Great. And if any try to desecrate the city by corrupting its future members while they are still on earth, their efforts are brought to nothing. (Matthew 13:41-43) Only "those written in the Lamb's scroll of life," the 144,000, will finally enter into New Jerusalem.*—Revelation 13:8; Daniel 12:3.

The River of Water of Life

19 The resplendent New Jerusalem will channel grand blessings to humankind on earth. This is what John next learns: *"And he showed me a river of water of life, clear as crystal, flowing out from the throne of God and of the Lamb down the middle of its broad way."* (*Revelation 22:1, 2a*) When does this "river"

---

* Note that "the Lamb's scroll of life" contains only the names of the 144,000 of spiritual Israel. Thus it differs from "the scroll of life" that includes those who receive life on earth.—Revelation 20:12.

---

15. What words of Revelation about New Jerusalem are similar to Isaiah's prophecy?
16. Who are "the nations" that will walk by means of the light of New Jerusalem?
17. Who are "the kings of the earth" who "bring their glory" into New Jerusalem?

18. (a) Who will be excluded from New Jerusalem? (b) Who only will be allowed to enter the city?
19. (a) How does John describe New Jerusalem as channeling blessings to humankind? (b) When does the "river of water of life" flow, and how do we know?

flow? Since it flows "out from the throne of God and of the Lamb," it could only be after the Lord's day began in 1914. That was the time for the event heralded by the blowing of the seventh trumpet and the grand announcement: "Now have come to pass the salvation and the power and the kingdom of our God and the authority of his Christ." (Revelation 11:15; 12:10) Previous to that date, "the Lamb" was not enthroned as Messianic King. Additionally, since the river runs through the broad way of New Jerusalem, the time of the vision's fulfillment must be after the destruction of Satan's world, when New Jerusalem 'comes down out of heaven from God.'—Revelation 21:2.

20 This is not the first time that life-giving water has been offered to mankind. When he was on earth, Jesus spoke of water that imparted everlasting life. (John 4:10-14; 7:37, 38) Further, John is about to hear the loving invitation: "The spirit and the bride keep on saying: 'Come!' And let anyone hearing say: 'Come!' And let anyone thirsting come; let anyone that wishes take life's water free." (Revelation 22:17) This invitation is being sounded even now, indicating that a measure of water of life is already available. But in the new world, those waters will flow from God's throne and through New Jerusalem as a veritable river.

21 What is this "river of water of life"? Literal water is a vital element for life. Without food a man can survive for a number of weeks, but without water he will die in about one week. Water is also a cleansing agent and vital for health. Thus, the water of life must represent something essential for the life and health of mankind. The prophet Ezekiel was also granted a vision of this "river of water of life," and in his vision, the river flowed out from the temple in Jerusalem and down into

the Dead Sea. Then, miracle of miracles! That lifeless, chemically saturated body of water was converted into freshwater teeming with fish! (Ezekiel 47:1-12) Yes, the visionary river brings back to life something that was previously dead, confirming that the river of water of life pictures God's provision through Jesus Christ for restoring perfect human life to the "dead" human race. This river is "clear as crystal," showing the purity and holiness of God's provisions. It is not like the blood-stained, death-dealing "waters" of Christendom.—Revelation 8:10, 11.

22 The river originates at "the throne of God and of the Lamb." This is appropriate, since the basis of Jehovah's life-giving provisions is the ransom sacrifice, and this was provided because Jehovah "loved the world so much that he gave his only-begotten Son, in order that everyone exercising faith in him might not be destroyed but have everlasting life." (John 3:16) The water of life also involves God's Word, which is spoken of as water in the Bible. (Ephesians 5:26) However, the river of water of life includes not only the truth but also every other provision of Jehovah, based on Jesus' sacrifice, for recovering obedient humans from sin and death and granting them everlasting life.—John 1:29; 1 John 2:1, 2.

23 During the Thousand Year Reign, the benefits of the ransom are applied fully through the priesthood of Jesus and his 144,-000 underpriests. Fittingly, then, the river of water of life flows through the middle of the broad way of New Jerusalem. This is composed of spiritual Israel, which along with Jesus makes up the true seed of Abraham. (Galatians 3:16, 29) Therefore, when the water of life flows in abundance through the

---

20. What indicates that a measure of water of life is already available?
21. What is represented by the "river of water of life," and how does Ezekiel's vision of this river help us to know?

22. (a) Where does the river originate, and why is this appropriate? (b) What is involved in the water of life, and what does this symbolic river include?
23. (a) Why is it fitting that the river of water of life flows through the middle of the broad way of New Jerusalem? (b) What divine promise to Abraham will be fulfilled when the water of life flows abundantly?

middle of the broad way of the symbolic city, "all nations of the earth" will have full opportunity to bless themselves by means of Abraham's seed. Jehovah's promise to Abraham will be completely fulfilled.—Genesis 22: 17, 18.

Trees of Life

[24] In Ezekiel's vision, the river even became a torrent, and the prophet saw growing on both sides of it all kinds of fruit-bearing trees. (Ezekiel 47:12) But what does John see? This: *"And on this side of the river and on that side there were trees of life producing twelve crops of fruit, yielding their fruits each month. And the leaves of the trees were for the curing of the nations." (Revelation 22:2b)* These "trees of life" must also picture part of Jehovah's provision for giving eternal life to obedient mankind.

[25] What bounteous provision Jehovah makes for responsive humans! Not only may they partake of those refreshing waters but they may pluck from those trees a continuing variety of sustaining fruits. Oh, if only our original parents had been satisfied with a similar "desirable" provision in Eden's Paradise! (Genesis 2:9) But now a global Paradise is here, and Jehovah even makes provision through the leaves of those symbolic trees for "the curing of the nations."* Far superior to any medicine, herbal or otherwise, that is dispensed today, the soothing application of those symbolic leaves will raise believing mankind to spiritual and bodily perfection.

[26] Those trees, well watered by the river, may additionally picture the 144,000 members of the Lamb's wife. While on earth these also drink of God's provision for life through Jesus Christ and are called "big trees of righteousness." (Isaiah 61:1-3; Revelation 21:6) They have already produced much spiritual fruitage to Jehovah's praise. (Matthew 21:43) And during the Thousand Year Reign, they will have a part in dispensing the ransom provisions that will serve for "the curing of the nations" from sin and death.—Compare 1 John 1:7.

No More Night

[27] Entry into New Jerusalem—surely, there could be no more wondrous privilege! Just think—those once lowly, imperfect humans will follow Jesus into heaven to become part of such a glorious arrangement! (John 14:2) John gives some idea of the blessings to be enjoyed by these, saying: *"And no more will there be any curse. But the throne of God and of the Lamb will be in the city, and his slaves will render him sacred service; and they will see his face, and his name will be on their foreheads." (Revelation 22:3, 4)* When the Israelite priesthood became corrupt, it suffered Jehovah's curse. (Malachi 2:2) Jerusalem's faithless "house" was pronounced abandoned by Jesus. (Matthew 23:37-39) But in New Jerusalem, "no more will there be any curse." (Compare Zechariah 14:11.) All its inhabitants have been tested in the fire of trials here on earth, and having gained the victory, they will have 'put on incorruption and immortality.' In their case, Jehovah knows, just as he knew with Jesus, that they will never fall away. (1 Corinthians 15:53, 57) Further, "the throne of God and of the Lamb" will be there, making the city's position secure for all eternity.

[28] Like John himself, all future members of that celestial city are "slaves" of God. As such,

---

* Notice that the expression "the nations" often refers to those who do not belong to spiritual Israel. (Revelation 7:9; 15:4; 20:3; 21:24, 26) The use of the expression here does not suggest that mankind will continue to be organized into separate national groups during the Thousand Year Reign.

24. What does John now see on both sides of the river of water of life, and what do they picture?
25. What bounteous provision does Jehovah make for responsive humans in the global Paradise?
26. What may the trees of life also picture, and why?

27. What further blessings does John mention for those privileged to enter into New Jerusalem, and why is it said that "no more will there be any curse"?
28. Why do members of New Jerusalem have God's name written on their forehead, and what thrilling prospect lies before them?

they have God's name prominently written on their forehead, identifying him as their Owner. (Revelation 1:1; 3:12) They will count it an inestimable privilege to render him sacred service as part of New Jerusalem. While Jesus was on earth, he made a thrilling promise to such prospective rulers, saying: "Happy are the pure in heart, since they will see God." (Matthew 5:8) How happy these slaves will be actually to behold and worship Jehovah in person!

29 John continues: *"Also, night will be no more, and they have no need of lamplight nor do they have sunlight, because Jehovah God will shed light upon them."* (Revelation 22:5a) Ancient Jerusalem, like any other city on earth, relied on the sun for light by day and on moonlight and artificial light by night. But in heavenly New Jerusalem, such lighting will be unnecessary. The city will be illuminated by Jehovah himself. "Night" may also be used in a figurative sense, referring to adversity or separation from Jehovah. (Micah 3:6; John 9:4; Romans 13:11, 12) There could never be that kind of night in the glorious, radiant presence of the almighty God.

30 John closes out this magnificent vision by saying of these slaves of God: *"And they will rule as kings forever and ever."* (Revelation 22:5b) True, at the end of the thousand years, the benefits of the ransom will have been applied to completion, and Jesus will present a perfected human race to his Father. (1 Corinthians 15:25-28) What Jehovah has in mind for Jesus and the 144,000 after that, we do not know. But Revelation assures us that their privileged sacred service to Jehovah will continue into all eternity.

Revelation's Happy Climax

31 The realization of this vision of New Jerusalem, the Lamb's bride, is the happy climax to which Revelation points, and fittingly so. All of John's first-century fellow Christians to whom the book was initially addressed looked forward to entering into that city as immortal spirit corulers with Jesus Christ. The remnant of anointed Christians still alive today on earth have the same hope. Thus Revelation moves on to its grand climax, as the completed bride is united with the Lamb. Next, by means of New Jerusalem, the benefits of Jesus' ransom sacrifice will be applied to mankind, so that eventually all faithful ones will enter into everlasting life. In this way the bride, New Jerusalem, as a loyal helpmeet to her Bridegroom King, will share in building up for eternity a righteous new earth—all to the glory of our Sovereign Lord Jehovah.—Matthew 20:28; John 10:10, 16; Romans 16:27.

32 What joy we feel, then, as we draw to the close of our consideration of the book of Revelation! We have seen the final efforts of Satan and his seed utterly frustrated and Jehovah's righteous judgments carried out to completion. Babylon the Great must go out of existence forever, to be followed by all other hopelessly corrupt elements of Satan's world. Satan himself and his demons will be abyssed and later destroyed. New Jerusalem will rule with Christ from the heavens as the resurrection and judgment proceed, and perfected mankind will finally come to enjoy everlasting life in the Paradise earth. How vividly Revelation portrays all these things! How it strengthens our determination to 'declare this everlasting good news as glad tidings to every nation and tribe and tongue and people' on earth today! (Revelation 14:6, 7) Are you expending yourself to the full in this great work?

33 With our hearts so full of gratitude, let us give attention to the concluding words of Revelation.

---

29. Why does John say of heavenly New Jerusalem that "night will be no more"?
30. How does John conclude the magnificent vision, and of what does Revelation assure us?
31. (a) What culmination is marked by the vision of New Jerusalem? (b) What does New Jerusalem accomplish for other faithful ones of mankind?

32, 33. What have we learned from Revelation, and what should be our heartfelt response?

Revelation and You

Start 9/28/92

ON READING the delightful description of New Jerusalem, you may be moved to ask: 'Can something so wonderful really come to be?' John answers that question by reporting the angel's next words: *"And he said to me: 'These words are faithful and true; yes, Jehovah the God of the inspired expressions of the prophets sent his angel forth to show his slaves the things that must shortly take place. And, look! I am coming quickly. Happy is anyone observing the words of the prophecy of this scroll.'"* (*Revelation 22:6, 7*) All the wonderful promises of Revelation will really be fulfilled! Speaking in the name of Jesus, the angel declares that Jesus is coming soon, "quickly." This must be Jesus' coming "as a thief" to destroy Jehovah's enemies and usher in the grand and happy climax of Revelation. (Revelation 16:15, 16) We should, therefore, conform our lives to the words of "this scroll," Revelation, to be pronounced happy at that time.

² After such a richness of revelation, it is understandable that John felt overwhelmed: *"Well, I John was the one hearing and seeing these things. And when I had heard and seen, I fell down to worship before the feet of the angel that had been showing me these things. But he tells me: 'Be careful! Do not do that! All I am is a fellow slave of you and of your brothers who are prophets and of those who are observing the words of this scroll. Worship God.'"* (*Revelation 22:8, 9;* compare Revelation 19:10.) This twice-stated warning not to worship angels was timely in John's day, when some evidently pursued such worship or claimed special revelations from angels. (1 Corinthians 13:1; Galatians 1:8; Colossians 2:18) Today, it highlights the fact that we must worship God alone. (Matthew 4:10) We should not corrupt pure worship with the worship of anyone or anything else.—Isaiah 42:5, 8.

³ John continues: *"He also tells me: 'Do not seal up the words of the prophecy of this scroll, for the appointed time is near. He that is doing unrighteousness, let him do unrighteousness still; and let the filthy one be made filthy still; but let the righteous one do righteousness still, and let the holy one be made holy still.'"*—*Revelation 22:10, 11.*

---

1. (a) What reassurance does the angel give John regarding all the wonderful promises in Revelation? (b) Who is it that says, "I am coming quickly," and when is this "coming"?

2. (a) How does John react to the richness of revelation, and what does the angel tell him? (b) What do we learn from the angel's words, "Be careful!" and, "Worship God"?

3, 4. What does the angel continue to tell John, and how has the anointed remnant obeyed his words?

"Outside are the dogs . . ."

STOP

> "Happy are those who . . . gain entrance into the city by its gates"

⁴ The anointed remnant today have obeyed the words of the angel. They have not sealed up the words of the prophecy. Why, the very first issue of *Zion's Watch Tower and Herald of Christ's Presence* (July 1879) set out comments on numerous verses of Revelation. As we noted in our opening chapter, the Watch Tower Society has over the years published other enlightening books on Revelation. Now we again draw the attention of all truth-lovers to the powerful Revelation prophecies and their fulfillment.

⁵ If people want to ignore the warnings and counsel in Revelation, well, let them do so! "He that is doing unrighteousness, let him do unrighteousness still." If it is their choice, those who are wallowing in the filth of this permissive age can die in that filth. Shortly, Jehovah's judgments will be executed to completion, starting with the destruction of Babylon the Great. Let meek persons be diligent to heed the prophet's words: "Seek Jehovah . . . Seek righteousness, seek meekness. Probably you may be concealed in the day of Jehovah's anger." (Zephaniah 2:3) As for those who are already dedicated to Jehovah, "let the righteous one do righteousness still, and let the holy one be made holy still."

The wise know that no temporary advantage coming from sin can compare with the lasting blessings to be enjoyed by those who pursue righteousness and holiness. The Bible says: "Keep testing whether you are in the faith, keep proving what you yourselves are." (2 Corinthians 13:5) Based on the course you choose and stay with, you will receive your reward.—Psalm 19:9-11; 58:10, 11.

---

5. (a) What if people want to ignore the warnings and counsel in Revelation? (b) What should be the response of meek and righteous ones?

REVELATION AND YOU

⁶ Jehovah, the King of eternity, now addresses readers of Revelation for the last time in the prophecy, saying: *"Look! I am coming quickly, and the reward I give is with me, to render to each one as his work is. I am the Alpha and the Omega, the first and the last, the beginning and the end. Happy are those who wash their robes, that the authority to go to the trees of life may be theirs and that they may gain entrance into the city by its gates. Outside are the dogs and those who practice spiritism and the fornicators and the murderers and the idolaters and everyone liking and carrying on a lie."* *—Revelation 22:12-15.*

---

6. What does Jehovah say as he addresses readers of Revelation for the last time in the prophecy?

⁷ Once again, Jehovah God emphasizes his eternal sovereignty and the fact that what he first purposes he will at last perform. He is "coming quickly" to execute judgment and will reward those earnestly seeking him. (Hebrews 11:6) His standards determine who will be rewarded and who will be rejected. The clergy of Christendom have acted like "speechless dogs," winking at the vices that Jehovah here describes. (Isaiah 56:10-12; see also Deuteronomy 23:18, *New World Translation Reference Bible,* footnote.) Certainly, they have 'liked and carried on' lying doctrines and dogmas and have totally ignored the

---

7. (a) For what is Jehovah "coming quickly"? (b) Why will the clergy of Christendom have no share in New Jerusalem?

counsel of Jesus to the seven congregations. Hence, they have no share in New Jerusalem.

8 Only those anointed Christians who truly "wash their robes" so as to be clean in Jehovah's eyes are privileged to "go to the trees of life." That is, they receive the right and title to immortal life in their heavenly position. (Compare Genesis 3:22-24; Revelation 2:7; 3: 4, 5.) After their death as humans, they gain entrance into New Jerusalem by resurrection. The 12 angels allow them in, while keeping out any who practice lies or uncleanness though claiming to have a heavenly hope.

The great crowd on earth also have "washed their robes and made them white in the blood of the Lamb" and need to maintain their clean standing. This they can do by avoiding the vices that Jehovah here warns against, as well as by taking to heart Jesus' admonition in his seven messages to the congregations.—Revelation 7:14; chapters 2 and 3.

9 After Jehovah, Jesus speaks. He addresses words of encouragement to righthearted ones who read Revelation, saying: *"I, Jesus, sent my angel to bear witness to you people of these things for the congregations. I am the root*

---

8. (a) Who only "go to the trees of life," and what does this mean? (b) How have the great crowd "washed their robes," and how do they retain a clean standing?

9. What words does Jesus speak, and to whom is his message and the whole of Revelation primarily directed?

and the offspring of David, and the bright morning star." (*Revelation 22:16*) Yes, these words are primarily "for the congregations." This is a message, first of all, for the congregation of anointed Christians on earth. Everything in Revelation is addressed primarily to anointed Christians, who will inhabit New Jerusalem. Through that congregation, the great crowd is also privileged to gain understanding of these precious prophetic truths.—John 17: 18-21.

¹⁰ Jesus Christ was entrusted with conveying Revelation to John and through him to the congregation. Jesus is both "the root and the offspring of David." He descended from David according to the flesh and thus is qualified to be King of Jehovah's Kingdom. He will also become David's "Eternal Father," and thus David's "root." (Isaiah 9:6; 11:1, 10) He is the permanent, immortal King in David's line, fulfilling Jehovah's covenant with David, and "the bright morning star" foretold in Moses' day. (Numbers 24:17; Psalm 89:34-37) He is the "daystar" that rises, causing the day to dawn. (2 Peter 1:19) All the wiles of the great enemy Babylon the Great were not able to prevent this glorious rising.

Say: "Come!"

¹¹ Now it is John's own turn to speak. Out of a heart brimming with appreciation for all that he has seen and heard, he exclaims: *"And the spirit and the bride keep on saying: 'Come!' And let anyone hearing say: 'Come!' And let anyone thirsting come; let anyone that wishes take life's water free."* (*Revelation 22:17*) The benefits of Jesus' ransom sacrifice will not be limited to the 144,000, for here is an open invitation. Jehovah's impelling spirit works through the bride class, so that the message continues to be sounded forth with all clarity: "Take life's water free." (See also Isaiah 55:1; 59:21.) Anyone who is thirsting for righteous-

---

10. Why did Jesus call himself (a) "the root and the offspring of David"? (b) "the bright morning star"?
11. What open invitation does John now present, and who may respond to it?

ness is invited to "come" and receive of Jehovah's bounty. (Matthew 5:3, 6) How privileged are all of the prospective earthly class who respond to this invitation of the anointed John class!

¹² Since the early 1930's, the growing number of the great crowd has been "hearing" —paying attention to the invitation. Like their anointed fellow slaves, they have attained to a clean standing before Jehovah. They long for the time when New Jerusalem will descend from heaven to channel blessings to humankind. Having heard the rousing message of Revelation, the great crowd not only say "Come!" but actively gather others to Jehovah's organization, training these also to proclaim: "Let anyone thirsting come." So the number of the great crowd continues to grow, as over 3,000,000 of them in more than 200 lands around the earth share with fewer than 9,000 of the anointed bride class in extending the invitation to "take life's water free."

¹³ Next, it is Jesus who speaks again, saying: *"I am bearing witness to everyone that hears the words of the prophecy of this scroll: If anyone makes an addition to these things, God will add to him the plagues that are written in this scroll; and if anyone takes anything away from the words of the scroll of this prophecy, God will take his portion away from the trees of life and out of the holy city, things which are written about in this scroll."*—*Revelation 22:18, 19.*

¹⁴ Those of the John class must draw attention to "the prophecy" of Revelation. They must not hide it or add to it. Its message must be preached openly, "from the housetops." (Matthew 10:27) Revelation is inspired of God. Who would dare change a word of what God himself has spoken and transmitted through the one who is now the reigning

---

12. How does the great crowd respond to the invitation of Revelation 22:17?
13. What warning does Jesus issue?
14. How does the John class view "the prophecy" of Revelation?

REVELATION CLIMAX

King, Jesus Christ? Certainly, such a person would deserve to lose out in the quest for life and suffer the plagues that must come upon Babylon the Great and upon the whole world.

¹⁵ Jesus now adds a final word of encouragement: *"He that bears witness of these things says, 'Yes; I am coming quickly.'"* (*Revelation 22:20a*) Jesus is "the faithful and true witness." (Revelation 3:14) If he bears witness to the visions of Revelation, they must be true. Both he and Jehovah God himself repeatedly stress the fact that they are coming "quickly," or soon, Jesus here saying that for the fifth time. (Revelation 2:16; 3:11; 22:7, 12, 20) The "coming" is to execute judgment on the great harlot, the political "kings" and all others who oppose "the kingdom of our Lord [Jehovah] and of his Christ."—Revelation 11:15; 16:14, 16; 17:1, 12-14.

¹⁶ Your knowing that Jehovah God and Jesus are coming quickly should encourage you to keep "close in mind the presence of the day of Jehovah." (2 Peter 3:12) Any seeming stability of the earth of Satan's system of things is illusory. Any seeming success that the heaven of the worldly rulers under Satan might achieve is transitory. These things are passing away. (Revelation 21:1) The only permanence is to be found in Jehovah, his Kingdom under Jesus Christ, and his promised new world. Never lose sight of that!—1 John 2:15-17.

¹⁷ May you, then, allow what you have learned from your study of Revelation to influence your life profoundly. Did not your glimpse into Jehovah's heavenly presence impress on you the transcendent glory and holiness of our Creator? (Revelation 4:1–5:14) What a privilege to serve such a God! May

your appreciation for his holiness move you to take very seriously Jesus' counsel to the seven congregations and avoid things such as materialism, idolatry, immorality, lukewarmness, apostate sectarianism, or anything else that could make your service unacceptable to Jehovah. (Revelation 2:1–3:22) The apostle Peter's words to the John class apply also in principle to the great crowd: "In accord with the Holy One who called you, do you also become holy yourselves in all your conduct." —1 Peter 1:15, 16.

¹⁸ Additionally, may you be moved to a renewed zeal as you proclaim "the year of goodwill on the part of Jehovah and the day of vengeance on the part of our God." (Isaiah 35:4; 61:2) Whether of the little flock or of the great crowd, may you have the fullest share possible in publicizing the pouring out of the seven bowls of Jehovah's anger, telling of God's judgments on Satan's world. At the same time, lend your voice to the joyful proclamation of the everlasting good news concerning the established Kingdom of Jehovah and his Christ. (Revelation 11:15; 14:6, 7) Be at this work urgently. And may a realization that we are in the Lord's day move many who are not yet serving Jehovah to join in the work of proclaiming the good news. May these also progress toward dedicating their lives to God with a view to baptism. Remember, "the appointed time is near"!—Revelation 1:3.

¹⁹ Thus, with John, we fervently pray: *"Amen! Come, Lord Jesus."* And John, the elderly apostle, adds: *"May the undeserved kindness of the Lord Jesus Christ be with the holy ones."* (*Revelation 22:20b, 21*) May it also be with all of you who read this publication. May you have faith that the grand climax of Revelation is at hand, so that you too can join us in a hearty *"Amen!"*

---

15. What is the significance of Jesus' words that he "bears witness of these things" and "I am coming quickly"?
16. Knowing that Jehovah God and Jesus are coming quickly, what resolute action should you take?
17. How should your appreciation of Jehovah's holiness affect you?

18. In what should you play as full a part as possible, and why is this work urgent today?
19. What are the closing words of the elderly apostle John, and how do you respond to them?

Learn More About God's Purposes for Mankind

Examine this thoroughly researched presentation of how life got here and what this means for the future.

Life—How Did It Get Here? By Evolution or by Creation? has been described as the finest science book for building appreciation for life and its complexities. It completely demolishes the teaching of evolution and irrefutably demonstrates the existence of an almighty Creator.

Learn how God will eliminate all causes of suffering and usher in a righteous new world.

You Can Live Forever in Paradise on Earth provides easily understood answers to such major questions as, Who is God? Why does he permit wickedness? What happens at death? Who go to heaven, and why? And it explains how you, too, may be able to live forever in an earthly Paradise.

Both these publications have 256 pages and are the same page size as this book, and each contains well over a hundred teaching illustrations, most in beautiful color. Copies will be sent to you for $3.00 (U.S.) each, postpaid. (Contributions subject to change.)

Send to Watch Tower, using one of these addresses:

ALASKA 99507: 2552 East 48th Ave., Anchorage. **AUSTRALIA:** Box 280, Ingleburn, N.S.W. 2565; Zouch Road, Denham Court, N.S.W. 2565. **BAHAMAS:** Box N-1247, Nassau, N.P. **BARBADOS:** Fontabelle Rd., Bridgetown. **BELIZE:** Box 257, Belize City. **CANADA L7G 4Y4:** Box 4100, Halton Hills (Georgetown), Ontario. **ENGLAND NW7 1RN:** The Ridgeway, London. **FIJI:** Box 23, Suva. **GERMANY, FEDERAL REPUBLIC OF:** Postfach 20, D-6251 Selters/Taunus 1. **GHANA:** Box 760, Accra. **GUYANA:** 50 Brickdam, Georgetown 16. **HAWAII 96819:** 2055 Kam IV Rd., Honolulu. **HONG KONG:** 4 Kent Road, Kowloon Tong. **INDIA:** Post Bag 10, Lonavla, Pune Dis., Mah. 410 401. **IRELAND:** 29A Jamestown Road, Finglas, Dublin 11. **JAMAICA:** Box 180, Kingston 10. **JAPAN:** 1271 Nakashinden, Ebina City, Kanagawa Pref., 243-04. **KENYA:** Box 47788, Nairobi. **LEEWARD ISLANDS:** Box 119, St. Johns, Antigua. **LIBERIA:** P.O. Box 171, Monrovia. **MALAYSIA:** 28 Jalan Kampar, Off Jalan Landasan, 41300 Klang, Sel. **NEW ZEALAND:** P.O. Box 142; 198 Mahia Rd., Manurewa. **NIGERIA:** PMB 001, Shomolu, Lagos State. **PAKISTAN:** 197-A Ahmad Block, New Garden Town, Lahore 16. **PANAMA:** Apartado 1835, Panama 9A. **PAPUA NEW GUINEA:** Box 636, Boroko, N.C.D. **PHILIPPINES, REPUBLIC OF:** P.O. Box 2044, Manila 2800; 186 Roosevelt Ave., San Francisco del Monte, Quezon City 3010. **SIERRA LEONE:** P. O. Box 136, Freetown. **SOUTH AFRICA:** Private Bag 2067, Krugersdorp, 1740. **SWEDEN:** Box 5, S-732 00 Arboga. **SWITZERLAND:** Ulmenweg 45; P.O. Box 225, CH-3602 Thun. **TRINIDAD AND TOBAGO, REP. OF:** Lower Rapsey Street & Laxmi Lane, Curepe. **UNITED STATES OF AMERICA:** 25 Columbia Heights, Brooklyn, N.Y. 11201. **WESTERN SAMOA:** P. O. Box 673, Apia. **ZAMBIA, REP. OF:** Box 21598, Kitwe. **ZIMBABWE:** 35 Fife Avenue, Harare.

1990 —
1/22 205 - 209
1/29 209 - 215

2/5   215 - 220
2/12 221 - 228
2/19 229 ⌣ 234
2/26 235 ⌣ 243

5/7/90 - 290 - 295 #
5/14/90 - 295 - 300
5/21/90 - 301 - 305
5/28/90 - 305 - 310

1989
7/24 68 TO 73
7/31 74 TO 79

11 - 6/89 142 -   18 ✓
11 - 13/89 148 TO   ✓
11 - 20/89 155 TO   ✓
11 - 27/89 161 - 16 ✓
12 - 4   165 TO 17
12 - 11/89 171 TO 176
12 - 8 - Pg. 177 TO 181
12/25/89 182 TO 186

Raiders of the Last Ark

external Love
internal Love
peace activating
your mind

Phreddie —
alm
Flowers
Cuban —

Could the
real Bittersweet ?
Ethel L